Lecture Notes in Computer Science 2095

Edited by G. Goos, J. Hartmanis and J. van Leeuwen

Springer
Berlin
Heidelberg
New York
Barcelona
Hong Kong
London
Milan
Paris
Singapore
Tokyo

Bernt Schiele   Gerhard Sagerer (Eds.)

Computer
Vision Systems

Second International Workshop, ICVS 2001
Vancouver, Canada, July 7-8, 2001
Proceedings

 Springer

Series Editors

Gerhard Goos, Karlsruhe University, Germany
Juris Hartmanis, Cornell University, NY, USA
Jan van Leeuwen, Utrecht University, The Netherlands

Volume Editors

Bernt Schiele
ETH Zentrum, IFW B26.1
8092 Zürich, Switzerland
E-mail: schiele@inf.ethz.ch

Gerhard Sagerer
Universität Bielefeld
Technische Fakultät, Angewandte Informatik
Postfach 100 131, 33501 Bielefeld, Germany
E-mail: sagerer@techfak.uni-bielefeld.de

Cataloging-in-Publication Data applied for

Die Deutsche Bibliothek - CIP-Einheitsaufnahme

Computer vision systems : second international conference ; proceedings /
ICVS 2001, Vancouver, Canada, July 7 - 8, 2001. Bernt Schiele ; Gerhard
Sagerer (ed.). - Berlin ; Heidelberg ; New York ; Barcelona ; Hong Kong ;
London ; Milan ; Paris ; Singapore ; Tokyo : Springer, 2001
   (Lecture notes in computer science ; Vol. 2095)
   ISBN 3-540-42285-4

CR Subject Classification (1998): I.4, I.2.9-10, I.5.4-5, I.3.1-2, D.2

ISSN 0302-9743
ISBN 3-540-42285-4 Springer-Verlag Berlin Heidelberg New York

Springer-Verlag Berlin Heidelberg New York
a member of BertelsmannSpringer Science+Business Media GmbH

http://www.springer.de

© Springer-Verlag Berlin Heidelberg 2001
Printed in Germany

Typesetting: Camera-ready by author, data conversion by PTP-Berlin, Stefan Sossna
Printed on acid-free paper   SPIN 10839427   06/3142   5 4 3 2 1 0

Organization

The *Second International Workshop on Computer Vision Systems, ICVS 2001*, held in Vancouver, Canada, July 7–8, 2001 was organized as an associated workshop of the International Conference on Computer Vision 2001.

Organizing Committee

General Co-chairs: Kevin Bowyer (Univ. of South Florida, USA)
                                             Henrik Christensen (KTH, Sweden)
Program Co-chairs: Bernt Schiele (ETH Zurich, Switzerland)
                                               Gerhard Sagerer (Univ. of Bielefeld, Germany)
Publication: Jorge Cabrera (ULPGC, Spain)

Program Committee

Claus Andersen (Dator A/S, Denmark)
Aaron Bobick (Gorgia Tech, USA)
Kevin Bowyer (Univ. of South Florida, USA)
Jorge Cabrera (ULPGC, Spain)
Henrik Christensen (KTH, Sweden)
Patrick Courtney (Visual Automation, UK)
James L. Crowley (INPG, France)
Ernst Dickmanns (Univ. BW Munich, Germany)
Rüdiger Dillmann (Univ. Karlsruhe, Germany)
Bruce Draper (Univ. Colorado, USA)
Jan-Olof Eklundh (KTH, Sweden)
Robert Fisher (Univ. of Edinburgh, UK)
Catherine Garbay (TIMC-IMAG, France)
Domingo Guinea (IAI-CSIC, Spain)
Kurt Konolige (SRI, USA)
Claus Madsen (Univ. Aalborg, Denmark)
Stefan Posch (Univ. Halle, Germany)
Alex Pentland (MIT, USA)
Claudio Pinhanez (IBM Watson, USA)
Gerhard Sagerer (Univ. of Bielefeld, Germany)
Giulio Sandini (Univ. Genova, Italy)
Bernt Schiele (ETH Zurich, Switzerland)
Chris Taylor (Univ. Manchester, UK)
Monique Thonnat (INRIA Sophia-Antipolis, France)
Mohan Trivedi (UC San Diego, USA)
John Tsotsos (York Univ., Canada)
David Vernon (NUIM, Ireland)

Preface

Following the highly successful International Conference on Computer Vision Systems held in Las Palmas, Spain (ICVS'99), this second *International Workshop on Computer Vision Systems,* ICVS 2001 was held as an associated workshop of the International Conference on Computer Vision in Vancouver, Canada. The organization of ICVS'99 and ICVS 2001 was motivated by the fact that the majority of computer vision conferences focus on component technologies. However, Computer Vision has reached a level of maturity that allows us not only to perform research on individual methods and system components but also to build fully integrated computer vision systems of significant complexity. This opens a number of new problems related to system architecture, methods for system synthesis and verification, active vision systems, control of perception and action, knowledge and system representation, context modeling, cue integration, etc. By focusing on methods and concepts for the construction of fully integrated vision systems, ICVS aims to bring together researchers interested in computer vision systems.

Similar to the previous event in Las Palmas, ICVS 2001 was organized as a single-track workshop consisting of high-quality, previously unpublished papers on new and original research on computer vision systems. All contributions were presented orally. A total of 32 papers were submitted and reviewed thoroughly by program committee members. Twenty of them have been selected for presentation. We would like to thank all members of the organizing and program committee for their help in putting together a high-quality workshop.

The workshop was sponsored by the IEEE Computer Society.

We hope all participants enjoyed a successful and interesting workshop.

July 2001   Bernt Schiele and Gerhard Sagerer

Table of Contents

Real-Time Vision Modules

Recognition

Exploration and Navigation

A Vision System for Autonomous Ground Vehicles with a Wide Range of Maneuvering Capabilities

R. Gregor, M. Lützeler, M. Pellkofer, K.-H. Siedersberger, and E.D. Dickmanns

Institut für Systemdynamik und Flugmechanik,
Universität der Bundeswehr München (UBM),
D-85577 Neubiberg, Germany
http://www.unibw-muenchen.de/campus/LRT/LRT13/english/index.html

Abstract. This paper gives a survey on UBM's new Expectation-based Multi-focal Saccadic Vision (EMS-Vision) system for autonomous vehicle guidance. The core element of the system is a new camera arrangement, mounted on a high bandwidth pan and tilt head (TACC) for active gaze control. Central knowledge representation and a hierarchical system architecture allow efficient activation and control of behavioral capabilities for perception and action. The system has been implemented on commercial off-the-shelf (COTS) hardware components in both UBM test vehicles. Results from autonomous turn-off maneuvers, performed on army proving grounds, are discussed.

1 Introduction

Since nearly two decades autonomous systems are a topic of intense research. From the mid 80ies on, several national and international programs have been initiated all around the world, like AVCS in Asia, IVHS [1] and PATH in the United States or DRIVE and PROMETHEUS in Europe. The main goals in these programs have been to increase safety and efficiency in normal traffic. Thus, many research groups concentrated on the development of functionalities for autonomous road vehicles being able to interact with other vehicles in a co-operative manner. The key problem of an intelligent system is the acquisition of reliable and precise information about the actual situation. This includes information about ego-state as well as about position and velocity relative to the road and other road-users. Ego-state can be measured easily, but the determination of the vehicle's state relative to other objects and the geometry of these objects is much more difficult. Vision systems have proved their special aptitude for this kind of tasks, e.g. the determination of road curvature, without the need for expensive additional infrastructure. Countless approaches have been developed and often abandoned over the years. Impressive results have been demonstrated by the most successful groups, like from Carnegie Mellon University (CMU) C. Thorpe et al.[2], from University of Parma A. Broggi et al. [3], from the "Fraunhofer-Institut für Informations- und Datenverarbeitung" (IITB) [4] in

B. Schiele and G. Sagerer (Eds.): ICVS 2001, LNCS 2095, pp. 1–20, 2001.

Karlsruhe, from Daimler-Benz Forschung U. Franke et al. [5] and from UBM [6]. For the next step on the way to a really autonomous road vehicle, the navigation on road networks, more challenging problems like intersection recognition and complex driving maneuvers had to be solved. Only few groups have been able to present results from real driving tests like CMU [7], IITB [8] und UBM [9].

With the latest generation implementation, the Expectation-based Multi-focal Saccadic Vision (EMS-Vision) system, UBM has set a new course of development. Contrary to former implementations, mostly working with static configurations and optimized for specific tasks or domains, EMS-Vision is a flexible system, which is able to configure itself dynamically during operation depending on the actual situation. The explicit representation of the system's capabilities allows direct activation of specific capabilities just in time when needed. Special decision units responsible for different functions assign tasks to specialized experts and supervise their actions. Thus limited computational resources can be exploited very efficiently. The system has been implemented on standard, Intel-based PC hardware components running a general purpose operating system in both UBM test vehicles VAMoRs and VAMP.

The turn-off maneuver as an essential part of a complex driving mission is chosen to illustrate the interaction between the different modules.
The paper is organized as follows: Section 2 gives a review on the different hardware architectures used in former UBM systems. In section 3 the hardware concept of the EMS-Vision system is explained. While section 4 gives an overview over general system aspects, in section 5 and 6 individual components are explained in detail. In section 7 experimental results of an autonomous turn-off maneuver are presented. Section 8 concludes the contribution.

2   Development Steps at UBM

In 1985, after 8 years of simulation studies, UBM started to develop an autonomous vehicle based on the results achieved in the field of dynamic machine vision. At that time the computational needs could only be satisfied by specialized hardware. The system chosen then was based on an Intel MULTIBUS I architecture. It consisted of a maximum of 13 microprocessors Intel 80x86 and was extended by a videobus architecture. The system, called BVV, had been developed by the 'Institut für Meßtechnik' at UBM [10]. So called parallel processors (PP) were dedicated to feature extraction and on the other side of the MULTI-BUS, the object processors (OP) were used for recursive estimation purposes. For proper operation, the system was equipped with specialized firmware for bootstrapping and communication. Connection to the outside world was done via IEC-bus to a PC. This PC hosted the 'vehicle control' (VC) process and sensor and actuator interfaces to the vehicle. Problems with the bus-based architecture of the BVV were the restricted communication bandwidth, limited scalability and missing robustness.

In 1991 a new approach was taken based on the transputer concept, which satisfied all requirements like higher computing performance, higher communication bandwidth, compactness and robustness, a lower price, and a homogeneous system incorporating all interfaces and modules. In the last configuration, the overall system integrated in VaMP comprised about 60 transputers T-222 (16 bit, for image processing and communication) and T-800 (32 bit, for number crunching and knowledge processing). Additionally a PC host was needed.

Although the scalability of the transputer system had been quite satisfying, the overhead of developing parallel algorithms lead to the wish to have more computing power on the chip available. So the next generation of transputers, the T9000, in combination with a Transputer Image Processing (TIP) videobus system was chosen to be the next hardware platform. As the development of the T9000 was unpredictably delayed, the TIP system could only be used in conjunction with the earlier transputer generation. In 1995 the video processing nodes were substituted by IBM/Motorola PowerPC 601 based components with performance improvements per processor of more than one order of magnitude. However, as further developments of the TIP system had been stopped due to pin-incompatibility of the PowerPC 603 chip, a new hardware platform had to be found.

3 EMS-Vision

Based on the experience made with these systems and the results achieved, new goals were set for the development of EMS-Vision:

1. Exclusive use of COTS components to reduce hardware costs.
2. More processing power per node.
3. Recognize a greater variety of object classes.
4. Develop decision units to reach goal driven behavior and knowledge based control of perception subsystems.
5. Develop a uniform representation for all object classes.
6. Introduce a Dynamic Object-Data Base (DOB) for central storage of actual states of objects.

Several computer architectures have been investigated to find the appropriate hardware platform allowing the realization of EMS-Vision. The PC platform has finally been chosen, after the usability for automotive applications had been demonstrated with a prototype system. Although Windows NT does not supply any methods for hard real-time applications, it has shown sufficient for fulfilling the smoother real-time constraints here:

1. Applications with hard real-time constraints (control loops) are running on real-time hardware (transputer).
2. The 4D approach allows time-delay compensations.
3. Due to efficient image processing, CPU capacity is not exhausted (this would lead to indeterministic losses of cycles).

3.1   Sensor Concept

The EMS-Vision system design has been kept as general as possible to be able to cope with a variety of scenarios. Thus, the requirements for the vision system are manifold: Driving at high speeds requires large look-ahead distances on the trajectory planned in order to detect obstacles sufficiently early for collision avoidance. On uneven and rough terrain, inertial stabilization of the viewing direction is necessary in order to reduce motion blur in the images (especially the tele-ones).

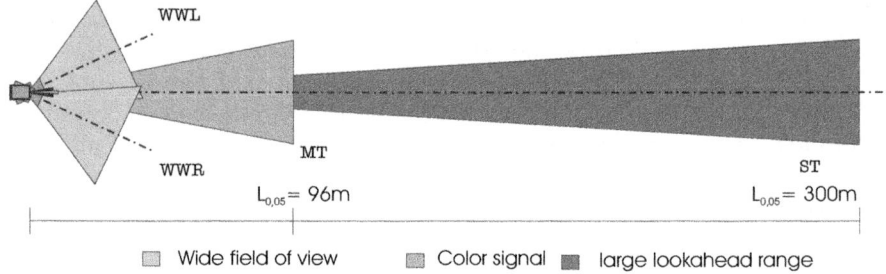

Fig. 1. MARVEYE camera configuration

In cluttered environments with many subjects moving in an unpredictable manner, a wide field of view is required for collision avoidance; the capability of stereo interpretation will help in these cases (in the near range) to understand the spatial arrangement and motion of objects quickly. All of these requirements have led to the design of the "Multi-focal, active/reactive Vehicle Eye" MARVEYE, taking advantage of the assembly of functions which nature combined into the vertebrate eye, closely interconnected to the vestibular system for inertial sensing. The MARVEYE camera arrangement combines a wide field of view (f.o.v.) nearby with central areas of high resolution. Coarse resolution monochrome peripheral vision with a wide f.o.v. ($> 100°$), realized by a pair of cameras in a divergent arrangement, is accompanied by high resolution foveal color imaging with a f.o.v. of 23°. A high sensitivity b/w-camera with a f.o.v. of $\sim 7°$ for large lookahead distances completes the system. Figure 1 shows the MARVEYE camera arrangement. At $L_{0.05}$ one pixel in the image corresponds to $5cm$ in the real world, so that a typical lane marking is covered by 3 pixels.

3.2   Hardware Concept

The MARVEYE camera configuration had major influence on the design of the computational part of the EMS-Vision system. As a PCI bus master transfer of one monochrome video image (768 by 572 pixels) into host memory takes approximately 12 ms (and the memory interface being blocked in the meantime), it was clear that for reaching a cycle time of $40ms$ a multi computer architecture would be necessary.

Figure 2 shows the actual hardware architecture.

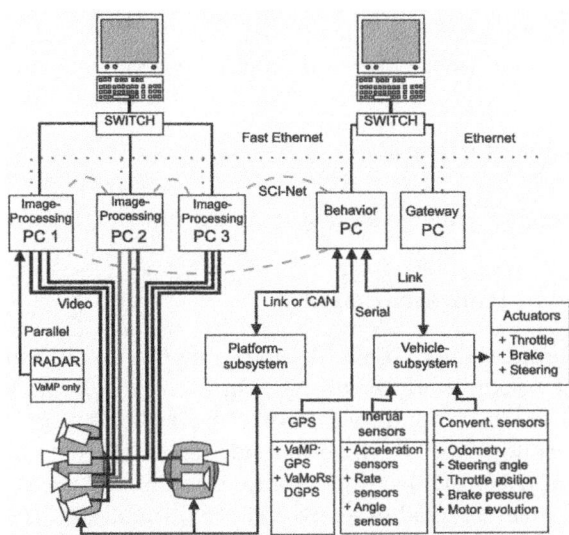

Fig. 2. Hardware architecture

The computational part of the EMS-Vision system is a PC-net with 4 computers (three "Image Processing PCs" and one "Behavior PC"). They are connected by SCI (Scalable Coherent Interface) for fast data exchange in real-time operation. Actually, two types of PCs are used, Dual Pentium II with 333MHz and Dual Pentium III with 450 MHz. The fifth PC ("Gateway PC") is used for consistent storage of system software only. Via Fast-Ethernet the system software is distributed to all other computers. The 10BaseT-Ethernet of the "Gateway PC" serves as a connection to external networks.

All "Image Processing PCs" are equipped with frame-grabbers for digitizing analog videostreams. The video signals of all cameras are synchronized. UBM's experimental vehicle VAMORS is equipped with a two axes pan-tilt head, whereas VAMP has two single axis pan heads, covering front and rear hemisphere. Sensors for angular position and rate for each axis are mounted on the head. Signals from these sensors are used by the "Platform Subsystem" to control gaze. This subsystem is connected to the "Behavior PC" by CAN bus or transputer-link. Via a transputer-link the "Vehicle Subsystem" is also coupled to the "Behavior PC". The "Vehicle Subsystem" consists of a small transputer net which guarantees real-time feedback control loops. Actuators for steering, brake and throttle are controlled by this subsystem. Additionally, inertial and odome-

try data and other sensor signals are read in. Another sensor directly connected
to the "Behavior PC" is a GPS receiver for global navigation.

Figure 2 shows that the entire computer network is connected to two termi-
nals. Although one terminal is sufficient for running the EMS-Vision system, the
second terminal is used for debugging and visualization purposes.

For time synchronized logging of digitized videostreams and vehicle sensor
data, a RAID-system has been integrated. The EMS-Vision system can be run
in a simulation mode where logged data can be replayed synchronously.

4   System Overview

This section presents some general system aspects.

4.1   Knowledge Representation

To perform complex tasks in dynamic environments, an autonomous agent needs
several kinds of background knowledge. On the one side, an expectation based
agent needs static background information about the objects in the environment
he will have to cope with. On the other side, an intelligent robot with a variety
of capabilities and (mostly) limited computational resources needs an internal
representation of these capabilities to achieve optimal performance. During operation, an internal representation of the outside world, the scene representation,
is aggregated dynamically by specified perception experts.

Dynamic knowledge representation and data exchange in the EMS-Vision
system is object oriented. It consists of four specific sections for the distributed
system:

Every computer in the system is represented by a computer object. This list
is generated dynamically during system bootup.

Every process in the system is represented by a process object. The process
objects contain both general information about the process itself and an interface for point to point communication. Each process object can at least
handle standardized administrative messages. Additionally, perception process objects contain information about the object classes they are specialized
for. An interface allows assigning new perception tasks to them or canceling
running tasks.

All nodes of the scene tree represent physical objects (sub-objects) or virtual
coordinate systems. Generally, the transformations between scene nodes are
described by homogeneous coordinate transformations (HCT), as standard
in computer graphics. HCTs can be used for the description of the relative
position (6DOF) between physical objects as well as for perspective projection
(Proj.) into an image coordinate system. Each scene node offers methods
for computing the HCT to its father node or vice versa. In this manner, an
arbitrary point in a specific object coordinate system can be transformed
into any other object coordinate system as long as all transformations are

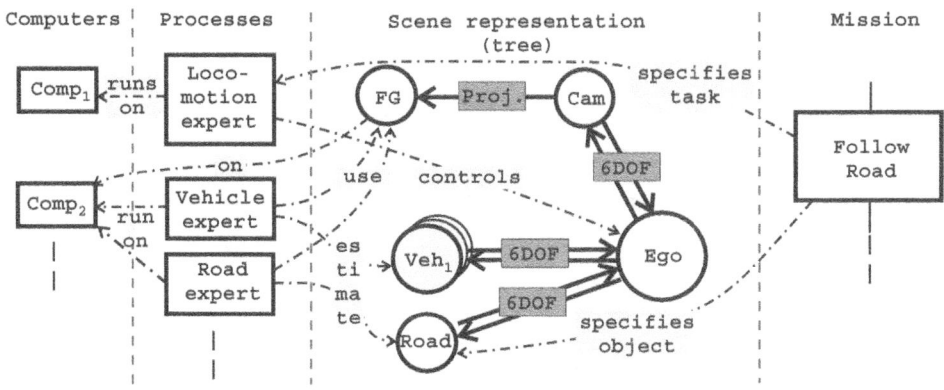

Fig. 3. The EMS-Vision data bases for dynamic knowledge

invertible, which perspective projection is not! Beside the relative position, scene nodes can also contain models for shape and dynamics or any other attributes of the objects represented, e.g. symbolic object information, meanings or control flow states. The scene tree is stored and managed by the **Dynamic Object Database**.

The mission plan describes the overall task. It is computed using digital maps containing roads and landmarks as background knowledge. It consists of a sequential list of mission elements, each containing one planned task for locomotion and an optional number of tasks for perception. During a mission, only one mission element can be valid at a time.

Figure 3 shows the principle organisation of the knowledge bases. The central element, the scene tree, contains an internal representation of the own vehicle (in this example condensed to one node Ego) and other objects in the real world (Road, Vehicles). The Ego node is connected to one camera node (Cam); the signals of this camera are digitized by a frame-grabber (FG).

The mission plan specifies the task "Follow Road" for the locomotion expert and gives a reference to the node containing road data. The locomotion expert controls the vehicle's motion. The perception modules aggregate data about physical objects within their specific field of expertise. They need access to digitized images and are therefore started on the computer equipped with the according frame-grabber.

4.2   General System Structure

A coarse overview of the general system structure is presented in figure 4. *Perception* modules process *sensor* signals and accumulate information about objects in the world (3D) and their dynamics relevant for the *mission* at hand. The *analysis* of all object data in conjunction with the state of the own subject and

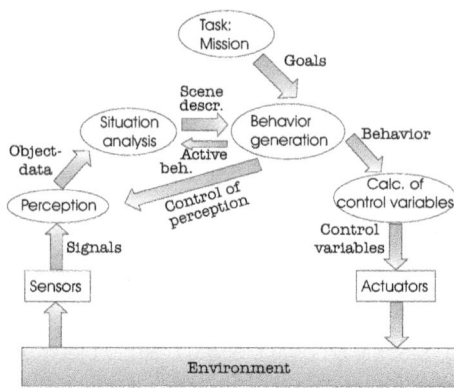

Fig. 4. System structure

its goals leads to a scene description. Based on this scene description, appropriate behavioral capabilities for locomotion and viewing direction are initiated and controlled to solve given tasks. Within active modules for behavioral capabilities control variables are calculated and commanded to the actuators. Additionally, *Behavior generation* controls active perception processes and assigns new perception tasks to specialized experts.

4.3   Decision Units

One of the most significant differences between the EMS-Vision system design and its predecessors is that a hierarchy of decision units (DUs), each specialized for a field of functions, is responsible for task assignment to specialized experts and for supervision and control of expert behavior.

For optimal resource exploitation, experts are started by the DUs just in time when needed and may be terminated after task completion. Three DUs have been designed and partially implemented at the moment, but the control structures used by the DUs have already been completed:

Behavior Decision for Gaze and Attention (BDGA) on the one side is responsible for task assignment to specialized perception experts. On the other side, it calculates optimal gaze strategies to keep the most important objects in the field of view (for details see M. Pellkofer [11]).

Behavior Decision for Locomotion (BDL) is responsible for triggering Vehicle Control (VC). Given complex task descriptions, e.g. "Turn right at intersection 1 onto cross-road 2", BDL realizes this task by initiating VC to perform adequate locomotion maneuvers (see K.-H. Siedersberger [12]).

Central Decision (CD) resides on the top level of the hierarchy, being that unit with highest authority for decision. If no autonomous driving mission is actually specified by the human operator, CD may decide autonomously, whether a stationary observation mission or an off-line data processing for model-refinement and map update shall be performed. During mission performance it supervises the actions of BDL and BDGA.

For conflict avoidance, tasks are ranked according to their relevance for the system. Minor conflicts within the field of functions of BDL and BDGA are directly solved there. Conflicts between BDL and BDGA, or conflicts that can not be solved under given constraints, are announced to CD. CD then may vary the constraints and leave conflict solution to BDL and BDGA, or determine and command a solution directly.

The following section describes the interaction between the experts for perception and locomotion and the DUs.

4.4 Control Flow

Task assignment in the EMS-Vision system can be divided into two parts: Locomotion and perception. During a mission, the mission expert provides the system with planned tasks for locomotion according to the mission plan and the actual situation. In general, all tasks are related to physical objects, like "road" following. Due to this, the major part of the interfaces for task assignment is related to objects as well. The interface for the interaction between BDGA and the perception experts is divided into an object related and a process related part. The process object of each perception process contains information about its capabilities and methods for task assignment. The perception object, in the computer science sense, allows direct control of the perception expert's operation on this object. The perception expert uses the object to transmit to BDGA its needs concerning gaze by specifying a fixation point in 3D object coordinates that should be centered in the image of a certain camera to provide optimal aspect conditions for object recognition (see section 5.4). Before tasks are assigned, the decision unit may start the qualified expert if necessary.

In order to initiate object recognition, simply the corresponding object is inserted into the scene tree and initialized with background knowledge. This object insertion is the signal for BDGA to assign the according perception task for this object to exactly one expert. For object tracking, another expert may be activated to achieve best estimation results. Of course, several objects may be recognized in parallel. Considering all objects with visible features in the scene tree, BDGA has to calculate an optimal gaze strategy for the perception of these objects. As a matter of fact, with multiple objects to be perceived in parallel, the requirements concerning gaze direction for all objects may conflict. In order to solve these conflicts, a relevance value is assigned to each object. The relevance of an object itself totally depends on the tasks, that actually are performed or that are planned to be performed based on these object data.

The experts specialized for actions assign the relevance value to the objects they need for task performance. For example, for BDL the own road is relevant for locomotion; perception modules only accumulate data about these objects.

This already gives a good relation between the relevance of objects for the same kind of tasks. Additionally, the relevance of different tasks for the complete system has to be considered. Therefore, different relevance ranges are allocated for different tasks. Within the system-wide relevance scale, all objects can be compared directly. This overall relevance range is divided into several parts, the relevance classes. Each expert is limited to a certain relevance class according to the relevance of the task performed. During operation, the relevance class of an object may change dynamically, if another expert needs this object for task performance.

In the sequel, the most important modules will be presented in detail.

5   Road Recognition

In this section, details on road recognition are presented. First the coordinate systems used for describing the position of road segments relative to the own vehicle are explained. Subsequently, the geometry models for road segments and intersections are explained. This leads to a description, how perception and gaze control interact.

5.1   Coordinate Systems

Building on the calling conventions introduced in [13], coordinate systems for the cross-road, index "cr", and the connecting segment, "cs" are added. In an ego-centered world description, the body-fixed coordinate system of the vehicle has its origin in the center of gravity (cg) with the x_f and z_f axes lying in the plane of symmetry of the vehicle. The "surface-oriented" coordinate system has its origin below the cg and its x_s-direction parallel to the local tangent of the road skeleton line; its $x_s - y_s$ plane is parallel to the local road surface. It thus holds the yaw angle, ψ_{s_cg}, between road and vehicle. The position of the cg relative to the road is described by a lateral offset (y_{r_s}) from the "surface" coordinate system. The "connect segment", describing the intersection of two road segments, has a longitudinal offset, x_{cs_r}, to the road-base coordinate system. It decreases as the vehicle approaches the intersection. The "cross-road" is linked to the "connect segment" by the turn-off angle ψ_{cr_cs}.

The scene tree for this road network is given in figure 5. Parts of the mapping geometry within the ego-vehicle are shown on the right hand side: cg, TACC-base, TACC, an example camera and a frame-grabber node jointly representing perspective mapping and the transformation of the image pixel array into a matrix of data in host memory. The left hand side shows the road network nodes with the surface oriented system, the actual road, the connect segment and the cross-road. Dynamic variables in this scene tree are the TACC pan- and tilt-angles ψ_{t_b} and θ_{t_b} besides the relative position of the vehicle to the road.

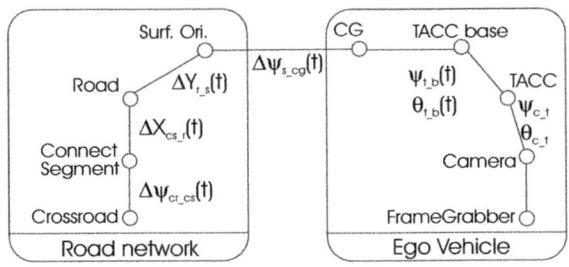

Fig. 5. Scene tree for road representation: Dynamic position parameters

5.2 Road Segment Geometry

The generic road model consists of a skeleton line and the road width perpendicular to this curve. The skeleton line is given by a horizontal clothoid (c_{0h}, c_{1h}). Clothoids are the trajectories wheeled vehicles follow, given constant steer-rate at constant speed. Special cases are straight lines ($c_{0h} = c_{1h} = 0$) and circular paths ($c_{0h} \neq 0$ and $c_{1h} = 0$). Allowing a linear change of road width along the path (b_1) results in a lookahead dependent formulation of the actual width. This differential geometric description results in a very compact parameterization, $[c_{0h}, c_{1h}, b_0, b_1, L]^T$, with L as the maximum segment length.

A birds-eye view of an example clothoidal band is given in figure 6. $P_r(l)$ denotes a point on the skeleton line, $\chi(l)$ the respective heading angle.

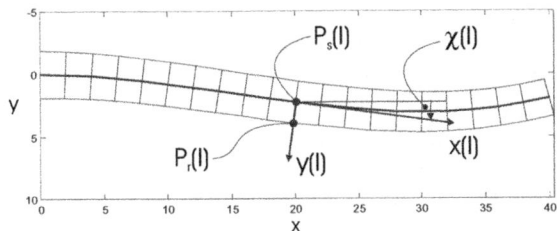

Fig. 6. Road model with $c_{0h} = 0.02\mathrm{m}^{-1}$, $c_{1h} = -0.0013\mathrm{m}^{-2}$, $b_0 = 3.75\mathrm{m}$, $b_1 = -0.02$ and $L = 40\mathrm{m}$

Additionally, for the near lookahead range, where segment curvature is negligible, a "local road" model is available, consisting of straight lines.

5.3 Connect Segment Geometry

The connecting segment is defined by the intersection of two road segments, e.g. the own road and a cross-road. The crossover point of the skeleton lines of the own road and the cross-road is the origin of the connecting segment. Its x_{cs}-axis is oriented parallel to the own road, the z_{cs}-axis perpendicular to the local surface and the y_{cs}-axis completes a right hand system. The geometry of the connecting segment is described by the road width of the two branching segments, their relative positions, the turn-off angle ψ_{cr_cs} and the inner radius of the curve r_{cr_cs} as geometry parameters. For an example of intersection geometry see fig. 7.

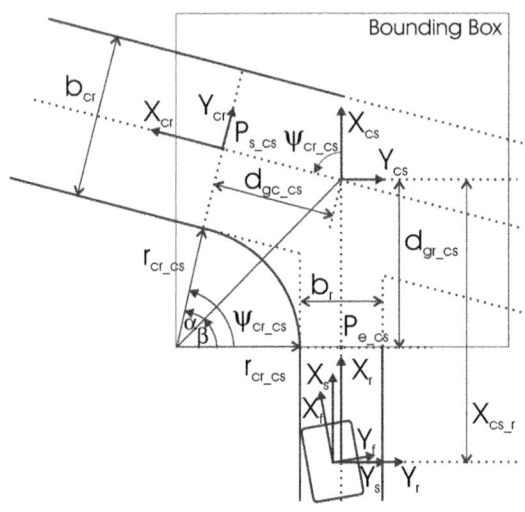

Fig. 7. Intersection geometry, with $\psi_{cr\_cs} = -75°$ and $b_{cr} \approx 2 \cdot b_r$

A bounding box, centered around the origin of the connect segment, is used as rough approximation for the intersection's geometry. Its size is given by $2 \cdot d_{gr\_cs}$ and $2 \cdot (r_{cr\_cs} + \frac{b_r}{2})$.

Commonly, road segments extend beyond the lookahead distance covered by the sensor system. Current information updates can only be acquired about the portion within this lookahead distance. This fact leads to a road representation moving with the vehicle cg. Intersections are a case where the lookahead distance can reach beyond the length of a road segment, e.g. at a T-junction. Intersections represent break points in road geometry description, because:

- Road segments end at intersections.
- The continuity assumptions underlying a road description with a single set of parameters can be violated at a crossing.

Thus, if the skeleton line of a road segment reaches into the area occupied by an intersection, the segment length has to be adjusted appropriately.

5.4   Regions of Attention

In order to determine optimal gaze for the recognition of an object, the geometrical description of object shape is not sufficient, as it gives no indication which characteristics of the object provide features for the sensor and the measurement method used. To solve this task, the perception expert itself communicates its needs by specifying a region of attention (RoA) in 3D object coordinates covering all object parts that essentially should be kept in a certain camera image. If the vision system comprises multiple cameras, the desired camera in which the RoA should be centered must be specified as well. The actual viewing direction can then be computed by the BDGA process in an optimal manner for all perception tasks, see [11]. For road objects, the RoA is a rectangle modeled by a set of parameters. The lookahead distance is adjusted by specifying a fixation point on the road skeleton line at a certain arclength l_{fp}. The rectangular RoA described by length l_{rec} (parallel to the local tangent of the skeleton line at l_{fp}) and width b_{rec} is centered around this fixation point.

5.5   Visual Perception

The perception modules are based on the 4D-approach to dynamic machine vision [14]. An internal model of relevant objects in the 3D world is built using parametric geometry and motion models. The model parameters must be determined from the image sequences originating from the MARVEYE camera configuration. In a recursive estimation loop the elements of the extended state vector $\hat{x}_{k-1}$ at time t_0 containing position and geometry parameters are used to predict the system state for time $t_0 + \Delta t$ by exploiting the transition matrix of the system Φ_{k-1} and the control input u_{k-1}, see equation (1). The transition matrix is known from the differential equations describing the applied motion models.

$$\overset{*}{x}_k = \Phi_{k-1}(\Delta t) \cdot \hat{x}_{k-1} + b_{k-1}(\Delta t) \cdot u_{k-1} \tag{1}$$

$$\overset{*}{p}_i = g_{3D \to 2D}(\overset{*}{x}_k, P_i) \tag{2}$$

Using these predicted model parameters x_k^* and the known mapping geometry, measurement points P_i on the object surface (3D) are projected into the respective images (2D) p_i^*. Measurement windows are centered around these dedicated positions in the image for extracting feature candidates with adapted parameters. A matching procedure links one of the measurement results to the expected feature p_i; the difference between measured and expected feature position is used to update the state vector with the Kalman filter gain matrix K_k (innovation step, eq. 3). Thus, a direct inversion of perspective mapping is avoided. Details on Kalman filtering can be found in [15]

$$\hat{x}_k = \overset{*}{x}_k + K_k(p_i - \overset{*}{p}_i) \tag{3}$$

5.6   Quality of Perception

State variables describing relative positions and geometry parameters represent one level of information for an intelligent autonomous agent. Additionally, the system requires information on how secure the perception modules are about the states supplied, see [11] for attention control issues and [12] for requirements for locomotion. For state estimation the well known technique of Extended Kalman Filtering is applied. The quality of estimation for each state is given by the variance, taken from the covariance matrices P of the filters, see Biermann [16].

Besides this information about the state of the filter, reliability information on the sensor input is required. This indicator of sensor performance dependends on the sensor type. Measurement reliability can be static, e.g. noise level for angular rate sensors, or dynamic, e.g. performance of image processing techniques. Two key quality indicators for model based image processing are:

1. the ratio of expected to matched features and
2. the sum of the absolute values of the differences between expected feature positions in the image and measured positions (residuals).

With the index of expected features i ranging from $1 \ldots m$ and the index of matched features j within $[1, n]$, the matched feature ratio is:

$$feat_{rat} = \frac{n}{m} \leq 1 \qquad (4)$$

Using the predicted feature position in 3-D camera-coordinates $Q^*(j)$ and projecting it onto the image plane gives $P^*(j)$. With the extracted position $P(j)$, the average residual is given by:

$$res_{sum} = \frac{1}{n} \sum_{j=1}^{n} |P^*(j) - P(j)| \qquad (5)$$

Low values of $feat_{rat}$ (eq. 4) indicate poor image quality, unsuitable parameterization of feature extraction or large differences between model assumptions and scene observed. Large values of the residual sum (eq.5) hint at model errors in geometry or system dynamics or at mismatches between features.

6   Gaze and Attention

A core element of EMS-Vision is the active gaze control unit consisting of a high bandwith pan and tilt head (TACC) (see section 3.2) with its embedded controller, the server process GazeControl (GC) and BDGA. In the sequel, these components are described.

GazeControl. is the executive part of the gaze control unit. It communicates with the embedded controller for the TACC and performs gaze maneuvers, monitors the performance of the active gaze maneuver and updates the TACC state and status in the scene tree. GC offers the following gaze maneuvers:

– With a smooth pursuit the angular motion between a camera and a physical object can be compensated, so that the object remains in the camera image.

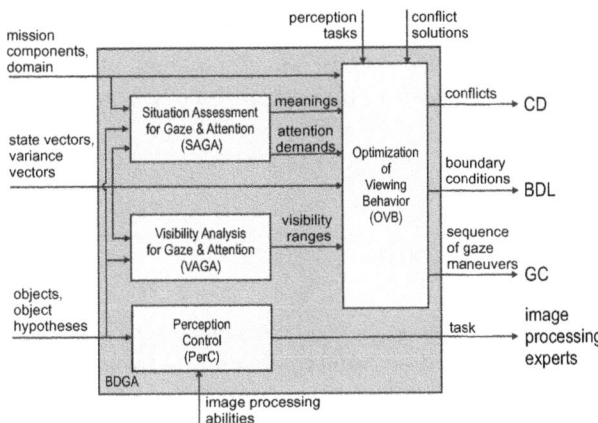

Fig. 8. BDGA

– With a saccade a physical object can be centered in the f.o.v. of a certain camera. This is favorable for getting high resolution images from objects far away.
– With a search path a systematic search for new objects in a certain 3-D area can be performed.

BDGA. is the planning part of the gaze control unit. It consists of four submodules: Situation Assessment for Gaze & Attention (SAGA), Visibility Analysis for Gaze & Attention (VAGA), Optimization of Viewing Behavior (OVB) and Perception Control (PerC).

SAGA uses the current and next mission elements in conjunction with domain information to add symbolic meanings to the object information. For effective exploitation of the pointing capability, the *attention demand*, a variable within the interval $[0, 1]$, is computed. It specifies the relevance of an object for gaze: An object with an *attention demand* of 1 will be regarded exclusively, an object with 0 will be ignored. The *attention demand* of all perception objects are normed, so that the sum of *attention demands* remains 1. The *attention demands* are evaluated by the optimization process OVB to calculate optimal gaze strategies. For task assignment, PerC evaluates the content of the dynamic knowledge bases in order to find the appropriate perception expert for each object to be perceived; it then sends a perception task to the expert specified for this class of object. The perception experts specify regions of attention RoAs (see section 5.4) for each perception object.

VAGA uses these RoAs to calculate visibility ranges for all objects. A visibility range is the angular range for both pan and tilt axis of the TACC, in which the RoA of an object is visible in a certain camera image. If one object is to be perceived only, the fixation point is centered directly in the according camera image.

If several objects have to be perceived and not all RoAs can be centered in the camera images in parallel, OVB calculates a sequence of smooth pursuits linked by saccades to satisfy the needs of all perception experts. Additional information may be be found in [11].

In the following section some results will be given.

7   Experimental Results

Autonomous turn-off maneuvers were conducted with the experimental vehicle VaMoRs on both unmarked campus roads and dirt roads on a military proving ground. Recognition of the intersection was fully integrated into the mission context, controlling the vehicle's locomotion and perception tasks. The viewing direction of the active pan-tilt head was controlled dynamically by the gaze control process based on fixation points and RoAs specified for each object.

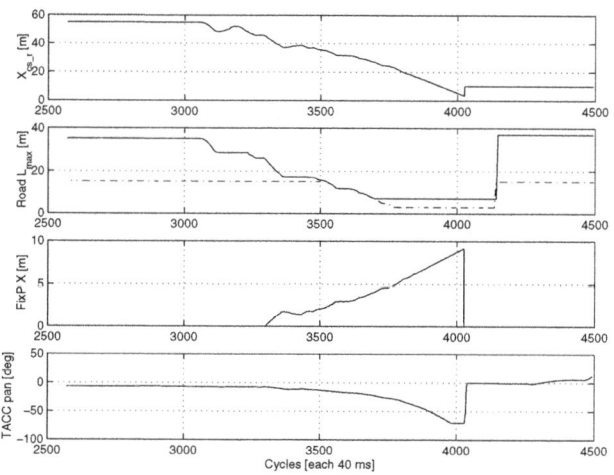

Fig. 9. Approaching a T-junction (from top to bottom): a) estimated distance, b) length of road and local-road segments, c) distance of fixation point into the cross-road d) resulting TaCC pan-angle.

Figure 9 shows data for approaching a T-junction. The top-most plot shows x_{cs_r}, the distance of the connect segment to the own vehicle. The estimated value decreases as the vehicle approaches the intersection. At cycle 4025, when the vehicle enters the intersection, the recognition of the cross-road is canceled and the objects for the own-road are reinitialized with state variables of the cross-road. The second row gives the length L_{max} for the Own Road and the Local Road segments (dashed). The third subplot shows the position of the fixation point as it moves along the skeleton line of the cross-road segment to improve the aspect ratio for perception. The lowest plot displays the resulting pan-angle of the TACC, ranging from $-7°$ to $-70°$.

Figure 10 shows the quality measures for the same experiment. In the initial phase of the approach, when the cross-road is still too small in the image to be tracked robustly, no estimation is conducted and the variance, depicted in the second subplot from the top is not valid. During cross-road tracking the variance decreases. In the final phase the position is updated by prediction only resulting in a cubic increase in variance. Image processing in the initial phase is characterized by occasional total loss of matched features and a high residual sum. In the tracking phase, the matched feature ratio remains above 75%.

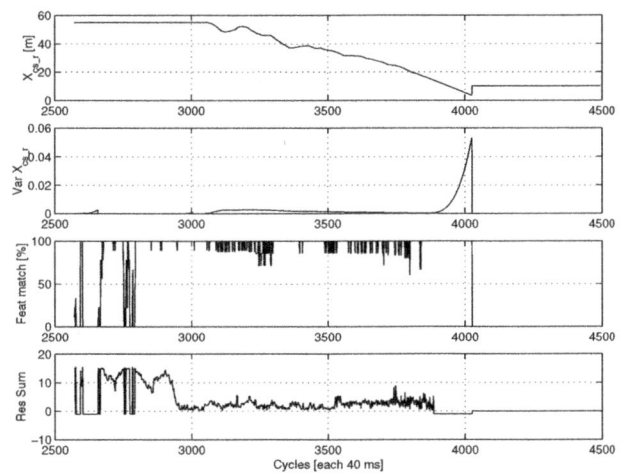

Fig. 10. Quality measures at an intersection (from top to bottom): a) estimated distance, b) distance variance c) matched feature ratio, d) residual sum

Figure 11 shows results for a different turn-off maneuver. During road following one object, the Local Road, is relevant for gaze only (bottom graph) and fixated directly. After 45 seconds, an object hypothesis for the cross-road is instantiated, so that the number of relevant objects increases. From that time on, VAGA calculates the visibility ranges for both the cross-road (second graph) and the Local Road (top graph). Because both visibility ranges do not overlap, OVB initiates a sequence of smooth pursuits for the two objects. At the transitions, saccades are performed and signaled to the perception experts (4th graph) for interruption of the measurements since motion blur will occur. After 65 seconds the Local Road is no longer visible and the cross-road is fixated only. After 76 seconds the vehicle enters the intersection and the scene tree is reorganized.

The top-most row, labeled (a), in figure 12 shows the initial phase of the approach; the left and middle column show images from the two wide angle cameras, the rightmost one is from the color-camera. Vertical search windows

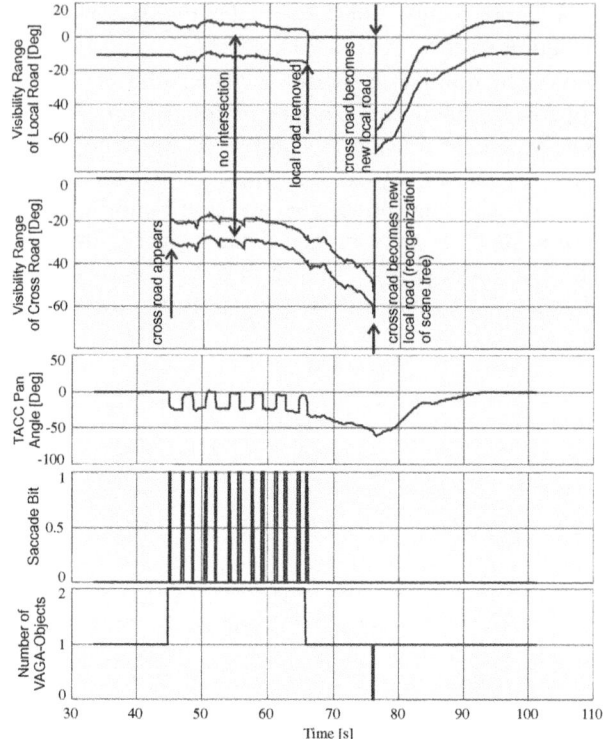

Fig. 11. Visibility Ranges

are applied at the expected position of the cross-road in the image. The Local Road segment is tracked in the wide-angle camera. The pan-tilt head is panning ∼ 5° to the left, facilitating cross-road detection; approximately 2/3 of the image at the expected cross-road position is devoted to the left of the own-road. This focusing has little effect on road detection near by, ((b) & (c)). The shortening of the lookahead range can be seen in the images of row (c), where no feature extraction windows are positioned on the inner radius of the curve. The last pair of images shows the new road being tracked after the turn-off maneuver has been completed.

8   Conclusions and Outlook

The system architecture presented here is considered to be rather general and scalable to actual needs. Aerospace applications for nap-of-the-earth helicopter guidance and for landing approaches have been investigated as well. The system may be used for driver assistance or for the implementation of autonomous missions. Adaptation to different types of vehicles is simple due to well-separated modules for the representation of specific knowledge. The approach is object

Fig. 12. Approaching an intersection, mild-tele camera (left) and right wide-angle camera (right); **(d)** after turn-off onto cross-road

oriented both in a computer science and in a physical sense. Physical objects are represented in 3-D space and time. Sensor data fusion is realized by proper modeling of sensors taking the statistical properties of the measurement process fully into account. The approach has large growth potential for more elaborate area-based image sequence processing with the powerful microprocessors to come, and for learning on an elevated level based on understanding processes in 3-D space and time.

References

1. Charles Thorpe, Todd Jochem, and Dean A. Pomerleau. Automated highways and the free agent demonstration. In *International Symposium on Robotics Research*, October 1997.

2. Todd M. Jochem, Dean A. Pomerleau, and Charles E. Thorpe. MANIAC: A next generation neurally based autonomous road follower. In *IEEE Conference on Intelligent Autonomous Systems IAS-3*. Pittsburgh, USA, February 1993.

3. Alberto Broggi, Massimo Bertozzi, and Alessandra Fascioli. The 2000 km test of the argo vision-based autonomous vehicle. *IEEE Intelligent Systems*, pages 55–64, January 1999.

4. H.-H. Nagel, W. Enkelmann, and G. Struck. FhG-Co-Driver: From Map-Guided Automatic Driving by Machine Vision to a Cooperative Driver Support. In *Mathematical and Computer Modeling, Vol. 22*, 1995.

5. U Franke. Real time 3D-road modeling for autonomous vehicle guidance. In P. Johanson and S. Olsen, editors, *Selected Papers of the 7th Scandinavian Conference on Image Analysis*, pages 277–284. World Scientific Publishing Company, 1992.

6. Ernst Dieter Dickmanns, Reinhold Behringer, Dirk Dickmanns, Thomas Hildebrandt, Markus Maurer, Frank Thomanek, and Joachim Schiehlen. The seeing passenger car 'VaMoRs-P'. In *Procs. of the Intelligent Vehicles Symposium 1994*, Paris, October 1994. IEEE Industrial Electronics Society.

7. Todd Jochem, Dean A. Pomerleau, and Charles Thorpe. Vision based intersection navigation. In *IEEE Symposium on Intelligent Vehicles*, Tokyo, Japan, September 1996.

8. F. Heimes, K. Fleischer, and H.-H. Nagel. Automatic generation of intersection models from digital maps for vision-based driving on innercity intersections. In *Procs. of the IEEE Intelligent Vehicles Symposium 2000* [17], pages 498–503.

9. N. Müller and S. Baten. Image processing based navigation with an autonomous car. In *Proc. Int. Conf. on Intelligent Autonomous Systems*, Karlsruhe, March 1995.

10. V. Graefe. Two multi-processor systems for low level real-time vision. In J. M. Brady, L. A. Gerhardt, and H. F. Davidson, editors, *Robotics and Artificial Intelligence*, pages 301–308. Sprinter-Verlag, 1984.

11. M. Pellkofer and E. D. Dickmanns. EMS-Vision: Gaze control in autonomous vehicles. In *Procs. of the IEEE Intelligent Vehicles Symposium 2000* [17].

12. K.-H. Siedersberger and E. D. Dickmanns. EMS-Vision: Enhanced Abilities for Locomotion. In *Procs. of the IEEE Intelligent Vehicles Symposium 2000* [17].

13. M. Lützeler and E. D. Dickmanns. Robust road recognition with MarVEye. In *Procs. of the 1998 IEEE Conference on Intelligent Vehicles*, Stuttgart, Germany, October 1998. IEEE Industrial Electronics Society.

14. E. D. Dickmanns and H. J. Wünsche. Dynamic vision for perception and control of motion. In B. Jaehne, H. Haußenecker, and P. Geißler, editors, *Handbook on Computer Vision and Applications*, volume 3. Academic Press, 1999.

15. Arthur Gelb, Joseph F. Kaspar, Raymond A. Nash, Charles F. Price, and Arthur A. Sutherland. *Applied Optimal Estimation*. The MIT Press, 12 edition, 1992.

16. C. L. Thornton and G. J. Bierman. UDU^T-covariance factorization for Kalman filtering. In C. T. Leondes, editor, *Control and Dynamic Systems: Advances in Theory and Applications*. Academic Press, Inc., New York, USA, 1980.

17. IEEE Intelligent Transportation Systems Council. *Procs. of the IEEE Intelligent Vehicles Symposium*, Detroit (MI), USA, October 2000.

A Framework for Generic State Estimation in Computer Vision Applications

Cristian Sminchisescu[1] and Alexandru Telea[2]

[1] INRIA Rhône-Alpes,
Institut National Polytechnique de Grenoble, France,
Cristian.Sminchisescu@inrialpes.fr,
[2] Eindhoven University of Technology,
Dept. of Mathematics and Computer Science, The Netherlands,
alext@win.tue.nl

Abstract. Experimenting and building integrated, operational systems in computational vision poses both theoretical and practical challenges, involving methodologies from control theory, statistics, optimization, computer graphics, and interaction. Consequently, a control and communication structure is needed to model typical computer vision applications and a flexible architecture is necessary to combine the above mentioned methodologies in an effective implementation. In this paper, we propose a three-layer computer vision framework that offers: a) an application model able to cover a large class of vision applications; b) an architecture that maps this model to modular, flexible and extensible components by means of object-oriented and dataflow mechanisms; and c) a concrete software implementation of the above that allows construction of interactive vision applications. We illustrate how a variety of vision techniques and approaches can be modeled by the proposed framework and we present several complex, application oriented, experimental results.

1 Introduction

Experimenting and building systems in computational vision poses several major challenges. First, such systems involve methodologies from various areas, such as object modeling, optimization, control theory, statistics and computer graphics. Secondly, a control and communication structure is necessary to build complete classes of vision application in terms of the above methodologies. Finally, in order to satisfy the different demands of particular vision applications, one needs a software architecture where they can be built in a complete, extensible, flexible and interactive manner.

These are some reasons for which relatively few generic-purpose vision software systems exist. Most such systems are monolithic software architectures built around specialized linear algebra or numerical optimization modules such as Netlib [13] and LAPACK [1], image processing tools such as SUSAN [18] and Intel's Image Processing Library [8], or basic visualization tools such as OpenGL [24] and Geomview [12]. Few such systems, if any, have a high-level architecture able to integrate the many aspects of a computer vision problem (computations, control, visualization, user interaction). Moreover, their design often lacks the simplicity, extensibility and completeness required

B. Schiele and G. Sagerer (Eds.): ICVS 2001, LNCS 2095, pp. 21–34, 2001.

to build various vision applications out of generic, reusable components. For instance, Intel's Open Source Computer Vision Library [8] offers various functionalities, such as camera calibration, image thresholding, image-based gesture recognition, but does not structure them in a modular, extensible, and customizable way. Target Jr [19], intended object-oriented, employs a one-way communication to its Netlib-based Fortran optimization routines. Since this control is hard-wired in its classes, Target Jr is not usable for applications that require user input or data monitoring during the optimization process. Finally, almost no computer vision software we know allows adding interactive manipulation and visualization of its data structures to the computational code in a simple, yet generic manner. Visual interactivity is important in several respects, such as the setting of correspondences between 3D vision models and 2D images, and for monitoring and control of the time evolution of vision applications.

Summarizing, many vision systems lack a generic control model. Secondly, they provide heterogenous functionalities that cannot be easily adapted to new application contexts.

In order to address these problems, we propose a generic high-level application model that covers a large class of vision approaches, a software architecture of this generic model that combines the flexibility, extensibility, and interactivity requirements, and an efficient and effective implementation of this architecture. The proposed application model is based on the idea that a large range of vision applications share the concept of generic optimal state estimation. Such applications involve:

- a *model* characterized by its state
- a generative *transformation* which predicts discretized model features in the observation space, based on a current state configuration
- an *association* of predicted and extracted features in the observation space to evaluate a configuration cost
- a *control strategy* that updates the model state such that the evaluation cost meets an optimality criterium

This application model is powerful enough to cover many techniques such as deformable models/dynamical systems, optimization based methods and sampling based methods, as well as combinations of them (mixed methods). The application model is flexible and extensible as it does not make any assumptions about the ways the model is represented or discretized, the type and number of extracted features (cues), how the association is done, and the underlying strategy used to estimate and evolve the model state. From the proposed model, we derive an architecture that provides desired extensibility, flexibility and modularity requirements in terms of object-oriented and dataflow mechanisms, and finally, we propose an implementation of the above architecture which allows building complex vision applications with visual parameter monitoring and interactive control.

The rest of the paper describes the proposed vision framework, as follows. Section 2 describes the generic vision application model we propose. Section 3 describes an architecture that combines the model's genericity with the flexibility, extensibility, and modularity requirements, and presents a concrete implementation of the architecture. Section 4 presents several vision applications constructed in the proposed framework.

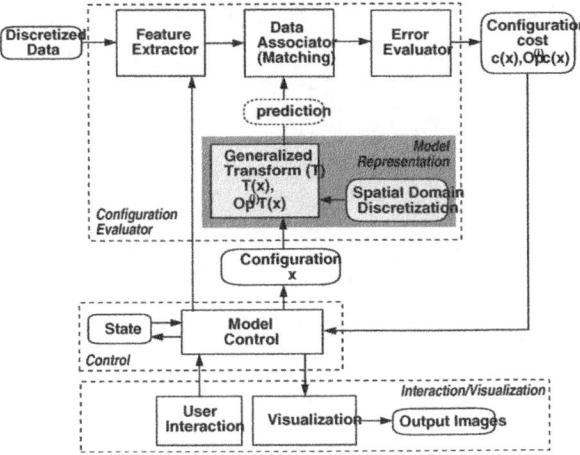

Fig. 1. Vision application model

2   Application Model

The proposed application model exploits the observation that many vision applications are based on the generic state estimation concept. This concept involves optimal estimates of a model's parameters based on a (possibly temporal) sequence of observations. In detail, our application model involves the following elements (see also Fig. 1 which depicts these elements and the data streams between them):

1. a "representational" *discretization* in a spatial domain.
2. a composite (generally non-linear) *generalized transformation* (T), parameterized in terms of the current configuration (typically an instance of the state) which generates predictions in the observation space for points in the discretized domain. This item and the previous one form the *model representation*.
3. a sequence of (possibly temporal) observations or extracted *features*.
4. a way to associate predictions to features to evaluate a *configuration cost* or higher order operators associated with it (their computation typically needs equivalent quantities of T).
5. a *strategy* to evolve the model state based on the evaluation of configuration costs or higher-order operators associated to it, such as its gradient or Hessian, in order to match an optimality criterium (see Fig. 1).
6. several *user interaction* and *visualization* components responsible for the application building and scene exploration, including interactive model-data couplings, 2D and 3D renderings, as well as classical graphics user interfaces (GUI).

The application model elements outlined above are detailed in the following sections.

2.1   Configuration Evaluator

The basic task of the configuration evaluator is to compute the cost of a configuration or higher order operators (gradient or Hessian) associated with it. Their evaluation

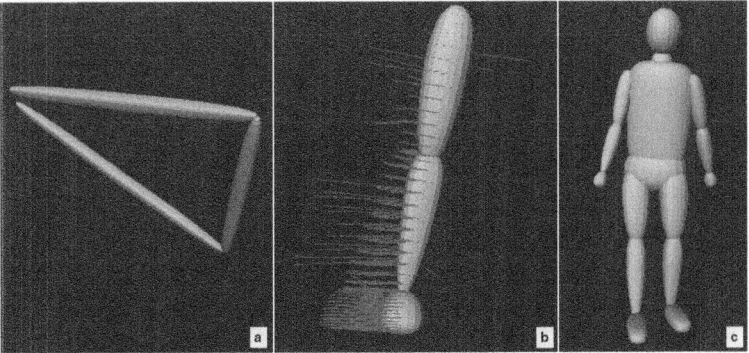

Fig. 2. Various hierarchical models used during tracking

is typically performed in terms of equivalent quantities computed for the model/data generalized transform (T).

Model Representation. The model is spatially discretized in a domain Ω. For any point $u \in \Omega$, we can compute a prediction in the observation space $x = T(q, u)$. The Jacobian matrix of the generalized transformation makes the connection between differential quantities in parameter and observation spaces:

$$\dot{x} = \frac{\partial T}{\partial q}\dot{q} = L\dot{q} \tag{1}$$

The process of model estimation involves a data association problem between individual model feature predictions r_i and one or more observations that we shall generically denote $\bar{r}_i$ (with additional subscripts if these are several). We refer to $\Delta r_i(x) = \bar{r}_i - r_i(x)$ as the feature prediction error.

Feature Extraction, Data Association and Error Evaluation. These components extract the various types of information used in vision applications. Typical datasets include 2D image data, namely edge/contour/silhouette information, optical flow information, or 3D range data obtained, for instance, from a multi-camera system.

A subsequent data associator or matching stage establishes correspondences between model predictions and data features. The matching is either explicit such as in the case of an optical flow module or a 3D model to range features, or implicit, when every predicted model feature has already a computed cost on a potential surface (see below and Fig. 3). In the case of explicit matched features a separate error evaluation stage computes the feature prediction error, based on a certain error distribution. Common error distributions include both well-known non-robust Gaussian ones and robustified ones that model the total (inlier plus outlier) distribution for the observation, e.g.:

$$\rho_i(s, \sigma) = \nu(1 - e^{-\frac{s}{\sigma^2}}) \tag{2}$$

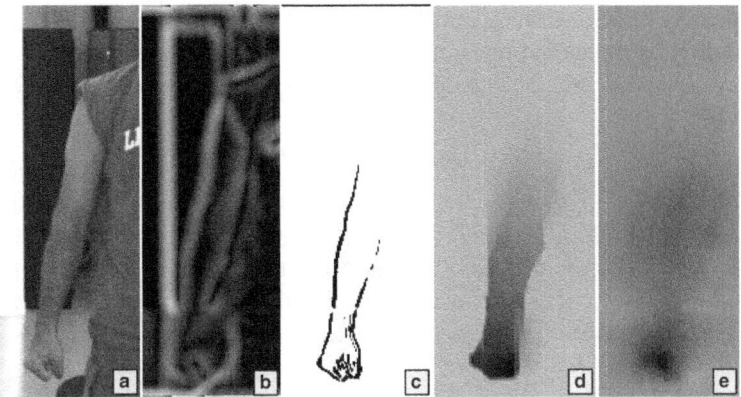

Fig. 3. Image processing operators: original image (a), edge detection (b), motion boundaries (c), robust flow in horizontal (d) and vertical (e) directions

where ν, σ control the outlier threshold and robust influence, respectively, s is the squared feature prediction error, $s = \Delta r_i W_i \Delta r_i^{\top}$, and W_i is a symmetric positive definite weighting matrix associated with feature i.

For implicit feature matching, let us consider the case of edges, where a potential surface can be build such that it has gaps in the places in the images corresponding to edge features or steep changes in intensity. The image potential is computed for every image frame from the image intensity $I(x, y)$ as follows:

$$\prod(x, y) = -\beta \, \| \nabla (G_\sigma * I)(x, y) \| \tag{3}$$

where σ determines the width of the Gaussian function G_σ, $*$ denotes the convolution operator, and β determines the potential surface steepness. The potential is generating a 2D force field, given by:

$$f_{image}(x, y) = -\nabla \prod(x, y) \tag{4}$$

2.2   State Representation and Control

The state representation and control components constitute the core of the application model. Various state representations correspond to various control strategies. Typical ones include unimodal, Gaussian state representation and multiple-hypothesis (sample-based) representations. Generic control strategies include:

- *continuous* ones (deformable models, continuous optimization) which generally assume unimodal state representation and evaluation of the cost function and its higher order operators (gradient, Hessian, etc.);
- *discrete* ones which only involve cost function evaluations and sampling methods for focusing the search effort;
- *mixed* strategies that involve a combination of the first two.

Regardless of the state representation and control employed, there is a unique interface between these components and the configuration evaluator (Fig. 1).

Dynamical Systems and Deformable Models. A deformable model estimates the state of the system by numerical integrating a synthetic dynamical system that encodes the fitting error. The Lagrangian equations governing its evolution can be written as:

$$M\ddot{q} + D\dot{q} + Kq = f_q, f_q = \int L^\top e \qquad (5)$$

where $M = \int \delta L^\top L$, $D = \int \gamma L^\top L$, and $K = diag(k_{si})$, with δ and γ being tuning parameters, k_{si} being the stiffness associated with the parameter i, and f_q are generalized "forces", acting on the state parameters and e is a distance error in the observation space (typically an $L2$ norm).

Continuous Optimization Based Methods. Optimization based methods perform a non-linear estimation in terms of the generalized transformation gradient and Hessian. Popular optimizers include second order damped Newton trust region methods that choose a descent direction by solving the regularized system [6]:

$$(H + \lambda W)\delta q = -g \qquad (6)$$

where W is a symmetric positive-definite matrix and λ is a dynamically chosen weighting factor. For robust error distribution specific gradient and Hessian approximations have to be derived in terms of the robustifiers [16]. For least squares problems, $g = \int L^\top e$ and $H \approx \int L^\top L$.

Sampling Methods. Sampling methods, usually known in vision under the generic name of CONDENSATION [3], are discrete methods that propagate the entire parameter distribution in time as a set of hypotheses, or samples, with their associated probability. In each frame, the entire distribution is resampled (i.e. recomputed and reweighted) based on new image observations. As these methods do not traditionally have a continuous component, evaluating the distribution in our scheme requires only the evaluation of a configuration, but no other associated higher-order operators. The computational burden lies in the strategies for sampling the parameter distribution in order to locate typical sets, i.e. areas where most of the probability mass is concentrated. Known strategies include importance, partitioned (Gibbs) or annealing based sampling methods (see [9]). We developed an uniform interface such that various discrete sampling methods can be parameterized by the search strategy.

Mixed Continuous/Discrete Methods. Mixed continuous/discrete methods have been proposed recently [16] in an effort to combine generic robustness properties of sample-based techniques with the local informed, accuracy and speed properties of continuous ones. The state is represented effectively as a set of hypotheses. In each frame, each hypothesis is subject to a continuous optimization followed by a hypothesis generation based on the uncertain directions of the continuous estimate. Finally, the current set of hypotheses is pruned and propagated to the next time step.

2.3   Interaction/Visualization

The interaction and visualization modules are responsible for scene exploration and manipulation, parameter monitoring and control, and interactive application building. While further details are provided in Section 3, we point out that the dual, simultaneous type of control, user driven vs. application driven, imposes particular demands on the system design, namely *consistency* and *control* problems: user input has to be consistently integrated and propagated into the application data structures (even during application driven execution), while the structuring of individual application components has to allow external interaction during the execution of their different operations. We address these problems by means of automatically enforcing dataflow consistency and by using object-orientation in order to design components with open, non-encapsulated, control.

3   Architecture

The above sections present a generic model that can accommodate a large class of vision applications. These applications share the conceptual structure described in Fig. 1 in terms of component functionalities and intercommunication. To make this application model viable, one must produce a software implementation of it that complies with the requirements of modularity, simple application construction and extension, and flexible control specification, discussed in the previous sections.

We have achieved the above combination by choosing a specific software architecture for implementing the discussed conceptual model. This architecture is based on the combination of two design principles: object-orientation and dataflow, as follows.

3.1   Object Orientation

Object orientation (OO) provides a sound, complete framework for modeling a system as a set of related software modules, by what is called a *class hierarchy* [7]. Specific mechanisms such as subclassing allow the incremental construction of application functionality by specializing a few basic concepts, as well as an effective reuse of the written code. In our case, we have implemented our vision application model as a C++ class library that specializes a few base classes that correspond to the generic concepts shown in Fig. 1. The fixed characteristics of the model, such as the data interfaces between the generic components in Fig. 1, reside the library's base classes. Subclasses add specific functionality to the basic components, in an orthogonal way. For example, different control strategies or model parameterizations, error evaluations, or feature detection techniques can be added easily, independently on each other, and without modifying the basic software architecture.

3.2   Dataflow

Object orientation effectively models the static, structural relations between the framework's components. To model the dynamic, control relations, we added the *dataflow* concept to the C++ classes. We structure a vision application as a network of classes that have data inputs, outputs, and an update operation. Application execution is driven by the network structure: once a class's input change, the class reads the new input, updates its output, and triggers the execution of the other classes connected to its output, thus enforcing the *dataflow consistency*. A dataflow architecture allows constructing complex control strategies in a simple, yet flexible way, by connecting together the desired components in the desired network. Keeping the vision computational code inside the components and the control strategy outside them, in the network structure, has two advantages: the vision components are simple to write, extend, and understand, and they are directly reusable in applications having different control scenarios.

3.3   Implementation

Writing a vision application in the above setup implies constructing and updating the desired dataflow network. We have made this process flexible, by integrating our vision C++ library in the VISSION dataflow application environment [20]. In VISSION, the dataflow networks are constructed interactively by assembling iconic representations of C++ classes in a GUI network editor (see Fig. 5 b). Figure 4 a,b show two such networks for the vision applications discussed in the next section. The graphical icons are actual subclasses of the vision components shown in Fig. 1.

Besides providing a simple, intuitive way to construct the application, this solution offers several other advantages as an implementation for our architecture. First, VISSION provides graphics user interfaces (GUIs) automatically for all the classes of a network, thus allowing for parameter changes and monitoring. Figure 5 a shows such an interface for the 3D range data tracking application discussed in the next section. Secondly, once a parameter is changed, the traversal and update of the dataflow network is performed automatically, thus enforcing the *dataflow consistency*. Thirdly, VISSION can dynamically load different C++ class libraries. Consequently, we integrated our vision library with the Open Inventor library which provides several direct manipulation tools and 2D and 3D viewers by which monitoring the time evolution of a vision experiment and setting up model-data correspondences can be done in a simple, interactive way, as described in the next section.

There exist several dataflow application environments similar to VISSION, such as AVS [22] or Khoros [25]. From an end user point of view, these environments offer the same visual programming, dataflow, and user interface facilities as VISSION. However, integrating our vision C++ library in such environments would pose several architectural problems. First, these environments are primarily designed to integrate C or FORTRAN code. Integrating C++ libraries, such as our vision library or the Open Inventor library, is a complex task. Secondly, these environments assume that the code to be integrated is developed based on an application programmer interface (API) provided by the environment. Such an API usually contains data types and functions via which the user code and the environment communicate. In our case, however, we wish to keep our vision library independent on a specific environment API. In this way, our vision library can be deployed in different environments, such as custom turnkey applications, with little or no modification.

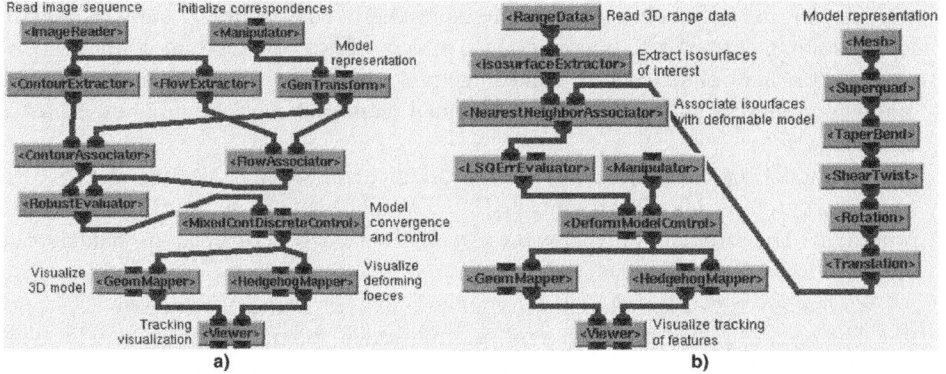

Fig. 4. Tracking networks for human motion (a) and 3D range data (b)

4 Applications

In this section we discuss applications involving shape estimation and tracking both on 2D monocular image data and 3D range data. These applications that we have implemented in our framework are typical examples for the state estimation approach based on temporal observations.

In order to model a large class of objects or structures, we have implemented a hierarchical multi-object parametric representation (see Fig. 2), by subclassing the model representational components (Fig. 1). More precisely, any node $u_i \in \Omega$ corresponding to one of the objects discretization domain can be transformed into a 3D point $p_i = p_i(x)$, and subsequently into an image prediction $r_i = r_i(x)$, by means of a composite nonlinear transformation:

$$r_i = T_i(x) = P(p_i = A(x_a, x_i, D(x_d, u_i))) \tag{7}$$

where D represents a sequence of parametric deformations which construct the corresponding part in a self-centered reference frame, A represents a chain of transformations that position the corresponding part in the hierarchy, and P represents the perspective projection of the camera, in case we work with 2D data. The entire transformation T (see Subsection 2.1) is assembled in terms of the individual transforms T_i.

4.1 2D Image-Based Temporal Estimation

In this subsection, we illustrate the flexibility of the presented framework by a temporal estimation application based on 2D image sequences. The examples we show involve various types of model representations, various types of feature extractors and data associators as well as different control strategies and interaction modules.

Human Body Tracking. We use human body motion sequences that consist of an arm and an entire human body motion (see Figs. 9 and 8). They both involve complex motions with significant self-occlusion, in cluttered backgrounds, including subjects wearing loose clothing. In order to accommodate the complexity of such an application, we have derived a novel mixed-type control method, combining robust (Eqn.2) continuous optimization and sampling along the uncertain directions of the continuous estimate (see Section 2.2).

For model representation, we use the hierarchical scheme mentioned above and superquadric ellipsoids with tapering and bending deformations as basic representational primitives. The estimation involves the articulations degrees of freedom, namely 6 for the arm and 30 for the human model.

We employ both edge and intensity features as cues during estimation. The optical flow has been extracted based on a robust multi-scale computation and the edges have been weighted based on the motion boundary map extracted from that computation (see Fig. 3). Furthermore, we used a multiple association scheme for the assignment of model contour predictions to image observations. Consequently, the Feature Extractor and Data Associator modules have been implemented by chaining together the corresponding Extractors/Associators for contours and optical flow, weighted accordingly (see Fig. 4 a).

A 3D model to 2D image Manipulator interaction module has been employed for specifying correspondences between the model joints and the subject joints in the image, in order to initialize the model in the first frame of the sequence. Subsequent estimation, both for the model initial pose and proportions as well as articulation parameters during the next frames, is fully automated based on image cues. Finally, the model geometry and deforming forces are visualized by the GeomMapper and the HedgehogMapper modules respectively, within an interactive Viewer module.

Incremental Model Acquisition and Tracking. The bicycle sequence in Figure 10 uses a mixed model representational structure and a control strategy based on deformable models for the state estimates (Section 2.2). Only contours are used as image cues initially, based on a single association scheme using implicit matching in a computed image potential (Section 2.1). User interaction was needed during model initialization as for the human sequence.

The tracking started with a minimal hierarchical model, a frame consisting of 3 parametric shapes. New model components, with different discretization and parameterizations, are discovered and recovered during tracking based on geometric consistency checks (see [17] for details). Particularly, lines moving consistently with the bicycle frame, but not part of the initial parameterization, are identified, reconstructed, and integrated in the model representation, and further used to improve the tracking robustness as additional cues. Reconstructed model (predicted) lines are displayed in red while image extracted lines (features) are displayed in green. New corresponding cues for line alignment are added to the existing ones (based on model contours). The extended model representation finally consists of heterogenous components: different discretizations (points and lines) and parameterizations (deformable shapes and rigid lines).

This application needs flexibility at all levels of the vision system: we need various representations and discretizations for model components, various feature extractors and data associators corresponding to each component prediction/observation couple,

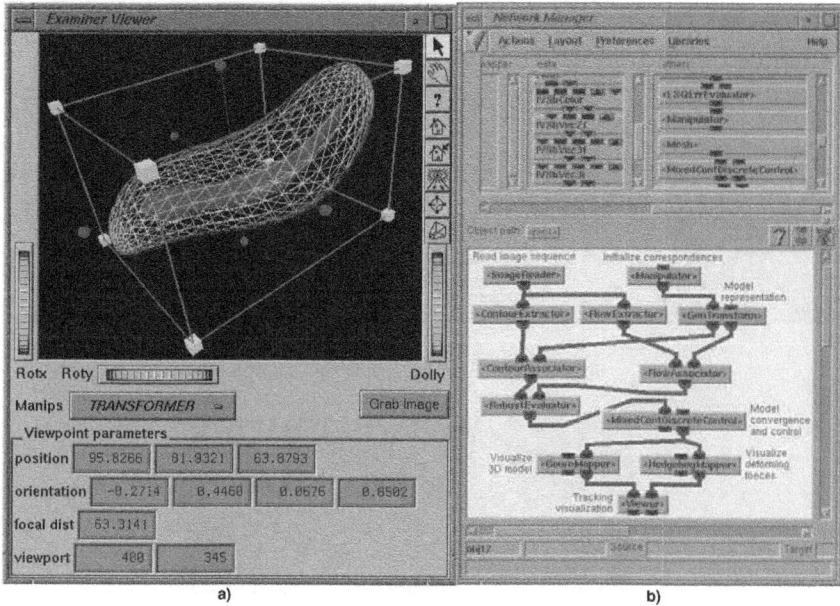

Fig. 5. Data viewer and model manipulator interface (a). A vision application in the visual dataflow network editor (b)

and a way to integrate each component contribution as a cue in the model control. For instance, in a deformbale model control, Jacobians corresponding to each component representational mapping need to be evaluated.

4.2   3D Flow Feature Tracking

In this section, we present a 3D feature tracking and reduced modeling application based on information extracted from fluid dynamics simulations. We employ a model representation based on a superquadric ellipsoid with tapering, bending, shearing and twisting parametric transformations. Next, we employ a control strategy based on deformable models (see Section 2.2). The application's network is shown in Fig. 4 a.

In this application, isosurfaces of vorticity magnitude are extracted from a 3D 128^3 time-dependent CFD dataset[1] by a specialized IsosurfaceExtractor module. In the first frame, a desired feature is selected for tracking. The model shape and position are adjusted to approximate the selected feature's geometry by using the GUIs and Manipulator tools mentioned in Sec. 3.3 (Fig. 5 a). Figures 6 e-h show the model convergence (rendered in wireframe) towards a given isosurface geometry, during the initialization phase. The model is first rigidly attracted towards the feature, then starts bending to approximate feature's snake-like form. We used a Data Associator based on nearest neighbor correspondences to match model discretized points to points on the isosurface of interest. Figures 6 a-d show several time instants after initialization when the tracking is

---

[1] Dataset courtesy of N. Zabusky, D.Silver and X. Wang [15]

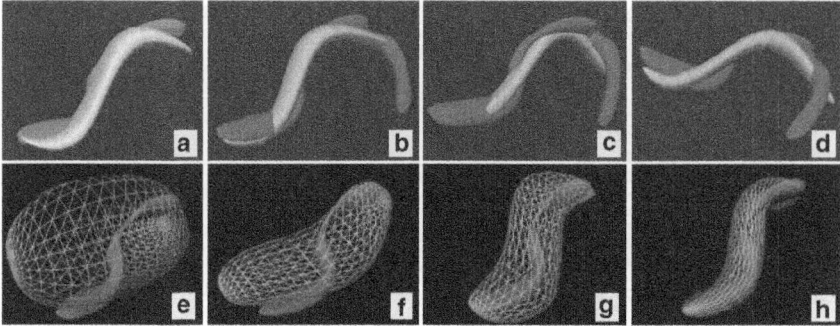

Fig. 6. 3D range data tracking examples

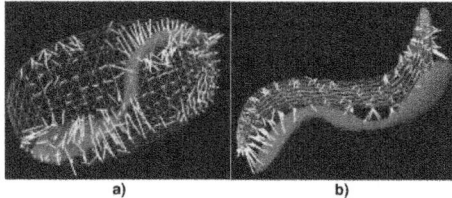

Fig. 7. 3D flow features, model, and deforming forces

automatic. The deforming forces for the initial, respectively converged model state, are shown in Fig. 6.

5   Conclusions

We have presented a layered framework for the modeling, design and implementation of integrated computer vision applications. Our proposal includes: (1) an application model in the form of generic state estimation, involving a control and communication structure able to cover a large class of vision paradigms; (2) an architecture able to support flexibility, extensibility and interactivity demands based on object-oriented and dataflow principles; and (3) an effective and efficient implementation of this architecture.

We have subsequently presented how various vision technique classes, like the ones based on dynamical systems/deformable models, continuous optimization, random sampling, as well as combination of them, can be naturally integrated in the proposed framework. Finally, we have presented several complex integrated vision applications which have been easily built within our framework.

References

1. E. ANDERSON, Z. BAI, C. BISCHOF ET AL, *LAPACK User's Guide*, SIAM Philadelphia, 1995.
2. A.BARR *Global and local deformations of solid primitives.* Comp. Graphics, 18:21-30, 1984.

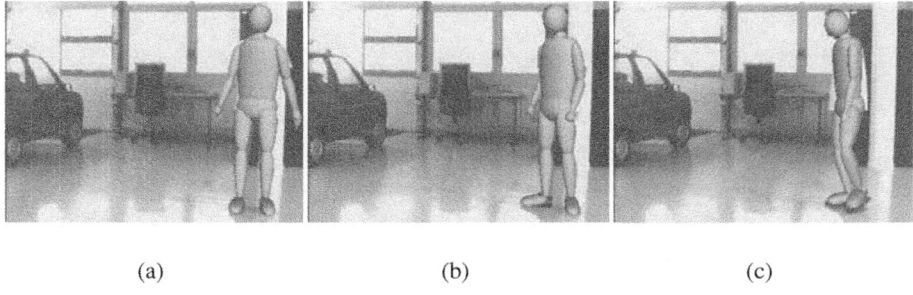

(a)   (b)   (c)

Fig. 8. Frames during human tracking sequence

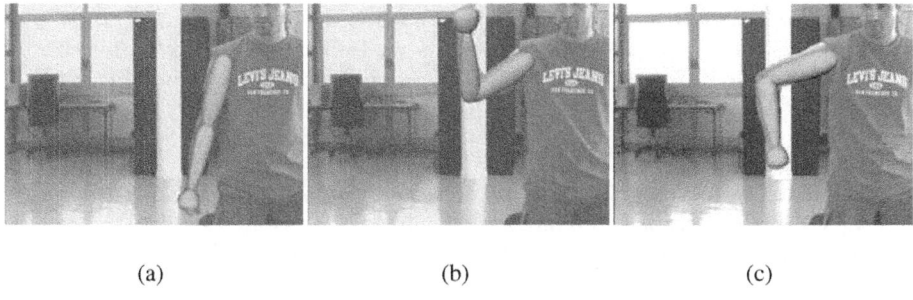

(a)   (b)   (c)

Fig. 9. Frames during hand tracking sequence

3. M.ISARD AND A.BLAKE *CONDENSATION – conditional density propagation for visual tracking.* IJCV, 29, 1, 5–28, (1998).
4. D.DECARLO AND D.METAXAS *Combining Information using Hard Constraints.* IEEE CVPR 1999.
5. E.DICKMANS AND V.GRAEFE *Applications of dynamic monocular machine vision.* Machine Vision and Applications, 1:241-261, 1988.
6. R.FLETCHER *Practical Methods of Optimization.* John Wiley, 1987.
7. E. GAMMA, R. HELM, R. JOHNSON, J. VLISSIDES, *Design Patterns: Elements of Reusable Object-Oriented Software*, Addison-Wesley, 1995.
8. INTEL OPEN SOURCE COMPUTER VISION LIBRARY, available at http://developer.intel.com/software/opensource/cvfl/
9. D.J.C.MACKAY *An Introduction to Monte Carlo Methods.* Learning in Graphical Models, M.Jordan editions, 1999.
10. D.METAXAS AND D.TERZOPOULOS *Shape and nonrigid motion estimation through physics-based synthesis.* IEEE TPAMI, 15(6):580-591, 1993.
11. A.PENTLAND *Automatic extraction of deformable part models.* IJCV, 4:107-126, 1990.
12. M. PHILLIPS, S. LEVY, AND T. MUNZNER *Geomview - An Interactive Geometry Viewer*, Notices A.M.S., October 1993.
13. NETLIB REPOSITORY *available at www.netlib.org*

(a)   (b)   (c)

Fig. 10. Model and incrementally recovered line feature tracking

14. F.SOLINA AND R.BAJCSY *Recovery of Parametric models from range images: the case of superquadrics with local and global deformations.* IEEE TPAMI, 12(2):131-146, 1990.
15. D. SILVER AND X. WANG *Tracking and Visualizing Turbulent 3D Features.* IEEE TVCG, 3(2), June 1997.
16. C.SMINCHISESCU AND B.TRIGGS *A Robust Multiple Hypothesis Approach to Monocular Human Motion Tracking*, submitted.
17. C.SMINCHISESCU, D.METAXAS, AND S.DICKINSON *Incremental Model-Based Estimation Using Geometric Consistency Constraints*, submitted.
18. S.M. SMITH AND J.M. BRADY *SUSAN - a new approach to low level image processing*, IJCV, 23(1):45-78, May 1997.
19. TARGETJR SOFTWARE AND DOCUMENTATION, available at http://www.targetjr.org/
20. A.C. TELEA, J.J. VAN WIJK, VISSION*: An Object Oriented Dataflow System for Simulation and Visualization*, Proc. IEEE VisSym'99, Springer, 1999.
21. D.TERZOPLOULOS, A.WITKIN, AND M.KASS *Constraints on deformable models:Recovering 3D shape and non-rigid motion.* Artificial Intelligence, 36(1):91-123,1988.
22. C. UPSON, T. FAULHABER, D. KAMINS, D. LAIDLAW, D. SCHLEGEL, J. VROOM, R. GURWITZ, AND A. VAN DAM, *The Application Visualization System: A Computational Environment for Scientific Visualization.*, IEEE Computer Graphics and Applications, July 1989, 30–42.
23. J. WERNECKE, *The Inventor Mentor: Programming Object-Oriented 3D Graphics with Open Inventor*, Addison-Wesley, 1993.
24. M. WOO, J. NEIDER, T. DAVIS, D. SHREINER, *The OpenGL Programming Guide*, 3rd edition, Adison-Wesley, 1999.
25. KHORAL RESEARCH INC., *Khoros Professional Student Edition*, Khoral Research Inc, 1997.

A Modular Software Architecture for Real-Time Video Processing[1]

Alexandre R.J. François and Gérard G. Medioni

Integrated Media Systems Center / Institute for Robotics and Intelligent Systems
University of Southern California, Los Angeles, CA 90089-0273
{afrancoi,medioni}@iris.usc.edu

Abstract. An increasing number of computer vision applications require on-line processing of data streams, preferably in real-time. This trend is fueled by the mainstream availability of low cost imaging devices, and the steady increase in computing power. To meet these requirements, applications should manipulate data streams in concurrent processing environments, taking into consideration scheduling, planning and synchronization issues. Those can be solved in specialized systems using ad hoc designs and implementations, that sacrifice flexibility and generality for performance. Instead, we propose a generic, extensible, modular software architecture. The cornerstone of this architecture is the Flow Scheduling Framework (FSF), an extensible set of classes that provide basic synchronization functionality and control mechanisms to develop data-stream processing components. Applications are built in a data-flow programming model, as the specification of data streams flowing through processing nodes, where they can undergo various manipulations. We describe the details of the FSF data and processing model that supports stream synchronization in a concurrent processing framework. We demonstrate the power of our architecture for video processing with a real-time video stream segmentation application. We also show dramatic throughput improvement over sequential execution models with a port of the pyramidal Lukas-Kanade feature tracker demonstration application from the Intel Open Computer Vision library.

1 Introduction

The past few years have seen a dramatic intensification of research activity in the field of video analysis, especially for motion analysis, stabilization, segmentation and tracking (see e.g. [4][1][13][3]). This was made possible in part by the mainstream proliferation of imaging devices and the steady increase in computing power. However, most video processing algorithms still operate off-line. Only a few real-time systems have been demonstrated (see e.g. [2][6][12]). Furthermore, in many cases, a (sometimes extrapolated) throughput of 5-10 frames per second (fps) is

---

[1] This research has been funded by the Integrated Media Systems Center, a National Science Foundation Engineering Research Center, Cooperative Agreement No. EEC-9529152, with additional support from the Annenberg Center for Communication at the University of Southern California and the California Trade and Commerce Agency.

considered "real-time", with the assumption that increasing computing power will eventually allow the same algorithms to perform at 30 fps. For direct scalability to be at least possible, the supporting systems must rely on multithreading to ensure that all the available computing power is utilized efficiently. Consequently, such difficult issues as scheduling, planning and synchronization, must be specifically and carefully addressed. In traditional real-time vision systems, those are handled with clever *ad hoc* designs and implementation techniques. Flexibility, generality and scalability may be sacrificed for performance. Temporally sensitive data handling is a major requirement in multimedia applications, although the emphasis is put on the capture/storage/transmission/display string. Examples are BMRC's Continuous Media Toolkit [11] and MIT's VuSystem [9], that both implement modular dataflow architecture concepts. Their control mechanisms, however, are more concerned with the circulation of data between processing modules (possibly distributed), and they do not provide a complete uniform processing model. We propose the *generic, extensible, modular* software architecture presented in figure 1. A *middleware layer* provides an abstraction level between the low-level services and the applications, in the form of software components. An *application layer* can host one or several data-stream processing applications built from instances of the software components in a data-flow based programming model.

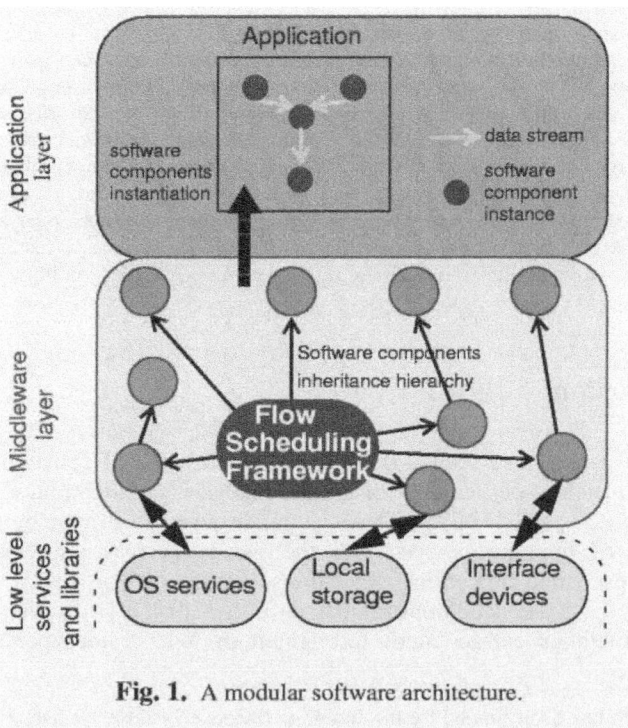

Fig. 1. A modular software architecture.

This paper is organized as follows: in section 2 we describe the Flow Scheduling Framework (FSF), cornerstone of our architecture, that defines a *common generic data and processing model* designed to support concurrent data stream processing.

Applications are built in a data-flow programming model, as the specification of data streams flowing through processing centers, where they can undergo various manipulations. In section 3, we demonstrate the power of our architecture for vision systems with a real-time video stream processing application and with comparative performance tests conducted with the pyramidal Lukas-Kanade feature tracker demonstration application from the Intel Open Computer Vision library. We conclude the paper in section 4 with a summary of our contribution.

2 The Flow Scheduling Framework (FSF)

The FSF is an extensible set of classes that provide basic synchronization functionality and composition mechanisms to develop data-stream processing components. The FSF specifies and implements a *common generic data and processing model* designed to support stream synchronization in a concurrent processing framework. Applications are built in a data-flow programming model, as the specification of data streams flowing through processing centers, where they can undergo various manipulations. This extensible model allows to encapsulate existing data formats and standards as well as low-level service protocols and libraries, and make them available in a system where they can inter-operate.

Dataflow processing models are particularly well suited to data-stream processing application specification. However, traditional dataflow models were not designed to handle on-line data streams, and thus are not directly applicable to our design. An application is specified as a dependency graph of processing nodes. In the traditional approach (see figure 2a), each processing node has a fixed number of inputs and outputs, each of a given data type. When all the inputs are available for a given node, they are processed to produce the node's outputs. This processing can be triggered either manually or automatically. The production of the outputs in one node triggers or allows the processing in other nodes, and the procedure is propagated down the graph until the final outputs are produced. This approach is adequate in the case of deterministic processing of static data. Input type checking can be done at application design time. A first problem arises when the data type of an input is known at design type, but not the number of objects of that type. This situation can be handled at the price of more complex structures. A deeper deficiency is the static model on which, ironically, dataflow programming is based: the "dataflow" is regulated off-line, implicitly. There is no support for on-line processing, time consistency or synchronization, and process parameters are not integrated in the data model which makes any type of feed-back impossible. Extending the static dataflow model to a dynamic, data stream model is not trivial: process inputs are no longer static, unique objects (e.g. a single image), but time samples entering the system at a given rate (e.g. the frames of a video stream). Consequently, as process completion order is not deterministic, data must be kept available in the system until all dependent processes have been completed. The straightforward extension to the static model, using local buffers in processing centers as described in figure 2b, although functional in simple cases, introduces several fundamental problems, such as the persistence of computed samples in the system and the collection of samples stored in independent buffers for data or process synchronization: if a process depends on data produced by several other processes, it should perform on synchronous inputs (i.e. data produced from the same sample), which requires, if buffers are used, to search all the buffers of all the input processes for samples with a particular time stamp. In order to avoid those problems, we introduce volatile carriers for synchronous data, called *pulses*, that are flowing down the stream paths (figure 2c). The color coding defined in figure 2 (green for processing, red for persistent data and blue for volatile data) is used consistently in the remainder of this paper.

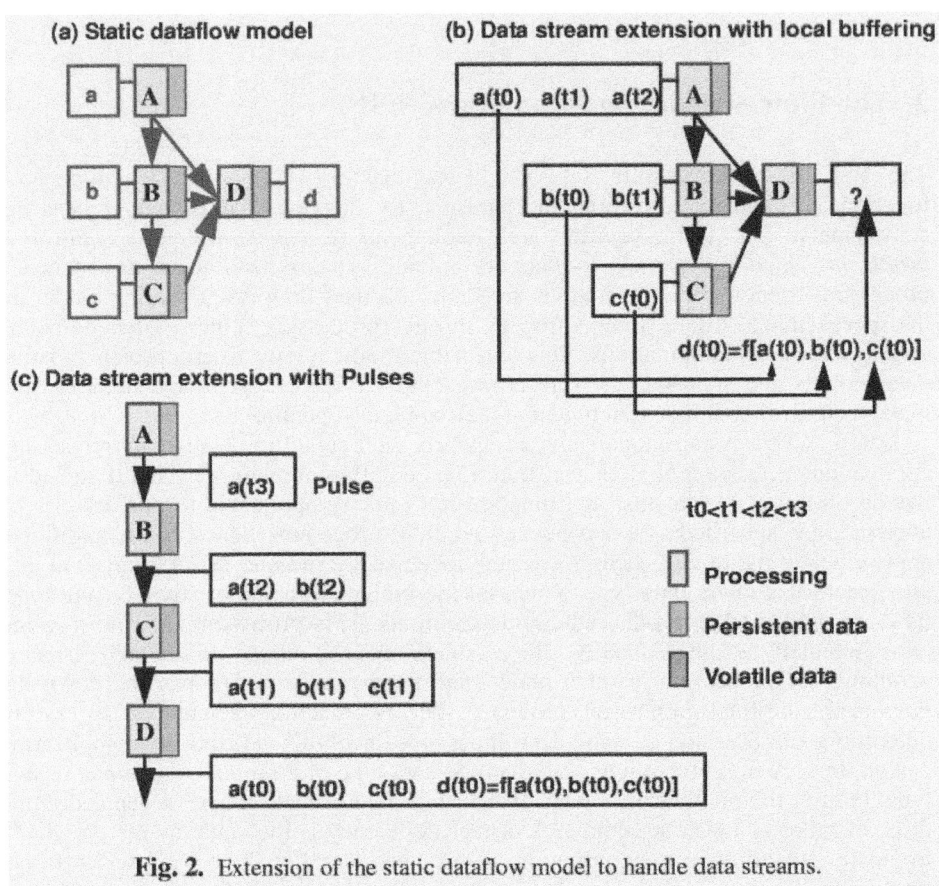

Fig. 2. Extension of the static dataflow model to handle data streams.

2.1   Overview of FSF Concepts

Information is modeled as data *streams*. A stream represents one or several synchronized objects, i.e. expressed in the same time referential. An application is specified by a number of streams of various origins and the manipulations they undergo as they pass through processing nodes called *cells*. *Intra-stream processes* include formatting, alteration and presentation. A stream can originate from local sources such as local storage or input devices, or can be received from a network. It can also be created internally as the result of the manipulation of one or several other streams. As a stream goes through different cells, it can be altered. After processing, a stream can be stored locally, sent to output devices or sent on a network. *Inter-stream operations* are necessary for synchronization, as time referential transformations require the exchange or re-organization of data across streams. Streams occur in an application as time samples, which can represent instantaneous data, such as samples describing the state of a sensor at a given time, or integrated data describing, at a given time, the state of one or several objects over a certain period of time. We make a distinction between *active streams*, that carry volatile information, and *passive streams*, that hold persistent data in the application. For example, the frames captured by a video camera do not necessarily need to remain in the application space after they have been processed. Process parameters however must be persistent during the execution of the application.

2.2   Data Model

We define a structure that we call *pulse*, as a carrier for all the data corresponding to a given time stamp in a stream. In an application, streams can be considered as pipes in which pulses can flow (in one direction only). The time stamp characterizes the pulse in the stream's time referential, and it cannot be altered inside the stream. Time referential transforms require inter-stream operations.

As a stream can represent multiple synchronized objects, a pulse can carry data describing time samples of multiple individual objects as well as their relationships. In order to facilitate access to the pulse's data, it is organized as a mono-rooted composition hierarchy, referred to as the pulse structure (see figure 5). Each node in the structure is an instance of a *node type* and has a *name*. The node name is a character string that can be used to identify instances of a given node type. The framework only defines the base node type that supports all operations on nodes needed in the processing model, and a few derived types for internal use. Specific node types can be derived from the base type to suit specific needs, such as encapsulating standard data models. Node attributes can be *local*, in which case they have a regular data type, or *shared*, in which case they are subnodes, with a specific node type. Node types form an inheritance hierarchy to allow extensibility while preserving reusability of existing processes.

2.3   Processing Model

We designed a processing model to manage generic computations on data streams. We define a generic cell type, called *Xcell*, that supports basic stream control for generic processing. Custom cell types implementing specific processes are derived from the Xcell type to extend the software component base in the system. In particular, specialized cell types can encapsulate existing standards and protocols to interface with lower-level services provided by the operating system, devices and network to handle for example distributed processing, low-level parallelism, stream presentation to a device, etc.

In an Xcell, the information carried by an active stream (*active pulses*) and a passive stream (*passive pulses*) is used in a process that may result in the augmentation of the active stream and/or update of the passive stream (see figure 3). Each Xcell thus has two independent directional stream channels with each exactly one input and one output. Part of the definition of the Xcell type and its derived types is the process that defines how the streams are affected in the cell. The base Xcell only defines a place-holder process that does not affect the streams.

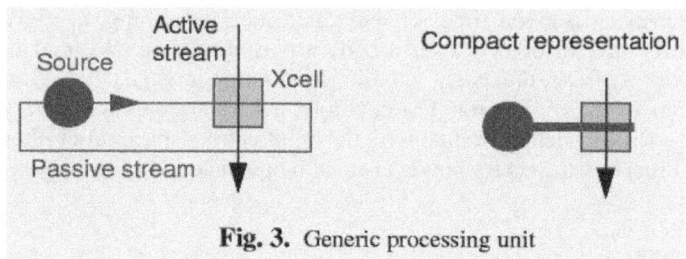

Fig. 3. Generic processing unit

Flow Control. In an Xcell, each incoming active pulse triggers the instantiation of the cell process, to which it is the input data. The process can only read the active pulse data and add new data to the active pulse (i.e. augment its structure). *Existing data cannot be modified.*

Process parameters are carried by the passive stream. A passive stream must form a loop anchored by exactly one source that produces a continuous flow of pulses repro-ducing its incoming (passive) pulses. The passive pulse arriving at the cell at the same time as the active pulse is used as parameters for the corresponding process instance. The process can access and may update both the structure and the values of the passive pulse.

When the process is completed, the active pulse is sent to the active output. The passive pulse is transmitted on the passive output, down the passive loop, to ultimately reach the source where it becomes the template for generated pulses. Note that the continuous pulsing on passive loops is only a conceptual representation used to provide a unified model. Furthermore, in order to make application graphs more readable, passive loops are represented in compact form as self terminating bidirectional links (see figure 3).

In this model, the processing of different active pulses of the same active stream can occur in parallel, as pulses are received by the cell. However, a given active pulse being processed in a cell is not output until the process is complete. This multithread-ing capability is necessary if real-time performance is to be met, as it allows to reduce the system latency and maximize the throughput (see figure 4). Concurrent execution, however, introduces the major burden of having to keep track of data relationships, in particular dependency and synchronization information. In our model, a cell cannot alter the time stamp of an active pulse: time referential transformations, such as buffering or pulse integration, require to make the active pulse data persistent *via* a passive loop, as described later.

Filtering. In an Xcell derived cell, the process is defined as a function that takes as input data an active pulse and a passive pulse, and may augment the active pulse and/or modify the passive pulse. The process description includes the specification of the associated input and parameter types, i.e. substructures to look for in the active and passive pulses structures respectively. When designing custom cells, corresponding local data types and node types must be defined if not already available. A partial structure type is specified as a *filter* or a composition hierarchy of filters (see figure 5). A filter is an object that specifies a node type, a node name and eventual subfilters corresponding to subnodes. The filter composition hierarchy is isomorphic to its target node structure. When an active pulse is received, the cell process input structure must be identified in the active pulse, and similarly the parameter structure must be identified in the passive pulse before the process can be started. Finding substructures in pulses is called filtering, and is a subtree matching operation. In order to provide efficient access to relevant data in the pulses, filtering operations return *handles*, that are used in the process for direct access to the relevant structure nodes. A handle is a pointer to a pulse node. Handles can be organized in composition hierarchies isomorphic to filter and node structures. A handle or composition hierarchy of handles is formed as the result of the filtering of a pulse's structure.

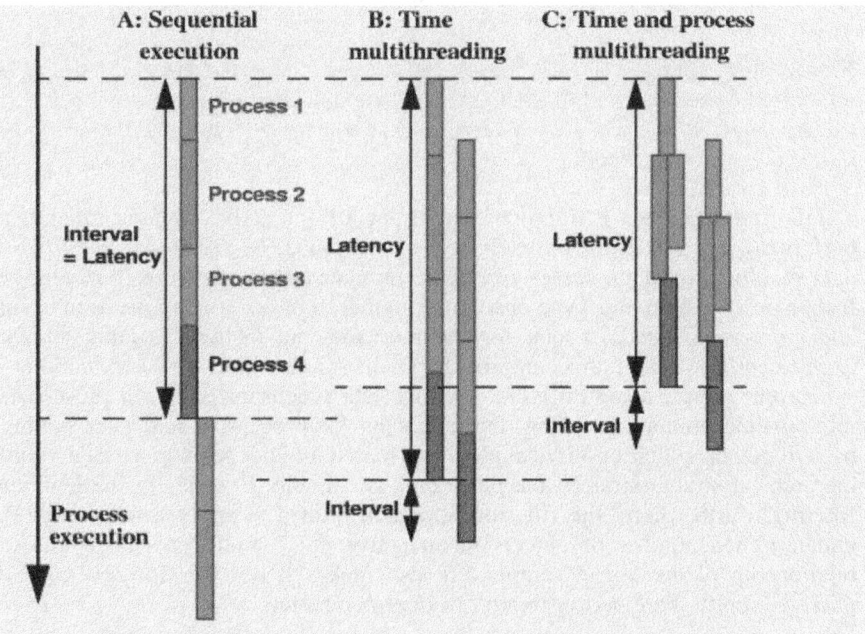

Fig. 4. Advantage of multithreading for temporally sensitive applications. Processes 2 and 3 are independent; Process 4 depends on both 2 and 3. With a sequential execution model, the processing lag also constrains the achievable rate (inversely proportional to the interval between the completion of the processes of two consecutive time samples). Multithreading separates the lag from the processing rate.

The Node names specified in filters to identify instances can be exact strings or string patterns to allow multiple matches. The filtering process thus returns a list of handles, one for each match. The interpretation of multiple matches in the active pulse is part of a specific process implementation. For example, the process can be applied to each match, thus allowing to define operations on objects whose count is unknown at design time.

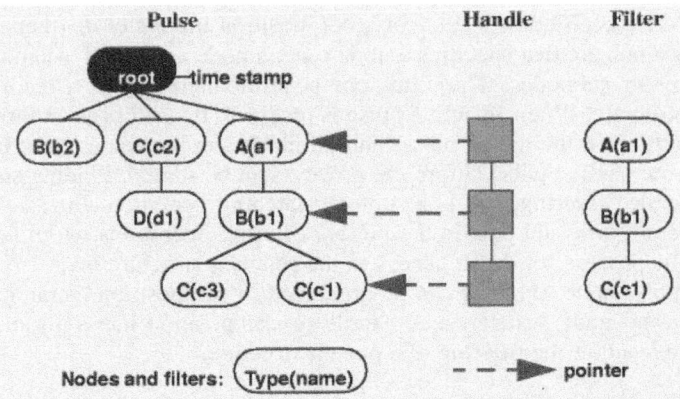

Fig. 5. Pulse filtering. To each process are associated input and parameter data types, in the form of substructures called filters, for which the incoming active and passive pulses structures (respectively) are searched. These filtering operations return handles, used during processing for direct access to relevant nodes.

Filtering efficiency is a major issue especially on active streams, since it must be performed independently on each new active pulse. In traditional dataflow models, data resulting from processes is not accumulated in a structure, but simply output from a processing node. Type checking can therefore occur at application design time, and there is no need to look for the relevant data in the incoming stream. After experimenting with this approach, we found that in applications where synchronization is a central issue, keeping data synchronized in our pulse structure is more efficient than separating data elements for processing and later having to put back together synchronous samples distributed in independent storage nodes. The hierarchical structuration of the pulse data is suitable for efficient implementation of filtering. Furthermore, the filtering approach allows to apply a same process to an undetermined number of objects in an active pulse while preserving the temporal relationship of the object samples. It also makes it possible for several cells on a passive loop to share part or totality of their parameters.

2.4   From Components to Applications

Stream Routing. An application is specified by a graph of cells with two independent sets of links: active and passive. Active and passive connections are different in nature, and cannot be interchanged.

There is no limitation on the number of cells on a same passive loop. Feed-back can thus be implemented either with cells that directly update their parameters in their process, or with separate cells for processing and update, if the update depends on some subsequent processes, as shown in figure 6. Updated parameters are used in processes as they become available on the corresponding passive loop, thus feed-back loops cannot create any interlock.

The set of active connections between the cells is a *dependency graph*. A cell using as input the result of another cell must be traversed after the cell on which it depends in order for its process to be executed (otherwise the filtering fails and pulses are transmitted without any process). Independent cells can be traversed in arbitrary order, and their processes can occur in parallel. To take advantage of this parallelism, we define the *Scell* type, which is a stream splitter (see figure 7). An Scell has one active input and two active outputs. Scells transmit incoming input active pulses on both active outputs simultaneously.

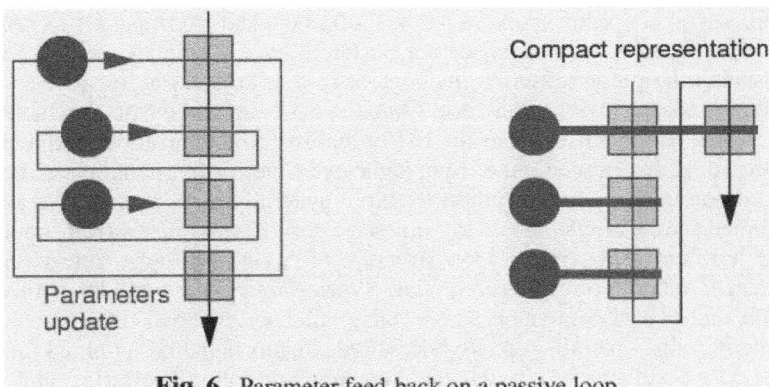

Fig. 6. Parameter feed-back on a passive loop

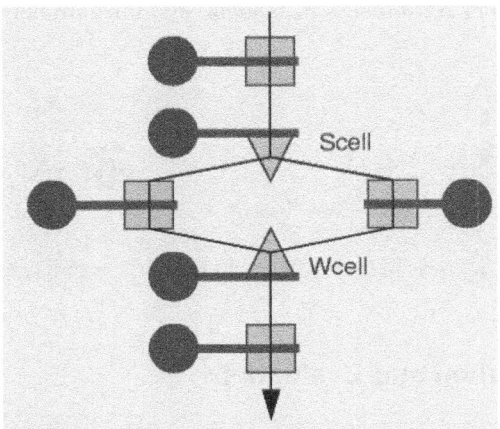

Fig. 7. Stream routing for parallel execution

The only local synchronization enforced in the cells is that an active pulse does not reach a given cell before it has been completely processed by the previous cell on the active path. In order to enforce this constraint when a stream follows several parallel paths, we introduce the *Wcell* (see figure 7), which has two active inputs and one active output. A Wcell is needed when a cell depends on several independent cells traversed in parallel: the Wcell waits until it receives the same pulse on both its active inputs before sending it to its active output.

There is no *a priori* assumption on the time taken by cell processes. If the processing time in the upstream cells varies from pulse to pulse, active pulses might reach a given cell out of order. If simple time consistency can be enforced in cell processes, more elaborate synchronization mechanisms are usually required.

Synchronization. In our framework, synchronization reduces to time referential transformations. As already pointed out, each active stream has its own time referential, to which the pulses' time stamps relate. All passive streams share the same system time referential. The time referential in a stream cannot be altered. Time referential transformations thus require the transfer of pulses across different streams. To do so, active pulses must be stored in a passive loop before they can be reintroduced in a different active stream. Intuitively, if any time reorganization of the active pulses is to occur, they must be buffered. The minimal setup required is presented in figure 8. Active pulses are buffered, by a specialized cell, to a passive loop in which the pulses describe the content of the buffer at a given time. Buffered pulses may undergo a time transform. Another specialized cell on the same passive loop can retrieve the pulses from the buffer and restitute them in an active stream at the desired rate, determined either by a dedicated timer or by incoming active pulses. This operation may involve resampling. More generally, if two active streams are to be combined in one single active stream (see figure 8), the pulses from both streams must be buffered in a passive loop structure after undergoing a time transform to place them in a common time referential. Synchronous pulses can be retrieved from the buffer and placed in a same active pulse, after an eventual time transformation. This pattern easily generalizes to several active streams being recombined into several different active streams. Although the time transformation, buffering and eventual resampling when de-buffering are generic concepts, the actual operations to carry are data (node) type and cell process dependent, and thus are not part of the framework definition.

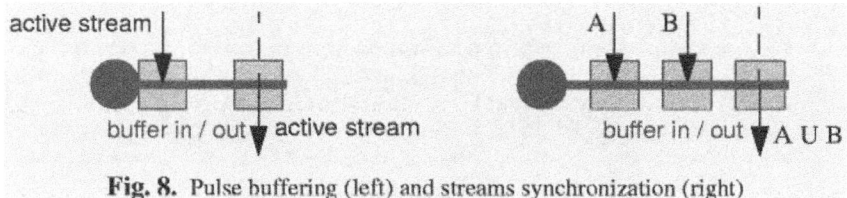

Fig. 8. Pulse buffering (left) and streams synchronization (right)

3   Implementation and Evaluation

We have implemented a prototype FSF in the form of a C++ library, made of a set of C++ classes implementing the basic cell and node types, pulses, filters and handles. All our developments are currently targeted at the Windows NT/2000 operating system, but the library can easily be ported to other multitasking operating systems. Note that this implementation does not feature any resource exhaustion control mechanism, which would require using Quality of Service functionalities from a real-time Operating System.

Using our prototype FSF library, we have developed two applications to illustrate the power of our design both in terms of application development and run-time performance. Building these application required to define a number of custom cells, together with the node types required for their parameters, and a few other node types for the basic data types manipulated in the applications. Many image processing operations are carried out using the Intel Image Processing Library [7], which we encapsulated in our system. For all reported experiments we used a dual Pentium III 550 MHz machine running Windows 2000.

3.1   Real-Time Video-Stream Segmentation

Our first demonstration is an adaptive color background model-based video-stream segmentation application, as described in [5]. The corresponding application graph is presented in figure 9. On frames 240x180 pixels, the application, which involves such expensive operations as the conversion of each RGB frame to the HSV color system, runs at 30 fps, a frame rate far superior to the one achieved in our previous stand alone implementations. The multithreaded processing model makes real-time processing possible by utilizing all the available processing power.

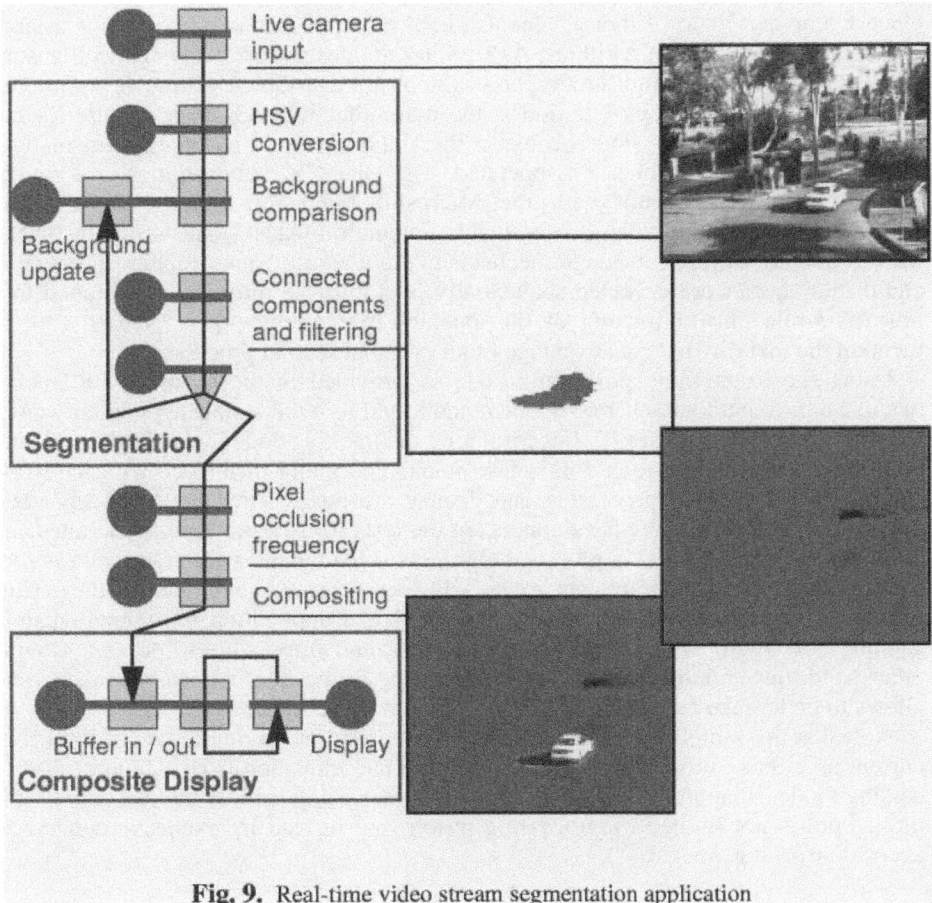

Fig. 9. Real-time video stream segmentation application

Implementing the different components needed to realize this application was simpler than in a stand-alone system, because of the well-defined structuration imposed by the FSF model. Consequently, the overall application was easier to put together. In particular, in a single thread implementation, the feed-back loop is very inefficient in terms of system throughput. Furthermore, if all the described node types and cells mentioned actually had to be developed, most of them are generic and can easily be re-used in other applications. As more modules are developed, less generic components will have to be implemented to realize a given application. Reversely, as new components are developed, they can be used in existing applications by substituting functionally equivalent cells.

3.2   Lukas-Kanade Tracker

Our second demonstration aims at emphasizing the importance of multithreading and synchronization issues in on-line and real-time processing. The recently released Intel Open Computer Vision Library (OpenCV) [8] contains the source code for a large number of useful vision algorithms. As a library, it does not offer any application support, although simple demonstration applications are distributed with it. A representative video processing demonstration is the pyramidal Lukas-Kanade feature tracker [10]. For our purpose, we do not consider the algorithm itself, nor its implementation, but rather the way in which it is operated. The OpenCV demonstration is a simple Windows application built with the Microsoft Fundation Classes (MFC). The dynamic aspect of the video processing is not multithreaded, and is driven by the MFC's display callback message mechanism. As a result, frame capture, processing and display cycles are executed sequentially, and thus the throughput is limited to a few fps while only a fraction of the available processing power is used (not to mention the inability to take advantage of an eventual second processor).

Using the exact same processing code as provided in the OpenCV LKTracker demo, we have built a tracker component and tested it in the simple application whose graph is presented in figure 10. Encapsulating the tracking code in our framework and building the application took only a few hours. The major difference with the MFC version is that capture, processing and display are now carried out by independent threads for each frame. We have conducted the tests for several input frame rates and number of tracked points. A plot of the processor load against the frame rate is presented in figure 11. The frame rate in the MFC demonstration is limited by the performance of subsystems of the machine on which the application is running (mainly capture card, main processor and display card), and impossible to control. On the other hand, our architecture allows to control the frame rate, is clearly scalable and allows to better take advantage of all the available processing power.

Note that this simple demonstration, although useful in making our point for a concurrent processing model, is also an example of bad transition from a sequential processing model. Inappropriate design of the tracking component is the reason why the throughput is not limited by processing power, but instead by exclusive concurrent access to tracking data.

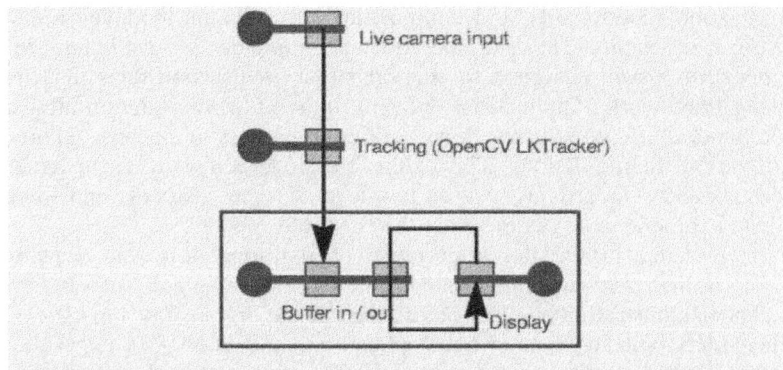

Fig. 10. OpenCV Lukas-Kanade tracker port to our multithreaded framework

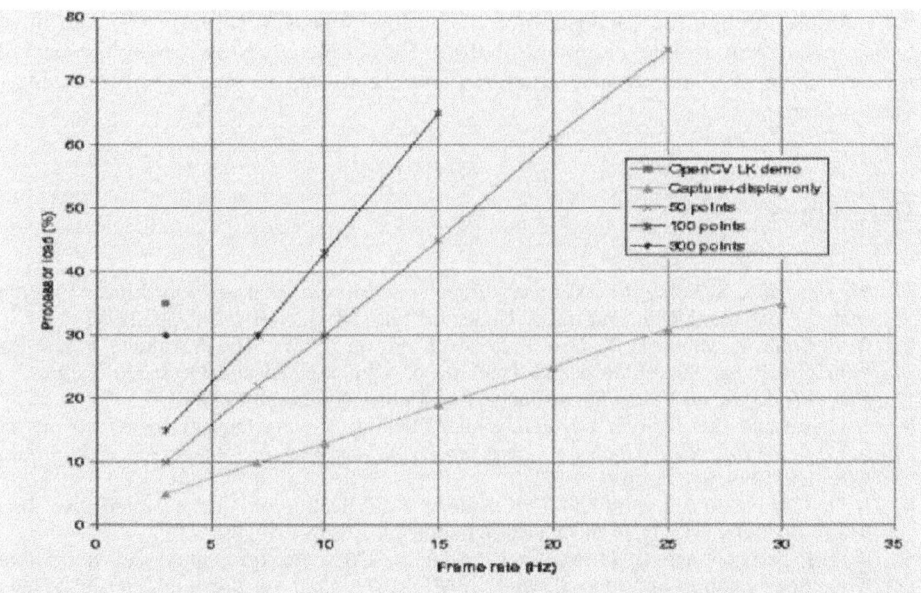

Fig. 11. Processor load against frame rate comparative results obtained with the OpenCV LKTracker demonstration for various frame rates and numbers of tracked points.

4 Conclusion

We have presented a generic, extensible, modular software architecture to support real-time vision applications. The cornerstone of this architecture is the Flow Scheduling Framework (FSF), an extensible set of classes that provide basic synchronization functionality and composition mechanisms to develop data stream processing components. The FSF specifies and implements a *common generic data and processing model* designed to support stream synchronization in a concurrent processing framework. Applications are built in a data-flow programming model, as the specification of data streams flowing through processing centers, where they can undergo various manipulations. This extensible model allows to encapsulate existing data formats and standards as well as low-level service protocols and libraries, and make them available in a system where they can inter-operate.

We have demonstrated the importance of multithreading and synchronization issues for on-line, real-time processing, and thus the relevance of our architecture design. The demonstration applications also prove the practicality and efficiency of its implementation, both in terms of development and execution. Our experiment results also confirm that concurrent processing of data streams not only requires a software architecture supporting synchronization and flow control mechanism, but also careful application design, as a straightforward port of the static (or batch), sequential version will usually prove inadapted to the dynamic model.

Future developments include the incorporation of relevant existing CV algorithms, for example through the encapsulation of the Intel OpenCV Library. We also intend to use this system as a development platform for computer vision research, especially for the design of dynamic data structures and algorithms for real-time processing of video streams.

References

1. M. Ben-Ezra, S. Peleg, M. Werman, "Real-Time Motion Analysis with Linear Programming," Computer Vision and Image Understanding, 78(1), April 2000, pp. 32-52.
2. T. E. Boult, R. Micheals, X. Gao, P. Lewis, C. Power, W. Yin and A. Erkan, "Frame-Rate Omnidirectional Surveillance and Tracking of Camouflaged and Occluded Targets," in Proc. Workshop on Visual Surveillance, Fort Collins, CO, June 1999.
3. I. Cohen and G. Medioni, "Detecting and Tracking Moving Objects for Video Surveillance," in *Proc. IEEE Conf. on Computer Vision and Pattern Recognition*, Fort Collins, CO, June 1999, vol. 2, pp. 319-325.
4. R. T. Collins, A. J. Lipton and T. Kanade, Special Section on Video Surveillance, IEEE Trans. on Pattern Analysis and Machine Intelligence, 22(8), August 2000.
5. A. R.J. François and G .G. Medioni, "Adaptive Color Background Modeling for Real-Time Segmentation of Video Streams," in *Proc. Int. Conf. on Imaging Science, Systems, and Technology*, Las Vegas, NA, June 1999, pp. 227-232.
6. I. Haritaoglu, D. Harwood and L. S. Davis, "W4: Real-Time Surveillance of People and Their Activities," IEEE Trans. on Pattern Analysis and Machine Intelligence, 22(8), August 2000, pp. 809-830.
7. Intel Image Processing Library, http://developer.intel.com/vtune/perflibst/ipl/
8. Intel Open Computer Vision Library, http://www.intel.com/research/mrl/research/cvlib/
9. C. J. Lindblad and D. L. Tennenhouse, "The VuSystem: A Programming System for Compute-Intensive Multimedia," IEEE Jour. Selected Areas in Communications, 14(7), September 1996, pp. 1298-1313.
10. B. D. Lucas and T. Kanade, "Optical Navigation by the Method of Differences," in Proc. Int. Joint Conf. on Artificial Intelligence, Los Angeles, CA, August 1985, pp. 981-984.

11. K. Mayer-Patel and L. A. Rowe, "Design and Performance of the Berkeley Continuous Media Toolkit," in Multimedia Computing and Networking 1997, pp. 194-206, Martin Freeman, Paul Jardetzky, Harrick M. Vin, Editors, Proc. SPIE 3020, 1997.
12. G. Medioni, G. Guy, H. Rom and A. François, "Real-Time Billboard Substitution in a Video Stream," *Multimedia Communications*, Francesco De Natale and Silvano Pupolin (Eds.), Springer-Verlag, London, 1999, pp. 71-84.
13. K. Toyama, J. Krumm, B. Brumitt and B. Meyers, "Wallflower: Principles and Practice of Background Maintenance," in *Proc. IEEE Int. Conf. on Computer Vision*, Corfu, Greece, September 1999, pp. 255-261.

MOBSY: Integration of Vision and Dialogue in Service Robots*

Matthias Zobel, Joachim Denzler, Benno Heigl, Elmar Nöth, Dietrich Paulus, Jochen
Schmidt, and Georg Stemmer

Lehrstuhl für Mustererkennung, Universität Erlangen-Nürnberg
Martensstr. 3, 91058 Erlangen, Germany
info@immd5.informatik.uni-erlangen.de,
http://www5.informatik.uni-erlangen.de

Abstract. MOBSY is a fully integrated autonomous mobile service robot system. It acts as an automatic dialogue based receptionist for visitors of our institute. MOBSY incorporates many techniques from different research areas into one working stand-alone system. Especially the computer vision and dialogue aspects are of main interest from the pattern recognition's point of view. To summarize shortly, the involved techniques range from object classification over visual self-localization and recalibration to object tracking with multiple cameras. A dialogue component has to deal with speech recognition, understanding and answer generation. Further techniques needed are navigation, obstacle avoidance, and mechanisms to provide fault tolerant behavior. This contribution introduces our mobile system MOBSY. Among the main aspects vision and speech, we focus also on the integration aspect, both on the methodological and on the technical level. We describe the task and the involved techniques. Finally, we discuss the experiences that we gained with MOBSY during a live performance at the 25th anniversary of our institute.

1 Introduction

In service robots many different research disciplines are involved, e.g. sensor design, control theory, manufacturing science, artificial intelligence, and also computer vision and speech understanding with dialogue. The latter two are especially important since service robots should serve as personal assistants. As a consequence service robots differ from other mobile robotic systems mainly by their intensive interaction with people in natural environments. In typical environments for service robots, like hospitals or day care facilities for elderly people, the demands on the interface between robot and humans exceed the capabilities of standard robotic sensors, like sonar, laser, and infra-red sensors. Thus, in many cases, computer vision as well as natural language dialogue components become essential parts of such a system.

In this paper we mainly concentrate on the following two aspects of a service robot: computer vision and natural language dialogue. We show a particular example application to demonstrate how a mobile platform becomes a service robot by integrating current research results from both areas into one system.

* This work was supported by the "Deutsche Forschungsgemeinschaft" under grant SFB603/TP B2,C2 and by the "Bayerische Forschungsstiftung" under grant DIROKOL.

B. Schiele and G. Sagerer (Eds.): ICVS 2001, LNCS 2095, pp. 50–62, 2001.

In contrast to other systems, e.g. [4,13], we do neither concentrate on the technical design of a mobile platform, nor on the learning ability of a mobile system in general [7]. Instead, we are mainly interested in the integration of vision and speech to improve the capabilities of such systems, and even to increase them.

Currently, we provide a fully functional human-machine-interface by natural language processing, that cannot be found for systems like MINERVA [24] or RHINO [7]. Several systems are known that include speech as one means for a human-machine-interface (e.g. [5]); they mostly use simple spoken commands. We provide a real dialogue component in our system that takes as input spoken language and thus allows for the most natural way of communication. An active vision system is used for localization of the platform in a natural environment without the need of adding artificial markers in the scene. Additionally, events are recognized based on the visual information acquired by the binocular camera system. Thus, the camera system is essential for the robot's functionality, and not just an anthropomorphic feature.

The paper is structured as follows. In the next section we formulate the task that we want MOBSY to execute. In Section 3 we shortly describe the involved techniques of our system, i.e. the computer vision, dialogue, and robotic modules. Especially, we emphasize self-localization based on visual information, because in general this is a typical problem for the classical sensors. Technical details on the whole service robot MOBSY are given thereafter in Section 4 as well as a short discussion on the integration process. We conclude in Section 5 with results and experiences that we gained when MOBSY was in action. Finally, we give an an outlook to future improvements and applications.

2 Task Description

As a test bed for our developments we chose a setup as it can be seen in Fig. 1. The scenario is an indoor area at our institute in front of the elevators. In this environment we want MOBSY to act as a mobile receptionist for visitors, i.e. it has to perform the following steps (cf. Fig. 2):

– MOBSY waits at its home position for one of the three doors of the elevators to open. It moves its head to see the doors in the sequence *left, middle, right, middle, left, ...*
– If a person arrives, MOBSY approaches it on the paths that are shown as lines in Fig. 1; during the approach it already addresses the person, introducing itself as a mobile receptionist, and asks the person not to leave.
– After arrival in front of the person, it starts a natural language information dialogue. Simultaneously, the binocular camera system starts to track the person's head to initiate a first contact.
– When the dialogue is finished, MOBSY turns around and returns to its home position where it has to reposition itself, as the odometric information is not very accurate.
– Then the waiting process for a new person to arrive resumes.

This main loop is repeated until MOBSY is stopped externally. Accomplishing the previously described steps requires the coordinated combination of

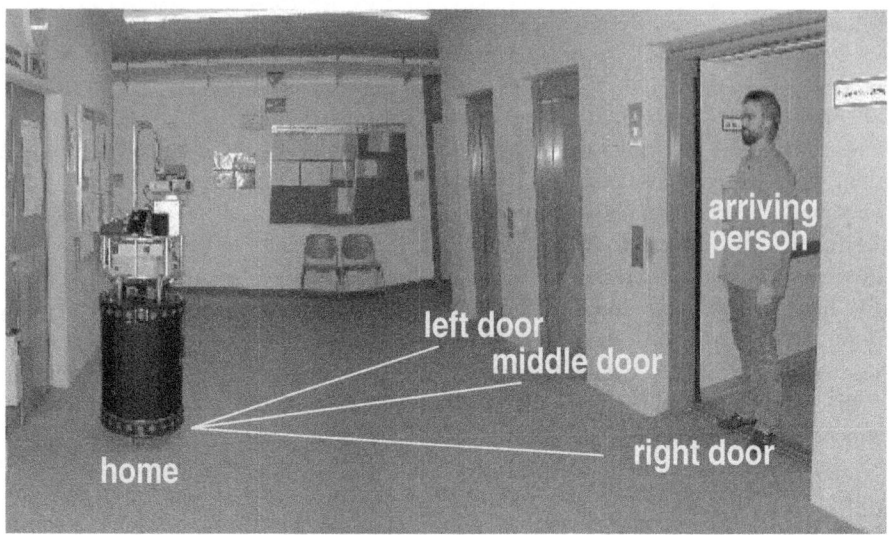

Fig. 1. Environmental setup for the task.

- object detection and classification,
- visual face tracking and camera control,
- natural language dialogue,
- robot navigation including obstacle avoidance, and
- visual self-localization and recalibration.

The methods we used for these five areas are described in more detail in the following section.

3   Modules

Object classification. For our scenario we expect visitors of our institute to arrive by one of three elevators. It follows, that the arrival of a person is necessarily preceded by the opening of one of the elevator doors. Therefore we use a person indicator mechanism based on distinguishing between open and closed elevator doors. For that purpose we decided to use a support vector machine (SVM) as the classification technique that is predestinated for solving two-class problems (cf. [23] for detailed description). The SVM takes as input color images of size 96×72 of the doors of the elevators and it returns *open* or *closed* as a result.

For training the SVM we compiled a training set of 337 images of elevator doors: manually labeled into 130 *closed* and 207 *open*. An elevator door is regarded as *open* in the range from open to half open, otherwise *closed*. The training phase results in 41 support vectors that determine the discriminating hyperplane between the two classes. We used SVM[light] [16] for the implementation of a SVM framework.

Of course, an open door is not sufficient to decide for the arrival of a person. Think of a visitor that wants to depart from the institute and an elevator door opens to pick

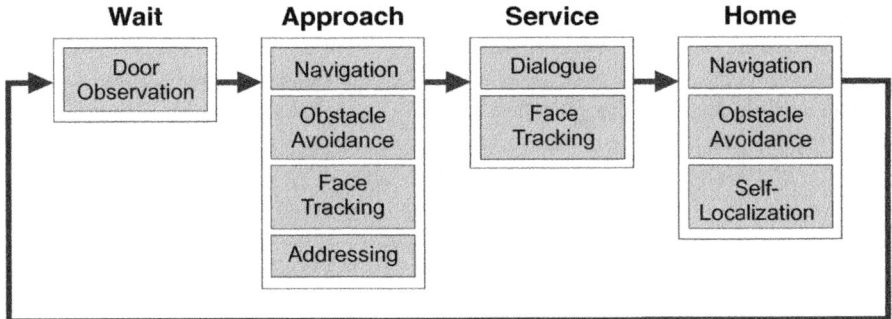

Fig. 2. Flowchart describing the main loop.

him up, or think of the situation of open doors but the elevator is empty. In our current implementation such a detection error would cause MOBSY to start to approach to that person, too. Therefore, this situation has to be intercepted in an appropriate way.

Face tracking. While MOBSY approaches an arrived person and during the dialogue phase, both cameras of the binocular vision system should fixate on the person's face to maintain contact. If the person moves slightly it should maintain the fixation. This makes the person feel that MOBSY's attention is focused on him. It could also be used for the system to validate visually if there is still a person it should serve, or if the person is already gone. Another aspect that is not yet realized is, that recognition of faces could also take place during tracking. Therefore two major problems must be solved: face detection and controlling the motion of the cameras. Face detection is based on discriminating skin colored regions from other areas in the images [8] by computing a color distance for each pixel. To reduce computation time we are using an image resolution of 96×72 pixels. The center of gravity of the skin colored pixels is assumed to be the position of the face in the image. From the determined face positions in each camera, steering commands can be calculated for the tilt and vergence axes of the binocular system to bring the face's positions into the centers of the images. Attention must be payed to the fact that no independent tilt motion is possible because of the mechanical constraints of the binocular camera system. To keep the motions smooth and to let them look more natural, the vergence motions are compensated by appropriate motions of the pan axis.

It is obvious, that skin color segmentation is not very specific to faces. But the following facts justify our choice. First, it is very likely that detected skin color in a height between approximately 1.60 m and 1.80 m is caused by a face, and second, it works very fast and robust.

Dialogue. When the robot has reached its position in front of the person, the dialogue module initiates the conversation with a greeting and a short introduction into MOBSY's capabilities. Our goal was to enable the robot to perform a natural language conversation with the user. For this purpose, the dialogue module consists of four sub-units which form a processing pipeline: for each utterance, the speech recognizer computes a hypothesis of the spoken word sequence. The word sequence is transformed into a semantic-pragmatic representation by the language understanding unit. In combination with the current dialogue-state, the semantic-pragmatic representation is used by the dialogue management for answer generation. The generated system prompt is transformed into an audible result by the speech synthesis unit. All sub-units of the dialogue module have to be designed to deal with high noise levels as well as with a diversity of the person's utterances. The noise level is partly caused by the environment of the robot, for example, the elevator doors, other people on the floor, and partly by the robot itself, because of its several built-in fans and electric motors. The person's utterances have an unusual high degree of diversity, because of MOBSY's job to welcome visitors. In addition to this, MOBSY is among the first 'persons' a visitor of the institute meets, so visitors usually do not get any introduction into the system, except by MOBSY itself. In the following, we describe in more detail, how the sub-units of the dialogue module meet these challenges. In order to remove the background noise before and after the user's utterance, speech recognition starts only if the energy level in the recorded signal exceeds a threshold for a predefined duration, and stops immediately after the energy level falls below a threshold for more than a fixed amount of time. High-frequency noise gets eliminated by a low-pass filter. Our robust continuous speech recognizer with a lexicon of 100 words uses mel-cepstra features and their derivatives. A more detailed description of the recognizer can be found in [11,12]. We initialized the acoustic models of the recognizer on training data of a different domain, and adapted them to the scenario with approx. 900 utterances of read speech. The recognizer uses a simple bigram model. The language understanding unit searches for meaningful phrases in the recognized word sequence. For additional information, please refer to [19]. Each phrase has a predefined semantic-pragmatic representation. Words that do not belong to meaningful phrases are ignored by the language understanding unit. This simple strategy results in a very high robustness to smaller recognition errors and user behavior. The dialogue management contains a memory for the state of the dialogue. It uses rules to choose a suitable system prompt based on the dialogue memory and the current input. For example, if the user asks, "Where can I find it?", the system provides information on the location of the item that it was asked for in a previous question. If the meaning of the recognized sentence does not fit to the dialogue memory, an error of the speech recognizer is assumed, and an appropriate answer is generated. In order to prevent the robot from stupidly repeating always the same prompts for greeting, etc. most system prompts are represented by a set of several different pre-recorded speech files. One speech file for the current prompt is chosen randomly and played. For maximum intelligibility, we decided to use the German Festival speech synthesis system [6,17] to record the system prompt speech files.

Navigation and obstacle avoidance. If MOBSY recognizes an arriving person, the robot moves straight to a predefined position in front of the door (cf. Fig. 1). While moving, MOBSY looks in the direction of its movement, thus facing the person waiting at the elevator. After the dialogue phase MOBSY returns straight to its initial position. Currently the navigation tasks are only implemented in a rudimentary way, i.e. no path planning nor other intelligent strategies are used. They will be integrated in a later stage of the project.

With the robot operating in an environment where many people are present, obstacle avoidance is essential. Non-detected collisions could be fatal, because of the robot's considerable weight. We use the infra-red and tactile sensors for the detection of obstacles. Thus we are able to detect persons at a distance up to 30 - 50 cm away from the robot, depending on the illumination of the room and the reflectivity of the peoples' clothes. The tactile sensors are used for reasons of safety only, i.e. they react as a last instance in cases where the infra-red sensors fail. If an obstacle is detected MOBSY stops immediately and utters a warning that it cannot move any further.

Self-localization. For self-localization we use a neon tube that is mounted at the ceiling. By analyzing an image of the lamp we can calculate its direction as well as its position relative to the robot. Knowing the desired direction and position from measurements in advance, correcting movements can be determined to reposition the robot to its true home.

Fig. 3 shows the 3-D configuration that is used here. The position of the lamp is defined by the end point p_1 and a second distinct vector p_2 on the lamp which can be chosen arbitrarily. We move one of the stereo cameras such that it points to the presumed position of p_1 and take an image as shown in Fig. 4. If the lamp is not fully visible in the first view we perform a heuristic search for it. The extraction of the projections q_1 and q_2 of p_1 and p_2 into the image can be done easily by analyzing the binarized image. Note that q_2 may be located arbitrarily on the line. We approximate a line by doing linear regression using the bright points and find the visible end point by a simple search along this line.

The coordinate system is defined to be such that its origin corresponds to the projection center of the camera, the z-axis is perpendicular to the floor, and the y-axis points to the front of the robot. It is also assumed that the camera center is at the intersection of the pan and tilt axes of the binocular camera system and that it also intersects the rotation axis of the robot. In reality, these axes do not intersect exactly, but this approximation works fine in our experiments.

We determine the intrinsic camera parameters using Tsai's calibration method [25] in advance and keep the focal lengths constant during operation. With this knowledge and the knowledge about the pan and tilt angles of the stereo head we can determine the vectors p_1' and p_2' from the image points q_1 and q_2. These vectors point to the lamp-points p_1 and p_2 and may have arbitrary scales.

The plane E_1 is defined to be parallel to the floor. The plane E_2 contains both, the origin and the line that describes the lamp. The vector v is defined to point in the direction of the intersection of these two planes and can be calculated by the formula $v = (p_1' \times p_2') \times (0\,0\,1)^{\mathrm{T}}$.

From our setup we can measure the desired coordinates p_{d} of the lamp's end point relative to the coordinate system and also the desired direction v_{d} of the lamp (in our example $v_{\mathrm{d}} = (0, -1, 0)^{\mathrm{T}}$). If the robot would be located at the desired position, p_{d} would point to the same direction as p_1' and v_{d} to the same direction as v. If they are not the same, the robot must be rotated by the angle $-\alpha$. The necessary corrective translation can be determined by rotating p_1' by α around the z-axis, scaling the result to the size of p_{d}, and subtracting p_{d}.

For the general case of vision based localization and navigation we already presented a method using lightfields as scene models [15] and particle filters for state estimation [14]. Since currently a self–localization is necessary only, when the robot is back in its

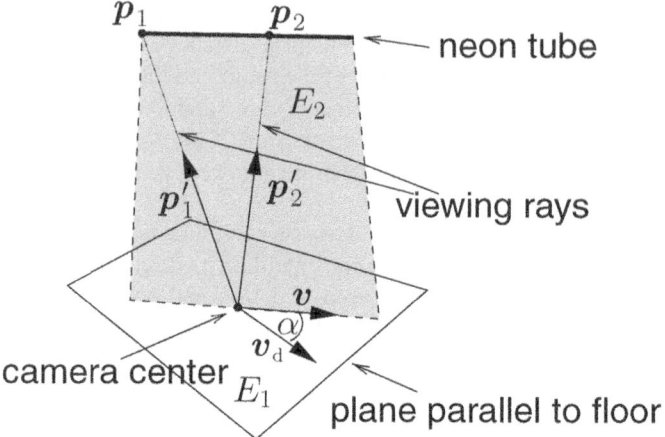

Fig. 3. 3-D configuration for self-localization.

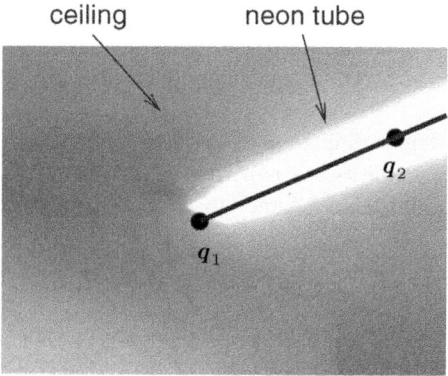

Fig. 4. Image of a lamp used for self-localization.

home position, a iterative self–localization over time is not suited. Later on, when the robot is also used to bring visitors to offices of people, we will substitute the current module with the lightfield based localization framework.

4   System Design

In this section we present the design of our autonomous mobile platform in more detail. At first we explain the most important hardware components, followed by a description of the software integration process.

Robot hardware. MOBSY is designed to be completely autonomous. All equipment for proper operation must be carried by MOBSY, e.g. additional batteries, axis controllers,

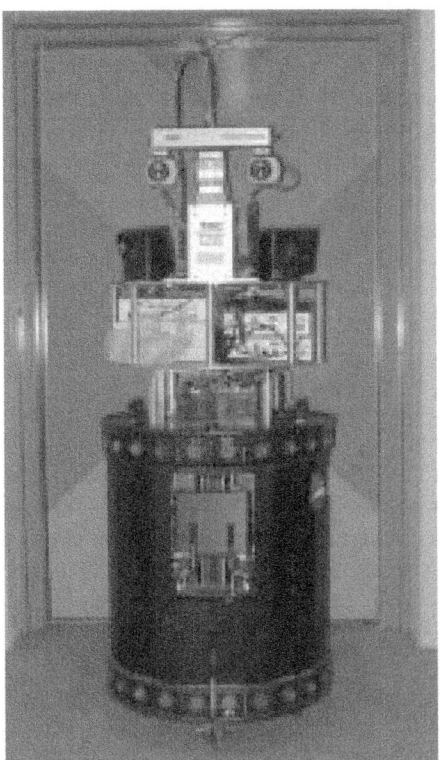

Fig. 5. MOBSY the autonomous mobile service robot.

speakers, etc. The freedom in system design is restricted by the mobile platform itself, i.e. the lower part of MOBSY that contains the drive. The robot is a cylindrically shaped XR4000 from Nomadic Technologies. Inside the platform there are two PCs running under Linux. One of the PCs is responsible for motion and sensor control, the other PC, a dual Pentium II 300 MHz, is used for all high level tasks like vision, path planning, speech recognition.

On top of this "out of the box" platform XR4000, we mounted a two-storied rack for carrying all additional equipment (cf. Fig. 5), because there is no room left inside the platform itself. Especially all components of the vision system (controllers for the head's axes, cameras, batteries, the head itself) require most of the available space. Integrating the vision system was also the most challenging part in our system design.

One advantage of the chosen rack solution is that the "level of interaction" is lifted from the platform's height to one that is more similar to a human being. Among other aspects, height is an important step to let a person forget about that he is interacting with a robot but rather with a human vis-a-vis.

The vision system that we use is a 10 DOF Bisight/Unisight binocular system from HelpMate Robotics. Because no display is connected to the PCs while the platform is in operational mode, and therefore no images from the cameras could be investigated online, we mounted two small LCD panels for monitoring what the cameras see.

Also on the most upper level of the rack we mounted the interface for the dialogue component, i.e. microphone and two loudspeakers. The microphone has a high degree of directivity that helps to make the speech recognition process more robust against high background noise.

Software integration. Configuring or programming pattern analysis systems is a time consuming task that requires specialized knowledge on the effects of signal process-ing algorithms as well as knowledge about the implementation and interfaces. Software developers for image processing today have the choice from several programming lan-guages suited for their needs, e.g. C, C++, Java, Fortran, etc. Speech processing is mostly done in C. Several libraries for image processing routines are available for each of these languages. The larger the application gets that uses such libraries, the higher is the importance of well-structured software.

Summarizing from the modules and algorithms described in the previous sections, the requirements for a common software platform include implementations of Hidden Markov Models for word recognition, statistical classifiers for images and speech, hard-ware interfaces for digitizers of sound and video, controllers for motors, filters for 1D and 2D signals, Kalman and particle filters for tracking objects in images or to model temporal events in sound, just to mention some.

As vision and speech analysis is carried out from the signal level up to an interpreta-tion, a knowledge-based or model driven system is required that should also be shared wherever possible. High demands on efficiency result from the real-time constraints imposed to parts of the processing chain.

As the flowchart in Fig. 2 indicates, there exist two levels on which an integration of software is necessary.

- The task level, indicated in Fig. 2 by the boxes named *wait*, *approach*, *service*, and *home* and the arrows that connect them.
- The modules level that is indicated by the gray shaded boxes.

Depending on the level, different integration techniques are appropriate.

On the most abstract level, the task level, the overall behavior of the system is determined and integration focuses mainly on the combination of the modules to build the correct sequence. The tasks are solved sequentially. In our system, the module sequence is scheduled and synchronized by the Unix shell. For example, the module *addressing* is started when the module *door observation* reports an arrived person. Parallelism is achieved by the Unix process mechanisms that allow of background processes and the controlled stopping of processes by signaling. Proceeding like this has one important advantage: exchanging modules is relatively simple. We experienced this, when we had to replace our first revision of the door detection that used color histograms by the more effective technique based on SVM.

On the second level, the modules level, that defines the functionality of the system, integration is not that simple. The modules are executed simultaneously and require synchronization. For example, for face tracking computer vision and active camera control have to be carried out in one process. As each module represents a research task on its own in our institute, a separate solution is required for each. On the other hand, as re-inventing the wheel too many times delays real scientific and technical progress, the contributors were urged to share software from the very beginning of their implementation. For over a decade such cooperation lead to integration of partially divergent work, as e.g. shown for object recognition and tracking in [10].

As we have shown in [21,22], class hierarchies in C++ can be used to encapsulate actors that are used in active vision. As our system is equipped with an active camera, these classes are used to rotate camera axes. A similar abstract interface is used for robot control and hides controller details; some details on the class hierarchy for these hardware interfaces can be found in [20]. This is useful for the navigation and obstacle avoidance module. Robot control and image analysis have thus been successfully integrated. Synchronization and message passing on the control level for robotic hardware have simply been possible by the use of threads. Other class hierarchies provide the common interfaces for the required algorithms mentioned in the beginning of this section, such as classifiers and Hidden Markov Models. Currently no knowledge base is used in the vision system of our autonomous robot, but a common knowledge-based system applied simultaneously in vision and speech has already been established, as demonstrated in [18,2]. The modules of our vision software system are to some extent portable to other software systems, as the experiments on the system ADORE [3] prove, when this system was used to work with our algorithms to generate hypotheses for object recognition in an office room (see the article B. Draper et. al. on *Adapting Object Recognition Across Domains: A Demonstration* in this volume).

Currently, there has to be little time-critical interaction and information exchange between the dialogue and the face tracking modules. Therefore we preferred to separate the dialogue part from the robotic and vision tasks. It turned out to be sufficient to run the dialogue and face tracking processes in parallel on the task level.

5 Conclusion and Future Work

First we would like to mention that our system operated for more than 2 hours without any human intervention at the 25th anniversary of our institute. The robot had to deal with many people coming out of the elevator or standing around while talking to each other, thus generating a high noise level (cf. Fig. 6; many more images and movies are available from the web site [1]). The robustness is regarded as a great success, especially since the whole integration process took only about two man-months.

In this contribution we introduced MOBSY as an example of an autonomous mobile service robot, acting as a receptionist for visitors of our institute. Research results from many different areas were combined into one fully operational system that has demonstrated its functionality during a two hour real-time performance at our crowded institute. Currently, MOBSY is often in use for further demonstrations.

Increasingly, the aspect of smart interaction with people plays an important role in service robotics. Therefore natural language dialogue and computer vision components have to be integrated with classical robotic sensors.

Safety is one of the major topics when autonomous mobile systems deal with people, especially if there are many of them. Due to the short range of the used infra-red sensors,

Fig. 6. MOBSY operating at the 25th anniversary.

we were forced to move MOBSY at relatively low speed, so that the platform stops early enough in front of a detected obstacle or person. This leads to the drawback, that it takes a relatively long time, approximately five seconds, for the robot to reach its destinations in front of the elevator doors. People arriving at the institute may leave the elevator and go away because they are not aware of the mobile receptionist. Therefore we introduced that MOBSY addresses the person immediately after it was detected. This reduced the number of situations where dialogue module started to talk to a closed elevator door. If however this case happened, a timeout in the dialogue module recognizes the absence of a person and initiates the homing of the platform. This simple attention mechanism will be replaced in the future by a visual module that checks for the presence of people.

The definition of evaluation criteria for the performance of a system like MOBSY is not a trivial task. Of course it would be possible to evaluate the reliability and accuracy of each of the system's subunits, but there exist additional aspects concerning the whole system, that cannot be expressed by a simple number, for example, the acceptance by the users. Currently, this topic remains under further investigations.

In the future we will extend the capabilities of MOBSY. Beside the classical robotic tasks we will especially focus on the vision and dialogue components of the robot. For example, we want the platform to guide visitors to the employees or to special places of the institute, based on visual tracking and navigation. Beyond pure navigation, our robot should be able to press the button to call the elevator, if someone wants to leave the institute. Pressing the button requires the ability of MOBSY to visually localize it and to press it with a gripper.

References

1. http://www5.informatik.uni-erlangen.de/~mobsy.
2. U. Ahlrichs, J. Fischer, J. Denzler, Ch. Drexler, H. Niemann, E. Nöth, and D. Paulus. Knowledge based image and speech analysis for service robots. In *Proceedings Integration of Speech and Image Understanding*, pages 21–47, Corfu, Greece, 1999. IEEE Computer Society.
3. J. Bins B. Draper and K. Baek. Adore: Adaptive object recognition. In Christensen [9], pages 522–537.

4. R. Bischoff. Recent advances in the development of the humanoid service robot hermes. In *3rd EUREL Workshop and Masterclass - European Advanced Robotics Systems Development*, volume I, pages 125–134, Salford, U.K., April 2000.
5. R. Bischoff and T. Jain. Natural communication and interaction with humanoid robots. In *Second International Symposium on Humanoid Robots*, pages 121–128, Tokyo, 1999.
6. A. Black, P. Taylor, R. Caley, and R. Clark. The festival speech synthesis system, last visited 4/10/2001. http://www.cstr.ed.ac.uk/projects/festival.html.
7. W. Burgard, A.B. Cremers, D. Fox, D. Hähnel, G. Lakemeyer, D. Schulz, W. Steiner, and S. Thrun. The interactive museum tour-guide robot. In *Proceedings of the Fifteenth National Conference on Artificial Intelligence*, pages 11–18, Madison, Wisconsin, July 1998.
8. Douglas Chai and King N. Ngan. Locating facial region of a head-and-shoulders color image. In *Proceedins Third IEEE International Conference on Automatic Face and Gesture Recognition*, pages 124–129, Nara, Japan, 1998. IEEE Computer Society Technical Commitee on Pattern Analysis and Machine Intelligence (PAMI).
9. H. Christensen, editor. *Computer Vision Systems*, Heidelberg, Jan. 1999. Springer.
10. J. Denzler, R. Beß J. Hornegger, H. Niemann, and D. Paulus. Learning, tracking and recognition of 3D objects. In V. Graefe, editor, *International Conference on Intelligent Robots and Systems – Advanced Robotic Systems and Real World*, volume 1, pages 89–96, München, 1994.
11. F. Gallwitz. *Integrated Stochastic Models for Spontaneous Speech Recognition*. Phd-thesis, Technische Fakultät der Universität Erlangen-Nürnberg, Erlangen. to appear.
12. F. Gallwitz, M. Aretoulaki, M. Boros, J. Haas, S. Harbeck, R. Huber, H. Niemann, and E. Nöth. The Erlangen Spoken Dialogue System EVAR: A State-of-the-Art Information Retrieval System. In *Proceedings of 1998 International Symposium on Spoken Dialogue (ISSD 98)*, pages 19–26, Sydney, Australia, 1998.
13. U. Hanebeck, C. Fischer, and G Schmidt. Roman: A mobile robotic assistant for indoor service applications. In *Proceedings of the IEEE RSJ International Conference on Intelligent Robots and Systems (IROS)*, pages 518–525, 1997.
14. B. Heigl, J. Denzler, and H. Niemann. Combining computer graphics and computer vision for probabilistic visual robot navigation. In Jacques G. Verly, editor, *Enhanced and Synthetic Vision 2000*, volume 4023 of *Proceedings of SPIE*, pages 226–235, Orlando, FL, USA, April 2000.
15. B. Heigl, R. Koch, M. Pollefeys, J. Denzler, and L. Van Gool. Plenoptic modeling and rendering from image sequences taken by a hand-held camera. In W. Förstner, J.M. Buhmann, A. Faber, and P. Faber, editors, *Mustererkennung 1999*, pages 94–101, Heidelberg, 1999. Springer.
16. Th. Joachims. Making large-scale support vector machine learning practical. In Schölkopf et al. [23], pages 169–184.
17. Gregor Möhler, Bernd Möbius, Antje Schweitzer, Edmilson Morais, Norbert Braunschweiler, and Martin Haase. The german festival system, last visited 4/10/2001. http://www.ims.uni-stuttgart.de/phonetik/synthesis/index.html.
18. H. Niemann, V. Fischer, D. Paulus, and J. Fischer. Knowledge based image understanding by iterative optimization. In G. Görz and St. Hölldobler, editors, *KI–96: Advances in Artificial Intelligence*, volume 1137 (Lecture Notes in Artificial Intelligence), pages 287–301. Springer, Berlin, 1996.
19. E. Nöth, J. Haas, V. Warnke, F. Gallwitz, and M. Boros. A hybrid approach to spoken dialogue understanding: Prosody, statistics and partial parsing. In *Proceedings European Conference on Speech Communication and Technology*, volume 5, pages 2019–2022, Budapest, Hungary, 1999.
20. D. Paulus, U. Ahlrichs, B. Heigl, J. Denzler, J. Hornegger, and H. Niemann. Active knowledge based scene analysis. In Christensen [9], pages 180–199.

21. D. Paulus and J. Hornegger. *Applied pattern recognition: A practical introduction to image and speech processing in C++*. Advanced Studies in Computer Science. Vieweg, Braunschweig, 3rd edition, 2001.
22. D. Paulus, J. Hornegger, and H. Niemann. Software engineering for image processing and analysis. In B. Jähne, P. Geißler, and H. Haußecker, editors, *Handbook of Computer Vision and Applications*, volume 3, pages 77–103. Academic Press, San Diego, 1999.
23. B. Schölkopf, Ch. Burges, and A. Smola, editors. *Advances in Kernel Methods: Support Vector Learning*. The MIT Press, Cambridge, London, 1999.
24. S. Thrun, M. Bennewitz, W. Burgard, A. Cremers, F. Dellaert, D. Fox, D. Hahnel, C. Rosenberg, J. Schulte, and D. Schulz. Minerva: A second-generation museum tour-guide robot. In *Proceedings of the IEEE International Conference on Robotics Automation (ICRA)*, pages 1999–2005, 1999.
25. R.Y. Tsai. A versatile camera calibration technique for high-accuracy 3d machine vision metrology using off-the-shelf tv cameras and lenses. *IEEE Journal of Robotics and Automation*, 3(4):323–344, 1987.

A Handwriting Recognition System Based on Visual Input*

Markus Wienecke, Gernot A. Fink, and Gerhard Sagerer

Bielefeld University, Faculty of Technology
33594 Bielefeld
{mwieneck,gernot,sagerer}@techfak.uni-bielefeld.de

Abstract. One of the most promising methods of interacting with small portable computing devices such as personal digital assistants is the use of handwriting. However, for data acquisition touch sensitive pads, which are limited in size, and special pens are required. In order to render this communication method more natural Munich & Perona [11] proposed to visually observe the writing process on ordinary paper and to automatically recover the pen trajectory from video image sequences. On the basis of this work we developed a complete handwriting recognition system based on visual input. In this paper we will describe the methods employed for pen tracking, feature extraction, and statistical handwriting recognition. The differences compared to classical on-line recognition systems and the modifications in the visual tracking process will be discussed. In order to demonstrate the feasibility of the proposed approach evaluation results on a small writer independent unconstrained handwriting recognition task will be presented.

1 Introduction

In the field of human computer interaction the ultimate goal is to make interaction with computing machinery possible without the need for special input devices such as keyboard or mouse. Therefore, more natural modalities of communication such as speech, gesture, and handwriting are investigated. However, in order to capture a person's writing, again a combination of special input devices is necessary, namely touch sensitive pads and special pens. As handwriting is currently mostly used for the interaction with small personal digital assistants (PDAs) also the size of the input field is severely restricted. Therefore, a promising alternative might be to retain ordinary pen and paper to produce handwritten text and capture the writing process by observing it using a video camera — an idea first envisioned by Munich & Perona in 1996 [11].

In contrast to traditional methods to obtain so called on-line handwriting data — i.e. the dynamically sampled trajectory of the pen — an approach based on visual observation will be faced with severe difficulties in obtaining the trajectory data. As a consequence the input data of the recognition process itself

---

* This work was partially supported by the German Research Foundation (DFG) within project **Fi799/1**.

B. Schiele and G. Sagerer (Eds.): ICVS 2001, LNCS 2095, pp. 63–72, 2001.

might be erroneous or noisy. Therefore, a subsequent recognition model has to be robust against the inherent limitations of the data acquisition method.

In this paper we present a complete handwriting recognition system based on visual input. A short review of related work in on-line handwriting recognition will be given in the following section. The architecture of our system will be described in section 3. Additionally, it will be shown in which respects the capabilities of our system go beyond the original work by Munich & Perona [11], which did not yet include a recognition module. The methods employed for tracking a pen in video data, extracting robust features, and for statistical recognition will be discussed in subsequent sections.

2   Related Work

In handwriting recognition usually two different research areas are distinguished[1]. When the handwritten text, which has been produced by ordinary writing on paper, is subsequently digitized for automatic processing using some sort of image acquisition device, so called off-line recognition is performed. Handwriting data is thus viewed as some special sort of images to be analyzed. On-line handwriting recognition, however, deals with dynamic data describing the motion of the pen as observed during the writing process. For recording such pen trajectories mostly special digitizing tablets are used. In contrast to off-line data the dynamics of the writing process can be exploited for the analysis of on-line pen trajectories.

Earlier approaches to recognition of on-line handwriting applied segmentation-based methods in combination with sophisticated classification techniques (cf. e.g. [16]). In more recent work, however, so called segmentation-free approaches based on Hidden-Markov-Models (HMMs) were successfully applied to the task and gained growing interest in the research community (e.g. [12,9,5]). This is certainly to some extent due to the fact that the HMM technology reached a state of maturity in the context of speech recognition (cf. e.g. [7]), where hardly any fundamentally different approaches are pursued today. As pen-trajectory data can also be viewed as a time series of samples transferring the HMM approach from speech recognition to the domain of on-line handwriting recognition is almost straight forward — a fact that has also been explicitly pointed out by some authors (e.g. [15]).

As for the acquisition of trajectory data special devices are necessary the investigation of alternative methods for obtaining on-line handwriting data seems promising. Munich & Perona [11] first proposed to use a video-based approach. Handwriting can thus be produced with an ordinary pen on paper. The writing process is observed by a video camera and the pen trajectory is automatically extracted from the recorded image sequence. In the original work the feasibility of the video-based tracking was demonstrated. However, even in more recent work [10] handwriting recognition based on video input was not investigated.

---

[1] For an overview of the field of handwriting and character recognition see e.g. [2].

A comparable approach using video-based data acquisition was recently proposed in [1]. Difference images are used to obtain the ink trace left on the paper during writing. Using an existing recognition system results on a small writer dependent task are presented.

3   System Architecture

The proposed complete system for handwriting recognition based on the visual observation of the writing process consists of four major building blocks depicted in Fig. 1. It shares modules for feature extraction from pen trajectory data as well as for recognition of handwritten characters or words with most current on-line handwriting recognition systems. However, the trajectory data can't be obtained directly from a special device such as a digitizing tablet but are the results of a method for tracking the pen tip in image sequences during the process of writing. We use a slightly modified version of the approach developed by Munich & Perona [11]. The most important modification is to include a completely automatic procedure for finding the pen initially before the actual writing starts. This feature is of fundamental importance in order to make the interaction with such a system as natural as possible.

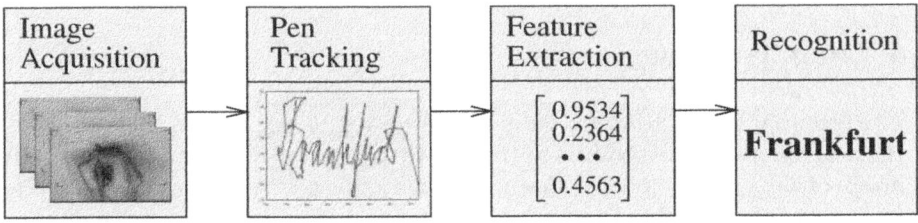

Fig. 1. Architecture of the video based handwriting recognition system.

The image sequences from which the pen trajectory is obtained during writing are captured using a standard video camera working in interlaced PAL mode. We obtain 50 frames per second with a resolution of 768×288 pixels. As the pen tip needs to be clearly visible in every single image the positioning of the camera has to be considered carefully. We found the setup show in Fig. 2 to provide a good compromise between the different requirements. It allows the user to write in a rather natural position. The writing space visible in the video images covers an area of approximately 18×13 cm so that the writing of multiple word instances or even short portions of text can be observed. As the camera can't be positioned directly above the writing area the scene is observed from an angle of approximately 65 degrees. An illumination that proved to be sufficient for our purposes is provided by two ordinary table lamps. During video based handwriting recognition the digitizing tablet shown in Fig. 2 is not used. However,

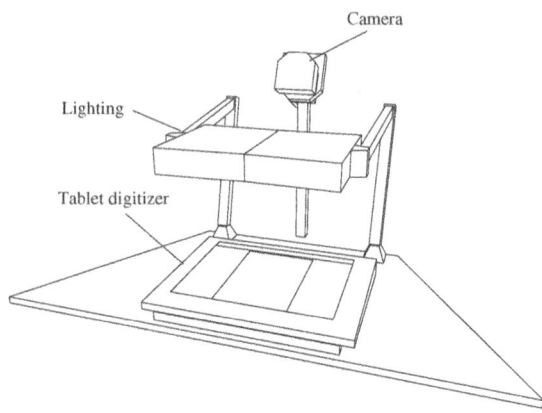

Fig. 2. Hardware setup of the video based handwriting recognition system: The digitizing tablet is only used to collect supplementary data.

it serves as a means to record precise pen trajectories as a sort of ground truth data for comparison with the results of video based tracking. Larger amounts of training material are also captured much more easily using the digitizing tablet.

4   Pen Tracking

The essential information for online handwriting recognition is the trajectory of the pen tip, hence the position of the pen tip has to be determined in every single image of the video sequence. The architecture of our system for video-based pen-tracking is illustrated in Fig. 3. In most parts it is based on the system developed by Munich & Perona [11], except for changes in the initial pen finding module and the Kalman filter. Additionally, a different approach for the pen up/down classification is used.

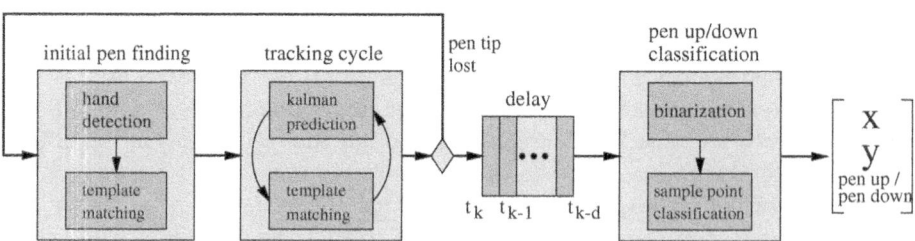

Fig. 3. Architecture of tracking system: The time-consuming template matching in the initial finding step works on the entire image whereas during the tracking process only a small cut will be used. In order to prevent occlusions pen-up/down classification is performed with a certain delay. The output vector consists of the position of the pen tip and pen-up/down information.

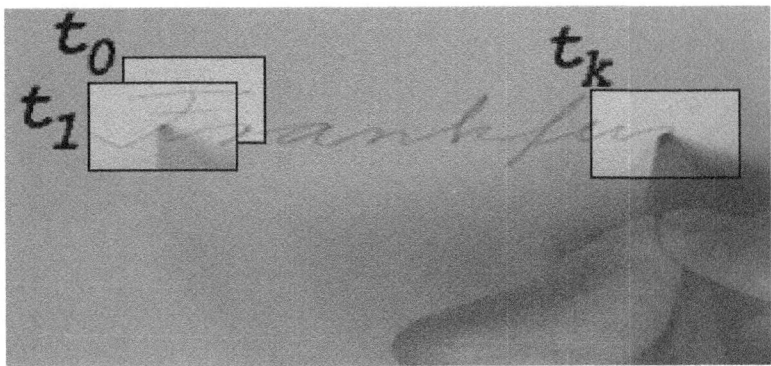

Fig. 4. Tracking: The search window for the template matching is illustrated for the time steps t_0, t_1 and the current frame t_k during the writing of the word *"Frankfurt"*.

An important step towards system usability is to automate the initial pen finding and the recovery of the tracking process when the pen is lost. Therefore, the initial pen finding procedure was designed to require very little user cooperation. In order to reduce the response time as much as possible, the initialization is subdivided into two parts: First, a fast hand detection module notices if the scene changes significantly, e.g. a hand moves into the scene. This is achieved by calculating the difference image of two consecutive frames. If the difference image yields regions with high activity the initial template matching will be performed as the second part of the initial pen finding. This step is time-consuming and cannot be performed in real time. A speed-up is attained by using a pyramidal scheme for comparing a set of template images of the pen tip with the current image. However, the user must not move the pen for about three seconds during this initial template matching phase.

The pen tip is assumed to be found, if the difference between the template and the image falls below a certain threshold. In order to increase the robustness of the template matching, a contrast enhancement is carried out by normalizing the intensity values of the templates and the image. This approach compensates well for variations in the lighting conditions.

After the initial pen position is determined, the pen tip has to be tracked during the whole writing process. In order to achieve real time performance the search space for the template matching is reduced by predicting the expected position of the pen tip in the succeeding video image using a Kalman filter. The position of the pen tip is then estimated by performing a template matching in a small region around the predicted position (Fig. 4). If the pen tip cannot be found, the processing returns to the initial finding procedure.

The Kalman filter represents a model of the kinematic motion of the pen tip, assuming that it may be described as a superposition of a constant velocity term and white noise, which compensates for the time-varying acceleration. For efficiency reasons we use a realization of the Kalman filter a proposed by Kohler

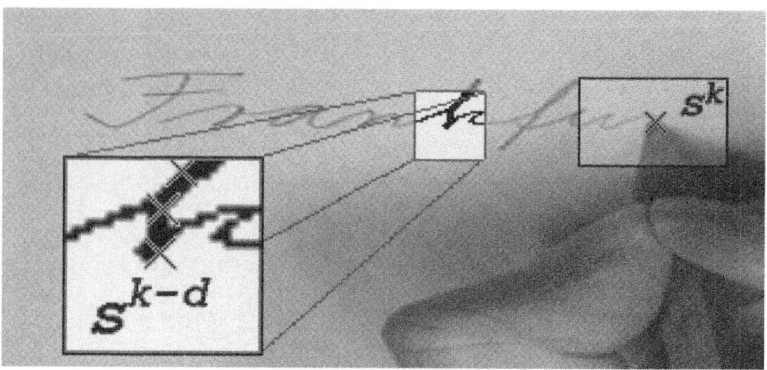

Fig. 5. Pen-up/down classification: The gray crosses mark the positions of the pen-tip found by the template matcher. The image is binarized in a small surrounding of the point s^{k-d}, extracted d frames ago, assuming that the ink trace is usually dark against the background.

[8]. In contrast to the method originally used in [11] the internal model is split up into two independent components for horizontal and vertical motion.

The method described so far is capable of tracking the pen tip in image sequences regardless of whether it is actually writing on paper or moved to another position during a so called pen-up phase. However, for the recognition process the distinction between the two writing modes is extremely important. Therefore, we use an approximate method for deciding between pen-up and pen-down strokes, assuming that the ink trace is usually dark against the background.

A small region surrounding the calculated pen position is binarized using a threshold that is automatically determined from the bimodal intensity histogram of that region [13]. If intensity values falling below that threshold can be found in the vicinity of the line connecting adjacent pen positions, this segment of the pen trajectory will be classified as pen-down and as pen-up otherwise. Additionally, if the intensity histogram is not bimodal, we assume that there is no ink trace visible in the region and classify the segment of the trajectory as pen-up.

In order to prevent occlusions by the pen tip or the writer's hand we perform the pen-up/down classification with a certain time delay, so that the current position of writing is sufficiently far away from the part of the image that has to be analyzed. Experiments indicated that after approximately one second the distance between the current writing position and the image area previously occupied by the pen tip is sufficiently large (Fig. 5).

5   Feature Extraction

Before feature vectors are calculated some preprocessing steps are applied to the trajectory data, mainly in order to make the features to a certain degree independent of the device or method used for pen-tracking. Therefore, not only

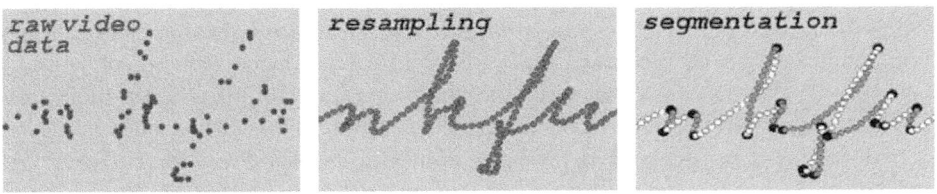

Fig. 6. Preprocessing: From left to right the raw samples obtained from the pen tracker, the resampled data, and the segmented trajectory are shown.

data obtained from the pen-tracking process described in the previous section can be used in the development of the video-based handwriting recognition system but also also traditional trajectory data obtained from a tablet digitizer.

After smoothing the trajectory by replacing each sample point with the mean value of its neighbors, the trajectory is spatially resampled using a linear interpolation scheme in order to compensate for device specific sampling frequencies and variations in the velocity of handwriting. This approach works well if trajectory data are sampled at higher frequencies of approximately 100 Hz and above which is common for tablet digitizers. However, when applied to the video-based tracking results sampled at only 50 Hz the method does not produce sufficiently smooth curves. In order to increase the smoothness we apply a momentum term, that considers the previous orientation of the vector connecting adjacent sample points.

The second step consists of partitioning the trajectory into stroke-like segments. The segmentation criterion is based on the local curvature and the vertical velocity of the pen tip, assuming that a high curvature or a low velocity signalize start and end points of handwritten strokes (Fig. 6). This idea goes back to the work of Plamondon & Maarse [14].

The main reason for segmenting the trajectory into stroke like entities is to allow the computation of writing-size invariant features — an important aspect for writer-independent systems. According to the work of Dolfing & Haeb-Umbach [3] an overlap of 50% of the segments was used for calculating 17 dimensional feature vectors, which include features like the sine and cosine of the mean writing direction, sine and cosine of the mean curvature, pen-up/down information, aspect ratio, and curliness of the segment as defined in [6]. In order to take the dynamics of the signal into account we also compute approximations of the derivatives of the above mentioned features. Inspired by [3] we additionally calculate so called delayed features, namely the sine and cosine of the change of writing direction and the relative change of writing size between the feature vectors at time t and $t - 2$.

6   Handwriting Recognition

For the design of statistical recognition systems the availability of a sufficiently large database of training samples is an important prerequisite. Ideally, for a video-based recognition system it would be desirable to obtain a large amount of image sequences recorded while observing a subject's writing of words or sentences. However, the recording of such video data requires much more effort and storage than the direct recording of trajectory data with a suitable device.

Therefore, we decided to use the digitizing tablet (Wacom UltraPad A3) shown in Fig. 2 for the recording of training and cross-validation data. Furthermore, for this first data acquisition effort we decided to limit recording to isolated words. The lexicon was somewhat arbitrarily chosen to comprise the names of large German cities[2].

Using the same hardware setup as during video-based tracking we recorded data from 13 subjects who were asked to write the complete list of 201 city names in random order on ordinary paper using a special ball-point pen that can be tracked by the digitizing tablet. For collecting a test set of video-based data this procedure was repeated with four different writers using visual pen tracking. As we wanted to obtain unconstrained handwritten data no instructions concerning the writing style were given.

For configuration, training, and decoding of Hidden-Markov-Models (HMMs) for the video-based handwriting recognition task we used the methods and tools provided by the ESMERALDA development environment [4]. From the recorded trajectories we selected the data of 7 writers for setting up a semi-continuous HMM-system with a shared codebook containing 256 Gaussian mixtures with diagonal covariance matrices. Models for 52 characters and 2 diacritical marks – namely dot for "i" and German umlauts and dash for "t" – were trained using standard Baum-Welch reestimation. As we do not apply stroke reordering after a word has been completely written we need to allow for different temporal relations between base characters and associated diacritic marks. Therefore, for every word including diacritic marks a set of different realizations is contained in the lexicon depending on whether diacritics immediately follow the base character or are added after the word has been completed. The overall recognition lexicon thus contains 335 entries.

On the cross-validation set of unconstrained handwritten data from 6 different writers using the digitizing tablet we achieved a recognition rate of 92.5%. For the evaluation of the video-based approach the training set was enlarged to comprise the data of 11 writers. On the test set of the 4 writers using visual pen tracking a recognition rate of 75.5% was achieved. 3.4% of the errors were introduced by the video-based pen tracking.

Fig. 7 shows recognition results obtained on typical video data. After the initial pen finding the tracking process performs quite well also on faster pen movements between words. However, during the writing of the word "Hamburg" the pen tip is lost, but the tracking process recovers quickly and proceeds normally afterwards.

---

[2] From a list of German city names and associated zip codes we selected those cities that were assigned more than one code resulting in a list of 201 different names.

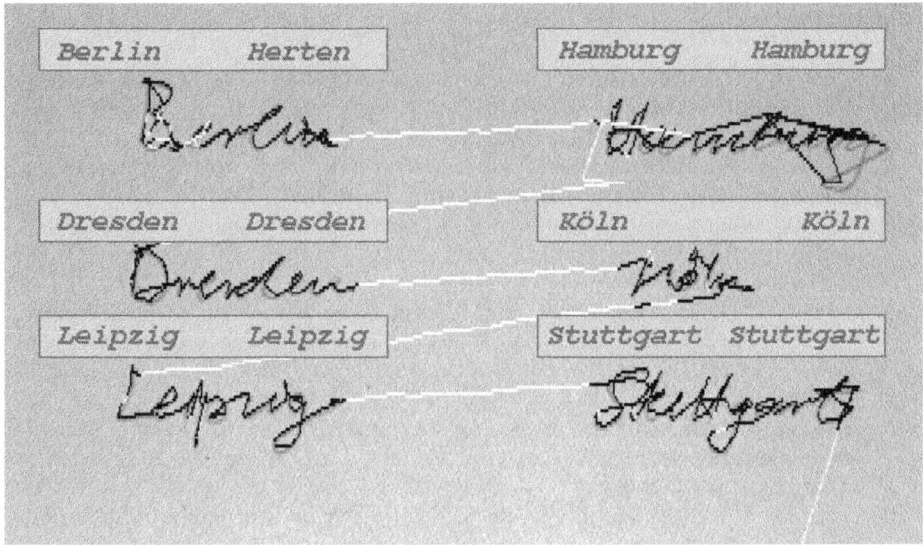

Fig. 7. Recognition results: A 6-word trajectory obtained from the pen tracker is super-imposed to the captured video image. The small boxes illustrate the words that were written on the left and the recognition results on the right hand side. Furthermore, this sequence demonstrates the robustness of the pen tracking and recovery, because during writing the letter *"g"* of the word *"Hamburg"*, the pen tip is lost, but after a few frames automatically recovered.

7   Conclusion

We proposed a complete on-line handwriting recognition system based on visual input. Pen trajectories are automatically extracted from video image sequences recorded during the observation of the writing process. The pre-processing and feature extraction methods applied generate a data representation which is to a certain extent robust against the limitations of the video-based pen tracking and facilitates writer independent recognition. Promising recognition results could be achieved for experiments on a writer independent unconstrained handwriting recognition task.

Acknowledgments. We would like to gratefully acknowledge the support of Mario Munich, formerly California Institute of Technology, and Pietro Perona, California Institute of Technology, who allowed us to use their software for visual pen-tracking in the development of our visual handwriting recognition system.

Additionally, we would like to thank Marc Hanheide, Birgit Möller, Thomas Plötz, and Frank Seifert, students of Computer Science, Bielefeld University, for enthusiastically developing a visual pen-tracking system during a project seminar.

References

1. H. Bunke, T. von Siebenthal, T. Yamasaki, and M. Schenkel. Online handwriting data acquisition using a video camera. In *Proc. Int. Conf. on Document Analysis and Recognition*, pages 573–576, 1999.
2. H. Bunke and P. S. P. Wang, editors. *Handbook of Character Recognition and Document Image Analysis*. World Scientific Publishing Company, Singapore, 1997.
3. J. G. A. Dolfing and R. Haeb-Umbach. Signal representations for hidden markov model based on-line handwriting recognition. In *Proc. Int. Conf. on Acoustics, Speech and Signal Processing*, volume IV, pages 3385–3388, München, 1997.
4. Gernot A. Fink. Developing HMM-based recognizers with ESMERALDA. In Václav Matoušek, Pavel Mautner, Jana Ocelíková, and Petr Sojka, editors, *Lecture Notes in Artificial Intelligence*, volume 1692, pages 229–234, Berlin Heidelberg, 1999. Springer.
5. Jianying Hu, Michael K. Brown, and William Turin. HMM based on-line handwriting recognition. *IEEE Trans. on Pattern Analysis and Machine Intelligence*, 18(10):1039–1044, 1996.
6. S. Jaeger, S. Manke, and A. Waibel. Npen++: An on-line handwriting recognition system. pages 249–260, Amsterdam, September 2000.
7. Frederick Jelinek. *Statistical Methods for Speech Recognition*. MIT Press, Cambridge, MA, 1997.
8. Markus Kohler. Using the kalman filter to track human interactive motion - modelling and initialization of the kalman filter for translational motion -. Technical Report 629, Informatik VII, University of Dortmund, January 1997.
9. John Makhoul, Thad Starner, Richard Schwartz, and George Chou. On-line cursive handwriting recognition using hidden markov models and statistical grammars. In *Human Language Technology*, pages 432–436. Morgan Kaufmann, 1994.
10. Mario E. Munich. *Visual Input for Pen-based Computers*. PhD thesis, California Institute of Technology, Pasadena, California, January 2000.
11. Mario E. Munich and Pietro Perona. Visual input for pen-based computers. In *Proc. Int. Conf. on Pattern Recognition*, volume 3, pages 33–37, Vienna, Austria, 1996.
12. Krishna A. Nathan, Jerome R. Bellegarda, David Nahamoo, and Eveline J. Bellegarda. On-line handwriting recognition using continuous parameter Hidden Markov Models. In *Proc. Int. Conf. on Acoustics, Speech and Signal Processing*, volume 5, pages 121–124, Minneapolis, 1993.
13. N. Otsu. A threshold selection method from gray-level histograms. *IEEE Trans. on Systems, Man, and Cybernetics*, 9:62–66, 1979.
14. Réjean Plamondon and Frans J. Maarse. An evaluation of motor models of handwriting. *IEEE Trans. on Systems, Man, and Cybernetics*, 19(5):1060–1072, 1989.
15. T. Starner, J. Makhoul, R. Schwartz, and G. Chou. On-line cursive handwriting recognition using speech recognition methods. In *Proc. Int. Conf. on Acoustics, Speech and Signal Processing*, volume 5, pages 125–128, Adelaide, 1994.
16. Charles C. Tappert, Ching Y. Suen, and Toru Wakahara. The state of the art in on-line handwriting recognition. *IEEE Trans. on Pattern Analysis and Machine Intelligence*, 12(8):787–808, 1990.

Integration of Wireless Gesture Tracking, Object Tracking, and 3D Reconstruction in the Perceptive Workbench

Bastian Leibe[1], David Minnen[2], Justin Weeks[2], and Thad Starner[2]

[1] Perceptual Computing and Computer Vision Group, ETH Zurich
Haldeneggsteig 4, CH-8092 Zurich, Switzerland
leibe@inf.ethz.ch
[2] Contextual Computing Group, GVU Center
Georgia Institute of Technology
{dminn,joostan,thad}@cc.gatech.edu

Abstract. The Perceptive Workbench endeavors to create a sponta-neous and unimpeded interface between the physical and virtual worlds. Its vision-based methods for interaction constitute an alternative to wired input devices and tethered tracking. Objects are recognized and tracked when placed on the display surface. By using multiple infrared light sources, the object's 3D shape can be captured and inserted into the virtual interface. This ability permits spontaneity since either preloaded objects or those objects selected at run-time by the user can become physical icons. Integrated into the same vision-based interface is the ability to identify 3D hand position, pointing direction, and sweeping arm gestures. Such gestures can enhance selection, manipulation, and navigation tasks. In previous publications, the Perceptive Workbench has demonstrated its utility for a variety of applications, including augmented reality gaming and terrain navigation. This paper will focus on the implementation and performance aspects and will introduce recent enhancements to the system.

Keywords. gesture, 3D object reconstruction, object recognition, tracking, computer vision, infrared, virtual reality

1 Introduction

Humans and computers have interacted primarily through devices that are con-strained by wires. Typically, the wires limit the distance of movement and in-hibit freedom of orientation. In addition, most interactions are indirect. The user moves a device as an analogue for the action to be created in the display space. We envision an untethered interface that accepts gestures directly and can ac-cept any objects the user chooses as interactors. In this paper, we apply our goal to workbenches, a subgroup of semi-immersive virtual reality environments.

Computer vision can provide the basis for untethered interaction because it is flexible, unobtrusive, and allows direct interaction. Since the complexity

B. Schiele and G. Sagerer (Eds.): ICVS 2001, LNCS 2095, pp. 73–92, 2001.

of general vision tasks has often been a barrier to widespread use in real-time applications, we simplify the task by using a shadow-based architecture.

An infrared light source is mounted on the ceiling. When the user stands in front of the workbench and extends an arm over the surface, the arm casts a shadow on the desk's surface, which can be easily distinguished by a camera underneath.

The same shadow-based architecture is used in the Perceptive Workbench [16] to reconstruct 3D virtual representations of previously unseen real-world objects placed on the desk's surface. In addition, the Perceptive Workbench can illuminate objects placed on the desk's surface to identify and track the objects as the user manipulates them. Taking its cues from the user's actions, the Perceptive Workbench switches between these three modes automatically. Computer vision controls all interaction, freeing the user from the tethers of traditional sensing techniques.

In this paper, we will discuss implementation and performance aspects that are important to making the Perceptive Workbench a useful input technology for virtual reality. We will examine performance requirements and show how our system is being optimized to meet them.

2   Related Work

While the Perceptive Workbench [16] is unique in its ability to interact with the physical world, it has a rich heritage of related work [1,13,14,20,23,31,32,34,39]. Many augmented desk and virtual reality designs use tethered props, tracked by electromechanical or ultrasonic means, to encourage interaction through gesture and manipulation of objects [3,1,23,29,34]. Such designs tether the user to the desk and require the time-consuming ritual of donning and doffing the appropriate equipment.

Fortunately, the computer vision community has taken up the task of tracking hands and identifying gestures. While generalized vision systems track the body in room- and desk-based scenarios for games, interactive art, and augmented environments [2,40], the reconstruction of fine hand detail involves carefully calibrated systems and is computationally intensive [19]. Even so, complicated gestures such as those used in sign language [28,35] or the manipulation of physical objects [25] can be recognized. The Perceptive Workbench uses such computer vision techniques to maintain a wireless interface.

Most directly related to the Perceptive Workbench, Ullmer and Ishii's "Meta-desk" identifies and tracks objects placed on the desk's display surface using a near-infrared computer vision recognizer, originally designed by Starner [31]. Unfortunately, since not all objects reflect infrared light and since infrared shadows are not used, objects often need infrared reflective "hot mirrors" placed in patterns on their bottom surfaces to aid tracking and identification. Similarly, Rekimoto and Matsushita's "Perceptual Surfaces" [20] employ 2D barcodes to identify objects held against the "HoloWall" and "HoloTable." In addition, the HoloWall can track the user's hands (or other body parts) near or pressed against its surface, but its potential recovery of the user's distance from the surface is relatively coarse compared to the 3D pointing gestures of the Perceptive Workbench. Davis and Bobick's SIDEshow [6] is similar to the Holowall except that it uses cast shadows in infrared for full-body 2D gesture recovery. Some augmented desks have cameras and projectors above the surface of the desk; they are designed to augment the process of handling paper or interact with models and widgets through the use of fiducials or barcodes [32,39]. Krueger's VideoDesk [13], an early desk-based system, uses an overhead camera and a horizontal visible light table to provide high contrast hand gesture input for interactions which are then displayed on a monitor on the far side of the desk. In contrast with the Perceptive Workbench, none of these systems address the issues of introducing spontaneous 3D physical objects into the virtual environment in real-time and combining 3D deictic (pointing) gestures with object tracking and identification.

3 Goals

Our goal is to create a vision-based user interface for VR applications. Hence, our system must be responsive in real-time and be suitable for VR interaction. In order to evaluate the feasibility of meeting this goal we need to examine the necessary performance criteria.

System Responsiveness. System responsiveness, the time elapsed between a user's action and the response displayed by the system [38], helps determine the quality of the user's interaction. Responsiveness requirements vary with the tasks to be performed. An acceptable threshold for object selection and manipulation tasks is typically around 75 to 100 ms [36,38]. System responsiveness is directly coupled with latency. It can be calculated with the following formula:

$$SystemResponsiveness = SystemLatency + DisplayTime \qquad (1)$$

System latency, often also called device lag, is the time it takes our sensor to acquire an image, calculate and communicate the results, and change the virtual world accordingly. Input devices should have low latency, ideally below 50 ms. Ware and Balakrishnan measured several common magnetic trackers and found them to have latencies in the range of 45 to 72 ms [36].

In our situation, system latency depends on the time it takes the camera to transform the scene into a digital image, image processing time, and network latency to communicate the results. Given an average delay of 1.5 frame intervals at 33 ms per interval to digitize the image results in a 50 ms delay. In addition, we assume a 1.5 frame interval delay in rendering the appropriate graphics. Assuming a constant 60 frame per second (fps) rendering rate results in an additional 25 ms delay for system responsiveness. Since we are constrained by a 75 ms overhead in sensing and rendering, we must minimize the amount of processing time and network delay in order to maintain an acceptable latency for object selection and manipulation. Thus, we concentrate on easily computed

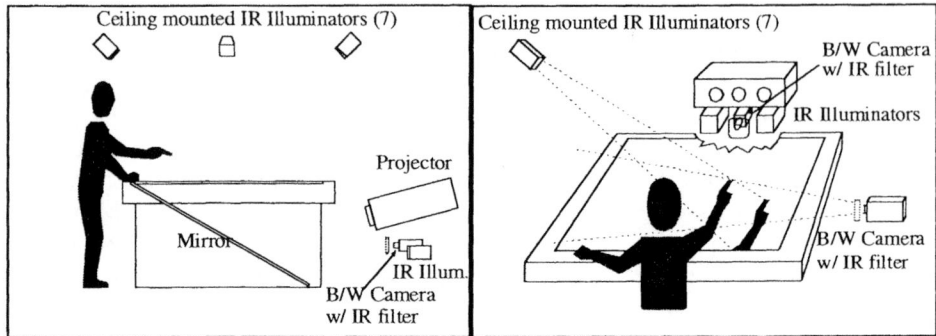

Fig. 1. Light and camera positions for the Perceptive Workbench. The top view shows how shadows are cast and the 3D arm position is tracked.

vision algorithms and a lightweight UDP networking protocol for transmitting the results.

Accuracy. With the deictic gesture tracking, we estimate that absolute accuracy will not need to be very high. Since the pointing actions and gestures happen in the three dimensional space high above the desk's surface, discrepancies between a user's precise pointing position and the system's depiction of that position is not obvious or distracting. Instead, it is much more important to capture the trend of movement and allow for quick correctional motions.

For the object tracking, however, this is not the case. Here, the physical objects placed on the desk already give a strong visual feedback and any system response differing from this position will be very distracting. This constraint is relatively easy to satisfy, though, since the task of detecting the position of an object on the desk's surface is, by nature, more accurate than finding the correct arm orientation in 3D space.

4   Apparatus

The display environment for the Perceptive Workbench builds on Fakespace's immersive workbench [37]. It consists of a wooden desk with a horizontal frosted glass surface on which an image can be projected from behind the workbench.

We placed a standard monochrome surveillance camera under the projector to watch the desk's surface from underneath (see Figure 1). A filter placed in front of the camera lens makes it insensitive to visible light and to images projected on the desk's surface. Two infrared illuminators placed next to the camera flood the desk's surface with infrared light that is reflected back toward the camera by objects placed on the desk.

We mounted a ring of seven similar light sources on the ceiling surrounding the desk (Figure 1). Each computer-controlled light casts distinct shadows on the desk's surface based on the objects on the table (Figure 2a). A second infrared camera and another infrared light source are placed next to the desk to provide a side view of the user's arms (Figure 3a). This side camera is used solely for recovering 3D pointing gestures.

Note that at any time during the system's operation, either the ceiling lights, or the lights below the table are active, but not both at the same time. This constraint is necessary in order to achieve reliable detection of shadows and reflections.

We decided to use near-infrared light since it is invisible to the human eye. Thus, illuminating the scene does not interfere with the user's interaction. The user does not perceive the illumination from the infrared light sources underneath the table, nor the shadows cast from the overhead lights. On the other hand, most standard charge-coupled device (CCD) cameras can still see infrared light, providing an inexpensive method for observing the interaction. In addition, by equipping the camera with an infrared filter, the camera image can be analyzed regardless of changes in (visible) scene lighting.

We use this setup for three different kinds of interaction:

- Recognition and tracking of objects placed on the desk surface based on their contour
- Tracking of hand and arm gestures
- Full 3D reconstruction of object shapes from shadows cast by the ceiling light-sources.

For display on the Perceptive Workbench we use OpenGL, the OpenGL Utility Toolkit (GLUT) and a customized version of a simple widget package called microUI (MUI). In addition, we use the workbench version of VGIS, a global terrain visualization and navigation system [37] as an application for interaction using hand and arm gestures.

5 Object Tracking & Recognition

As a basic precept for our interaction framework, we want to let users manipulate the virtual environment by placing objects on the desk surface. The system should recognize these objects and track their positions and orientations as they move over the table. Users should be free to pick any set of physical objects they choose.

The motivation behind this is to use physical objects in a "graspable" user interface [9]. Physical objects are often natural interactors as they provide physical handles to let users intuitively control a virtual application [11]. In addition, the use of real objects allows the user to manipulate multiple objects simultaneously, increasing the communication bandwidth with the computer [9,11].

To achieve this tracking goal, we use an improved version of the technique described in Starner et al. [27]. Two near-infrared light-sources illuminate the desk's underside (Figure 1). Every object close to the desk surface (including the user's hands) reflects this light, which the camera under the display surface can

Fig. 2. (a) Arm shadow from overhead IR lights; (b) resulting contour with recovered arm direction.

see. Using a combination of intensity thresholding and background subtraction, we extract interesting regions of the camera image and analyze them. We classify the resulting blobs as different object types based on a 72-dimensional feature vector reflecting the distances from the center of the blob to its contour in different directions.

Note that the hardware arrangement causes several complications. The foremost problem is that our two light sources under the table can only provide uneven lighting over the whole desk surface. In addition, the light rays are not parallel, and the reflection on the mirror surface further exacerbates this effect. To compensate for this, we perform a dynamic range adjustment. In addition to a background image, we store a "white" image that represents the maximum intensity that can be expected at any pixel. This image is obtained by passing a bright white (and thus highly reflective) object over the table during a one-time calibration step and instructing the system to record the intensity at each point. The dynamic range adjustment helps to normalize the image so that a single threshold can be used over the whole table. An additional optimal thresholding step is performed for every blob to reduce the effects of unwanted reflections from users' hands and arms while they are moving objects. Since the blobs only represent a small fraction of the image, the computational cost is low.

In order to handle the remaining uncertainty in the recognition process, two final steps are performed: detecting the stability of a reflection and using tracking information to adjust and improve recognition results. When an object is placed on the table, there will be a certain interval when it reflects enough infrared light to be tracked but is not close enough to the desk's surface to create a recognizable reflection. To detect this situation, we measure the change in size and average intensity for each reflection over time. When both settle to a relatively constant value, we know that an object has reached a steady state and can now be recognized. To further improve classification accuracy, we make the assumption that objects will not move very far between frames. Thus, the closer

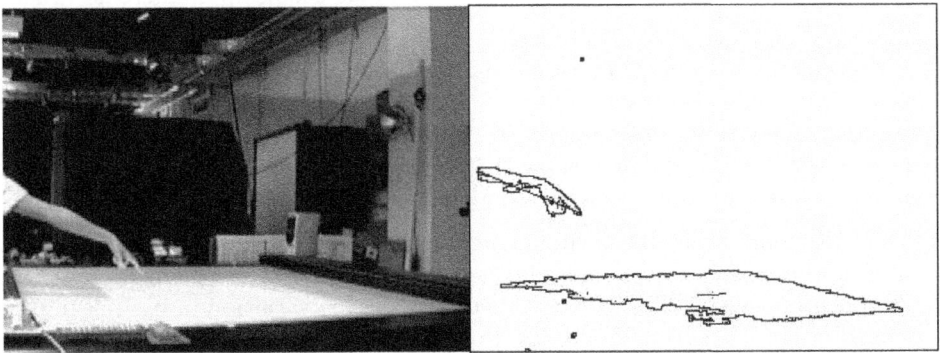

Fig. 3. (a) Image from side camera (without infrared filter); (b) arm contour from similar image with recovered arm direction.

a blob is to an object's position in the last frame, the more probable it is that this blob corresponds to the object and the less reliable the recognition result has to be before it is accepted. In addition, the system remembers and collects feature vectors that caused some uncertainty (for example, by an unfamiliar orientation that caused the feature vector to change) and adds them to the internal description of the object, thus refining the model.

In this work, we use the object recognition and tracking capability mainly for cursor or place-holder objects. We focus on fast and accurate position tracking, but the system may be trained on a different set of objects to serve as navigational tools or physical icons [31]. A future project will explore different modes of interaction based on this technology.

6   Deictic Gesture Tracking

Following Quek's taxonomy [18], hand gestures can be roughly classified into symbols (referential and modalizing gestures) and acts (mimetic and deictic gestures). Deictic (pointing) gestures depend strongly on location and orientation of the performing hand. Their meaning is determined by the location at which a finger is pointing, or by the angle of rotation of some part of the hand. This information acts not only as a symbol for the gesture's interpretation, but also as a measure of the extent to which the corresponding action should be executed or to which object it should be applied.

For navigation and object manipulation in a virtual environment, many gestures will have a deictic component. It is usually not enough to recognize that an object should be rotated – we will also need to know the desired amount of rotation. For object selection or translation, we want to specify the object or location of our choice just by pointing at it. For these cases, gesture recognition methods that only take the hand shape and trajectory into account will not suffice. We need to recover 3D information about the users' hands and arms in relation to their bodies.

In the past, this information has largely been obtained by using wired gloves or suits, or magnetic trackers [3,1]. Such methods provide sufficiently accurate results but rely on wires tethered to the user's body or to specific interaction devices, with all the aforementioned problems. We aim to develop a purely vision-based architecture that facilitates unencumbered 3D interaction.

With vision-based 3D tracking techniques, the first issue is to determine what information in the camera image is relevant – that is, which regions represent the user's hand or arm. What makes this difficult is the variation in user clothing or skin color and background activity. Previous approaches on vision-based gesture recognition used marked gloves [8], infrared cameras [22], or a combination of multiple feature channels, like color and stereo [12] to deal with this problem, or they just restricted their system to a uniform background [33]. By analyzing a shadow image, this task can be greatly simplified.

Most directly related to our approach, Segen and Kumar [24] derive 3D position and orientation information of two fingers from the appearance of the user's hand and its shadow, co-located in the same image. However, since their approach relies on visible light, it requires a stationary background and thus cannot operate on a highly dynamic back-projection surface like the one on our workbench. By using infrared light for casting the shadow, we can overcome this restriction.

The use of shadows solves, at the same time, another problem with vision-based architectures: where to put the cameras. In a virtual workbench environment, there are only few places from where we can get reliable hand position information. One camera can be set up next to the table without overly restricting the available space for users. In many systems, in order to recover three dimensional information, a second camera is deployed. However, the placement of this second camera restricts the usable area around the workbench. Using shadows, the infrared camera under the projector replaces the second camera. One of the infrared light sources mounted on the ceiling above the user shines on the desk's surface where it can be seen by the camera underneath (see Figure 4). When users move an arm over the desk, it casts a shadow on the desk surface (see Figure 2a). From this shadow, and from the known light-source position, we can calculate a plane in which the user's arm must lie.

Simultaneously, the second camera to the right of the table (Figures 3a and 4) records a side view of the desk surface and the user's arm. It detects where the arm enters the image and the position of the fingertip. From this information, the computer extrapolates two lines in 3D space on which the observed real-world points must lie. By intersecting these lines with the shadow plane, we get the coordinates of two 3D points – one on the upper arm, and one on the fingertip. This gives us the user's hand position and the direction in which the user is pointing. We can use this information to project an icon representing the hand position and a selection ray on the workbench display.

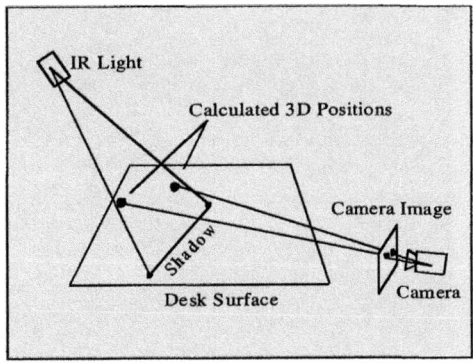

Fig. 4. Principle of pointing direction recovery.

Obviously, the success of the gesture-tracking capability relies heavily on how fast the image processing can be done. Fortunately, we can make some simplifying assumptions about the image content. We must first recover arm direction and fingertip position from both the camera and the shadow image. Since the user stands in front of the desk and the user's arm is connected to the user's body, the arm's shadow should always touch the image border. Thus, our algorithm exploits intensity thresholding and background subtraction to discover regions of change in the image. It also searches for areas in which these regions touch the desk surface's front border (which corresponds to the shadow image's top border or the camera image's left border). The algorithm then takes the middle of the touching area as an approximation for the origin of the arm (Figures 2b and Figure 3b). Similar to Fukumoto's approach [10], we trace the shadow's contour and take point farthest away from the shoulder as the fingertip. The line from the shoulder to the fingertip reveals the arm's 2D direction.

In our experiments, the point thus obtained was coincident with the pointing fingertip in all but a few extreme cases (such as the fingertip pointing straight down at a right angle to the arm). The method does not depend on a pointing gesture, but also works for most other hand shapes, including a hand held horizontally, vertically, or in a fist. These shapes may be distinguished by analyzing a small section of the side camera image and may be used to trigger specific gesture modes in the future.

The computed arm direction is correct as long as the user's arm is not overly bent (see Figure 3). In such cases, the algorithm still connects the shoulder and fingertip, resulting in a direction somewhere between the direction of the arm and the one given by the hand. Although the absolute resulting pointing position does not match the position towards which the finger is pointing, it still captures the trend of movement very well. Surprisingly, the technique is sensitive enough so that users can stand at the desk with their arm extended over the surface

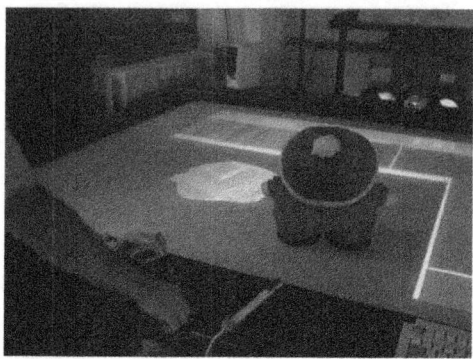

Fig. 5. Real object inserted into the virtual world. The figure shows a reconstruction of the doll in the foreground.

and direct the pointer simply by moving their index finger without any arm movement.

6.1   Limitations and Improvements

Figure 3b shows a case where segmentation based on color background sub-traction in an older implementation detected both the hand and the change in the display on the workbench. Our new version replaces the side color camera with an infrared spotlight and a monochrome camera equipped with an infrared-pass filter. By adjusting the angle of the light to avoid the desk's surface, the user's arm is illuminated and made distinct from the background. Changes in the workbench's display do not affect the tracking.

One remaining problem results from the side camera's actual location. If a user extends both arms over the desk surface, or if more than one user tries to interact with the environment simultaneously, the images of these multiple limbs can overlap and merge into a single blob. Consequently, our approach will fail to detect the hand positions and orientations in these cases. A more sophisticated approach using previous position and movement information could yield more reliable results, but at this stage we chose to accept this restriction and concentrate on high frame rate support for one-handed interaction. In addition, this may not be a serious limitation for a single user for certain tasks. A recent study shows that for a task normally requiring two hands in a real environment, users have no preference for one versus two hands in a virtual environment that does not model effects such as gravity and inertia [23].

7   3D Reconstruction

To complement the capabilities of the Perceptive Workbench, we want to be able to insert real objects into the virtual world and share them with other

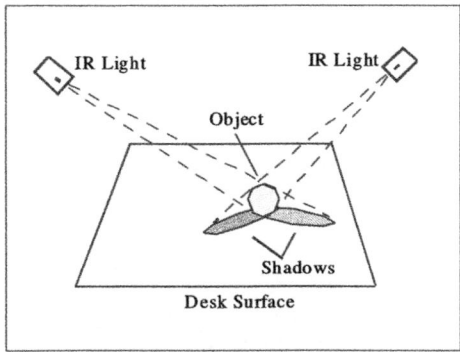

Fig. 6. Principle of the 3D reconstruction.

users at different locations (see Figure 5). An example application for this could be a telepresence or computer-supported collaborative work (CSCW) system. This requires designing a reconstruction mechanism that does not interrupt the interaction. Our focus is to provide a nearly instantaneous visual cue for the object, not necessarily on creating a highly accurate model.

Several methods reconstruct objects from silhouettes [26,30] or dynamic shadows [5] using either a moving camera or light source on a known trajectory or a turntable for the object [30]. Several systems have been developed for reconstructing relatively simple objects, including some commercial systems.

However, the necessity to move either the camera or the object imposes severe constraints on the working environment. Reconstructing an object with these methods usually requires interrupting the user's interaction with it, taking it out of the user's environment, and placing it into a specialized setting. Other approaches use multiple cameras from different viewpoints to avoid this problem at the expense of more computational power to process and communicate the results.

In this project, using only one camera and multiple infrared light sources, we analyze the shadows cast by the object from multiple directions (see Figure 6). Since the process is based on infrared light, it can be applied independently of the lighting conditions and with minimal interference with the user's natural interaction with the desk.

To obtain the different views, we use a ring of seven infrared light sources in the ceiling, each independently switched by computer control. The system detects when a user places a new object on the desk surface, and renders a virtual button. The user can then initiate reconstruction by touching this virtual button. The camera detects this action, and in approximately one second the system can capture all of the required shadow images. After another second, reconstruction is complete, and the newly reconstructed object becomes part of the virtual world. Note that this process uses the same hardware as the deictic

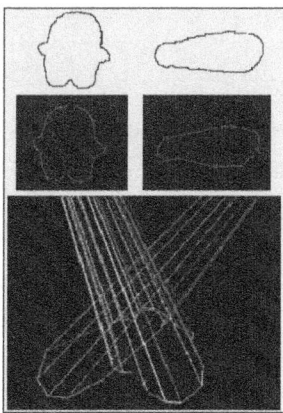

Fig. 7. Steps of the 3D reconstruction of the doll from Figure 5, including the extraction of contour shapes from shadows and the intersection of multiple view cones (bottom).

gesture-tracking capability discussed in the previous section, and thus requires no additional cost.

Figure 7 shows a series of contour shadows and a visualization of the reconstruction process. By approximating each shadow as a polygon (not necessarily convex) [21], we create a set of polyhedral "view cones" extending from the light source to the polygons. The intersection of these cones creates a polyhedron that roughly contains the object.

Intersecting nonconvex polyhedral objects is a complex problem, further complicated by numerous special cases. Fortunately, this problem has already been extensively researched and solutions are available. For the intersection calculations in our application, we use Purdue University's TWIN Solid Modeling Library [7]. Recently, a highly optimized algorithm has been proposed by Matusik et al. that can perform these intersection calculations directly as part of the rendering process [17]. Their algorithm provides a significant improvement on the intersection code we are currently using, and we are considering it for a future version of our system.

Figure 8c shows a reconstructed model of a watering can placed on the desk's surface. We chose the colors to highlight the different model faces by interpreting the face normal as a vector in RGB color space. In the original version of our software, we did not handle holes in the contours. This feature has since been added by constructing light cones for both the object contours and for those representing holes. By inspecting the pixels adjacent to the outside of the contour, we can distinguish between the two types of borders. Then, rather than intersecting the light cone with the rest of the object, we perform a boolean differencing operation with the cones formed from the hole borders.

7.1 Limitations

An obvious limitation to our approach is that we are confined to a fixed number of different views from which to reconstruct the object. The turntable approach permits the system to take an arbitrary number of images from different viewpoints. In addition, not every nonconvex object can be exactly reconstructed from its silhouettes or shadows. The closest approximation that can be obtained with volume intersection is its visual hull, that is, the volume enveloped by all the possible circumscribed view cones. Even for objects with a polyhedral visual hull, an unbounded number of silhouettes may be necessary for an exact reconstruction [15]. However, Sullivan's work [30] and our experience have shown that usually seven to nine different views suffice to get a reasonable 3D model of the object.

Exceptions to this heuristic are spherical or cylindrical objects. The quality of reconstruction for these objects depends largely on the number of available views. With only seven light sources, the resulting model will appear faceted. This problem can be solved either by adding more light sources, or by improving the model with the help of splines.

In addition, the accuracy with which objects can be reconstructed is bounded by another limitation of our architecture. Since we mounted our light sources on the ceiling, the system can not provide full information about the object's shape. There is a pyramidal blind spot above all flat, horizontal surfaces that the reconstruction can not eliminate. The slope of these pyramids depends on the angle between the desk surface and the rays from the light sources. Only structures with a greater slope will be reconstructed entirely without error. We expect that we can greatly reduce the effects of this error by using the image from the side camera and extracting an additional silhouette of the object. This will help keep the error angle well below 10 degrees.

8 Performance Analysis

8.1 Object and Gesture Tracking

Both object and gesture tracking currently perform at an average of between 14 and 20 frames per second (fps). Frame rate depends on both the number of objects on the table and the size of their reflections. Both techniques follow fast motions and complicated trajectories.

To test latency, we measured the runtime of our vision code. In our current implementation, the object tracking code took around 43 ms to run with a single object on the desk surface and scaled up to 60 ms with five objects. By switching from TCP to UDP, we were able to reduce the network latency from a previous 100 ms to approximately 8 ms. Thus, our theoretical system latency is between 101 and 118 ms. Experimental results confirmed these values.

For the gesture tracking, the results are in the same range since the code used is nearly identical. Measuring the exact performance, however, is more difficult because two cameras are involved.

Table 1. Reconstruction errors averaged over three runs (in meters and percentage of object diameter).

	Cone	Pyramid
Maximal Error	0.0215 (7.26%)	0.0228 (6.90%)
Mean Error	0.0056 (1.87%)	0.0043 (1.30%)
Mean Square Error	0.0084 (2.61%)	0.0065 (1.95%)

Even though the system responsiveness (system latency plus display lag) exceeds the envisioned threshold of 75 to 100 ms, it still seems adequate for most (navigational) pointing gestures in our current applications. Since users receive continuous feedback about their hand and pointing positions, and most navigation controls are relative rather than absolute, users adapt their behavior readily to the system. With object tracking, the physical object itself provides users with adequate tactile feedback. In general, since users move objects across a very large desk, the lag is rarely troublesome in the current applications.

Nonetheless, we are confident that some improvements in the vision code can further reduce latency. In addition, Kalman filters may compensate for render lag and will also add to the tracking system's stability.

8.2 3D Reconstruction

Calculating the error from the 3D reconstruction process requires choosing known 3D models, performing the reconstruction process, aligning the reconstructed model and the ideal model, and calculating an error measure. For simplicity, we chose a cone and pyramid. We set the centers of mass of the ideal and reconstructed models to the same point in space, and aligned their principal axes.

To measure error, we used the Metro tool developed by Cignoni, Rocchini, and Scopigno [4]. It approximates the real distance between the two surfaces by choosing a set of 100,000 to 200,000 points on the reconstructed surface, then calculating the two-sided distance (Hausdorff distance) between each of these points and the ideal surface. This distance is defined as $\max(E(S_1, S_2), E(S_2, S_1))$ with $E(S_1, S_2)$ denoting the one-sided distance between the surfaces S_1 and S_2:

$$E(S_1, S_2) = \max_{p \in S_1}(dist(p, S_2)) = \max_{p \in S_1}(\min_{p' \in S_2}(dist(p, p'))) \qquad (2)$$

The Hausdorff distance corresponds directly to the reconstruction error. In addition to the maximum distance, we also calculated the mean and mean-square distances. Table 1 shows the results. In these examples, the relatively large maximal error was caused by the difficulty in accurately reconstructing the tip of the cone and the pyramid.

Improvements may be made by precisely calibrating the camera and lighting system, adding more light sources, and obtaining a silhouette from the side camera to eliminate ambiguity about the top of the surface. However, the system meets its goal of providing virtual presences for physical objects in a timely manner that encourages spontaneous interactions.

8.3   User Experience

To evaluate the current usability of the system, we performed a small user study with the goal of determining the relative efficiency and accuracy of the object tracking capability. We designed a task that required users to drag virtual balls of various sizes to specified locations on the table's surface with the help of physical "cursor" objects. The system recorded the time required to complete the task of correctly moving four such balls.

Although the number of participants was too small to yield significant quantitative results, we discovered several common problems users had with the interface. The main difficulties arose from selecting smaller balls, both because of an imprecise "hot spot" for physical interactors, and because the physical object occluded its virtual representation. By designing a context-sensitive "crosshair" cursor that extended beyond the dimensions of the physical object, we were able to significantly increase performance in those cases. In the future, we plan to conduct a more thorough user study, with more participants, that also measures the usability of the gesture tracking subsystem.

9   Putting It to Use: Spontaneous Gesture Interfaces

All the components of the Perceptive Workbench – deictic gesture tracking, object recognition, tracking, and reconstruction – can be seamlessly integrated into a single, consistent framework. The Perceptive Workbench interface detects how users want to interact with it and automatically switches to the desired mode.

When users move a hand above the display surface, the system tracks the hand and arm as described in Section 6. A cursor appears at the projected hand position on the display surface, and a ray emanates along the projected arm axis. These can be used in selection or manipulation, as in Figure 8a. When users place an object on the surface, the cameras recognize this and identify and track the object. A virtual button also appears on the display (indicated by the arrow in Figure 8b). By tracking the reflections of objects near the table surface, the system determines when the hand overlaps the button, thus selecting it. This action causes the system to capture the 3D object shape, as described in Section 7.

Since shadows from the user's arms always touch the image border, it is easy to decide whether an object lies on the desk surface. If the system detects a shadow that does not touch any border, it can be sure that an object on the desk surface was the cause. As a result, the system will switch to object-recognition and tracking mode. Similarly, the absence of such shadows, for a certain period, indicates that the object has been taken away, and the system can safely switch back to gesture-tracking mode. Note that once the system is

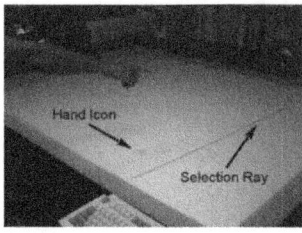 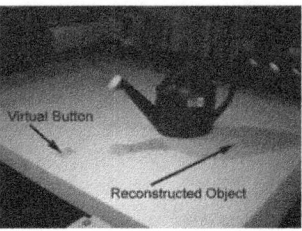 

Fig. 8. (a) Pointing gesture with hand icon and selection ray; (b) Virtual button rendered on the screen when object is detected on the surface; (c) Reconstruction of this watering can.

in object-recognition mode, it turns off the ceiling lights, and activates the light sources underneath the table. Therefore users can safely grab and move objects on the desk surface, since their arms will not cast any shadows that could disturb the perceived object contours.

These interaction modes provide the elements of a perceptual interface that operates without wires and without restrictions on the objects. For example, we constructed a simple application where the system detects objects placed on the desk, reconstructs them, and then places them in a template set where they are displayed as slowly rotating objects on the workbench display's left border. Users can grab these objects, which can act as new icons that the user can attach to selection or manipulation modes or use as primitives in a model building application.

An Augmented Reality Game. We created a more elaborate collaborative interface using the Perceptive Workbench in an augmented reality game. Two or more game masters can communicate with a person in a separate space wearing an augmented reality headset (Figure 9a). The workbench display surface acts as a top-down view of the player's space. The game masters place different objects which appear to the player as distinct monsters at different vertical levels in the game space. While the game masters move the objects around the display surface, this motion is replicated by monsters in the player's view, which move in their individual planes. The player's goal is to defeat these monsters by performing Kung Fu gestures before they can reach him. For a more detailed description of this application, see Starner et al. [27,16].

3D Terrain Navigation. A second application uses the Perceptive Workbench's deictic gesture tracking capability to interface with the VGIS global terrain navigation system [37]. Users choose the direction of navigation by pointing and can change the direction continuously (Figure 9b). Moving the hand toward the display increases the speed toward the earth and moving it away increases the speed away from the earth. Panning and rotating can be accomplished by

Fig. 9. Applications: (a) Two game masters controlling virtual monsters; (b) Terrain navigation using deictic gestures; (c) A virtual instantiation of the workbench.

making lateral gestures in the direction to be panned or by making a rotational arm gesture. Currently, users choose these three modes by keys on a keyboard attached to the workbench, while the extent of the action is determined by deictic tracking. We are experimenting with a system where the modes are selected via gesture.

Telepresence and CSCW. As another application of the Perceptive Workbench, we built a simple telepresence system. Using the sample interaction framework described at the beginning of this section, users can point to any location on the desk, reconstruct objects, and move them across the desk surface. All of their actions are immediately applied to a VR model of the workbench mirroring the current state of the real desk (Figure 9c). Thus, when performing deictic gestures, the current hand and pointing position appear on the model workbench as a red selection ray. Similarly, the reconstructed shapes of objects on the desk surface are displayed at the corresponding positions in the model. This makes it possible for coworkers at a distant location to follow the user's actions in real-time, while having complete freedom to choose a favorable viewpoint.

10   Future Work

Many VR systems use head-tracked shutter glasses and stereoscopic images to get a more immersive effect. In order to make these systems fully wireless, we need to apply vision-based methods to also track the user's head. At present, we are researching inexpensive and robust ways to do this that still meet the performance criteria. Results from Ware and Balakrishnan [36] suggest that, in contrast to fully immersive systems where users wear a head-mounted display and relatively small head rotations can cause large viewpoint shifts, semi-immersive systems do not impose such high restrictions on head-movement latency. In fact, since the head position is much more important than the head orientation in these systems, latency can even be slightly larger than with the gesture and object tracking.

In addition, we will work on improving the latency of the gesture-rendering loop through code refinement and the application of Kalman filters. For the recognition of objects on the desk's surface, we will explore the use of statistical methods that can give us better ways of handling uncertainties and distinguishing new objects. We will also employ hidden Markov models to recognize symbolic hand gestures [28] for controlling the interface. Finally, as hinted by the multiple game masters in the gaming application, several users may be supported through careful, active allocation of resources.

11   Conclusion

The Perceptive Workbench uses a vision-based system to enable a rich set of interactions, including hand and arm gestures, object recognition and tracking, and 3D reconstruction of objects placed on its surface. Latency measurements show that the Perceptive Workbench's tracking capabilities are suitable for real-time interaction.

All elements combine seamlessly into the same interface and can be used in various applications. In addition, the sensing system is relatively inexpensive, using standard cameras and lighting equipment plus a computer with one or two video digitizers, depending on the functions desired. As seen from the multiplayer gaming, terrain navigation, and telepresence applications, the Perceptive Workbench encourages an untethered and spontaneous interface that encourages the inclusion of physical objects in the virtual environment.

Acknowledgements. This work is supported in part by funding from Georgia Institute of Technology's Broadband Institute. We thank Brad Singletary, William Ribarsky, Zachary Wartell, David Krum, and Larry Hodges for their help building the Perceptive Workbench and interfacing it with the applications mentioned above. We also thank Brygg Ullmer, Jun Rekimoto, and Jim Davis for their discussions and assistance. In addition we thank Paul Rosin and Geoff West for their line segmentation code, the Purdue CADLab for TWIN, and Paolo Cignoni, Claudio Rocchini, and Roberto Scopigno for Metro.

References

1. O. Bimber. Gesture controlled object interaction: A virtual table case study. In *7th Int'l Conf. in Central Europe on Computer Graphics, Visualization, and Interactive Digital Media (WSCG'99)*, volume 1, Plzen, Czech Republic, 1999.
2. A. Bobick, S. Intille, J. Davis, F. Baird, C. Pinhanez, L. Campbell, Y. Ivanov, and A. Wilson. The kidsroom: A perceptually-based interactive and immersive story environment. *PRESENCE: Teleoperators and Virtual Environments*, 8(4):367–391, August 1999.
3. R. Bolt and E. Herranz. Two-handed gesture in multi-modal natural dialogue. In *ACM Symposium on User Interface Software and Technology (UIST'92)*, pages 7–14, 1992.

4. P. Cignoni, C. Rocchini, and R. Scopigno. Metro: Measuring error on simplified surfaces. *Computer Graphics Forum*, 17(2):167–174, June 1998.

5. D. Daum and G. Dudek. On 3-d surface reconstruction using shape from shadows. In *IEEE Conference on Computer Vision and Pattern Recognition (CVPR'98)*, pages 461–468, 1998.

6. J.W. Davis and A.F. Bobick. Sideshow: A silhouette-based interactive dual-screen environment. Technical Report TR-457, MIT Media Lab Tech Report, 1998.

7. Computer Aided Design and Graphics Laboratory (CADLAB). *TWIN Solid Modeling Package Reference Manual*. School of Mechanical Engineering, Purdue University, http://cadlab.www.ecn.purdue.edu/cadlab/twin, 1995.

8. K. Dorfmueller-Ulhaas and D. Schmalstieg. Finger tracking for interaction in augmented environments. Technical Report TR-186-2-01-03, Vienna University of Technology, 2001. submitted to Computer Graphics Forum.

9. G.W. Fitzmaurice, H. Ishii, and W. Buxton. Bricks: Laying the foundations for graspable user interfaces. In *Proceedings of CHI'95*, pages 442–449, 1995.

10. M. Fukumoto, K. Mase, and Y. Suenaga. Real-time detection of pointing actions for a glove-free interface. In *Proceedings of IAPR Workshop on Machine Vision Applications*, Tokyo, Japan, 1992.

11. H. Ishii and B. Ullmer. Tangible bits: Towards seamless interfaces between people, bits, and atoms. In *Proceedings of CHI'97*, pages 234–241, 1997.

12. C. Jennings. Robust finger tracking with multiple cameras. In *Proc. of the International Workshop on Recognition, Analysis, and Tracking of Faces and Gestures in Real-Time Systems*, pages 152–160, 1999.

13. M. Krueger. *Artificial Reality II*. Addison-Wesley, 1991.

14. W. Krueger, C.-A. Bohn, B. Froehlich, H. Schueth, W. Strauss, and G. Wesche. The responsive workbench: A virtual work environment. *IEEE Computer*, 28(7):42–48, July 1995.

15. A. Laurentini. How many 2d silhouettes does it take to reconstruct a 3d object? *Computer Vision and Image Understanding (CVIU)*, 67(1):81–87, July 1997.

16. B. Leibe, T. Starner, W. Ribarsky, Z. Wartell, D. Krum, B. Singletary, and L. Hodges. Toward spontaneous interaction with the perceptive workbench. *IEEE Computer Graphics & Applications*, 20(6):54–65, Nov. 2000.

17. W. Matusik, C. Buehler, S. Gortler, R. Raskar, and L. McMillan. Image based visual hulls. In *Proceedings of SIGGRAPH 2000*, 2000.

18. F.K.H. Quek. Eyes in the interface. *Image and Vision Computing*, 13(6):511–525, Aug. 1995.

19. J.M. Rehg and T. Kanade. Visual tracking of high dof articulated structures: an application to human hand tracking. In *Third European Conference on Computer Vision (ECCV'94)*, pages 35–46, 1994.

20. J. Rekimoto and N. Matsushita. Perceptual surfaces: Towards a human and object sensitive interactive display. In *Workshop on Perceptual User Interfaces (PUI'97)*, 1997.

21. P.L. Rosin and G.A.W. West. Non-parametric segmentation of curves into various representations. *IEEE Transactions on Pattern Analysis and Machine Intelligence*, 17(12):1140–1153, 1995.

22. Y. Sato, Y. Kobayashi, and H. Koike. Fast tracking of hands and fingertips in infrared images for augmented desk interface. In *Proc. of the Fourth IEEE International Conference on Automatic Face and Gesture Recognition*, pages 462–467, 2000.

23. A.F. Seay, D. Krum, W. Ribarsky, and L. Hodges. Multimodal interaction techniques for the virtual workbench. In *Proceedings CHI'99 Extended Abstracts*, pages 282–283, 1999.
24. J. Segen and S. Kumar. Shadow gestures: 3d hand pose estimation using a single camera. In *IEEE Conference on Computer Vision and Pattern Recognition (CVPR'99)*, volume 1, pages 479–485, 1999.
25. R. Sharma and J. Molineros. Computer vision based augmented reality for guiding manual assembly. *PRESENCE: Teleoperators and Virtual Environments*, 6(3):292–317, 1997.
26. S.K. Srivastava and N. Ahuja. An algorithm for generating octrees from object silhouettes in perspective views. *Computer Vision, Graphics, and Image Processing: Image Understanding (CVGIP:IU)*, 49(1):68–84, 1990.
27. T. Starner, B. Leibe, B. Singletary, and J. Pair. Mind-warping: Towards creating a compelling collaborative augmented reality gaming interface through wearable computers and multi-modal input and output. In *IEEE International Conference on Intelligent User Interfaces (IUI'2000)*, 2000.
28. T. Starner, J. Weaver, and A. Pentland. Real-time american sign language recognition using desk and wearable computer based video. *IEEE Transactions on Pattern Analysis and Machine Intelligence*, 20(12):1371–1375, 1998.
29. D. Sturman. *Whole-hand Input*. PhD thesis, MIT Media Lab, 1992.
30. S. Sullivan and J. Ponce. Automatic model construction, pose estimation, and object recognition from photographs using triangular splines. *IEEE Transactions on Pattern Analysis and Machine Intelligence*, 20(10):1091–1097, 1998.
31. B. Ullmer and H. Ishii. The metadesk: Models and prototypes for tangible user interfaces. In *ACM Symposium on User Interface Software and Technology (UIST'97)*, pages 223–232, 1997.
32. J. Underkoffler and H. Ishii. Illuminating light: An optical design tool with a luminous-tangible interface. In *Proceedings of CHI'98*, pages 542–549, 1998.
33. A. Utsumi and J. Ohya. Multiple-hand-gesture tracking using multiple cameras. In *IEEE Conference on Computer Vision and Pattern Recognition (CVPR'99)*, volume 1, pages 473–478, 1999.
34. R. van de Pol, W. Ribarsky, L. Hodges, and F. Post. Interaction in semi-immersive large display environments. In *Proceedings of Virtual Environments'99*, pages 157–168, 1999.
35. C. Vogler and D. Metaxas. Asl recognition based on coupling between hmms and 3d motion analysis. In *Sixth International Conference on Computer Vision (ICCV'98)*, pages 363–369, 1998.
36. C. Ware and R. Balakrishnan. Reaching for objects in vr displays: Lag and frame rate. *ACM Transactions on Computer-Human Interaction*, 1(4):331–356, 1994.
37. Z. Wartell, W. Ribarsky, and L.F. Hodges. Third-person navigation of whole-planet terrain in a head-tracked stereoscopic environment. In *IEEE Virtual Reality '99 Conference*, pages 141–149, 1999.
38. B. Watson, N. Walker, W. Ribarsky, and V. Spaulding. The effects of variation of system responsiveness on user performance in virtual environments. *Human Factors*, 40(3):403–414, 1998.
39. P. Wellner. Interacting with paper on the digital desk. *Communications of the ACM*, 36(7):86–89, 1993.
40. C. Wren, A. Azarbayejani, T. Darrell, and A. Pentland. Pfinder: Real-time tracking of the human body. *IEEE Transactions on Pattern Analysis and Machine Intelligence*, 19(7):780–785, 1997.

Towards Robust Multi-cue Integration for Visual Tracking

Martin Spengler and Bernt Schiele

Perceptual Computing and Computer Vision Group
Computer Science Department
ETH Zurich, Switzerland
{spengler,schiele}@inf.ethz.ch

Abstract. Even though many of today's vision algorithms are very successful, they lack robustness since they are typically limited to a particular situation. In this paper we argue that the principles of sensor and model integration can increase the robustness of today's computer vision systems substantially. As an example multi-cue tracking of faces is discussed. The approach is based on the principles of self-organization of the integration mechanism and self-adaptation of the cue models during tracking. Experiments show that the robustness of simple models is leveraged significantly by sensor and model integration.

1 Introduction

In the literature several algorithms are reported for precise object tracking in real-time. However, since most approaches to tracking are based on a single cue they are most often restricted to particular environmental conditions which are static, controlled or known a priori. Since no single visual cue will be robust and general enough to deal with a wide variety of environmental conditions their combination promises to increase robustness and generality. In this paper we argue that in order to obtain robust tracking in dynamically changing environments any approach should aim to use and integrate different cues. Complementary cues allow tracking under a wider range of different conditions than any single cue alone. Redundant cues on the other hand allow to evaluate the current tracking result and therefore allow to adapt the integration mechanism and the visual cues themselves in order to allow optimal integration.

In our belief, optimal context-dependent combination of information will be key to the long-term goal of robust object tracking. In order to enable robustness over time it is essential to use multiple cues simultaneously. Most approaches – based on multiple cues – only use one cue at a time therefore optimizing performance rather than robustness. Using multiple cues simultaneously allows not only to use complementary and redundant information at all times but also allows to detect failures more robustly and thus enabling recovery.

This paper introduces a general system framework for the integration of multiple cues. The ultimate goal of the framework is to increase and enable robust

B. Schiele and G. Sagerer (Eds.): ICVS 2001, LNCS 2095, pp. 93–106, 2001.
© Springer-Verlag Berlin Heidelberg 2001

object tracking in dynamically changing environments. The general framework exploits two methodologies for the adaptation to different conditions: firstly the integration scheme can be changed and secondly the visual cues themselves can be adapted. Adapting the visual cues allows to adapt to different environmental changes directly. Changing the integration scheme reflects the underlying assumption that different cues are suitable for different conditions. Based on this general framework two different approaches are introduced and experimentally analyzed.

This paper discusses the development of a system which aims at robust tracking through self-adaptive multi-cue integration. *Democratic Integration* introduced by Triesch and Malsburg [15] may be seen as an example of such a system. Section 4 introduces and discusses a modified version of Democratic Integration. The approach is evaluated experimentally and several shortcomings are identified. In particular, the original approach is limited to the tracking of a single target which leads to the proposition of a second system (Sect. 5). In this system multi-hypotheses tracking and multi-cue integration is realized by means of CONDENSATION, a conditional density propagation algorithm proposed by Isard and Blake [2]. Expectation maximization (EM) is used to obtain more reliable probability densities of the single-cue observations. Again, experimental results are reported and discussed.

2 Related Work

Although it is well known that the integration of multiple cues is a key prerequisite for robust biological and machine vision, most of today's tracking approaches are based on single cues. Even approaches which are called multi-cue in the literature often do not use their cues in parallel or treat them as equivalent channels. On the contrary, many approaches try to select the "optimal" cue for the actually perceived context. Also common is to use a single, predominant cue supported by other, often less reliable cues.

The layered hierarchy of vision based tracking algorithms proposed by Toyama and Hager [13,12] is a good example for the cue selection approach. Their declared goal is to enable robust, adaptive tracking in real-time. Different tracking algorithms are selected with respect to the actual conditions: Whenever conditions are good, an accurate and precise tracking algorithm is employed. When conditions deteriorate more robust but less accurate algorithms are chosen. Crowley and Berard [5] have proposed to use three different tracking algorithms in a similar way as proposed by Toyama and Hager.

Isard and Blake proposed the now popular CONDENSATION algorithm [8]. The original algorithm – well suited for simultaneous multi-hypotheses tracking – has been extended [9] by a second *supportive* cue (color in their case) which allows to recover from tracking failures. CONDENSATION and its derivative ICON-DENSATION possess two important properties: CONDENSATION is able to track multiple target hypotheses simultaneously which is important in the presence of multiple targets but also for recovery from tracking failure. In addition, CON-

DENSATION is well suited for concurrent integration of multiple visual cues even though not explicitly proposed by Isard and Blake.

Democratic Integration, an approach proposed by Triesch and Malsburg [15] implements *concurrent* cue integration: All visual cues contribute simultaneously to the overall result and none of the cues has an outstanding relevance compared to the others. Again, robustness and generality is a major motivation for the proposal. Triesch et al [14] convincingly argue for the need for adaptive multi-cue integration and support their claims with psychophysical experiments. Adaptivity is a key point in which democratic integration contrasts with other integration mechanisms. Following the classification scheme of Clark and Yuille [4], democratic integration implements weakly coupled cue integration. That is, the used cues are independent in a probabilistic sense[1]. Democratic integration and similar weakly coupled data fusion methods are also closely related to voting [11]. The weighted sum approach of democratic integration may be seen as weighted plurality voting as proposed in [10]. A more thorough analysis of the relations between sensor fusion and voting can be found in [3].

In the following section we propose a general system framework. We strongly believe that a robust and reliable tracking system has to have at least three key properties: Multi-cue integration, context-sensitive adaptivity and the ability to simultaneously pursue multiple target hypotheses. Due to its interesting and favorable properties we have chosen democratic integration as an exemplary implementation of the general approach. In order to track multiple target hypotheses simultaneously, we integrated CONDENSATION into our system as well. The combination of these two promising approaches leads to a tracking system which has all three above mentioned key properties.

3   General System Framework

This section describes the general system framework based on the integration of multiple cues. The ultimate goal of the framework is to enable robust tracking in dynamically changing environments. Visual cues should be complementary as well as redundant as motivated above. An important aspect of the general framework is that it is adaptable depending on the actual context. In order to adapt the system optimally the actual tracking results are evaluated and fed back to the integration mechanism as well as to the visual cues themselves. This allows to adapt the integration and the visual cues optimally to the current situation.

The general system framework is depicted in Fig. 1. Based on a series of images (called sensor data $s(t)$ in the following) N visual cues $p_1, \ldots, p_N$ are implemented. Each visual cue estimates the target's state vector individually. These estimations are then fused by the multi-cue integration unit into a single probability density p_C. Based on this probability density the multi-cue state estimator estimates potential target positions $\{\hat{\mathbf{x}}_1(t), \ldots, \hat{\mathbf{x}}_K(t)\}$. These estimated

---

[1] Due to the feedback loop of democratic integration its cues are not entirely independent anymore but indirectly coupled by the result they agreed upon.

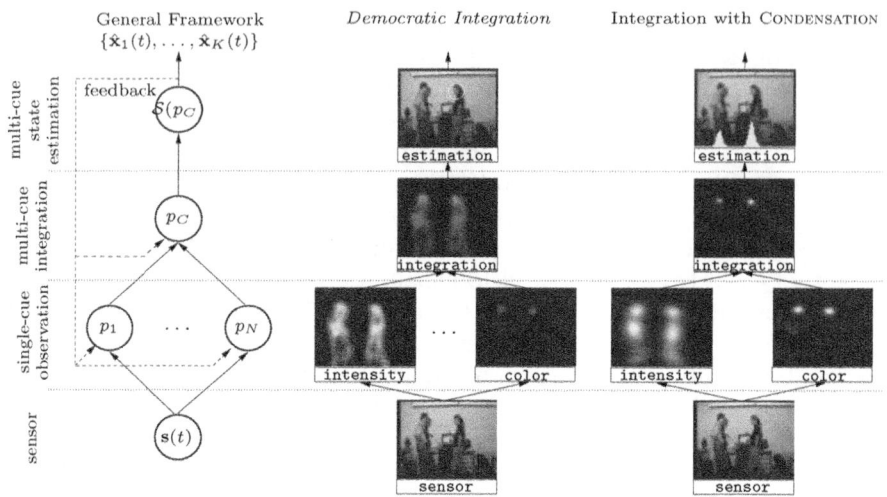

Fig. 1. General Framework A general framework for self-organizing multi-cue integration is depicted in the left column. The column in the middle illustrates *Democratic Integration*, one of the implementations of the general framework discussed in this paper. The right column is a similar illustration for the second implementation, integration with CONDENSATION.

target positions as well as the probability density p_C are then fed back to the multi-cue integration unit and the visual cues in order to adapt their internal states aiming to improve the overall performance. The proposed formulation is general and flexible with respect to different visual cues as well as different integration mechanisms. Also any feedback mechanism may be used enabling for example to use high level knowledge about the particular object or environment. Following Fig. 1 we introduce notations for the different stages of the framework:

Sensor: Temporally sorted sequence of vectors $\mathbf{s}(t)$ in the sensor or signal space $\mathbb{R}^m$, i.e. $\mathbf{s}(t) \in \mathbb{R}^m$. Example: In the remainder of the paper we use image sequences of dimension $m = image\_width \cdot image\_height$.

Single-cue Observation: Temporally sorted sequence of probability maps for each visual cue estimating the n-dimensional state vector of the target. More specifically every sensor space vector $\mathbf{s}(t)$ is projected onto a n-dimensional probability distribution $p_j(\mathbf{x}|t)$. Example: If the system ought to estimate the two-dimensional position of the object the dimension n is 2. When $\mathcal{M}_j$ denotes the mapping function $\mathcal{M}_j : \mathbb{R}^m \mapsto \mathbb{R}^n$ with parameterization $\mathbf{r}_j(t)$, the response of a single cue j is given by:

$$p_j(\mathbf{x}|t) = \mathcal{M}_j(\mathbf{s}(t); \mathbf{r}_j(t)) \tag{1}$$

Multi-cue Integration: Parameterized combination of N observation probability distributions $p_j(\mathbf{x}|t)$, with vector $\mathbf{r}_C(t)$ denoting the parameterization at time t:

$$p_C(\mathbf{x}|t) = \mathcal{C}(p_1(\mathbf{x}|t), \ldots, p_N(\mathbf{x}|t); \mathbf{r}_C(t)). \tag{2}$$

Multi-cue State Estimation: Select K state vectors $\hat{\mathbf{x}}_k(t)$ according to problem specific rules. As an example, a multi-cue state estimation rule might pick the local maxima of the combined probability distribution $p_C(\mathbf{x}|t)$. Note the distinction between the integration mechanism which results in the probability distribution $p_C(\mathbf{x}|t)$ and the state estimation which chooses appropriate candidates using that probability distribution.

$$\mathcal{S}(p_C(\mathbf{x}|t)) \rightarrow \{\hat{\mathbf{x}}_1(t), \hat{\mathbf{x}}_2(t), \ldots, \hat{\mathbf{x}}_K(t)\} \tag{3}$$

Feedback. The set $\mathcal{S}(p_C(\mathbf{x}|t))$ of estimated target state vectors as well as the probability distribution $p_C(\mathbf{x}|t)$ are fed back to the multi-cue integration unit and the single-cue observation units in order to adapt their parameterizations $\mathbf{r}_C(t)$ and $\mathbf{r}_j(t)$.

4 Democratic Integration

Democratic Integration, the first implementation of our general system framework, was originally proposed by Triesch at. al. [15]. Five visual cues agree upon a common position estimation. The individual cues are then evaluated on this estimation in order to determine their weights for the following time step. Additionally, every single cue adapts its internal model to increase the system's overall performance. At every moment two fundamental assumptions must be fulfilled: First, consensus between the individual cues must be predominant. Second, environmental changes must only affect a minority of the visual cues.

4.1 System Description

Sensor & Single-cue Observation. Democratic Integration currently works on two-dimensional color images. The system's sensor module (see Fig. 1 middle column) captures a sequence of color images $\mathbf{s}(t)$ and dispatches them to the attached single-cue observation units. These map the images to two-dimensional saliency maps $p_i(\mathbf{x}|t)$ expressing the observation's probability for every position $\mathbf{x}$. *Democratic Integration* implements the following single-cue observations:

The *intensity change cue* $p_{int}(\mathbf{x}|t)$ detects motion in a gray-level image $\mathbf{s}(t)$ relative to its predecessor $\mathbf{s}(t-1)$. Motion is thus pixel-wise defined as the difference of intensity between two subsequent images. *Skin color detection* $p_{col}(\mathbf{x}|t)$ calculates for every pixel the probability of skin color. More specifically human skin color is modeled as a specific subspace of the HSI[2] color space. Depending

---

[2] Hue, Saturation, Intensity; see [6]

only on the system's target position estimations $\hat{\mathbf{x}}(t)$, the *motion prediction cue* $p_{mot}(\mathbf{x}|t)$ predicts the target's future motion to maintain motion continuity. In contrast to the original paper [15] we implemented a motion prediction unit using *Kalman filtering*. In order to determine potential head positions, the *shape template matching cue* $p_{tmp}(\mathbf{x}|t)$ correlates the gray-level input image $\mathbf{s}(t)$ and a head template for every position in the input image. The *contrast* $p_{con}(\mathbf{x}|t)$ cue extracts contrast pixel-wise from the input image $\mathbf{s}(t)$. Contrast, defined over the pixel's neighborhood, is compared to a adaptive model of contrast in order to detect pixels with salient contrast. All visual cues except the intensity change cue can be adapted.

Multi-cue Integration & Multi-cue State Estimation. *Democratic Integration* implements context-dependent multi-cue integration by means of a weighted sum of the cues' probability densities:

$$p_C(\mathbf{x}|t) = \mathcal{C}(p_{int}(\mathbf{x}|t), p_{col}(\mathbf{x}|t), p_{mot}(\mathbf{x}|t), p_{tmp}(\mathbf{x}|t), p_{con}(\mathbf{x}|t); \mathbf{r}_C(t))$$
$$= \sum_i \omega_i \cdot p_i(\mathbf{x}|t) \tag{4}$$

Adapting the weights ω_i dynamically with respect to the cues' former performance opens the possibility to react on alternating situations. Conforming with the general system framework introduced in Sect. 3, *Democratic Integration* provides a multi-cue state estimation scheme:

$$\hat{\mathbf{x}}(t) = \arg\max_{\mathbf{x}}\{p_C(\mathbf{x}|t)\} \tag{5}$$

That is, the estimated target position is defined as the maximal response of the combined probability distribution $p_C(\mathbf{x}|t)$. This choice of a multi-cue state estimation is reasonable when the probability distribution $p_C(\mathbf{x}|t)$ has a single non-ambiguous maxima. However, the target state estimation scheme fails as soon as multiple hypotheses with similar probability emerge.

Feedback. Once the system is initialized, *Democratic Integration* provides means to adjust its parameters with respect to the current situation. As outlined in Sect. 3, unsupervised self-adaptation occurs in two different levels:

1. **Self-organized Multi-cue Integration** Adapting the integration mechanism itself makes it possible to select those visual cues which are reliable in the current context and to suppress the other ones. In *Democratic Integration*, this selection mechanism is implemented by the following dynamics:

$$\tau \cdot \dot{\omega}_i(t) = q_i(t) - \omega_i(t) \tag{6}$$

where $q_i(t)$ is a normalized quality measurement of cue i relative to the estimation $\hat{\mathbf{x}}(t)$ and τ is a constant determining how fast the weights ω_i are adapted. Quality measurement $q_i(t)$ is defined as the normalized distance between response $p_i(\hat{\mathbf{x}}(t)|t)$ and average response $\langle p_i(\mathbf{x}|t)\rangle$.

2. **Auto-adaptive Single-cue Observation** In analogy to the feedback loop for the multi-cue integration, the models of the single-cue observations are adapted by the following dynamics:

$$\tau_i \cdot \dot{\mathbf{r}}_i(t) = \mathfrak{f}(\mathbf{s}(\hat{\mathbf{x}}(t))) - \mathbf{r}_i(t) \tag{7}$$

where $\mathfrak{f}(\mathbf{s}(\hat{\mathbf{x}}(t)))$ extracts a suitable feature vector from image $\mathbf{s}(t)$ at position $\hat{\mathbf{x}}(t)$. Again, time constant τ_i controls the speed for adapting the model/parameters $\mathbf{r}_i(t)$.

As is, the feedback mechanism relies on the decision for a single target position estimate $\hat{\mathbf{x}}(t)$. The system is therefore limited to single target tracking and incapable of tracking multiple targets or even multiple target hypotheses. This is a major shortcoming of *Democratic Integration* as we will see in the experiments.

4.2 Analysis of *Democratic Integration*

Color-change Sequence. The color change sequence (Fig. 2) challenges the two most important visual cues for *Democratic Integration*, intensity change and skin color detection. Both of them start with initial reliabilities $\omega_{int} = \omega_{col} = 0.5$ whereas the remaining cues have initial weights 0.0. This setup expresses the a priori knowledge one has about the task: Tracking skin colored regions which are in motion.

After an initial period of convergence toward balanced weights, the ambient illumination changes abruptly from white to green (see Fig. 2, frame 24). Hence skin color detection fails completely and intensity change's reliability is also decreased for several frames. However, motion prediction is able to compensate. As soon as the lighting regains constancy (frame 30), intensity change becomes reliable again and its weight is increased. Skin color detection fails until the skin color model has adapted to the new conditions (frame 40). Afterward its weight increases too, converging toward former equilibrium. When the subject leaves the scene (frame 50), tracking is lost and the weights are re-adapted toward their default values. Shape template matching and contrast have only supporting character in this sequence.

Soccer Sequence. The soccer sequence depicted in Fig. 3 challenges *Democratic Integration* since it is captured in an uncontrolled environment. Furthermore, different potential targets appear and disappear over time. Similar to the color-change sequence discussed above, the weights converge toward an equilibrium in an initial period. When the tracked subject leaves the scene in frame 38, tracking is lost and re-adaptation toward default weights begins. After re-entrance (frame 53), the system continues to track the target. Failure of skin color detection between frame 60 and frame 80 is compensated by the remaining cues, namely motion prediction and contrast. After the skin color cue has recovered, a period of convergence lasts until the target's occlusion in frame 123 causes reorganization. Finally, tracking is lost when the target disappears and the weights are re-adapted toward their default values.

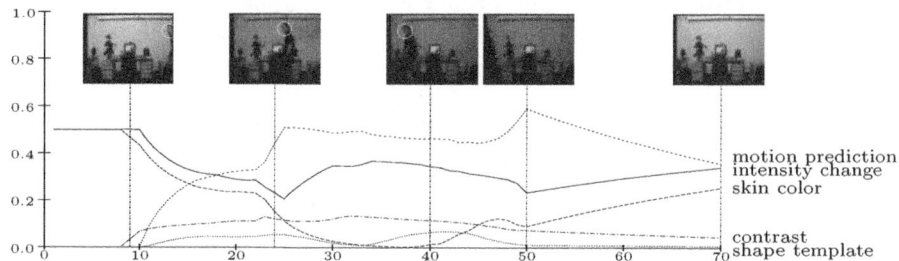

Fig. 2. Color-change sequence. This sequence primarily challenges the intensity detection cue and the skin color detection cue. Both are influenced by the radical change of ambient lighting from white to green in frame 24. Furthermore, this sequence illustrates the dynamic parameter adaptation vividly. See text for a detailed discussion.

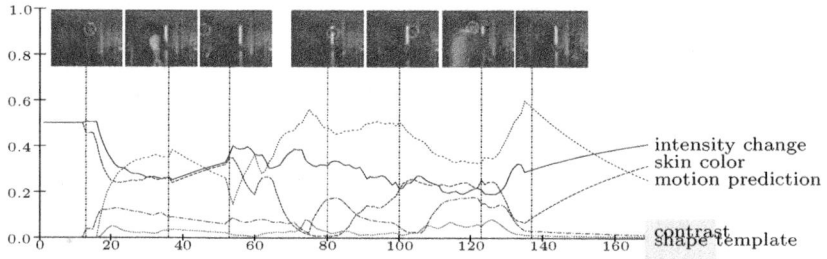

Fig. 3. Soccer sequence. This sequence challenges the tracking system in two ways. First, the sequence was captured under "real" conditions, i.e. outside the labor with its cooperative illumination and background conditions. Second, there are multiple subjects in the scene appearing and disappearing over time. Furthermore, some of the subjects play soccer in front of the camera. This causes fast movements and abrupt direction alternations. See text for a more detailed discussion of this sequence.

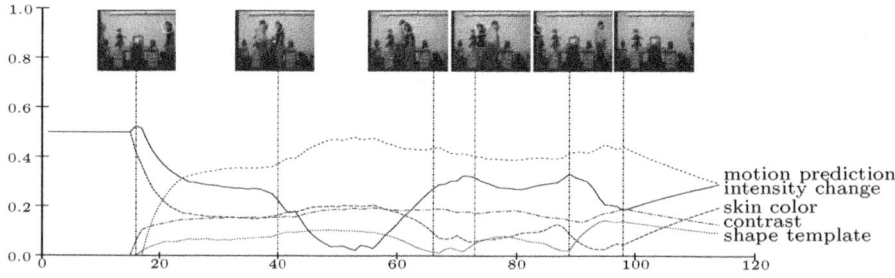

Fig. 4. Two person sequence. This sequence addresses the problem of simultaneous multiple targets. There are two main problems arising from the presence of multiple potential targets: First, the multi-cue state estimator has to choose one particular target due to the single-target limitation. Second, depending on the estimation heuristic, the tracker is likely to "jump" between two or more visible targets. A detailed discussion of this section is provided in the text.

Two Person Sequence. Looking at the problem of simultaneous tracking of multiple potential targets, this sequence shows more than one subject simultaneously. Also, the two subject cross, occluding one another. Due to the delay between arrival of subject one and subject two, the system is able to lock on subject one. The initial period of stable equilibrium lasts until the two subjects begin to shake hands in frame 40. At this point they do not move anymore and therefore the intensity change cue looses weight. Tracking continues although subject one is occluded by subject two when they cross. After a second period of equilibrium, the weights converge toward their default values after both targets have left the scene. Throughout the entire sequence, subject one is tracked successfully. Since the system can track only one target at any time it is rather unpredictable which subject is tracked after they met. This exemplifies that the system is inherently limited to single target tracking.

Discussion. In the experiments, *Democratic Integration* proved the concept of dynamic context-dependent multi-cue integration as a promising technique to achieve reliable tracking under uncontrolled conditions. Under steady conditions, the system converges toward an equilibrium whereas sudden changes in the environment provoke re-organization of the system. As expected, failure of a visual cue is compensated by other cues in order to maintain continuous tracking. Several cues are able to recover after a failure by adapting their internal states to the changed situation.

Nevertheless, *Democratic Integration* has several major shortcomings: The most obvious one is the system's inherent limitation to single target tracking. That is, *Democratic Integration* is not able to track multiple (potential) targets simultaneously. Furthermore, self-organizing systems like *Democratic Integration* are likely to fail in cases where they start tracking false positives. In such cases the system may adapt to the wrong target resulting in reinforced false positive tracking. A third problem is that the different initial parameters are set based on personal experience only. In the future we plan to employ machine learning techniques.

5   Integration with Condensation

In this section we propose a second implementation of the general system framework. It aims to improve the integration scheme to overcome shortcomings identified in the previous section. In particular integration by means of CONDENSATION [2] is used allowing to track multiple hypotheses simultaneously. This enables to track multiple subjects as shown in the experiments with the two person sequence. Also multiple hypotheses tracking is less affected by false positives since no decision is made about the "true" target positions.

5.1   System Description

Sensor & Single-cue Observation. In order to conform with the general system framework (Sect. 3), integration with CONDENSATION replaces multi-cue integration, multi-cue state estimation and feedback of *Democratic Integration*. Sensor and single-cue observation basically remain the same. Only intensity change and skin color detection are used in the following. Template matching and contrast cue have been removed without substitution because they had no major impact in the previous experiments. Motion prediction is no longer maintained as separate visual cue but is now part of the multi-cue integration.

As a novelty, probability densities $p_{int}(\mathbf{x}|t)$ and $p_{col}(\mathbf{x}|t)$ are approximated by mixtures of Gaussians in order to cluster the saliency maps.

$$p(\mathbf{x}|t) = \sum_{i=1}^{M} p(i|t) \cdot p(\mathbf{x}|i,t) \tag{8}$$

where M denotes the number of Gaussians in the mixture. Factor $p(i|t)$ weights Gaussian $p(\mathbf{x}|i,t)$. Clustering is performed by means of *expectation maximization* (EM), an iterative algorithm adjusting means $\boldsymbol{\mu}_i$, variances σ_i^2 and weights $p(i|t)$ of the mixture's Gaussians in order to maximize the log-likelihood E of N randomly drawn samples $p(\mathbf{x}_j|t)$, $j = 1 \ldots N$.

$$E = -\ln(\prod_{j=1}^{N} p(\mathbf{x}_j|t)) = -\sum_{j-1}^{N} \ln \left[\sum_{i=1}^{M} p(i|t) \cdot p(\mathbf{x}_j|i,t) \right] \tag{9}$$

In order to minimize E, EM requires iteratively applied update rules for $\boldsymbol{\mu}_i$, σ_i^2, and $p(i|t)$. For the special case of a mixture of Gaussians closed forms of these rules exist [1]. They can be obtained by maximizing E relative to means $\boldsymbol{\mu}_i$, standard deviation σ_i, and weight $p(i|t)$, i.e. by solving the following equations: $\frac{\partial E}{\partial \boldsymbol{\mu}_i} = 0$, $\frac{\partial E}{\partial \sigma_i} = 0$, $\frac{\partial E}{\partial p(i|t)} = 0$.

If the mixture's parameters $\boldsymbol{\mu}_i$, σ_i^2, and $p(i|t)$ for time step t are used to initialize EM approximation for time step $t + 1$ *motion continuity* emerges as a most welcomed side effect. In contrast to *Democratic Integration* where motion continuity is only provided by the motion prediction cue, it is now maintained by each visual cue individually. For time step 0 the mixtures coefficients are initialized randomly.

Multi-cue Integration, Multi-cue State Estimation, and Feedback. The combined probability distribution $p_C(\mathbf{x}|t)$ is in the new multi-cue integrator represented by a set of N samples $(\mathbf{x}_j^{(t)}, \pi_j^{(t)})$ approximating the integrated observations $\tilde{p}_C(\mathbf{x}|t)$ asymptotically with increasing N (see Grenander et. al. [7]). Maintained by the conditional density propagation algorithm CONDENSATION, $p_C(\mathbf{x}|t)$ is able to simultaneously track multiple hypotheses over time. For time step t probability density $p_C(\mathbf{x}|t)$ is computed by three subsequent elements:

1. **Resampling** Sample set $p_C(\mathbf{x}|t-1)$ is resampled by drawing (with replacement) N times a sample from $p_C(\mathbf{x}|t-1)$. A sample j is selected with probability $\pi_j^{(t-1)}$. Thus it is likely that samples with high probability $\pi_j^{(t-1)}$ are chosen more than once and others not at all. This leads to a new sample set

of size N with samples accumulated in regions where the former probability distribution $p_C(\mathbf{x}|t-1)$ had high probabilities. In order to deal with potential targets emerging in sparsely sampled regions the resampling algorithm may "inject" a given amount of new samples not related to $p_C(\mathbf{x}|t-1)$. In our implementation 10% of the N new samples are not resampled from $p_C(\mathbf{x}|t-1)$ but generated randomly. This random generation process might be guided by the cues directly.

2. **Prediction** A *motion model* is applied to every element of the newly sampled set $p_C(\mathbf{x}|t)$. Therefore the samples are subjected to *deterministic drift* followed by *stochastic diffusion*. In our implementation, the motion model consists of a simple linear extrapolation of sample position $\mathbf{x}_j^{(t-1)}$ (deterministic drift) followed by *Brownian motion* which lightly jitters the sample's position.

3. **Evaluation** The new samples are weighted by computing every sample's probability $\pi_j^{(t)}$ defined by the distribution $\tilde{p}_C(\mathbf{x}|t)$, the weighted sum of intensity change cue and skin color detection:

$$\tilde{p}_C(\mathbf{x}|t) = \omega_{int} \cdot p_{int}(\mathbf{x}|t) + \omega_{col} \cdot p_{col}(\mathbf{x}|t) \qquad (10)$$

The weights ω_{int} and ω_{col} are currently held constant because the new integration scheme is not able to provide reasonable input for the integration's self-organization (single-target vs. multi-target).

Having probability distribution $p_C(\mathbf{x}|t)$, extraction of potential hypotheses can be done in different ways: One adequate method is to project $p_C(\mathbf{x}|t)$ to the coordinate axes of the target's state space and assuming all combinations of local maxima as potential hypotheses. Cross-checking with one or more of the reliable single-cue observations eliminates false positives. Clustering with EM is another feasible state estimation method resulting in state estimations and corresponding confidence intervals.

In contrast to *Democratic Integration*, currently integration with CONDENSATION does not use an explicit feedback loop. The cues and the integration scheme are non-adaptive due to the conflict arising from the single hypothesis character of these components and the multiple hypotheses produced by integration with CONDENSATION. Nevertheless a nice feature of CONDENSATION is its inherent feedback loop: The resampling phase of every CONDENSATION iteration works on its predecessor's sample set.

5.2   Analysis of Integration with Condensation

Two person sequence. In order to compare with *Democratic Integration*, the same two person sequence has been evaluated for integration with CONDENSATION (Fig. 5). Subject one enters the scene in frame 11 and the new integration algorithm immediately generates a corresponding hypothesis. Until subject two enters the scene in frame 21 CONDENSATION accumulates samples for subject one. Subject two is reliably detected and tracked upon its entry. Since most of

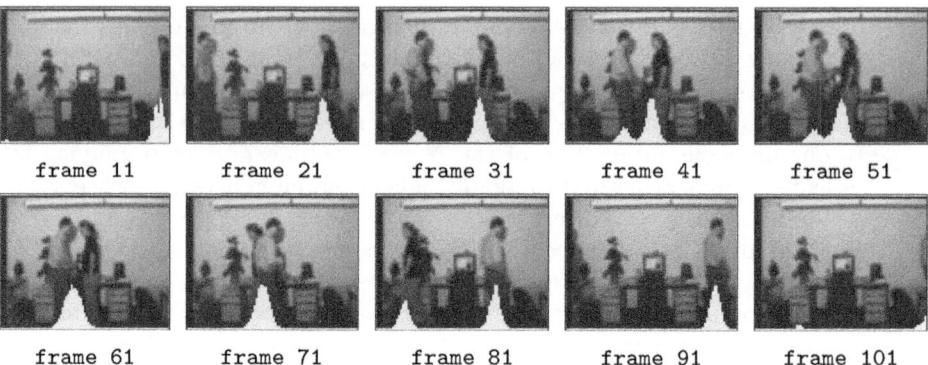

| frame 11 | frame 21 | frame 31 | frame 41 | frame 51 |
| frame 61 | frame 71 | frame 81 | frame 91 | frame 101 |

Fig. 5. Two person sequence. Using the same series of images as Fig. 4, this figure illustrates the tracking behavior of integration with CONDENSATION. The aim of simultaneous tracking of multiple targets is achieved by this approach: Both potential hypotheses emerge although they have not equal weight. Furthermore, the two hypotheses merge and even split during and after crossing of the subjects as they are supposed to do. See text for an in-depth discussion of this sequence

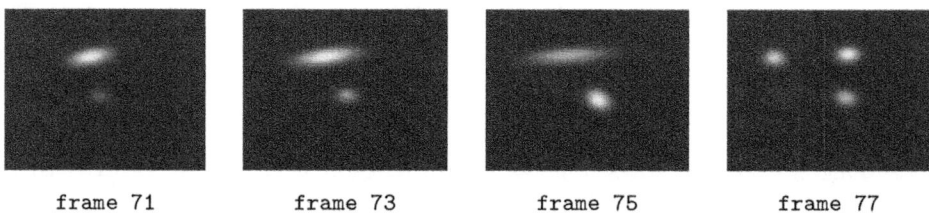

| frame 71 | frame 73 | frame 75 | frame 77 |

Fig. 6. Clustered probability density of skin color detection cue for frames 71 to 77 of the two person sequence. After the subjects have crossed, the Gaussians are stretched and finally torn apart (frame 77). A similar effect can be observed for intensity change cue.

the scene is sparsely sampled, tracking of subject two is delayed for a couple of frames until sample injection ignites accumulation and therefore a hypothesis emerges. Dominated by subject one, the hypothesis for subject two is unable to gain an equivalent number of associated samples.

When the two subjects cross after hand shaking, their hypotheses fuse into a single one (frame 61). This single observation does not immediately split into two hypotheses when the two subjects are separated again (frame 81). This delay is not caused by the integration scheme but by a malfunction of the visual cues. EM clustering holds the single target observation upright but stretches the Gaussians variance in order to approximate the observed saliency map accurately (Fig. 6).

Finally, the hypothesis splits and tracks the two subjects until they leave the scene. In the case of a disappearing subject, CONDENSATION reliably discards the corresponding hypothesis.

Discussion. Evaluation of the two person sequence shows that integration with CONDENSATION is able to overcome the single-target limitation of *Democratic Integration*. Potential targets are detected and tracked reliable even when they temporally occlude each other. A problem of this new approach is the delayed recovery of the two subjects' hypotheses after their re-separation. This "over-stretching" problem is not a shortcoming of the integration algorithm but of the visual cues' implementations and might be overcome by dynamic adding and removing of Gaussians in the mixtures.

Although multi-cue integration itself is non-adaptive, there is some inherent self-organization in CONDENSATION: The probability-guided resampling of the sample set causes accumulation of samples at regions with high probability. That is, potential hypotheses that prove as promising are automatically reinforced whereas false hypotheses are discarded after a short time. Furthermore, random sample injection can be taken as a bootstrapping mechanism. Due to the injection of new samples, emerging of sample accumulation is possible.

6   Conclusion

A general system framework of context-dependent multi-cue integration has been introduced as a means to obtain robust tracking in dynamically changing environments. Implementation of the framework showed to be adequate to increase the reliability and robustness of tracking. *Democratic Integration*, the first implementation of the framework, shows convergence toward an equilibrium under steady conditions. Distractions of visual cues are compensated by the less affected cues. *Democratic Integration* however is limited to track a single target even though several might be present. This limitation is primarily induced by the self-organization mechanisms which depends on the estimation of a single target position. Another shortcoming of *Democratic Integration* is false positive tracking: when the system locks on a wrong target it adapts itself toward this false positive. Reinforced by its self-adaptation mechanism the system will most often not recover from this failure and continue to track the wrong target.

The second implementation of the general system framework is based on CONDENSATION which enables simultaneous tracking of multiple hypotheses. This primarily tackles the single-target limitation but also the false positive tracking problem of *Democratic Integration*. Experiments show that this scheme reliably detects and tracks multiple hypotheses even under challenging conditions. Maintaining multiple hypotheses over time explicitly avoids locking on a particular target and therefore prevents wrong adaptation caused by false positive tracking.

Future work will address localized adaptation of the visual cues as well as of multi-cue integration. Although CONDENSATION implicitly uses self-organization, superposition of complementary visual cues will be adaptive again in order to increase the system's robustness. For the same reason adaptivity is introduced for the visual cues again. Furthermore, the system will be enhanced by new complementary cues, taking advantage of the system's modularity.

References

[1] Christopher M. Bishop. *Neural Networks for Pattern Recognition.* Oxford University Press, 1999.

[2] Andrew Blake and Michael Isard. *Active Contours: The Application of Techniques from Graphics, Vision, Control Theory and Statistics to Visual Tracking of Shapes in Motion.* Springer, 1998.

[3] C.G. Bräutigam. *A Model-Free Voting Approach to Cue Integration.* PhD thesis, Dept. of Numerical Analysis and Computing Science, KTH (Royal Institute of Technology), August 1998.

[4] J. Clark and A. Yuille. *Data fusion for sensory information processing.* Kluwer Academic Publishers, Boston, Ma. – USA, 1994.

[5] J.L. Crowley and F. Berard. Multi-modal tracking of faces for video communications. In *IEEE Conference on Computer Vision and Pattern Recognition*, 1997.

[6] Rafael C. Gonzalez and Richard E. Woods. *Digital Image Processing.* Addison-Wesley Publishing Company, 1993.

[7] Ulf Grenander, Y. Chow, and Daniel M. Keenan. *HANDS: A Pattern Theoretic Study of Biological Shapes.* Springer, 1991.

[8] M. Isard and A. Blake. Condensation – conditional density propagation for visual tracking. *International Journal of Computer Vision*, 29(1):5–28, 1998.

[9] M. Isard and A. Blake. Icondensation: Unifying low-level and high-level tracking in a stochastic framework. In *ECCV'98 Fifth European Conference on Computer Vision, Volume I*, pages 893–908, 1998.

[10] D. Kragić and H. I. Christensen. Integration of visual cues for active tracking of an end-effector. In *IROS'99*, volume 1, pages 362–368, October 1999.

[11] B. Parhami. Voting algorithms. *IEEE Transactions on Reliability*, 43(3):617–629, 1994.

[12] K. Toyama and G.Hager. Incremental focus of attention for robust vision-based tracking. *International Journal of Computer Vision*, 1999.

[13] K. Toyama and G. Hager. Incremental focus of attention for robust visual tracking. In *IEEE Conference on Computer Vision and Pattern Recognition*, 1996.

[14] J. Triesch, D.H. Ballard, and R.A. Jacobs. Fast temporal dynamics of visual cue integration. Technical report, University of Rochester, Computer Science Department, September 2000.

[15] Jochen Triesch and Christoph von der Malsburg. Self-organized integration of adaptive visual cues for face tracking. In *Proceedings of the Fourth IEEE International Conference on Automatic Face and Gesture Recognition*, 2000.

Real Time Visual Cues Extraction for Monitoring Driver Vigilance

Qiang Ji[1] and Xiaojie Yang[2]

[1] Department of Electrical, Computer, and Systems Engineering
Rensselaer Polytechnic Institute
[2] Department of Computer Science
University of Nevada at Reno

Abstract. This paper describes a real-time prototype computer vision system for monitoring driver vigilance. The main components of the system consists of a specially-designed hardware system for real time image acquisition and for controlling the illuminator and the alarm system, and various computer vision algorithms for real time eye tracking, eyelid movement monitoring, face pose discrimination, and gaze estimation. Specific contributions include the development of an infrared illuminator to produce the desired bright/dark pupil effect, the development a digital circuitry to perform real time image subtraction, and the development of numerous real time computer vision algorithms for eye tracking, face orientation discrimination, and gaze tracking. The system was tested extensively in a simulating environment with subjects of different ethnic backgrounds, different genders, ages, with/without glasses, and under different illumination conditions, and it was found very robust, reliable and accurate.

1 Introduction

The ever-increasing number of traffic accidents in the U.S. due to a diminished driver's vigilance level has become a problem of serious concern to society. Drivers with a diminished vigilance level suffer from a marked decline in their abilities of perception, recognition, and vehicle control and therefore pose serious danger to their own life and the lives of other people. For this reason, developing systems actively monitoring a driver's level of vigilance and alerting the driver of any insecure driving conditions is essential to accident prevention.

People in fatigue exhibit certain visual behaviors easily observable from changes in facial features like the eyes, head, and face. To make use of these visual cues, an increasingly popular and non-invasive approach for monitoring fatigue is to assess a driver's vigilance level through visual observation of his/her physical conditions using a camera and state-of-the-art technologies in computer vision. Several studies have shown the feasibility and promise of this approach [9], [13], [3], [14]. For example, study by Ueno et al [14] showed that the performance of their system is comparable to those of techniques using physiological signals. The current efforts in this area, however, focus on using only a single

B. Schiele and G. Sagerer (Eds.): ICVS 2001, LNCS 2095, pp. 107–124, 2001.

visual cue such as eyelid movement or line of sight or head orientation to characterize driver's state of alertness. The system relying on a single visual cue may encounter difficulty when the required visual features cannot be acquired accurately or reliably. It is therefore important to simultaneously use multiple visual cues to improve the detection accuracy and robustness.

We develop a real-time prototype computer vision system that can simultaneously extract multiple visual cues in real time to characterize one's level of vigilance. Specifically, our system monitors in real time, from video images of the subject's face obtained from a remotely installed camera, certain visual behaviors that typically characterize a person's level of fatigue. The specific visual behaviors we monitor include eyelid movements, face orientation, and gaze.

Figure 1 gives an overview of our visual cues extraction system for driver fatigue monitoring. The system starts with an initialization to perform certain calibration and to compute some nominal parameters. The system then performs pupil detection and tracking, which is then used for eyelid movement monitoring, gaze estimation, and face orientation determination respectively.

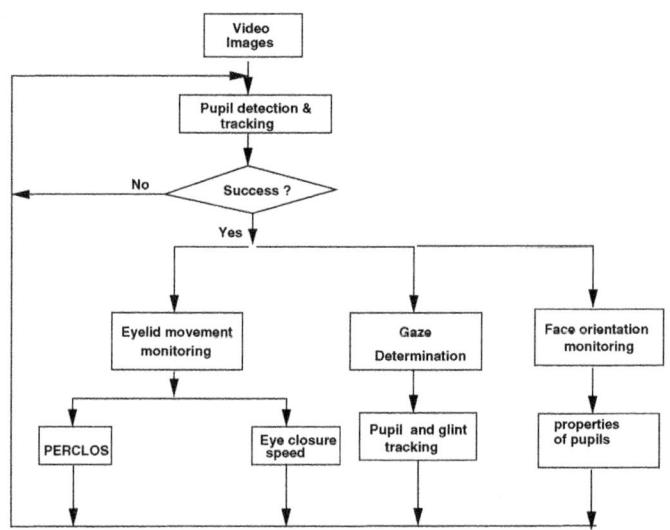

Fig. 1. Overview of the driver vigilance monitoring system

2   Image Acquisition

Image understanding of visual behaviors starts with image acquisition. The purpose of image acquisition is to acquire the video images of the driver face in real time. The acquired images should have relatively consistent photometric

property under different climatic/ambient conditions and should produce distinguishable features that can facilitate the subsequent image processing. To meet
these requirements, we built a special infrared (IR) illuminator and choose a
IR-sensitive CCD camera for image acquisition. According to the original patent
from Hutchinson [7], the use of IR illuminator allows to produce the bright-pupil
effect, which will be used for pupil detection and tracking.

Our IR illuminator consists two sets of IR LEDs, distributed evenly around
two concentric rings (8LED's in each ring) as shown in Figure 2. The center of
both rings coincides with the camera optical axis. Both rings are in the same
plane and mounted on the front of camera.

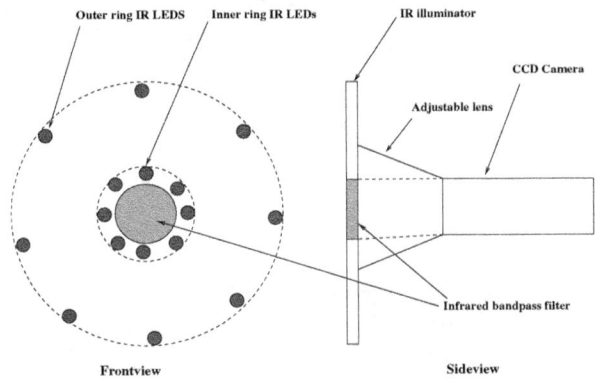

Fig. 2. IR light Source Configuration

The IR light source illuminates the user's eye and generates two kinds of
pupil images: bright and dark pupil images as shown in Figure 3. The bright
pupil image is produced when the inner ring of IR LEDs is turned on and the
dark image is produced when the outer ring is turned on. Note the glint [1] appears
on both the dark and bright pupil images. Figure 4 presents additional examples
of the acquired images using the image acquisition system described above. These
images demonstrate the robustness of the system in that the desired bright-pupil
effect is clear for images at different distances, orientations, magnifications, with
and without glasses. It even works to certain degree with Sun glasses.

3   Pupil Detection and Tracking

The goal of pupil detection and tracking is for subsequent eyelid movements
monitoring, gaze determination, and face orientation estimation. A robust, accurate, and real-time pupil detection is therefore crucial. Pupil detection and

---

[1] the small bright spot near the pupil, produced by corneal reflection of the IR illuminator.

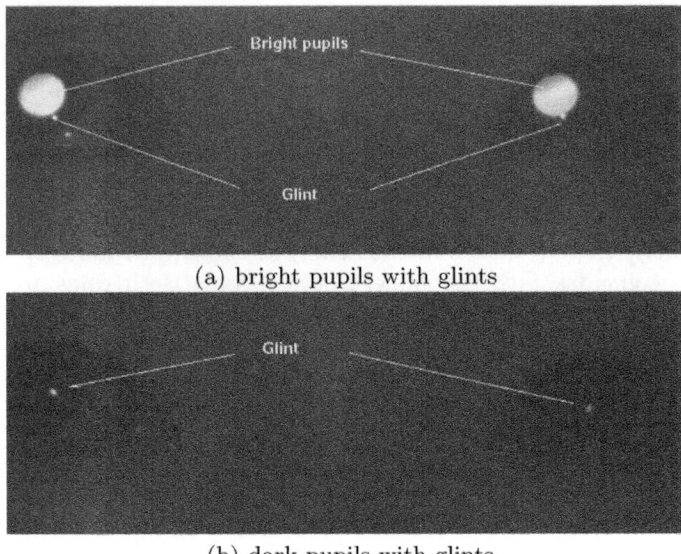

(a) bright pupils with glints

(b) dark pupils with glints

Fig. 3. Bright and dark pupil image

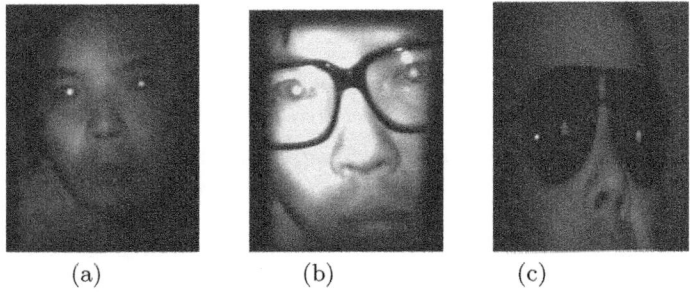

(a)   (b)   (c)

Fig. 4. Examples of the acquired images with the desired bright pupil effect. (a) without glasses, (b) with glasses; (c) with Sun glasses.

tracking starts with pupil detection. Figure 5 gives an overview of the pupil tracking system. Pupil tracking can be divided into two stages: pupil detection and pupil tracking as discussed below.

3.1   Pupil Detection

Pupil detection involves locating pupils in the image. The detection algorithm starts with an initialization to obtain the background image and to record the nominal pupil size and intensity. Following the initialization, a preprocessing is applied to minimize interference from illumination sources other than IR illuminator. This includes Sun light and ambient light interference. Figure 6 shows an image where parts of the background look very bright, almost as bright as

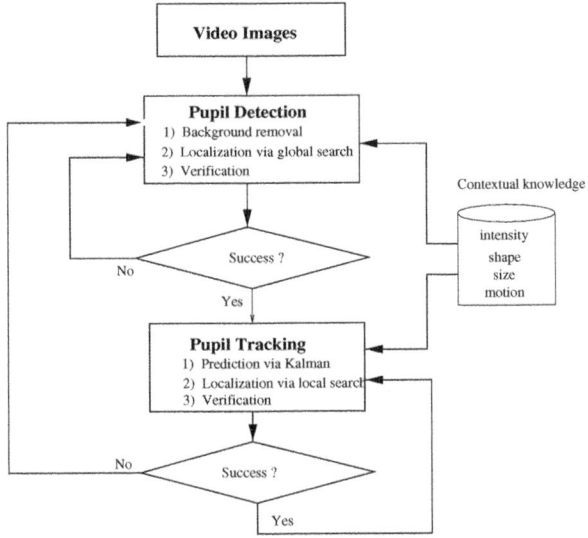

Fig. 5. Pupil detection and tracking system flowchart

the pupil. This must be eliminated or they may adversely affect pupil detection. Their removal is accomplished by subtracting the image with only ambient light from the one illuminated by both the infrared illuminator and the ambient light. The resultant image, as shown in Figure 6 contains the illumination effect from only the infrared illuminator. A micro-controller with a video decoder has been built to perform real image subtraction. The controller separates each incoming interlaced image frame from the camera into even and odd fields and alternately turns the inner ring on for the even field and off for the odd field. The difference image is then produced by subtracting the odd field from the even field. The images shown in Figure 6 are such produced.

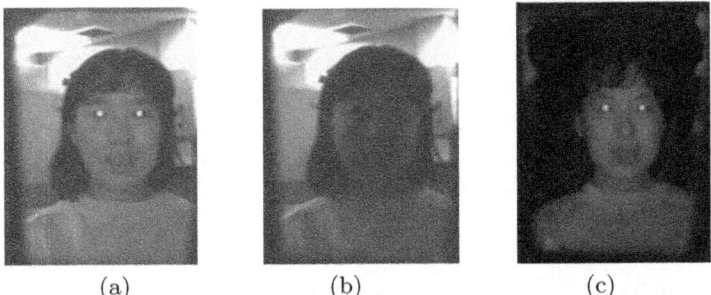

(a)   (b)   (c)

Fig. 6. Background Removal via Image Subtraction: (a) the image obtained with both ambient and IR light (even field); (b) the image obtained with only ambient light (odd field); and (c) the image resulted from subtraction (b) from (a)

3.2   Determining the Initial Pupils Positions

Given the image resulted from the background removal procedure, pupils may be detected by searching the entire image to locate two bright regions that satisfy certain size, shape, and distance constraints. To do so, a search window scans through the image. At each location, the portion of the image covered by the window is examined to determine the number of modality of its intensity distribution. It is assumed that the intensity distribution follows an unimodal distribution if the pupil is not covered by the window and follows a bimodal intensity distribution if the window includes the pupil as shown in Figure 7 (a) and its intensity histogram in (b), where there are two distinctive peaks, one representing background and the other representing pupil. The two peaks must also be sufficiently apart from each other.

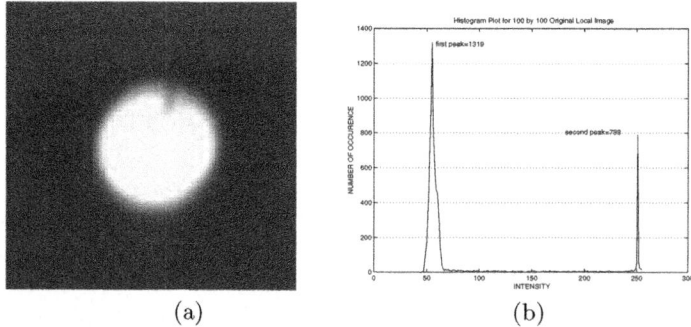

(a)   (b)

Fig. 7. An original subimage containing a pupil (a); and its histogram plot (b), which follows a bimodal distribution.

A thresholding is then applied to the window image if its intensity distribution is determined to be bimodal. The threshold is determined automatically by minimizing Kullback information distance [10]. This yields a binary image consisting of binary blob that may contain a pupil. The binary blob is then validated based on its shape, size, its distance to the other detected pupil, and its motion characteristics to ensure it is a pupil. The validation step is critical since some regions of the image such as the glares of the glasses (see Figure 8)) are equally bright. They may be mistaken for pupils without the verification procedure. The window moves to next position if the validation fails. The centroids of the blob are returned as the position of the detected pupil if the validation succeeds. This then repeats to detect another pupil.

3.3   Pupil Tracking via Kalman Filtering

Given the detected pupils in the initial frames, pupils can then be tracked from frame to frame in real time. Tracking can be done more efficiently by using the location of the pupil in previous frames to predict the location of the face in

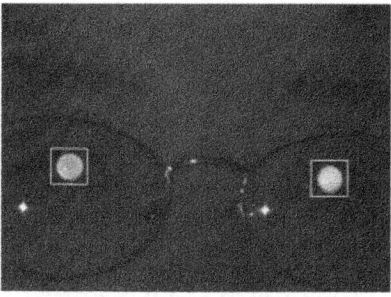

Fig. 8. The glares on the eye frame are equally as bright as the pupils. Verification can eliminate them from being considered as pupils.

future frames based on Kalman filtering [2], assuming that the person's pupil will not undergo significant locational change in two consecutive frames.

Briefly, our pupil tracking method based on Kalman filtering can be formalized as follows. A sequence of image frames is captured. The image sequence is sampled at each frame t, which is then processed to determine pupil position. The motion of a pupil at each time instance (frame) can be characterized by its position and velocity. Let (c_t, r_t) represent the pupil pixel position (its centroid) at time t and (u_t, v_t) be its velocity at time t in c and r directions. The state vector at time t can therefore be represented as $x_t = (c_t\ r_t\ u_t\ v_t)^t$.

The system can therefore be modeled as

$$\mathbf{x}_{t+1} = \phi \mathbf{x}_t + \mathbf{w_t} \tag{1}$$

where $\mathbf{w_t}$ represents system perturbation.

If we assume pupil movement between two consecutive frames is small enough to consider the motion of pupil positions from frame to frame uniform, the state transition matrix can be parameterized as

$$\phi = \begin{bmatrix} 1 & 0 & 1 & 0 \\ 0 & 1 & 0 & 1 \\ 0 & 0 & 1 & 0 \\ 0 & 0 & 0 & 1 \end{bmatrix}$$

We further assume that a fast feature extractor estimates $\mathbf{z}_t = (\hat{c}_t, \hat{r}_t)$, the pupil position at time t. Therefore, the measurement model in the form needed by the Kalman filter is

$$\mathbf{z}_t = H\mathbf{x}_t + v_t \tag{2}$$

For simplicity and since z_t only involves position, we have

$$H = \begin{bmatrix} 1 & 0 & 0 & 0 \\ 0 & 1 & 0 & 0 \end{bmatrix}$$

and v_t represents measurement uncertainty. Specifically, the position of current frame t, $z_t = (c_t, r_t)$, is estimated as

$$\hat{c}_t = c_{t-1} + (c_{t-1} - c_{t-2}) \tag{3}$$
$$\hat{r}_t = r_{t-1} + (r_{t-1} - r_{t-2}) \tag{4}$$

where (c_{t-1}, r_{t-1}) and (c_{t-2}, r_{t-2}) are the actual pupil pixel coordinates estimated at frames t-1 and t-2.

Given the state model in equation 1 and measurement model in equation 2 as well as some initial conditions, the state vector x_{t+1}, along with its covariance matrix Σ_{t+1}, can be updated from the measurement images using Kalman filter [11]. While x_{t+1} gives predicted pupil position, Σ_{t+1} gives the uncertainty of the estimated pupil position, which determines local search area. Figure 9 graphically illustrates the principle of Kalman filtering.

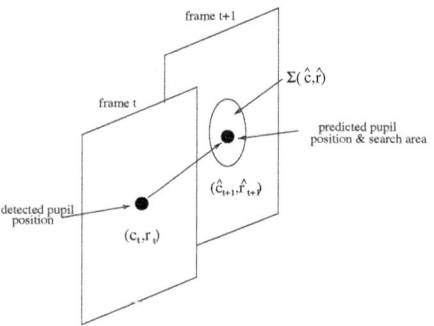

Fig. 9. Pupil detection and tracking using Kalman filtering

3.4   Tracking Results

The Kalman filter tracker has been implemented and tested. A tracking speed as high as 15-18 frames per second for an image size of 640 × 480 is achieved with a SUN 300 MHZ workstation (Ultra 30). The pupil detection and tracking software is found to be rather robust under different face orientations and distances and can quickly recover from tracking failures. For pupils temporarily out of the camera view, it can instantly relocate the pupils as soon as they reappear in the camera view It also works well for pupil with glasses. For a real time video demo of our pupil tracking system, please refer to *http://www.cs.unr.edu/~qiangji/fatigue.html*. Figure 10 shows the trajectory of the real and estimated pupil position in 30 consecutive frames using Kalman filter.

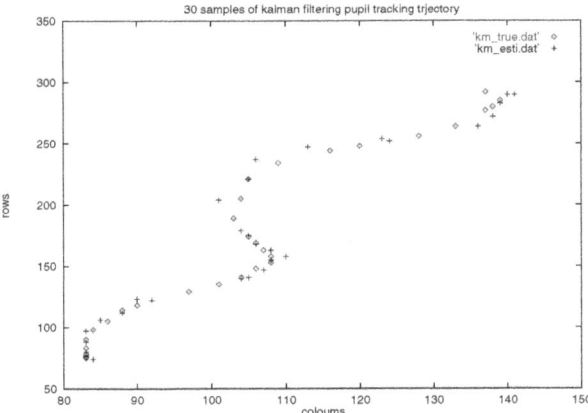

Fig. 10. Trajectory of the real and estimated pupil position in 30 consecutive frames. Crosses indicate the pupil positions estimated by Kalman filter. Small circles indicate the actual tracked pupil positions. It's apparent that the two pupil positions match very well.

4   Eyelid Movement Parameters

The primary purpose of pupils tracking is to monitor eyelid movements and to compute two ocular parameters: PERCLOS and AECS. PERCLOS measures percentage of eye closure over time. It has been found to be the most valid ocular parameter for characterizing driver fatigue [4]. AECS measures the average eye closure/opening speed, i.e., the amount of time needed to fully close the eyes and to fully open the eyes. To obtain these measurements, our algorithm continuously tracks the subject's pupils and determines in real time the amount of eye closure based on the the the area of the pupils that have been occluded by the eyelids.

To produce realistic real data, a human subject deliberately blinks her eyes differently in front of our system to simulate different levels of fatigue. The first experiment studied the difference in eye closure speed between an alert individual and drowsy individual. Our study indicates that the eye closure speed for a drowsy person can be more than eight times slower than that of an alert individual. The second experiment lasted for 6 minutes, with the subject being alert during the first 2.5 minutes and being fatigue afterwards. The goal of this experiment is to study: 1) whether the change in fatigue level can be detected by both parameters; 2) whether the two parameters correlate. Our system recorded the eyelid movement and computed the two parameters over the period in real time. Figure 11 (a) ane (b) plot running average PERCLOSE and AECS parameters over the entire 6 minute period.

Fig. 11 (a) shows that in the early session of the simulation (before 150000 ms or 2.5 minutes), PERCLOS is measured below 30%, which represents the alert state. However, beyond 150,000 ms, PERCLOS measures over 40%, a significant increase, representing the fatigue state. Interestingly enough, Fig. 11 (b) follows

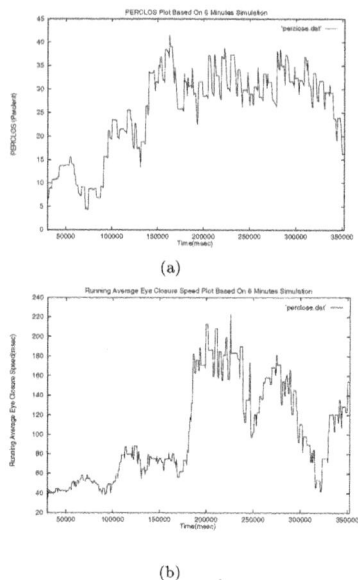

(a)

(b)

Fig. 11. Running average PERCLOS (a) and AECS (b) measurements over 6 minutes

the similar trend, i.e., it takes much shorter time to close the eyes when the subject is alert (before 150,000 ms) and much longer time to close when the subject is drowsy (after 150,000 ms). We can conclude from this experiment: 1) both parameters can detect different levels of vigilance; 2) PERCLOS and AECS covariate, which demonstrates the two parameters correlate to certain degree.

In summary, we have successfully developed a prototype hardware and software system that tracks pupils and computes PERCLOS and AECS parameters in real time. This is a very significant progress in that 1) it is real time; 2) it is robust; 3) it computes the most valid fatigue measure, a measure recommended by the US Department of Transportation for monitoring driver fatigue; 4) it is non-invasive, it can be executed without the knowledge of the user due to its use of infrared illumination. For a real time demo, please refer to http://www.cs.unr.edu/~qiangji/fatigue.html.

5   Face (Head) Pose Estimation

Face pose determination is concerned with computation of 3D face orientation and position. Face pose contains information about one's attention, gaze, and level of fatigue. The nominal face orientation while driving is frontal. If the driver's face orientation is in other directions (e.g., down or sideway) for an extended period of time, this is either due to fatigue or inattention. Face pose estimation, therefore, can detect both fatigue and inattentive drivers.

We propose a new model-based approach. Our approach recovers 3D face pose from a monocular view of the face with full perspective projection. Our study shows that there exists a direct correlation between 3D face pose and properties of pupils such as pupils size, inter-pupil distance, pupils shape, and average pupil intensities. Figure 12 shows pupil measurements under different head orientations. It is apparent from these images that

- The inter-pupil distance decreases as the face rotates away from the frontal orientation.
- The ratio between the average intensity of two pupils either increases to over one or decreases to less than one as face rotates away.
- The shapes of two pupils become more elliptical as the face rotates away.
- The sizes of the pupils also decrease as the face rotates away.

The above observations serve as the basis for estimating face orientation from pupils.

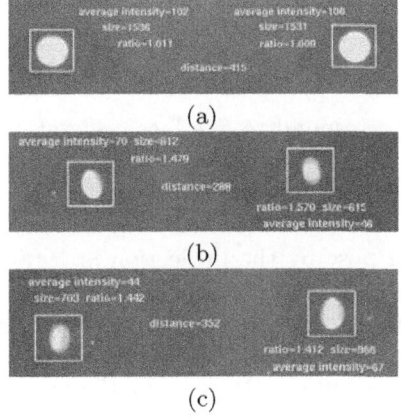

Fig. 12. Pupil images for different head orientations: (a) frontal; (b) left; and (c) right

5.1   Algorithm for Head Orientation Monitoring

Based on the above observations, we can develop a face pose estimation algorithm by exploiting the relationships between face orientation and these parameters. We build a so-called *Pupil Feature Space* (PFS) which is constructed by seven pupil features: inter-pupil distance, sizes of left and right pupils, intensities of left and right pupils, and ellipse ratios of left and right pupils. To make those features scale invariant, we further normalize those parameters by dividing over according values of the front view. Figure 13 shows sample data projections in PFS, from which we can see clearly that there are distinctive clusters of different poses in the PFS. Note that although we can only plot 3-dimensional space here, PFS is constructed by seven features, in which the clusters will be more distinctive. So a pose can be determined by the projection of pupil properties in PFS.

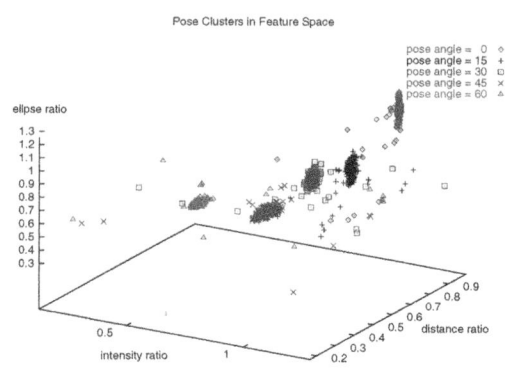

Fig. 13. Face pose clusters in pupil feature space

The five clusters correspond to five face orientations respectively. It is clear that there exist five distinctive clusters, representing each of five face orientations. Given sufficient training data, we are able to identify five distinctive clusters.

When determining pose by the projection in PFS, we need to find a representation of the PFS by which different pose classes are the most apart from each other. A well known method to achieve this goal is principal component algorithm (PCA), or eigen space algorithm, which is to find the principal components of the distribution of poses, or the eigenvectors of the covariance matrix of the set of poses. The eigenvectors are ordered, each one accounting for a different amount of the variation among the poses, and each individual pose can be represented exactly in terms of a linear combination of the eigenvectors.

Before pose estimation, we need training data to build the eigen PFS, and store several models representing typical poses, which are, in our experiments, varies every 15° from −45° to 45°. Figure 14 shows the distribution of the models in eigen PFS, where again, a 3-dimensional projection is used while the actual dimensions of the eigen PFS is 7. The face orientation of an input face can then be mapped to one of the seven clusters based on its Euclidean distance to the center of each cluster.

We developed a software based on the above idea to determine where the heads turn to and will warn the driver by sounding alarm if certain threshold is exceeded. Figure 15 shows the running average face pose estimation for a period of 6 minutes. As can be seen, most times during this period, face pose is frontal. But there are times when an extended period of time is spent on other directions

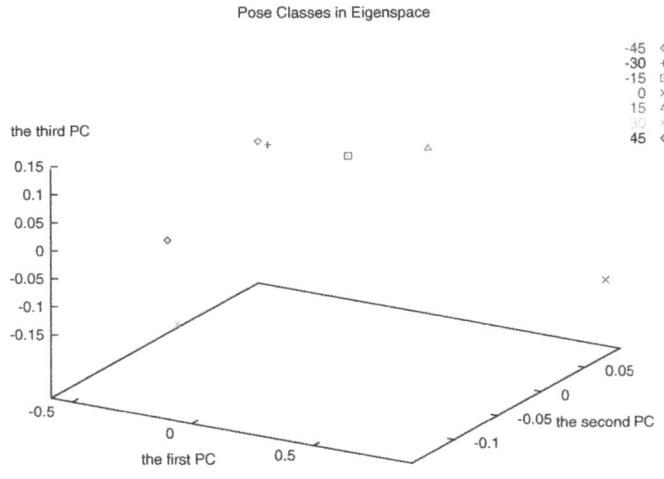

Fig. 14. Projection of pose classes in eigen PFS

(left or right), representing inattention. For a real-time demo of the face orientation determination, refer to http://www.cs.unr.edu/~qiangji/fatigue.html.

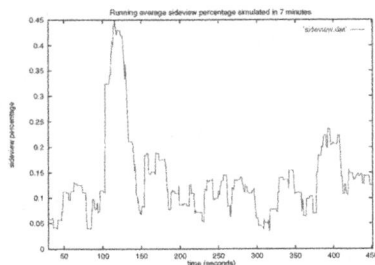

Fig. 15. Face Orientation Monitoring Over Time

6   Eye-Gaze Determination and Tracking

Gaze has the potential to indicate a person's level of vigilance. A fatigue individual tends to have a narrow gaze. Gaze may also reveal one's needs and attention. Gaze estimation is important not only for fatigue detection but also for identifying a person's focus of attention which can be used in the area of human-computer interaction.

Of the numerous techniques proposed for gaze estimation [1] [15], [12], the one proposed by Ebisawa [5] appears very promising and is directly applicable to this project. Their technique estimates the gaze direction based on the relative position between pupil and the glint. Based on an improvement of this technique, we have developed a video-based, contact-free eye-gaze estimation algorithm that can: 1)track and detect the eye position from the face image in real time; 2)estimate the gaze direction by computing the Cartesian Coordinates difference ·of the glint center and the pupil center; 3) map the pixel coordinates difference into screen coordinates (mm).

6.1   Pupil and Glint Detection and Tracking

The gaze estimation algorithm consists of three parts: pupil-glint detection and tracking, calibration, and gaze mapping. For this research, the gaze of a driver can be quantized into nine areas: frontal, left, right, up, down, upper left, upper right, lower left and lower right, as shown in Figure 16. Gaze estimation starts with pupil-glint detection and tracking. For gaze estimation, we continue using the IR illuminator as shown in Figure 2. To produce the desired pupil effects, the two rings are turned on and off alternately via a micro-controller to produce the so called bright and dark pupil effect as shown in Figure 3 (a) and (b). The pupil looks bright when the inner ring is turned on as shown in Fig. 3 (a) and the pupil looks dark when the outer ring is turned on as shown in Fig. 3 (b). Note glint appears on both images. Algorithm-wise, glint can be detected much more easily from the dark image since both glint and pupil appear equally bright and sometimes overlap on the bright pupil image. This explains why we need both the dark and bright pupil images.

Given a bright pupil image, the pupil detection and tracking technique described in section 3 can be directly applied for pupil detection and tracking. The location of a pupil at each frame is characterized by its centroid. Only one pupil needs to be tracked since both pupils give the same gaze direction. Given the dark pupil image, the pupil detection and tracking technique can be adapted to detect and track glint. The center of glint can be computed and is used to specify the location of the glint. Figure 17 gives an example of bright pupils (a); dark pupils with glint (b); and the detected pupil and glint (c).

6.2   Gaze Mapping

Given the relative position between pupil and glint, the screen (actual) coordinates of the gaze can be determined via a linear mapping procedure. The conventional approach for gaze mapping only uses coordinates displacement of pupil center and glint position [6] [8] as a pupil-glint vector. The main drawback with this method is that the subject must keep his or her head stationary, or the glint position in the image will change. In practice, it is difficult to keep head still and the existing gaze tracking methods will produce incorrect result if the head moves, even slightly. Head movement must therefore be incorporated in the

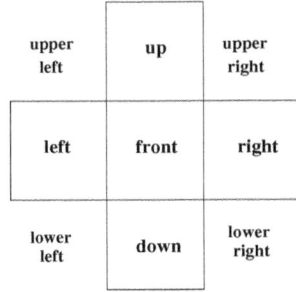

Fig. 16. The quantized eye gaze regions

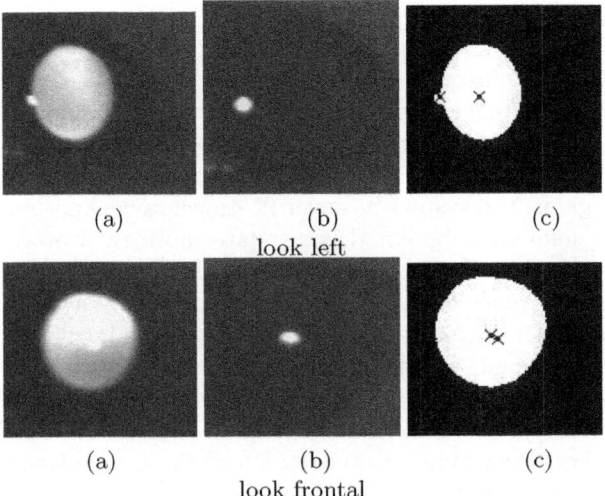

Fig. 17. Relative spatial relationship between glint and bright pupil center used to determine eye-gaze position. (a) bright pupil images, (b) glint images; (c) pupil-glint relationship generated by superimposing glint to the thresholded bright pupil images.

gaze estimation procedure. In this section, we introduce a new gaze estimation procedure that tolerates slight translational head movement.

According to our mapping procedure, the pupil-glint vector is represented by

$$\mathbf{g} = \begin{bmatrix} \Delta x \ \Delta y \ g_x \ g_y \ 1 \end{bmatrix}$$

where Δx and Δy are the pupil-glint displacement, g_x and g_y are the glint image coordinates. Unlike the existing methods which only uses Δx and Δy, our procedure also includes the glint position. This effectively reduces the head movement influence. The coefficient vector $\mathbf{c}$ is represented by

$$\mathbf{c} = \begin{bmatrix} \alpha \ \beta \ \gamma \ \lambda \ \theta \end{bmatrix}^T$$

Assuming the gaze point is located at one of the nine locations on the screen as illustrated in Figure 16. The pupil-glint vector measured during runtime can be mapped to the image screen locations through following equations:

$$i = \mathbf{g} \cdot \mathbf{c} = \alpha \Delta x + \beta \Delta y + \gamma g_x + \lambda g_y + \theta$$

where i is the gaze region index from 1 to 9 representing one of nine directions. The coefficients α, β, γ, λ, and θ are determined via a simple calibration procedure.

6.3   Experimental Results and Analysis

The gaze tracker is currently running on Sun Ultra10 (300 MHz) in real time. In operation, the subject faces directly to camera and changes his or her gaze direction after finishing calibration. Our study shows that the gaze estimation procedure is accurate. Of the 100 samples representing the subject fixing on different gaze regions, the system has over 95% accuracy. Another experiment was conducted to simulate different driving state: normal, drowsy and inattention and to study gaze distribution. 200 data samples were taken for each case. The gaze distributions plots are in Figure 18. Fig. 18 (a) shows most gaze points are located in region 5 (frontal), which reflects normal driving case. Fig. 18 (b) shows most gaze points are located in region 8 (lower center), which reflects drowsy driving case. Fig. 18 (c) shows most gaze points are distributed in region 4 (middle left), 5 (frontal), and 6 (middle right), which reflects inattentive driving case. For a real-time demonstration of the gaze estimation, please refer to http://www.cs.unr.edu/~qiangji/fatigue.html.

7   Conclusions

Through research presented in this paper, we developed an non-intrusive prototype computer vision system for real-time monitoring a driver's vigilance. We focus on developing the necessary hardware and imaging algorithms that can simultaneously extract multiple visual cues that typically characterize a person's level of fatigue. These visual cues include eyelid movement, gaze, and face orientation. The main components of the system consists of a hardware system for real time acquisition of video images of the driver and various computer vision algorithms and their software implementations for real time eye tracking, eyelid movement parameters computation, face pose discrimination, and gaze estimation.

Each part of our fatigue monitor system was tested extensively in a simulating environment with subjects of different ethnic backgrounds, different genders, ages, and under different illumination conditions. The system was found very robust, reliable and accurate. We are now collaborating with Honda

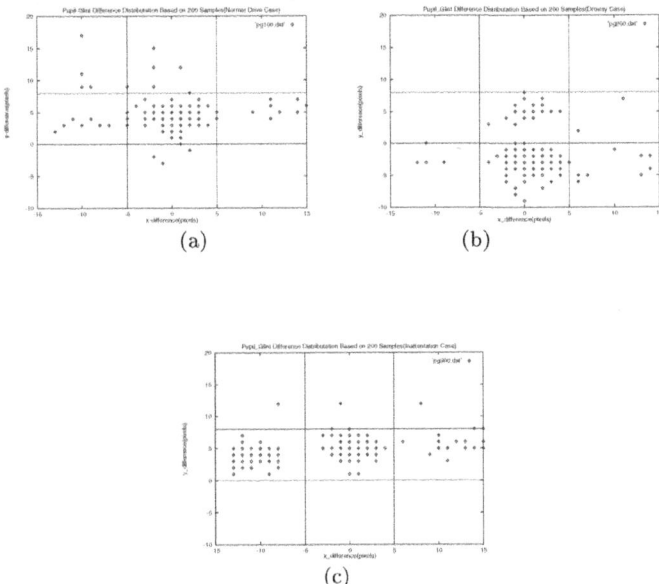

Fig. 18. Gaze distribution (a) under normal driving. Gaze most times are frontal; (b) fatigue driving, gaze looks down most time; and (3) inattentive driving, gaze looks away sometimes

to port the codes to PC and to install in a vehicle to evaluate its performance under real world driving conditions.

References

1. S. Baluja and D. Pomerleau. Non-intrusive gaze tracking using artificial neural networks. *Technical Report CMU-CS-94-102, Carnegie Mellon University*, 1994.
2. A. Blake, R. Curwen, and A. Zisserman. A framework for spatio-temporal control in the tracking of visual contours. *Int. Journal of Computer Vision*, 11(2):127–145, 1993.
3. S. Boverie, J. M. Leqellec, and A. Hirl. Intelligent systems for video monitoring of vehicle cockpit. *1998 International congress and exposition ITS: Advanced controls and vehicle navigation systems*, pages 1–5, 1998.
4. D. F. Dinges, M. Mallis, G. Maislin, and J. W. Powell. Evaluation of techniques for ocular measurement as an index of fatigue and the basis for alertness management. *Department of Transportation Highway Safety publication 808 762*, April, 1998.
5. Y. Ebisawa. Unconstrained pupil detection technique using two light sources and the image difference method. *Visualization and Intelligent Design in Engineering*, pages 79–89, 1989.
6. T. E. Hutchinson. Eye movement detection with improved calibration and speed. *United States Patent [19]*, (4,950,069), 1988.

124   Q. Ji and X. Yang

7. T. E. Hutchinson. Eye movement detection with improved calibration and speed. *U.S. patent 4950069*, April, 1990.
8. T. E. Hutchinson, K. White, J. R. Worthy, N. Martin, C. Kelly, R. Lisa, , and A. Frey. Human-computer interaction using eye-gaze input. *IEEE Transaction on systems,man,and cybernetics*, 19(6):1527–1533, 1989.
9. T. Ishii, M. Hirose, and H. Iwata. Automatic recognition of driver's facial expression by image analysis. *Journal of JSAE*, 41(12):1398–1403, 1987.
10. J. Kittler, J. Illingworth, and J. Foglein. Threshold selection based on simple image statistic. *Computer vision, graphics, and image processing*, 30:125–147, 1985.
11. P. S. Maybeck. *Stochastic Models, Estimation and Control*, volume 1. Academic Press, Inc, 1979.
12. R. Rae and H. Ritter. Recognition of human head orientation based on artificial neural networks. *IEEE Transactions on Neural Networks*, 9(2):257–265, 1998.
13. H. Saito, T. Ishiwaka, M. Sakata, and S. Okabayashi. Applications of driver's line of sight to automobiles-what can driver's eye tell. *Proceedings of 1994 Vehicle navigation and information systems conference, Yokohama, Japan, Aug. 1994*, pages 21–26, 1994.
14. H. Ueno, M. Kaneda, and M. Tsukino. Development of drowsiness detection system. *Proceedings of 1994 Vehicle navigation and information systems conference, Yokohama, Japan, Aug. 1994*, pages 15–20, 1994.
15. G. Yang and A. Waibel. A real-time face tracker. *Workshop on Applications of Computer Vision*, pages 142–147, 1996.

Radar and Vision Data Fusion for Hybrid Adaptive Cruise Control on Highways

U. Hofmann, A. Rieder, and E.D. Dickmanns

Institut für Systemdynamik und Flugmechanik,
Universität der Bundeswehr München (UBM),
D-85577 Neubiberg, Germany
ulrich.hofmann@unibw-muenchen.de
http://www.unibw-muenchen.de/campus/LRT/LRT13/english/index.html

Abstract. A system for hybrid adaptive cruise control (HACC) on high speed roads designed as a combination of a radar-based ACC and visual perception is presented. The system is conceived to run on different performance levels depending on the actual perception capabilities. The advantages of a combination of the two sensor types are discussed in comparison to the shortcomings of each single sensor type. A description of the visual lane detection and tracking procedure is given, followed by an overview of the vehicle detection, hypothesis generation and tracking procedure. Enhanced robustness is achieved by cooperative estimation of egomotion and the dynamics of other vehicles using the lane coordinate system as common reference. Afterwards, the assignment of vehicles to lanes and the determination of the relevant vehicle for the longitudinal controller is described.

1 Introduction

At present great effort is put into the development of driver assistance and comfort systems like lane departure warning, stop-and-go traffic assistance, convoy driving or adaptive cruise control (ACC). Unfortunately, these efforts mostly result in independent solutions for each task which do not communicate their knowledge among each other.

The EMS[1]-Vision system of UBM bundles the information different experts extract from sensor data and makes it available for all other experts. As a spin-off of the overall system architecture [1], UBM designed, in cooperation with an automotive supplier[2], a system for hybrid adaptive cruise control. It is a combination of a radar-based ACC system and visual perception for vehicle as well as lane detection and tracking.

---

[1] Expectation-based Multi-focal Saccadic

[2] We thank our project partner for supplying their profound knowledge on radar-based ACC to the project.

B. Schiele and G. Sagerer (Eds.): ICVS 2001, LNCS 2095, pp. 125–138, 2001.

2   System Specification

This HACC system is a comfort system designed for motorways and similar roads with white lane markings on both sides of all lanes. This is a wellknown domain where the expected obstacles are restricted to road vehicles. The own car (Ego) shall be driven manually in the lateral direction and is controlled autonomously in the longitudinal direction. A desired speed is set by the human driver. The computer controls the velocity of the car in such a manner, that a specified safety distance to other vehicles (OV) is kept and the difference between the desired and the actual velocity is as small as possible. It is in the driver's responsibility to choose the lane of the road and he has to decide whether to overtake or not. E.g. if there is another vehicle in front of the Ego driving with a velocity slower than the desired speed, the Ego slows down and follows with the speed of the leading car. The accelerations commanded by the velocity controller are restricted to a level, that the passengers feel comfortable. The safety distance to the OV ahead shall not be smaller than e.g 1.6sec · velocity of the own car. The HACC is not a security system. The driver always has to be aware of the traffic situation. He is legally responsible for all actions of the car. The driver can overrule the HACC system at any time. The maximal pressure of the braking system the HACC may command limites to deceleration -2.5m/s^2. That implies that HACC is not able to command emergency braking.

3   Scalable Performance

The system designed is able to operate at different performance levels as depicted in figure 1. The initial system status is given when no cruise control is active, the human driver himself controls the velocity and the heading direction.

A first performance step is that the conventional radar-based ACC system is activated. The decision whether an OV might be relevant, which means driving ahead of the Ego in the own lane with a velocity smaller than that of the Ego, is made using the so called driving tube. This driving tube is fixed parallel to the longitudinal axis of the Ego. Its curvature is estimated from the relative speeds of the 4 wheels using ABS-sensor signals. The system has no knowledge about the relative position to the real lanes.

A second performance step is that the OV hypotheses generated by the radar module are validated by vision and the lateral positions relative to the Ego as well as the dimensions of the OVs are determined. If the validation is successful, the OVs are inserted into the scene tree as the central knowledge representation scheme for physical objects in the system (see Chapter 6). All objects are tracked by vision. Also at the second performance step no information about the position and shape of the lane is available.

At the third performance step, additionally, the detection and tracking of the own lane and the assignment of the validated OVs to a lane (the own and the two adjoining lanes) takes place.

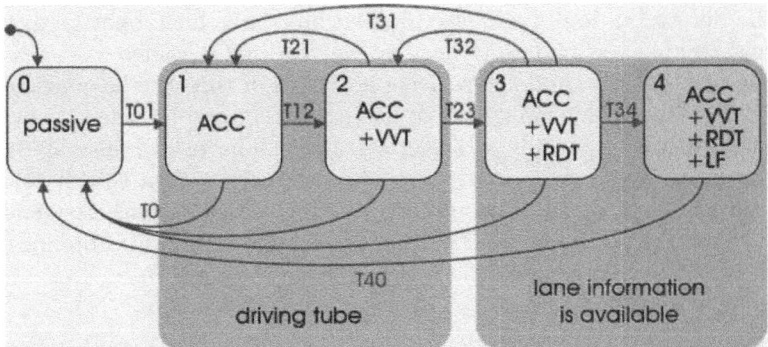

Fig. 1. Scalable performance steps ACC = radar-based Adaptive Cruise Control, VVT = visual Vehicle Validation and Tracking, RDT = Road Detection and Tracking, LF = Lane Follow

A forth performance step could be to follow a lane completely autonomous. This step was not in the scope of the project, but is a standard ability in UBM's EMS-Vision system.

The desired performance level is set by the driver via the human machine interface (HMI). In figure 1 the transitions Txx between the different performance levels stand for conditions which have to be met for a performance level change. T01 has to check whether the radar module is ready to perform the ACC task. Transition T12 verifies that vision is present and the VVT process is already delivering data. Transition T23 checks whether automatic lane detection is completed and the RDT process tracks the lane. If the RDT process stops tracking and starts a new automatic detection of the lane while the system is running at performance level 3, the system changes via transition T32 to level 2 until T23 is satisfied. If the weather or lighting conditions are not suitable for vision, the system changes via T21 or T31 to performance level 1. If the radar is not active or the driver overrules the computer, the system always changes via T0 to performance level 0. If the desired performance level is 4 the system can change via T34 to level 4 and may end the autonomous mode via T40 if the ACC is not active, the driver overrules the system or lane tracking fails.

4   Sensor Properties

The reason for a combination of a radar-based ACC with a vision system is to overcome the shortcomings of a pure radar-based ACC system and of a pure vision-based ACC as well. Shortcomings for the radar system are:

- Reflections on crash barriers can lead to false alarms.
- Two vehicles driving side by side with nearly the same speed are hardly distinguishable and may appear as only one obstacle, which is assigned to one lane. That means a vehicle or motorcycle beside a truck can be invisible for the radar.

- The determination of the lateral position of a vehicle relative to the Ego is considerably less precise than of the logitudinal distance.
- The own position and the relative positions of the OVs have no reference to the real lanes. This makes the decision whether an obstacle is relevant or not very difficult, especially at larger distances. The risk of false alarms is high.
- The radar-based ACC used suppresses vehicles with a velocity slower than a threshold value and oncoming traffic for vehicle hypothesis generation. A so tuned conventional ACC system is not able to handle stop-and-go traffic.

On the other hand

- a radar system is independent of weather and lighting conditions.
- The determination of the distances and relative velocities to OVs is very precise.

Advantages of the vision system are the ability to:

- determine the lateral positions of OVs relative to the Ego with high accuracy;
- determine the dimensions/shapes of OVs. This enables classification of obstacles and to make a model-based prediction of its possible behavior;
- detect and track the own lane.

As a consequence it is possible to:

- determine the shape of the own lane;
- determine the position of the Ego relative to the own lane;
- recognize a lane change depending on the yaw angle and horizontal offset of the Ego´s center of gravity (CG) relative to the center of the lane;
- determine the positions of OVs relative to the own lane.

The drawbacks are:

- Measurement results depend on the weather and lighting conditions.
- A vision only ACC has difficulties in determining the distances to OVs in longitudinal direction, because range information is lost in perspective projection. Consequently, it is rather difficult to get a precise value for the relative velocity.

Radar and vision have complementary properties. A combination of both leads to better overall system performance.

5   Sensors and Hardware Used

As experimental platform UBM´s Mercedes 500 SEL, dubbed VaMP, is used. See figure 2 and [1].

For this project, the vehicle has been equipped with a radar system, which is attached to the center of the front bumper (See figure 3). It has one radar club with a viewing angle of $\pm 4°$, and it is able to measure the relative velocity and distance to other vehicles in a range from 2 to 130 meters with an accuracy of

Fig. 2. Experimental vehicle VaMP

±1.5m. The radar-based ACC module uses data of the ABS-sensors to calulate the curvature of the trajectory of the own vehicle.

The system is able to observe the environment in front of the car with several cameras, which are mounted on a pan camera platform (See figure 4). From this MarVEye camera configuration [1] only the video data of the high sensitive black-and-white camera (third camera from left) and the intensity signal of the 3-chip color camera (second camera from left) are evaluated. The platform is not active. This bifocal camera configuration is equipped with a wide-angle lens on the b/w-camera with a horizontal viewing angle of ±22° and a tele lens on the 3-chip color camera with a viewing angle of ±5.5°. For image processing each second field (half image) is taken with a resolution of 768x286 pixels every 40msec.

Fig. 3. Radar

Fig. 4. Camera platform

Only one of the 3 image processing PCs available in the whole system is used for the vision tasks here. On this computer (comp2) the VVT, the RDT and the Radar process are running (See figure 5). The Radar process is the interface to the radar hardware. The actuators get their commands via the controller PC (comp1) where the locomotion expert is running (for details see [1]).

6   Scene Tree

The scene tree is the internal representation of the outside world. All nodes of the scene tree represent physical objects or virtual coordinate systems. The transformations between scene nodes are described by homogeneous coordinate transformations (HCT). HCTs can be used for describing the relative pose (6 degrees of freedom = 6DOF) between physical objects as well as for perspective projection into the image coordinate systems. For details see [1]. In figure 5, the connections between the scene representation, the processes and the computers used are depicted. E.g. the positions and dynamics of other vehicles are estimated relative to the coordinate system of the current own lane. This coordinate system lies in the middle of the lane, tangential to the lane and moves along the lane at constant distance ahead of the own car. The position and motion of the own car is also described relative to the lane coordinate system. Using the HCTs, e.g. the positions of OVs relative to the Ego can be calculated.

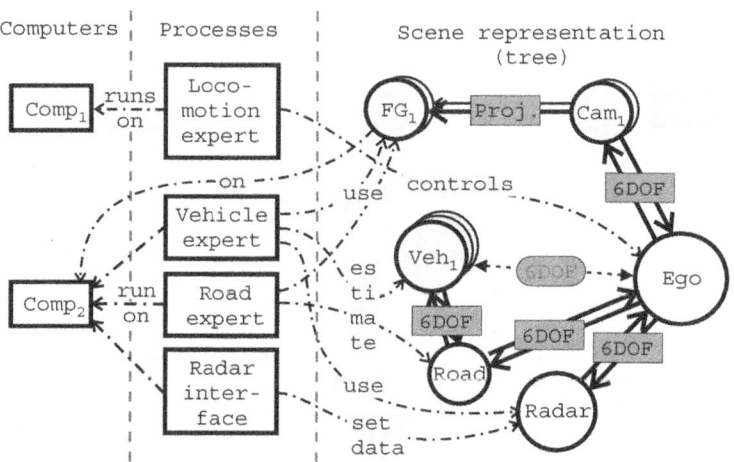

Fig. 5. EMS-Vision data bases: hybrid adaptive cruise control

7   Overview of Lane Detection and Tracking

Lane detection and tracking uses horizontal search windows to extract lane markings from grey-level images. Lane markings are characterized by dark-bright-dark grey-level transitions which match an expected width and orientation at expected positions. The expected positions and orientations of the lane markings are calculated from timestep to timestep using a 3D-model of the lane which is projected into the image plane. The differences between the measured and the expected positions are taken to innovate the 3D-model. In order to initalize the tracking process, a setup phase is necessary first. Lane markings are detected by extracting their edges. Therefore the correlations between ternary masks of the kind [-1,-1,-1,0,+1,+1,+1] and the grey-level values along the search paths are calculated. A grey-level transition from dark to bright results in a maximum, and from bright to dark in a minimum correlation value. For the decision on a max or min, a suitable grey-level threshold has to be found first. Therefore, the value for a threshold is successively decreased until sufficiently many maxima and minima are found and the threshold is larger than an allowed minimal value. Hence, two regression lines through the left and right lane markings are calculated. This is done using the image of the wide-angle camera only, because on motorways and similar roads the influence of lane curvature is negligible at near distances (6-30m). Under the assumptions that the postion of the Ego relative to a lane has a horizontal offset smaller than half the lane width and a yaw angle smaller e.g. 5 degree, the following items are calulated from the regression lines:

- the horizontal offset of the Ego´s CG relative to the skeleton line (center of the lane),
- the yaw angle between the longitudinal axis of the Ego and the tangent at the skeleton line measured at the CG as well as
- the lane width.

These first approximations are taken as starting values for the Extended Kalman Filter (EKF) [2]. During this automatic lane detection the driving tube is used for the decision on the relevance of OVs. The lane geometry is described by a moving average clothoid model. For details see [3] or [4]. The state variables which are estimated by the EKF can be differentiated in two kinds:

- The shape parameters of the model, which are the horizontal and vertical curvature, the lane width and their changes.
- The position parameters, which are the horizontal offset of the CG of the Ego to the skeleton line, the yaw angle and the pitch angle of the vehicle body relative to the lane.

By successively increasing the lookahead distance from near to far distances, the model reliably approaches the real lane markings by determining their curvatures. In the wide-angle image, the search windows are set in a manner, that the lookahead distance in 3D-space ranges from 6 to 40m, and for the tele-image from 30 to 100m. If the number of extracted features in the tele-image is less than a certain minimal number for several cycles, the lookahead distance is shortened and afterwards successively extended from near to far. This increases the robustness of lane tracking.

Before feature extraction is started, all search windows are checked whether a vehicle obscures the expected lane markings. To do this, the bounding box for each OV is tested whether it intersects with any search window. If an intersection exists, the search window is clipped (figure 6). If the resulting search path is too short this measurement is disabled.

Fig. 6. Clipping of search windows using bounding boxes of OVs

8   Vehicle Detection, Hypothesis Generation, and Tracking

In order to control the velocity of the Ego correctly, the HACC system has to detect all vehicles, which are potential obstacles. New vehicle hypotheses are generated by evaluating the radar measurements. Within the radar module a preprocessing of the radar measurements takes place where reflections with a similar distance, relative velocity and amplitude are grouped together. The radar system creates a list of potential vehicles every 60msec. These measurements first have to be assigned to the existing OV hypotheses of the scene tree. This is accomplished by defining a capture area around each OV hypothesis and assigning all radar measurements to it which lie within it (See figure 7, for details see [5]).

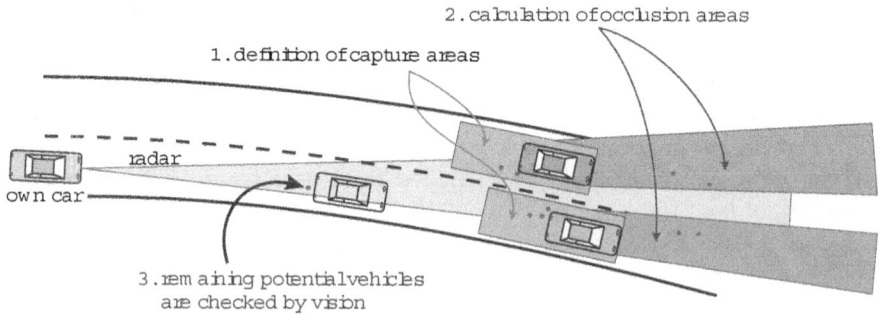

Fig. 7. Vehicle hypothesis generation

The existing vehicle hypotheses are sorted with respect to the distance from Ego. Then, the angular range covered by each vehicle hypothesis is calculated, and the radar measurements left over are checked whether they lie in such an area with a larger distance than the corresponding vehicle hypothesis. If this is true, the measurement is rejected. Remaining radar measurements, which could not be assigned to an existing vehicle hypothesis or occlusion area, are candidates for new vehicle hypotheses. These are checked by vision. If the validation is successful, a new vehicle hypothesis is added to the scene tree. If a hypothesis is not updated neither by radar nor by vision for several cycles it is removed from the scene tree. All vehicle hypotheses in the scene tree are tracked. At the position of a candidate for a new vehicle hypothesis a box model is initialized to fit the shape of the potential vehicle. The orientation of the box in 3D is assumed to be parallel to the lane at this distance. Depending on the yaw angle relative to the Ego the length or the width of the box is estimated. Furthermore, the lateral position and lateral velocity, the longitudinal position, speed and acceleration is estimated via EKF for each OV (for details see [5]). As already mentioned in section 6 the positions and dynamics of OVs and the egomotion are estimated relative to the lane coordinate system. This means that implicitly a separation between the dynamics of the Ego and of OVs is performed, which results in an enhanced robustness during the tracking of OVs.

9 Vehicle of Relevance

In order to decide which object is relevant for the longitudinal controller, it is substantial to determine the positions and the future behavior of other vehicles relative to the Ego. The relevance decision is made with the implicit assumption that OVs keep their lane most of the time, by assigning them to the lanes of the road.

The pure radar-based ACC system (performance level one) can only use the driving tube for the relevance decision. The driving tube is fixed with the longitudinal axis of the own vehicle. Its only parameter is the curvature which is calculated from the speeds of the 4 wheels measured with the ABS-sensors. It has no reference to the real lane geometry. See figure 8.

Movements inside the lane result in an alternating curvature of the driving tube. To reduce this behavior, the curvature of the driving tube is calculated by lowpass filtering. As a consequence, the driving tube lags behind or overshoots the value of the real lane curvature if the steering angle changes strongly. The decision for relevance using the driving tube easily leads to false alarms, especially at far distances. E.g. if the Ego passes a vehicle in a left curved lane, it could become the relevant vehicle if the driving tube changes its curvature because of steering angle perturbations of the Ego within the lane.

Figure 9 shows the driving tube and the lane model during a lane change. It can be seen, that at near distances (6 − 30m) on high speed roads the driving tube can be approximated by a straight lane, because the curvature has nearly

Fig. 8. Driving tube (bright overlay) and lane model (dark) while the Ego is driving near the right border of the lane, but still inside the lane

no influence. At far distances a relevance decision based on the driving tube would definitely be wrong.

In contrast, the visual lane detection and tracking process is able to calculate the position of the Ego relative to the lane with 6DOF and is able to determine the shape parameters of the lane. For the assignment of OVs to the lanes and the decision of their relevance, three cases can be differentiated:

1. Ego is driving inside the own lane and no lane change is indicated or assumed.
2. Ego is driving inside the own lane and a lane change to the left is assumed or notified by the left indicator.
3. Ego is driving inside the own lane and a lane change to the right is assumed or notified by the right indicator.

The detection of a lane change can be done by observing the yaw-angle and the horizontal offset of the Ego. If the predicted horizontal offset of the Ego at a lookahead distance of 10m is larger than 60% of the lane width, a lane change is assumed.

In case 1 the relevance decision area (RDA) is identical to the current own lane. See figure 10a. A vehicle will be assigned to the own lane if the horizontal offset is smaller than half the width of the lane. If a vehicle is already assigned to the own lane, it is associated with it as long as the horizontal offset is smaller than half the width of the lane plus half the width of the vehicle.

During a lane change it is reasonable to hang on to the current own lane for lane tracking until the CG has a horizontal offset larger than half the lane width and then to change the tracked lane. But performing the relevance decision with respect to the current lane will not lead to satisfactory behavior, because the Ego will leave the lane within a short time. During and after the lane change its velocity has to be controlled in consideration of the vehicles in the desired lane.

Fig. 9. Driving tube and lane model while performing a lane change

Normally, an overtake maneuver (case 2) is performed for driving faster than in the current lane. In order to overtake, a strong acceleration is needed at the beginning of the maneuver. Therefore, human drivers mostly accept a safety distance shorter than otherwise chosen. That means, increasing the velocity is performed by decreasing the safety distance in the current lane. The switch for the left indicator could be used for starting acceleration by shortening the allowed safety distance to the leading vehicle.

Simultaneously, the RDA should be extended to the desired lane. Its width in the current lane should be successively decreased as function of the horizontal offset. See figure 10b. As long as the CG of the Ego is inside the current own lane, the width of the RDA ranges from that part of the own lane, which is still covered by the vehicle shape, over the complete width of the desired lane. The extended RDA is parallel to the skeleton line of the current lane. If the horizontal offset of the Ego is larger than half the lane width, the new lane becomes the own lane and the RDA becomes identical to the new own lane. See figure 10c. Case 3 is nearly the same as case 2, but no acceleration by shortening the safety distance in the current lane is allowed.

Afterwards, all OVs are sorted according to their distance to the Ego and only the nearest OV within the RDA is set to be relevant. The velocity and distance to the relevant OV is communicated to the vehicle controller for the longitudinal motion for adjusting the speed of the Ego in a way that the convoy distance is larger than a desired value, e.g. 1.6sec · velocity of the own car.

10   Experimental Results

In figure 11, a lane change from the middle lane to the right lane is manually performed. You can see on the left of the images the image of the wide-angle

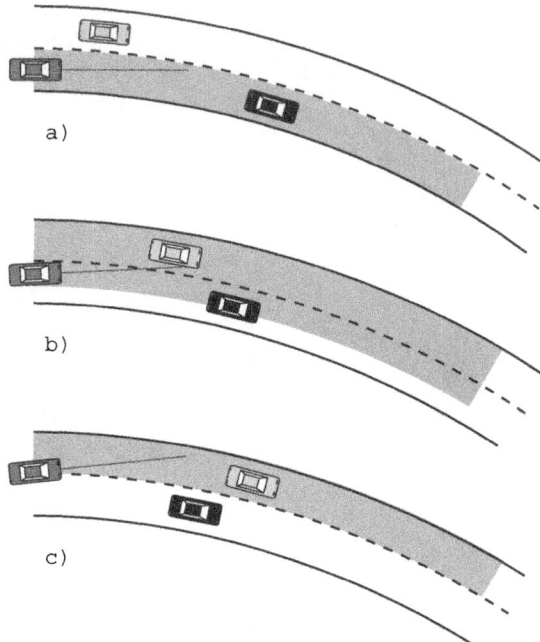

Fig. 10. Relevance decision area as function of the horizontal offset

camera and on the right the image of the tele camera. The image on top shows the own car following the OV with the velocity of the vehicle ahead and the desired safety distance. The relevant vehicle is marked with a red box (dark), while other tracked vehicle hypotheses are characterized by gray boxes (bright). The second image shows the own car just one timestep before the center of gravity of the own car crosses the lane markings. The relevant vehicle is still the vehicle ahead in the middle lane. The third image is just after the lane change is performed. The relevant vehicle has changed from the middle lane to the vehicle ahead in the right lane (dark box). And the lower image illustrates the approach to the vehicle ahead.

11   Conclusions and Outlook

The combination of radar and vision leads to a system with enhanced performance, capable of handling several tasks jointly using a common knowledge base. The system can select an appropriate level of performance depending on the hardware status or the performance of the experts. Monitoring the performance of the vision experts takes the weather and lighting conditions implicitly into account. Lane departure warning can be performed easily using the knowledge about the position of the Ego relative to the own lane. The implicit separation between egomotion and the dynamics of OVs using the lane coordinate system

Fig. 11. Lane change to the right

as common reference clearly improves the robustness of vehicle tracking. Convoy driving using activated lateral control is possible if the speed of the leading car is sufficently large such that it is not suppressed by radar measurement preprocessing. For speeds slower than that, first experiments are being under way using trinocular stereovision for handling stop-and-go traffic (for details see [5]).

References

1. R. Gregor, M. Lützeler, M. Pellkofer, K. H. Siedersberger, and E. D. Dickmanns. A vision system for autonomous ground vehicles with a wide range of maneuvering capabilities. In *this volume*.
2. G. J. Bierman. *Factorization Methods for Discrete Sequential Estimation*, volume 128 of *Mathematics in science and engineering*. Academic Press, Inc., 1977.

3. E. D. Dickmanns. Dynamic computer vision for mobile robot control. In *Proc. 19th Int. Symp. and Expos. on Robots*, Sydney (Australia), November 1988.
4. Reinhold Behringer. Visuelle Erkennung und Interpretation des Fahrspurverlaufs durch Rechnersehen für ein autonomes Straßenfahrzeug. In *Fortschrittsberichte*, volume 310. VDI Verlag, Düsseldorf, Germany, 1996.
5. André Rieder. *Fahrzeuge Sehen*. PhD thesis, Universität der Bundeswehr München, Fakultät für Luft- und Raumfahrttechnik, 2000. (im Druck).

Combining EMS-Vision and Horopter Stereo for Obstacle Avoidance of Autonomous Vehicles

K.-H. Siedersberger[1], M. Pellkofer[1], M. Lützeler[1], E.D. Dickmanns[1],
A. Rieder[2], R. Mandelbaum[2], and L. Bogoni[2]

[1] Institut für Systemdynamik und Flugmechanik,
Universität der Bundeswehr München (UBM),
D-85577 Neubiberg, Germany
http://www.unibw-muenchen.de/campus/LRT/LRT13/english/index.html
[2] Sarnoff Corporation
Princeton, New Jersey, USA
http://www.sarnoff.com

Abstract. A novel perception system for autonomous navigation on low level roads and open terrain is presented. Built within the framework of the US-German AutoNav project, it combines UBM's object oriented techniques, known as the 4D approach to machine perception (EMS-Vision), with Sarnoff's hierarchical stereo processing.
The Vision Front End 200, a specially designed hardware device for real-time image processing, computes and evaluates 320×240 pixel disparity maps at 25 frames per second. A key element for this step is the calculation of the horopter, a virtual plane that is automatically locked to the ground plane. For improved reliability, the VFE 200 results are integrated over time in a grid-based terrain representation. Obstacle information can then be extracted. The system's situation assessment generates a situation representation that consists of so-called situation aspects assigning symbolic attributes to scene objects. The behavior decision module combines this information with knowledge about its own body and behavioral capabilities to autonomously control the vehicle.
The system has been integrated into the experimental vehicle VaMoRs for autonomous mobility through machine perception. In a series of experiments, both positive and negative obstacles could be avoided at speeds of up to 16km/h (10mph).

1 Introduction

Driving on well-kept roads by visual feedback has become so mature that first products appear on the market. Computing power at affordable costs, volume and electric power consumption is coming along that will allow driving off-road and determining the vertical surface structure in real time while driving on uneven terrain. As a first step, detecting ditches (negative obstacles for wheeled vehicles) has been attacked. It is of major concern in the Demo III project of the US-Army [1].

B. Schiele and G. Sagerer (Eds.): ICVS 2001, LNCS 2095, pp. 139–156, 2001.
© Springer-Verlag Berlin Heidelberg 2001

In a joint US-German project 'Autonav' (1995 - present) the 'Pyramid Vision Technology' (VFE 200) developed by Sarnoff Corporation [2], [3] has been integrated with the basic structure of EMS-Vision [4], [5] developed by UBM. Real-time, full video-rate stereo interpretation has been achieved in a closed guidance loop with the test vehicle VaMoRs. The combined system is described in chapters 2 and 3. While chapter 4 sketches the new approach to situation assessment and behavior decision, chapter 5 discusses first experimental results for avoiding both positive and negative obstacles (on a dirt road respectively on a grass surface).

2   The EMS-Vision System

2.1   4D Approach

The UBM perception modules, e.g. for road- or vehicle detection, are based on the 4D-approach to dynamic machine vision [6]. An internal model of relevant objects in the 3D world is built using parametric geometry and motion models. Position and geometry parameters of the required objects must be determined from the image sequences originating from the MARVEYE-camera configuration. In a recursive estimation loop the elements of the state vector $\hat{x}_{k-1}$ at time t_0 containing position and geometry parameters are used to predict the system state for time $t_0 + \Delta t$ by exploiting the system's transition matrix Φ_{k-1} and the control input u_{k-1}, see equation (1). The transition matrix is known from the differential equations describing the applied motion models.

$$\overset{*}{x}_k = \Phi_{k-1}(\Delta t) \cdot \hat{x}_{k-1} + b_{k-1}(\Delta t) \cdot u_{k-1} \qquad (1)$$

$$\overset{*}{p}_i = g_{3D \to 2D}(\overset{*}{x}_k, P_i) \qquad (2)$$

Using these predicted model parameters $\overset{*}{x}_k$ and the known mapping geometry, measurement points P_i on the object surface (3D) are projected into the respective images (2D) $\overset{*}{p}_i$. Measurement windows are centered around these positions $\overset{*}{p}_i$ in the image for extracting feature candidates. A matching procedure links one of the measurement results to the expected feature p_i; the difference of measured feature position to expected feature position is used to update the state vector with the Kalman filter gain matrix K_k (innovation step, eq. 3). Details on Kalman filtering can be found in [7]. Thus an inversion of the perspective mapping is avoided.

$$\hat{x}_k = \overset{*}{x}_k + K_k(p_i - \overset{*}{p}_i) \qquad (3)$$

2.2   Hardware

The key sensor of the EMS-Vision system is the multi-focal active/reactive vehicle eye, called MARVEYE. This is a camera arrangement of up to four cameras with three different focal lengths (fig.1). Two cameras, equipped with wide-angle lenses, set up as a horizontal stereo pair with parallel or skewed optical axes. The skewed arrangement is used for tight maneuvering on low order roads and early detection of overtaking vehicles. The parallel setup is utilized for vertical curvature recognition and obstacle detection in off-road scenarios using stereo processing. On the third and fourth camera mild and strong tele-lenses are mounted. The image resolution of the tele cameras is 3 resp. 10 times higher than the resolution of the wide-angle cameras. The high resolution camera images and the corresponding different look-ahead distances are useful for identifying new objects, estimating object states and parameters with high precision, road curvature estimation and landmark navigation.

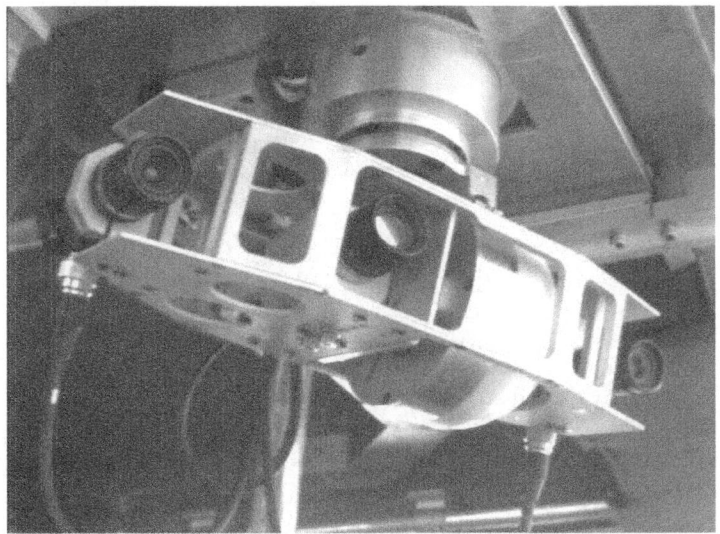

Fig. 1. MarVEye with parallel wide-angle cameras and one tele camera

The MARVEYE camera configuration is mounted on a pan-tilt camera head (TACC), so that the gaze control unit of the EMS-Vision system can point the tele cameras to an arbitrary part of the front hemisphere. The TACC supports fast gaze shifts, so-called saccades, soft camera turns for smooth pursuit of a moving target and inertial stabilization to compensate vehicle body motion in the frequency range of 0.7-2Hz.

The TACC is mounted in UBM's experimental vehicle VAMORS, a van MB 508D, behind the windscreen. The "Gaze Subsystem" is connected with the "Behavior PC" (fig.2). Additionally, this PC is coupled via a transputer-link with the "Vehicle Subsystem", a small transputer net for real-time control (25-200Hz) of the vehicle. All actuators, like steering, brake and throttle, are controlled by this subsystem. Otherwise some sensors, especially inertial and odometry sensors for dead reckoning and inertial guidance, are read in.

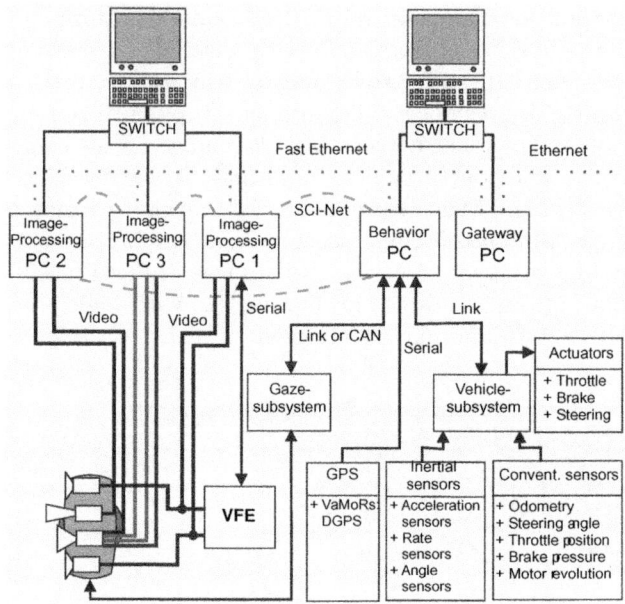

Fig. 2. EMS-Vision hardware with VFE integrated

The "Behavior PC" is part of the computational unit of the EMS-Vision system, which is a PC cluster with 4 computers (the "Behavior PC" and three "Image Processing PCs"). They are connected by SCI (Scalable Coherent Interface) for fast data exchange in real-time operation. An overview on the overall EMS-Vision system is given in [4] and [5].

Usually, each "Image Processing PC" is equipped with a frame-grabber for digitizing analog videostreams. Additionally, the "Image Processing PC1" is connected to Sarnoff's Visual Front End 200 (VFE 200) for robust stereo image processing. Figure 2 shows the hardware architecture of the EMS-Vision system with VFE integrated.

Robust stereo matching is computationaly costly. To achieve real-time performance, Sarnoff has built the VFE 200. It is a stand-alone video processing system, that captures the images of two cameras and passes them through a series of processors arranged in a pipeline architecture. Each processor is able to perform a specific operation on one or two images, such as warping, gaussian or laplacian filtering, subsampling, application of lookup tables, or correlation. With the algorithm described in section 3.1 the system is able to compute a 320 by 240 disparity map at full frame rate (30Hz with NTSC, 25Hz with PAL). The communication with the PC cluster is done via serial line at 57600 bytes per second. This limited bandwidth does not allow to send disparity maps to the PC, so their evaluation has to be done inside the VFE. For those types of non-standard operations four general purpose processors are provided.

2.3   Software

As described in the last section, the EMS-Vision system is a distributed system with a scalable net of PC's and certain subsystems. The processes running on the PCs are dynamically started and stopped. On every PC, an instance of the so-called dynamic knowledge representation (DKR) process runs in the background. The DKR processes distribute the dynamic knowledge representation in the system (see section 2.4) and communicate with each other via SCI. If changes in knowledge appear in one DKR process, the changes are sent to all other DKR processes, so that their knowledge representations remain consistent. Every DKR process possesses a time counter, showing the current system time. The time counters of the DKR processes are automatically synchronized. This is a precondition for having an unequivocal time everywhere in the system and for assigning meaningful time stamps to dynamic data. The other processes on the PCs, called client processes, register themselves on the local DKR process in order to get a scalable part of the knowledge representation mirrored. If a client process makes changes on its local knowledge representation, these changes are automatically sent to the local DKR process, and this, in turn, sends the changes to the DKR processes on the other computers. If a DKR process receives an update from an other DKR process, it automatically updates the mirrored knowledge representations of its local client processes. The client processes communicate with the DKR process via shared memory.

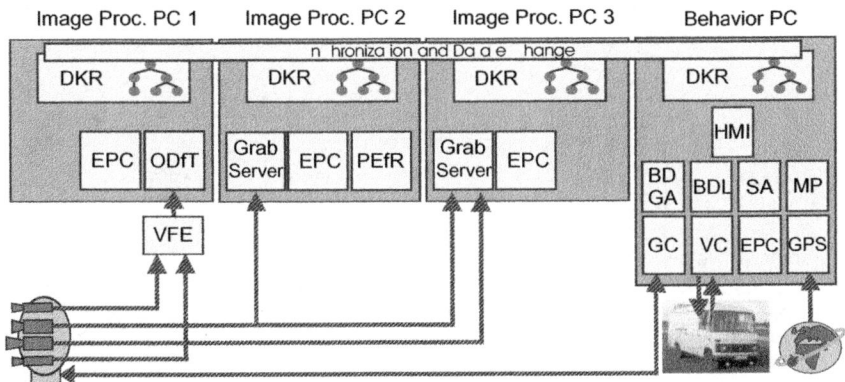

Fig. 3. Process mapping

In Figure 3 the process configuration used for autonomous driving missions described in this paper is presented. The VFE uses the parallel wide-angle cameras and sends their results to the Obstacle Detection for Terrain (ODfT) process. The ODfT process is responsible for the communication with the VFE. It transforms the scene representation common to all processes in the EMS-Vision framework to parameters that control the stereo matching and obstacle extraction process on the VFE. It also processes the obstacle information coming from the VFE, integrates it over time, and inserts and updates detected obstacles in the scenetree (see section 4.1). The 4D-Perception Expert, in this case handling the road objects (PEfR), runs on the second image processing PC and uses the mild tele camera. The Embedded PC Daemon (EPC), running on every PC, allows remote process control.

The following processes are located on the Behavior PC. The processes Behavior Decision for Gaze and Attention (BDGA) and Gaze Control (GC) perform active gaze control. Locomotion of the vehicle is controlled by the processes Behavior Decision for Locomotion (BDL) and Vehicle Control (VC). The Situation Assessment (SA) process generates symbolic information and meanings of objects. With the Mission Planning (MP) module, a mission plan can be generated for autonomous driving. A Human Machine Interface (HMI) allows the user to interact with the system.

2.4 Knowledge Representation

The DKR process shares the dynamic scene representation in the whole system. This dynamic knowledge representation of the EMS-Vision system is structured in a tree-like and object oriented manner (see fig.4).

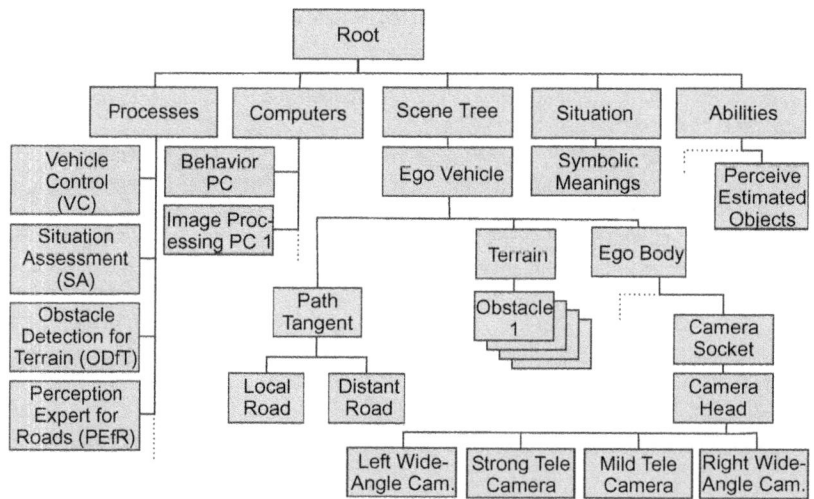

Fig. 4. Knowledge representation

- Every process in the system is represented by a process object. The process objects contain both general information about the process and an interface for point to point communication.
- Every computer in the system is represented by a computer object. This list is generated dynamically during system bootup.

- The scene tree is the key element of the dynamic knowledge representation. Its nodes represent physical objects, sub-objects or virtual coordinate systems. Transformations between scene nodes are described by homogeneous coordinate transformations (HCT). HCTs can be used for the description of the relative position (6DOF) between physical objects as well as for perspective projection into an image coordinate system. Due to the HCTs, an arbitrary point in a specific object coordinate system can be transformed into another object coordinate system or into a certain camera image. Scene nodes can also contain models for shape and dynamics or any other attributes of the represented object. Scene nodes, describing parts of the autonomous vehicle, like cameras, camera head or vehicle body, are static parts of the scene tree. On the other hand, external physical objects like roads, terrain and obstacles are temporary parts of the scene tree.
- In the situation branch of fig.4, symbolic meanings of single objects or groups of object are represented. Especially, an interface is offered for getting a list of references to scene objects with a specific meaning or for getting all meanings of a certain object in the scene.
- The abilities of the system and of system components are also part of dynamic knowledge representation. For example, the BDGA module offers the ability to fixate perceived objects with active gaze control.

3   Real-Time Time-Integrated Horopter Stereo

Stereo vision allows the extraction of 3D information from multiple pairs of images, which are taken by cameras at two or more different locations. The classical stereo setup described in section 2.2 has been used. Cameras are horizontally separated by a baseline of $b = 0.3$ m with parallel optical axes. The 1/3" cameras with 16 mm lenses correspond to a focal length of $f = 800$ pxl. The field of view covers about 24 degrees.

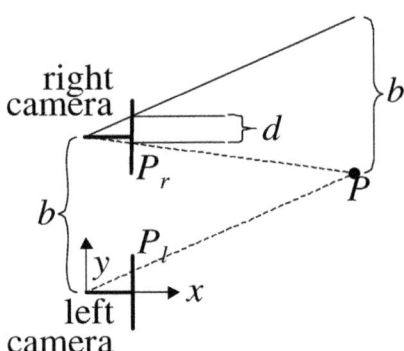

Fig. 5. Stereo camera setup

Given the two projections P_l in the left and P_r in the right camera of a point P in space, position P can be derived. According to figure 5 the relation between the distance x of P and the disparity d between the two projections P_l and P_r of P can be desribed as

$$d = \frac{bf}{x}; \qquad \frac{\partial x}{\partial d} = -\frac{bf}{d^2} = -\frac{x^2}{bf} \qquad (4)$$

In contrast to other sensors like radar or ladar, which determine range by measuring the time of flight of a signal, the range resolution of a stereo sensor depends significantly on the distance x. Quantitative analysis of our stereo algorithm showed that disparity can be measured with an accuracy of one quarter of a pixel. This means a range resolution of 3cm at a distance of 5m, but only a range resolution of 0.4m at 20m.

3.1 Horopter Stereo

A hierarchical stereo algorithm is used that first uses an affine transformation to align the images of left and right cameras and then determines the disparity for each pixel individually. This two step approach has two major advantages:

- It compensates for effects that are caused by the tilted viewing angle from which a ground vehicle perceives the terrain. Usually, disparities are large at the bottom of the image where close points can be seen, and diminish towards the top of the image where the horizon can be seen. After applying the affine transformation, disparity is uniform throughout the image, which simplifies further processing steps.
- It eliminates the need for accurate calibration for the determination of disparity. Thus, small rotations of the cameras or variations in the baseline do not impair the correspondence search.

Affine Prewarping. If two cameras are looking at a plane from different positions, then it can be obtained the left camera image from the right one by using an affine transformation [9]:

$$\begin{bmatrix} y_l \\ z_l \end{bmatrix} = \begin{bmatrix} a\ b\ c \\ d\ e\ f \end{bmatrix} \cdot \begin{bmatrix} y_r \\ z_r \end{bmatrix} \qquad (5)$$

On the other hand, given an affine transformation between two images, there exists exactly one plane in 3D space that causes this image motion. This plane is called the horopter. If a relatively flat terrain is assumed, then it is useful to interpret the image motion between the stereo cameras as a composition of an affine, introduced by a horopter approximation of the ground, and variations introduced by deviations from the planar ground assumption.

To determine the affine image motion, we use a hierarchical approach which was first described in [8]. This algorithm reduces the image resolution by repeatedly applying a gaussian filter and subsampling. Note that a single pixel in the low resolution image corresponds to a region in the original image. Starting from an initial guess which is based on the knowledge about the geometry of the scene, an iterative process calculates the alignment starting at the low resolutions before refining it at higher resolutions [10].

Correspondence. After applying the affine transformation the disparity for each individual pixel by standard correlation methods (SSD) can be determined. To estimate the quality of the measurement we compare the correlation results for the images at different resolutions as well as the the autocorrelation of the image with itself. Thresholds help to eliminate low correlation peaks.

3.2   Obstacle Detection

The obstacle detection step is performed as a post-processing phase following the generation of the disparity map produced by the stereo algorithm. It can be presented as a classification problem for regions of a disparity map.

The classification algorithm presented here takes advantage of the chosen horopter-based disparity computation. In this intererpetation, the disparity map consists of the residual parallax relative to the horopter plane in front of the vehicle, rather than the absolute parallax relative to the image plane. The rough classification of the disparity map relative to the identified ground plane labels positive disparities, which lie above the plane, as positive obstacles, and negative disparities, which lie below the plane, as negative obstacles.

The algorithm can be split into two parts. First, the dominant plane is identified. Second, the disparities are clustered and labeled.

Dominant Plane Identification. The identification of the dominant plane is obtained in the following steps:

1. Partition the disparity map into regions.
   The regions may vary both in size and shape. The smallest dimension should be chosen to be representative of the terrain sensitivity desired; while shape can be chosen to weigh the support/sensitivity with respect to a chosen normal direction. In this implementation we chose non-overlapping regions measuring 5x5. The overall size of the disparity map was 320x240.
2. Initialize a binary dominant plane mask (DPM).
   By introducing a mask, it is possible to eliminate areas having no valid disparities.
3. Fit the plane for each region.
   This step computes the normals for each region.
4. Filter normals with respect to x-component.
   The filtering is performed with respect to the attitude of the vehicle. In our case, the horizontal plane defining the pose of the cameras coincides with that of the vehicle, hence patches which have a strong x-component are selected. This operation allows eliminating portions of the disparity map

which might yield a large dominant plane which does not coincide with a *drivable*-dominant plane. Clearly when approaching a wall or a large vertical barrier, we want the classification process to be able to identify it as an obstacle rather than the dominant plane.

5. Histogram into n_x bins and identify the peak.
   Regions are sorted binned according to their angular orientation.
6. Eliminate from DPM all regions that are not in the neighborhood of the X-peak.
   Thus, regions which have x-component approximately parallel to the normal direction of the vehicle are kept.
7. Histogram into n_z bins and identify the peak.
   This sorting bins regions according to angular orientation of tilt.
8. Eliminate from DPM all the regions that are not in the neighborhood of the Z-peak. This processing is more important when driving off-road when the terrain can present a gradual descent or ascent. In flat areas, this process will effectively return no dominant peak. When no peak is present all the regions are kept.
9. Fit a plane common to all regions remaining in the DPM.

Object detection. Once the dominant plane has been identified, labels and measurements can be computed. First the pixels are grouped according to their disparity. Each component with a disparity bigger than a threshold $d_{\text{pos}}(z)$ is considered a positive obstacle, while each component with a disparity less than $d_{\text{neg}}(z)$ a negative obstacle. The two different threshold values are functions of the vertical image coordinate z so that the scene geometry can be taken into account.

$$d_{\text{pos}}(z) - c_{\text{pos}}z \text{ and } d_{\text{neg}}(z) = c_{\text{neg1}} \frac{z^2}{c_{\text{neg2}} + z} \tag{6}$$

The constants c_{pos}, c_{neg1} and c_{neg2} can be derived from the minimum obstacle size that has to be detected. Components that cover an image area that is large enough to be considered as an obstacle are surrounded by a rectangular bounding box. All of the processing steps described above (prewarping, correspondence, obstacle detection) are performed by the VFE within 240ms. The resulting bounding boxes are then sent to the PC for time integration.

3.3   Time Integration

The above algorithm is considerably more robust when the temporal information is also included. The non-real-time simulations show that integration is more effective if it is done in earlier processing stages. But since those algorithms are not yet implemented on the VFE, and the limited communication bandwidth between the VFE and the PC cluster does not allow disparity maps to be transmitted, we decided to do time-integration on an object level. Namely, obstacles are reported only after they appear in consecutive frames.

For this reason we represent the terrain as a two-dimensional grid. Each cell covers an area of 0.25x0.25m. Using the known geometry of the vehicle and the cameras, it is determined:

- the field of view, i.e. the terrain cells that are currently visible for the stereo camera pair.
- the obstacle regions based on the current image pair. Therefore, the terrain cells that lie within the bounding boxes around obstacles that were calculated in the disparity image (see section 3.2) are determined.

For each cell (i, j) an obstacle measurement $q_{i,j}$ is defined:

$$q_{i,j} = \frac{\text{Number of times reported as obstacle}}{\text{Number of times seen}} \qquad (7)$$

All cells whose obstacle measurement exceeds a threshold are considered candidates for terrain obstacles.

4 Situation Assessment and Behavior Decision

4.1 From Grid Based to Object Orientated Representations

Representation for autonomous vehicles is mostly done in one of the follwoing two ways:

Object oriented: This approach is most popular in structured environments (indoors, on-road driving). The ego vehicle and the world around it are represented as a collection of objects. Each object is assigned a label (eg. table, road, motorcycle), which characterizes its shape, dynamics and other attributes. By using expectations about how objects look and behave, perception and control can be done most efficiently. The 4D approach is a perfect example of an object oriented representation.

Grid based: In unstructured environments labeling is of great difficulty and limited profit. Labels like "bush" carry almost no information about the object's shape, color or danger it represents to the ego-vehicle. Most decisions have to be based on shape and qualities such as pliability. Here, grid based approaches are more common, where the terrain is devided in cells and each cell carries a set of attributes (height, color, vegetation).

[11] first combined the two approaches. This allows to choose whichever form of representation is more suitable for a given object.

In our application the ego vehicle, its sensors and actuators are all represented in an object oriented way. The terrain is integrated in the scene tree as an object by assigning a geodetic coordinate system (gravity orientated) to the terrain. Knowing the position of single terrain points relative to the ego vehicle by inertial state estimation and dead reckoning, any position given in the grid can be transfered to a position relative to the ego vehicle as well as relative to any other object and vice versa. If a road is present in the terrain, it is represented as an object.

The internal representation for obstacle detection is done in a grid based way. Once neighboring cells of the terrain have been individually identified as obstacle candidates they are grouped together to form a terrain obstacle. These obstacles become separate objects in the scene representation.

4.2 Relevance of Obstacles and Situation Assessment

Objects like positive or negative obstacles being detected and represented in the scene tree are of special relevance for the behavior of the autonomous vehicle. If an obstacle is within the driving tube, an avoidance strategy must be generated to protect the vehicle from damage. Generally, the information *"the object lies within the driving tube"* is a symbolic meaning of the corresponding object. Symbolic meanings of objects are calculated by the Situation Assessment (SA) module. Within the Situation Assessment module symbolic meanings are calculated by so-called situation aspects. A situation aspect is defined as linguistic variable and consists of the following parts:

- With the name of a situation aspect, the human viewer can associate a symbolic statement which describes an aspect of the real situation.
- The linguistic valences are fuzzy sets and represent the intrinsic symbolic information. The degree of fulfillment of the valences lies in the interval [0,1].
- Data processing buffers and preprocesses data required for the calculation of the meanings from the scene tree.
- The membership functions use the preprocessed data to calculate the fulfillment of the valences.
- The data logic and the processing logic specify, whether the data processing or the membership function must be active in the current system cycle.
- The period of validity specifies, how long the meanings are valid.

For the avoidance of positive and negative obstacles described in section 5, three situation aspects are used:

- IsLyingAhead: The situation aspect IsLyingAhead possesses the valences TRUE and FALSE. The notation IsLyingAhead.TRUE stands for the valancy TRUE of the situation aspect IsLyingAhead and so on. The valences describe, whether the object is in front of the vehicle or not.
- IsRelativeToDrivingTube: It describes the position of an obstacle relative to the driving tube. The valences are On, Left and Right. The data processing of this situation aspect buffers and low pass filters the steering angle of the autonomous vehicle and the position of the obstacle relative to the center of gravity.
- NoOfObstacleOnDrivingTube: This one arranges the objects lying in the driving tube in a proper order. The valences are First, Second, Third and so on. In this situation aspect, only objects, for which the fulfillment of the valences

IsRelativeToDrivingTube.On and IsLyingAhead.True are greater than 0.5, are taken into account.

These three situation aspects operate in a predetermined order, so that NoOfObstacleOnDrivingTube can process the results of IsRelativeToDrivingTube and IsLayingAhead. Thus, the values of the situation aspects are graduated: the meaning NoOfObstacleOnDrivingTube.First implicates the meaning IsRelativeTo-DrivingTube.On.

Due to the fuzzy character of the valences, not only the discrete statement *"the meaning of the situation aspect is correct/not correct"* can be specified, but also the degree of correctness. Another advantage is, that continuous changes in situation aspects can be handled. For the avoidance of positive and negative obstacles, the vehicle control process requires the objects with the symbolic meaning IsRelativeToDrivingTube.On. Especially, the object with the greatest fulfillment of NoOfObstacleOnDrivingTube.First is used, to stop the vehicle in front of the object. Symbolic meanings, being used by other processes, are announced in the whole system by the situation assessment module.

4.3   Avoidance Strategy

If Situation Assessment determines that the situation aspect IsRelativeToDrivingTube.On is appropriate, i.e. an obstacle is in the path of the vehicle, Behavior Decision for Locomotion (BDL) requests a next meaning (NoOfObstacleOnDrivingTube). If the situation aspect NoOfObstacleOnDrivingTube.First applies, all data about this obstacle, which are administered in the scenetree, are retrieved. Using obstacle data, BDL decides if an evasion maneuver or a stop maneuver (if the obstacle is too big) has to be initiated. In the case of a stop maneuver, additional parameters are calculated:

– The distance to the stop point. This distance is calculated from the distance between the leading edge of the obstacle and the front bumper of the vehicle minus a security distance of 1 meter.
– The distance to the point at which braking with a constant and comfortable deceleration has to be activated so that the vehicle can be stopped as requested.
– The necessary deceleration if the distance to the obstacle is too small for braking with the comfortable deceleration.

BDL compares these distances with the actual distance to the obstacle and triggers Vehicle Control (VC) to execute the stop maneuver if the distances coincide. VC generates the control variable for the actuators and applies these. In the case of a stop maneuver, the necessary deceleration is controlled by the deceleration controller which is part of VC. The computed brake pressure, the control variable, is sent to the brake system and the vehicle brakes until the velocity is zero. Then, VC commands a constant, reduced brake pressure, the deceleration controller is deactivated and so the vehicle is in the standing mode.

5   Experimental Results

5.1   Avoiding Positive Obstacles in On-Road Driving

In this experiment the test vehicle VaMoRs is driving autonomously (longitudinal and lateral control) on a dirt road with 10mph. Position and orientation of the dirt road relative to the ego vehicle and road parameters like the road width are estimated by the PEfR process. The dirt road is centered in the image of the mild tele camera by active gaze control (fig.6a).

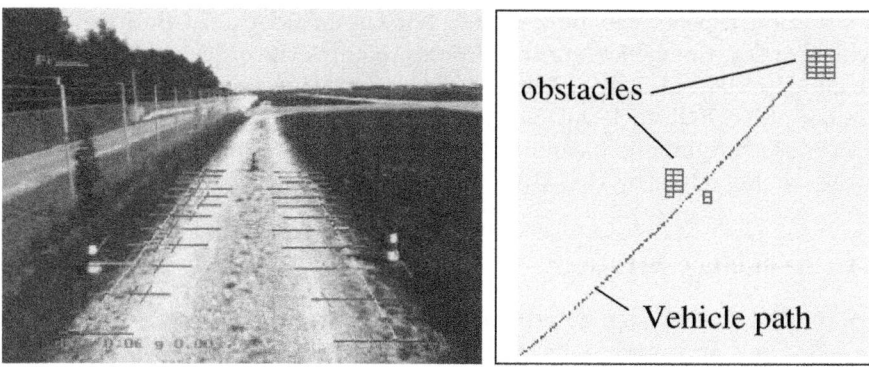

Fig. 6. Stopping in front of positive obstacles a) camera image and road detection b) grid base terrain representation with obstacles

Three pylons are placed in the environment of the dirt road. The first pylon is placed on the right roadside, the second pylon on the left roadside and the third one further down in the middle of the dirt road (see fig.6a).

Driving autonomously on the dirt road, these positive obstacles are detected by the VFE stereo process (see fig.6b). In the case of an obstacle, the ODfT process inserts a corresponding obstacle node in the scene tree. Obstacle nodes possess a shape model describing the size and form of the obstacle. If an obstacle node is inserted in the scene tree, SA uses the position and shape model of the obstacle and vehicle data to generate symbolic information about the obstacle in a cyclic manner. Especially, SA verifies using the situation aspect IsRelative-ToDrivingTube, whether the obstacle lies in the driving tube or not. For this situation aspect, the period of validity is 1 second.

Figure 7 shows data for a time period, in which the three pylons are detected. The first and the second pylon are detected at about 108 seconds and they are represented in the scene tree as obstacle 1 and 2 (fig.7a). As shown in figure 7b, the symbolic meaning IsRelativeToDrivingTube.Left has the greatest fulfillment for the obstacle 1. The plot of the situation aspect IsRelativeToDrivingTube.Right is not shown in this series of plots. BDL does not initiate an autonomous stop

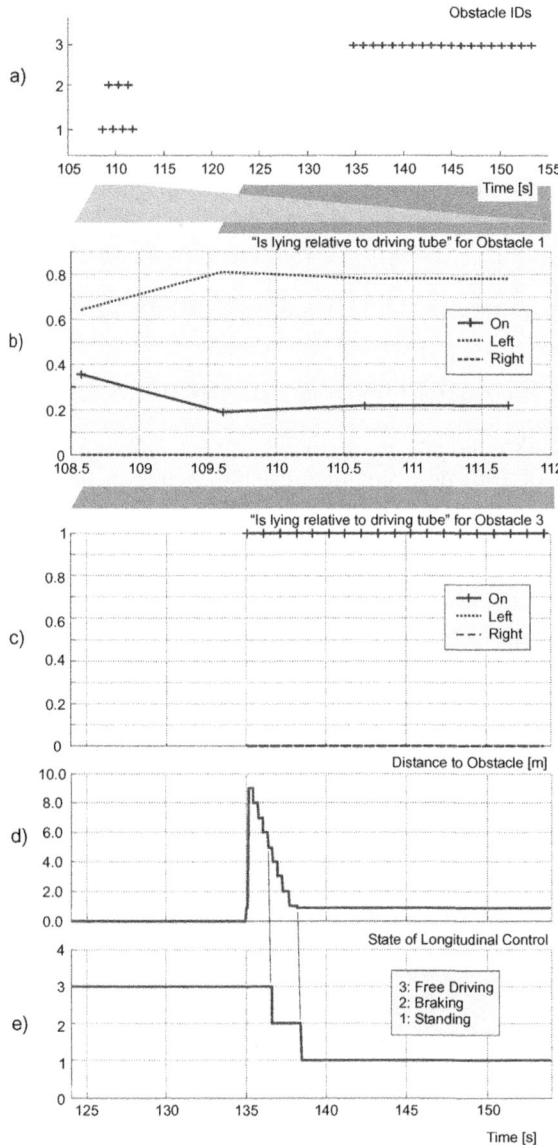

Fig. 7. Avoiding positive obstacles on a dirt road a) obstacle IDs in the scene tree b) situation aspect IsRelativeToDrivingTube for obstacle 1 c) situation aspect IsRelative-ToDrivingTube for obstacle 3 d) distance to obstacle e) states of longitudinal control

maneuver because the situation aspect IsRelativeToDrivingTube.On does not apply for obstacle 1 and 2 and so the vehicle passes these obstacles. After 135 seconds, the third pylon is detected. In figure 7c, it can be seen, that the meaning IsRelativeToDrivingTube.On has the greatest fulfillment for obstacle 3. Due to this, BDL initiates an autonomous stop maneuver.

At approx. 137 seconds VC starts braking because the distance to the obstacle coincides with the distance of the start point for braking (in this case approx. 5m, see fig.7d) that is calculated from parameters of the obstacle and the ego vehicle. The state of the longitudinal control is changed from state 3 (free driving) to state 2 (braking). When the vehicle comes to rest, VC changes the state of the longitudinal control to 1 (standing), see figure 7e. All the time, the lateral control is active and guides the vehicle on the dirt road. During longitudinal state 3 (free driving) the control of steering is deactivated, of course.

5.2 Avoiding Negative Obstacles in Off-Road Driving

Self occlusion makes negative obstacles very challenging for ground vehicles. From a distance of 20m no point deeper than 5cm can be seen in a ditch that is half a meter wide. Any algorithm which is able to detect such a ditch at this distance will cause a false alarm for every other depression of 5cm. Time-integration is therefore necessary to reduce false alarms. Figure8 shows an example. By enforcing object persistence while approaching a depression, real driving hazards can be distinguished from other depressions.

Fig. 8. Stopping in front of negative obstacle a) outside view b) grid based terrain representation with obstacles

The experimental vehicle performs an off-road mission with 10mph. The aim is to drive cross-country as long as no negative obstacles (i.e. ditches) are detected. The process configuration and control flow are identical to those of section 5.1, excepted that the PEfR process is passive and lateral control is done manually.

At approx. 324 second, the negative obstacle with Id 1004 is detected and this obstacle lies in the driving tube (see 9a), but for a few seconds this obstacle is the third closest, because some other obstacles are detected, which are closer to the ego vehicle. But these are removed, because they disappear over time.

After 327 seconds, object 1004 is now the first (closest) object relative to the ego vehicle (see fig.9b). Due to the situation aspect NoOfObstacleOnDriving-Tube.First, BDL initiates a stop maneuver in front of this ditch.

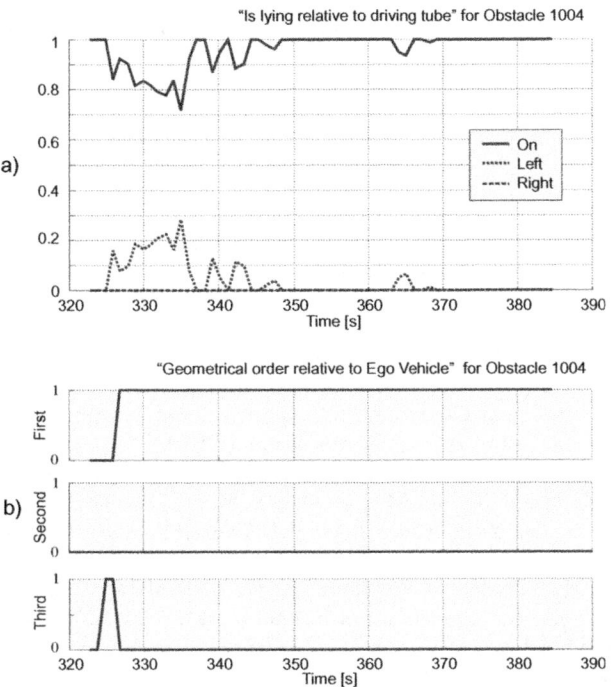

Fig. 9. Avoiding negative obstacles a) situation aspect IsLyingRelativeToDrivingTube b) geometrical order

6   Conclusions

The combination of 'Pyramid Vision Technology' (VFE 200, Sarnoff) and some basic components of the new EMS-Vision system installed in VaMoRs (UBM) has led to cutting edge results in real-time stereo vision in a transatlantic co-operation dubbed 'Autonav'. Full images of size 320 by 240 pixel can now be interpreted at video-rate with delay times similar to human vision (a few tenths of a second). Integration over time of a grid representation $((0.25m)^2$ cell size) derived from pixel-disparity results allows improving obstacle recognition. The robustly detected obstacles are inserted in the 'scene tree' as objects given by their extension and state relative to the autonomous vehicle in homogeneous coordinates. This is the object-oriented representation from which the standard procedures for 'situation assessment' and 'behavior decision' of EMS-Vision derive their guidance activities.

A small river-bed with the same grass texture on both sides could be detected reliably even under strong perturbations in pitch from uneven ground. For the detection of narrow ditches (60cm) solely by depth perception, sensitivity has to be tuned so high that false alarm rates are rather frequent. Time integration helps alleviating this problem under perturbations; speeds up to 10mph have been tested successfully. There is room for further improvements. Better results will become possible when color and edge features are interpreted in addition. This is planned for future activities.

References

1. P. Belluta, R. Manduchi, L. Matthies, K. Owens and A. Rankin: *Terrain Perception for DEMO III.* In Proceedings of the IEEE Intelligent Vehicles Symposium (IV), Dearborn, Michigan, U.S.A., October 2000.
2. R. Mandelbaum, M. Hansen, P. Burt, S. Baten: *Vision for Autonomous Mobility: Image Processing on the VFE-200.* Proceedings of the IEEE International Symposium on Intelligent Control (ISIC), International Symposium on Computational Intelligence in Robotics and Automation (CIRA), and Intelligent Systems and Semiotics (ISAS), Gaithersburg, Maryland, U.S.A., September 1998.
3. S. Baten, R. Mandelbaum, M. Lützeler, P. Burt, E.D. Dickmanns: *Techniques for Autonomous, Off-Road Navigation.* IEEE Intelligent Systems magazine, special issue on Vision-Based Driving Assistance, Nov-Dec. 1998, pp 57-65.
4. R. Gregor, M. Lützeler, M. Pellkofer, K.-H. Siedersberger, E.D. Dickmanns: *EMS-Vision: A Perceptual System for Autonomous Vehicles.* In Proceedings of the IEEE Intelligent Vehicles Symposium (IV), Dearborn, Michigan, U.S.A., October 2000.
5. R. Gregor, M. Lützeler, M. Pellkofer, K.-H. Siedersberger, E.D. Dickmanns: *A Vision System for Autonomous Ground Vehicles with a Wide Range of Maneuvering Capabilities.* In this volume.
6. E.D. Dickmanns and H.J. Wünsche: *Dynamic Vision for Perception and Control of Motion.* In B. Jaehne, H. Haußenecker and P. Geißler: Handbook on Computer Vision and Applications, volume 3, Academic Press, 1999.
7. A. Gelb, J.F. Kaspar, R.A. Nash, C.F. Price and A. Sutherland: *Applied Optimal Estimation.* The MIT Press, edition 12, 1992.
8. J.R. Bergen, P. Anandan, K. Hanna, R. Hingorani: *Hierarchical model-based motion estimation.* In Proceedings of the 2nd European Conference on Computer Vision, 1992.
9. N. Ayache: *Artificial Vision for Mobile Robots.* (Translation from French, 1989, INRIA), The MIT Press, London, 1991.
10. P. Burt, L. Wixson, G. Salgian: *Electronically Directed Focal Stereo.* In Proceedings of the International Conference on Computer Vision, 1995.
11. A. Bobick, R. Bolles, P. S. Schenker (ed.): *Multiple Concurrent Object Descriptions in Support of Autonomous Navigation.* In Proceedings SPIE Sensor Fusion, Vol. 1828, No. 5, Boston, MA, pp. 383-392, November 1992.

The CardEye: A Trinocular Active Vision System

Elsayed E. Hemayed, Moumen T. Ahmed, and Aly A. Farag

Computer Vision and Image Processing Laboratory
University of Louisville, KY 40292
{moumen,farag}@cvip.uofl.edu
http://www.cvip.uofl.edu

Abstract. The CardEye is an experimental, trinocular, 3D active vision system. Our goal is to create a flexible, precise tool for active vision research. The system uses an agile trinocular vision head that will be mounted on a robotic arm. The system has several degrees of freedom: pan, tilt, roll, vergence and variable baseline in addition to the automated zoom and focus of the cameras lenses. It utilizes an active lighting device to assist in the surface reconstruction process. After solving for the best system variables to image a surface, a novel multi-stage reconstruction algorithm is used to build a rich, complete 3D model of the surface. In this paper we describe the novel architecture of the system and its successful application to reconstruction of objects of varying surface characteristics.
...

1   Introduction

Representing the environment as 3D objects has drawn the attention of many vision researchers. Currently, there is enormous work in building 3D models for the spatial layout of the environment. The 3D model can be useful for many applications such as model building, object recognition, vehicle navigation, detection and tracking of objects. Most of the approaches proposed to solve this problem are inspired from the Marr paradigm that considers a static or a mobile sensor, but not a *controlled* one. Unfortunately, this approach seems to be inadequate to solve many problems where appropriate modifications of intrinsic and/or extrinsic parameters of the system sensors are necessary. That is why "active vision" has evolved as an alternative, new paradigm [1,2,3,4]. The aim of active vision is generally to elaborate control strategies in order to improve the perception task. Thus according to the specified task and to the data extracted from the acquired images, an active vision system might change its parameters (camera position and orientation, ocular parameters such as zoom, focus or aperture, etc.), and also the way data are processed (the applied algorithms). Therefore, an active system in general is more *relevant* to the application (usually because it is goal driven), more robust, and more accurate.

In this paper we present an active vision platform, the CardEye, designed and constructed in our laboratory for the development of active vision techniques.

B. Schiele and G. Sagerer (Eds.): ICVS 2001, LNCS 2095, pp. 157–173, 2001.

The system is flexible enough to be used for different visual tasks. The one of specific concern in this paper is 3D Euclidean reconstruction of objects with various surface characteristics within the working space of the system. Several features of the system are novel. The system has a novel architecture consisting of a trinocular head with several controllable parameters such zoom-lenses and active lighting device. To select values for these free parameters, a new sensor planning algorithm [5] solves for those parameters that maximize the effectiveness of the reconstruction process. In order to be able to extract 3D metric information from images acquired at the lens control parameters that are decided by the sensor planning module, the system uses a novel technique for zoom-lens camera calibration [6], which can capture the variations in the camera model parameters as continuous functions of lens settings. Last, but not least, the system employs a robust reconstruction approach [7,8] that combines structured-light, edge-based stereo and area-based stereo.

In the next section, we describe the architecture of the CardEye and its hardware components. Section 3 briefly outlines the system operation for surface reconstruction and shows different experimental results. Section 4 contains our conclusion and planned extensions.

2   System Architecture

The CardEye head is a computer-controlled, trinocular, multi-sensor, active vision system (Fig. 1). The goal in developing this system is to create a flexible, experimental platform for research on active computer vision. The system consists of an agile trinocular vision head that will be mounted on a robotic arm. The head has the controllable mechanical properties of vergence and variable baseline in addition to controllable zoom, focus and aperture of each camera. The arm will add the capabilities of pan, tilt and roll (in a sense, it functions similar to the human neck). The flexibility of the system and the availability of different sensors can assist in solving many problems in active vision research. As shown in Fig. 1, the head is completely implemented and functioning, and will be described next. Then an overview on the arm design and overall system simulations will follow.

2.1   Head Assembly

In contrast to many vision heads (e.g., Rochester head (University of Rochester) [9], FOVEA (University of Texas) [10], PennEyes (University of Pennsylvania) [11], BiSight (HelpMate Robotics Inc.) [12] and INRIA head (INRIA, France) [13]), the system makes use of a third camera to verify and improve the performance of visual task. The head has three Hitachi KP-M1 black and white CCD cameras with H10x11E Fujinon zoom lenses. Each camera can vary its zoom, focus and aperture settings under computer control. Although a right-angle, coplanar arrangement of the three cameras in a static head[1] simplifies the stereo

---

[1] See for example the Digiclops trinocular vision head commercially available from Point Grey Research Inc., Vancouver, British Columbia.

matching process [14], the expected system dynamics makes the alignment of that model rather difficult to adopt in case of an active head.

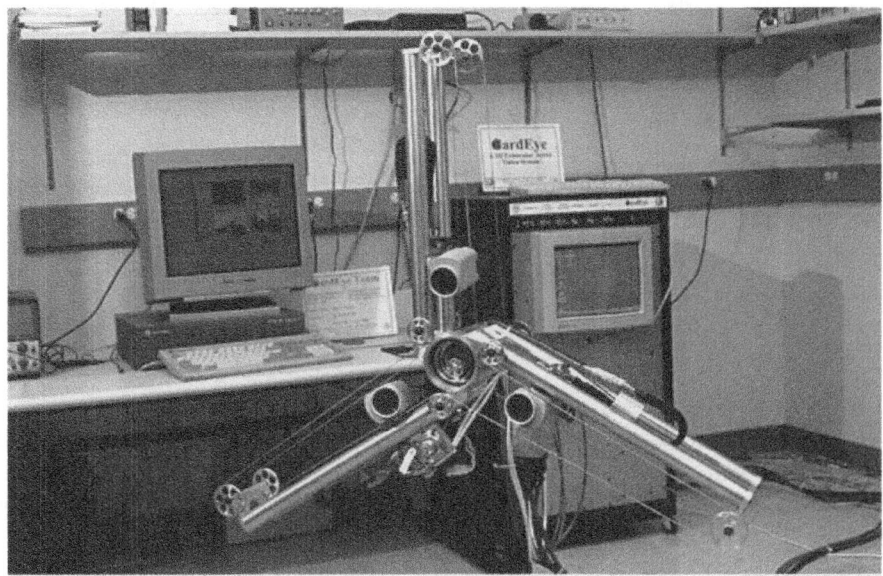

Fig. 1. CardEye trinocular active vision system. From left to right, the SGI machine for image processing, the trinocular head and the control circuitry cabinet.

As shown in the schematic diagram in Fig. 2(a), the cameras of the Card-Eye's head are organized in a coplanar, equilateral triangle arrangement. The main reason behind this arrangement is to make controlling the cameras' motion easier. The three cameras are coupled together such that only two high-current stepper motors are needed to control the cameras' position and orientation. If the two motors rotate in the same direction, the cameras can translate along their mounts to change the baseline distance. On the other hand, if the motors are stepped in opposite directions, the cameras rotate towards each other to fixate to a point. This is known as the vergence property. As such, this type of cameras arrangement and motion control represents a compromise between flexibility (due to many free parameters) and complexity (due to need to control all these parameters).

An active lighting device is mounted at the center of the trinocular head, see Fig. 2(b). This device consists of a laser generator, different diffractor filters mounted on a rotating drum, and a mounting mechanism having two small stepper motors to enable the device to change its orientation around the system vertical axis and to switch the filter. With the help of this device, structured-light techniques for surface reconstruction can be easily utilized in our system.

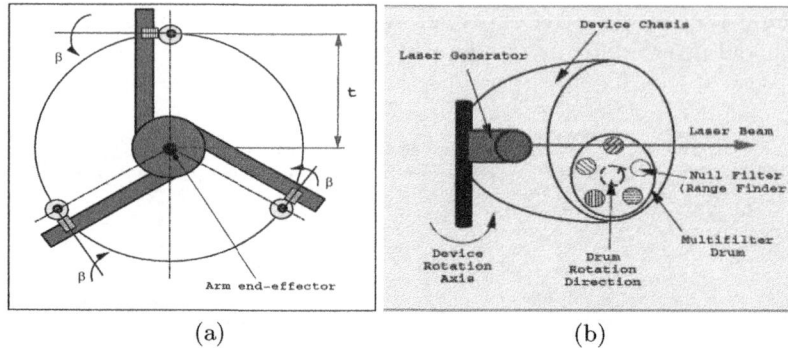

(a)   (b)

Fig. 2. CardEye Head: (a) Schematic diagram of the trinocular head, (b) Schematic diagram of the active lighting device at the head hub.

Currently, we are investigating the integration of this device with a ranger finder such that the two may use the same laser beam. The integrated device will be thus able to project a pattern on the environment and then measure its distance from the system. This will be very useful for the surface reconstruction process as well as system self-calibration.

2.2   Robotic Arm

The trinocular head is attached to the end-effector of a robotic arm with three segments and four joints - the base, elbow, shoulder and wrist, which provide pan, tilt and roll, respectively. The arm is to help the head to fixate at any point in the working space of the system. The three cameras of the trinocular head by themselves have only the capability to converge towards a point along the central line of the head (fixation line). The fixation line in the system represents the trajectory of the fixation points of the cameras. Therefore, to fixate at a certain spot of interest, the system first change the robotic arm joints to align the spot with the end-effector segment of the arm such that the fixation line of the head passes through the targeted spot. Then the cameras can translate and converge at the spot. Therefore once a target is defined for the system, the inverse kinematics of the system can be solved [15,16] to calculate a possible set of the arm joint angles which could be used to attain this given position and orientation.

In the current status of the system, the robotic arm has not been implemented yet. However, simulations (as illustrated in Fig. 3) have been used to test the coordination between the system parts, to justify the available degrees of freedom and to justify the solution of the system kinematics with different target locations.

Fig. 4 shows two fixation cases. In the first case, Fig. 4(a), the system fixates to a near target. In the second case, Fig. 4(b), the system fixates to a far target.

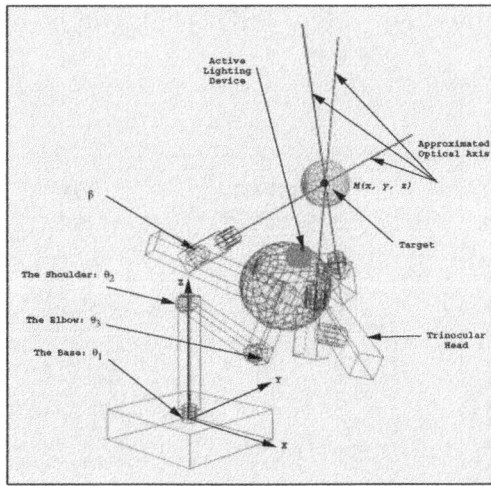

Fig. 3. CardEye simulated design (A trinocular head attached to three-segment robotic arm.)

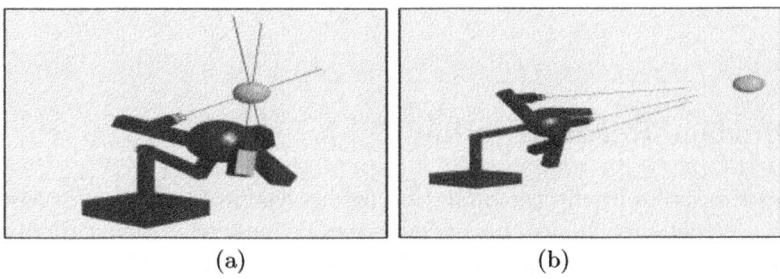

(a)   (b)

Fig. 4. Example of the system fixating to (a) a near target and (b) a far target.

2.3 Overall System

The system hardware includes powerful processors, a very fast network, precise controllers, robust vision sensors and special lighting devices. Combining these components enables the building of a fast, reliable system. Fig. 5 shows a schematic diagram of the system components and the links between them. As shown, the system is interfaced to a network of high-end workstations, PCs, an Onyx R10000 supercomputer and an ImmersaDesk visualization screen. The supercomputer is used for the computationally intensive algorithms, such as stereo correlation techniques. Using a Galileo video board, the Indigo2 snaps images (when needed) and performs simple image processing functions such as edge detection. The PCs are mainly used for controlling the system motors and the active lighting device. Currently, the components communicate with each other through the network sockets in a client/server environment. For future real time applications, a parallel network of DSP boards will be built and dedicated to the system.

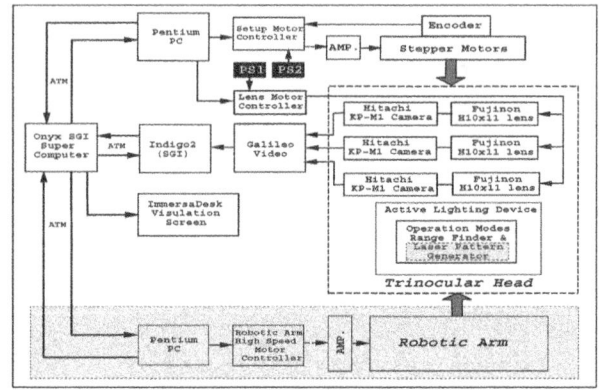

Fig. 5. Schematic diagram of the CardEye components (parts to be implemented in the next phase are shown shaded).

3   Surface Reconstruction

We next describe briefly the operation of the system for surface reconstruction. Given a target spot before the system, several images can be acquired to reconstruct the objects in the spot. Since the system is active, it is able to modify its variables to obtain the best possible images for the reconstruction task. Selecting these variables is by no means trivial since some task sub-goals are sometimes in conflict and since some other constraints have to be satisfied. The system first considers this problem, which is referred to as the sensor planning problem, to solve for these variables. The system uses this solution to adjust the head's cameras' position and orientation before images of the objects are taken. Our reconstruction approach is based on strong calibration, in a sense that a 3D Euclidean reconstruction can be performed. Therefore the three zoom-lens cameras are calibrated across continuous ranges of lens control parameters that cover the working space of the system, so that the camera parameters can be recovered at any lens setting requested by the sensor planning module. Moreover, our reconstruction approach benefit from the advantages of several basic reconstruction techniques such as feature-based stereo, area-based stereo and structured light in order that the system can handle objects with different surface characteristics (e.g., smooth, edgy, textureless, etc.). In the following, we briefly describe the sensor planning, calibration and reconstruction modules.

3.1   Sensor Planning

The sensor planning process [5] employs the targeted spot to generate the sensor parameters (vergence, baseline and cameras' zoom and focus) to achieve the goal of maximizing the effectiveness of the surface reconstruction from single frame of images. Some constraints are also imposed so that that the object be within the field of view and in focus for each camera. For effective reconstruction, the frame images should have a fairly large overlap area (required by stereo matching) and display adequate depth information (large disparity). The first sub-goal of the overlapping area tends to move the cameras as close as possible and as a result, maximizes the overlap surface area between the cameras. The second sub-goal is responsible for producing a compelling sensation of three-dimensionality and forces the cameras to move away from each other to create better depth information of the object. Obviously the two sub-goals are in conflict. Consequently, there exists a need to find the best sensor parameters that satisfy both sub-goals to a certain extent.

Fig.6 is used to illustrate the sensor planning approach. The figure describes the geometry of the CardEye head where the coordinate system is placed on the center of the head ($\mathbf{O}$). The three cameras are represented by their optical centers ($\mathbf{C'}, \mathbf{C''}, \mathbf{C'''}$). The z-axis is pointing outwards to an object at a distance d. The object is assumed to be inside a sphere that has a radius R. Estimates for R and d are assumed known a prior. It can be shown [5] that the overlap area between any cameras is directly related to the angle δ, see Fig.6(b), which is given by:

$$\delta = \pi - 2\tan^{-1}\left(\frac{\sqrt{3}t}{2d'}\right),\tag{1}$$

where the translation t is the distance between the cameras and the origin of the system, and $d' = \sqrt{d^2 + \frac{t}{2}^2}$. On the other hand, the total angular disparity of any two cameras, η, approximately equals [5]

$$\eta \approx \frac{\sqrt{3}Rt}{d'^2}\tag{2}$$

The product $\eta\,\delta$ is a good measure of how well the sensor parameters satisfy both criteria simultaneously. After considering its physical range, which is $0.1-0.6\ cm$ for the system, the value of t that maximizes the measure is solved for [5]. Moreover, by adjusting the vergence angle, all cameras can fixate on the same point in 3D space. The system's fixation point is the center $\mathbf{C}$ of the sphere. Once t is determined, the vergence angle can be given by $\beta = \tan^{-1}\left(\frac{t}{d}\right)$.

The sensor planning module finds next the zoom and focus settings of the three cameras, which will have same settings due to system symmetry. The field of view, α, of the camera is controlled by the zoom setting and is computed using the head's geometrical setup as

$$\alpha = \sin^{-1}\left(\frac{R}{\sqrt{t^2 + d^2}}\right)\tag{3}$$

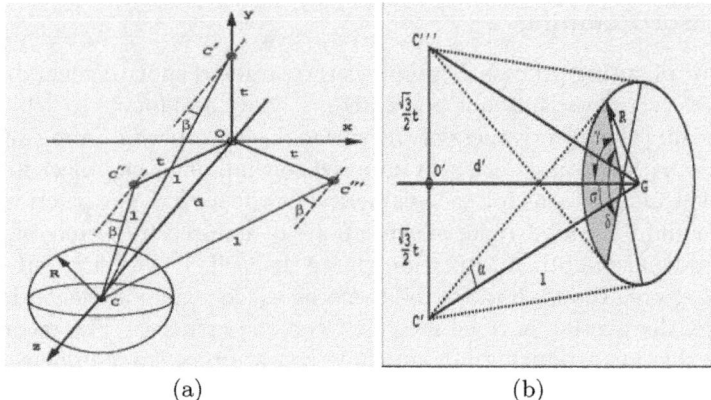

(a)   (b)

Fig. 6. (a) System geometry. The target for this system is a sphere with radius R. (b) Overlap area and angle δ.

The required field of view is converted to the right zoom motor setting after having previously established the relationship between the field of view angle and zoom motor activation signal by investigating several images acquired by the camera. Similarly, the proper focus setting of the active lens can be easily adjusted since a direct relationship is given in the lens data sheet.

The sensor planning algorithm was tested with simulations and real experiments. Fig. 7 illustrates the results for one experiment, the first row shows the images before applying the sensor planning, which showed small sized view of the object and were a little bit out of focus. The second row shows the images after applying the sensor planning to the system at distance $d = 1.7m$. Those images are well-focused and show more details of the object with the object being centered in the three images. The results of all our experiments, see [5], show that the presented sensor planning is capable of maintaining the object in the field of view and with relatively similar sizes at different distances from the system.

3.2   Zoom-Lens Camera Calibration

The CardEye uses three zoom-lens cameras, which need to be calibrated to know the camera model parameters at any lens setting (zoom and focus) as determined by the sensor planning module. Camera systems with automated zoom-lenses are inherently more useful than those with fixed-parameter (*passive*) lenses due to their flexibility and controllability. In such cameras, the image-formation process varies with the lens optical settings, thus many of the camera model parameters are non-linear functions of the lens settings. The calibration problem of these cameras relies on formulating functions that describe the relationships between the camera model parameters and the lens settings. As opposed to passive cameras, this raises several challenges [17]. First, the dimensionality of calibration

(a) Camera1   (b) Camera2   (c) Camera3

Fig. 7. Results of sensor planning applied to CardEye system. First row: before planning, second row: after planning with $d = 1.7m$.

data is large. A second challenge is the potential difficulty in taking measurements across a wide range of imaging conditions (e.g., defocus and magnification changes) that can occur over the range of zoom and focus control parameters.

The zoom-lens calibration approach, generally, involves first calibrating a conventional static camera model at a number of lens settings which span the lens control space using traditional calibration techniques. The calibrated model parameters (both intrinsic and extrinsic) at each lens setting can be stored in lookup tables and functional interpolation calculates values for intermediate lens settings (e.g., [18],[19]). An alternative approach is to model the parameter variations across continuous ranges of lens settings with functions fitted to the calibrated values [20],[17]. In [21], a combination of the two approaches was proposed; some parameters were stored in lookup tables while functions were formulated for the others.

To calibrate the Cardeye's cameras, we developed a neural framework [6] based on our novel neurocalibration approach [22], which cast the classical geometric (passive) camera calibration problem into a learning problem of a multi-layered feedforward neural network (MLFN). This framework consists of a number of MLFNs learning concurrently, independently and cooperatively, to capture the variations of model parameters across lens settings. Fig. 8 illustrates the central neurocalibration network and its associated MLFNs. This framework offers a number of advantages over other techniques (e.g., [17],[21]): it can capture complex variations in the camera model parameters, both intrinsic and extrinsic (as opposed to polynomials in [17]); it can consider any number/combination of lens control parameters, e.g., zoom, focus and/or aperture; all of the model parameters are fitted to the calibration data in a global optimization stage at the same time while minimizing the overall calibration error.

Since collecting the data needed for calibration is a tedious, time-consuming process, the integration of the active light device with a range finder would help

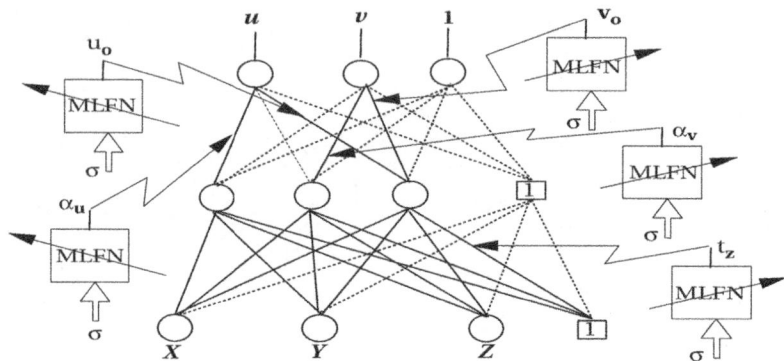

Fig. 8. Zoom lens calibration: five parameter MLFNs cooperate with the central neurocalibration net during the optimization, σ denotes the lens controllable parameters, (u_0, v_0) the principal point, α_u and α_v the image scale factors, t_z the z-component of the translation vector; The rest of the camera model parameters are represented by the central network weights; Dashed links in the central network designate link weights fixed during learning at 0 or 1.

the system collect the data automatically by itself without user supervision. This would make the system very flexible to re-calibrate whenever necessary. However, the automated data collection is more likely to introduce outliers in the data. Outlying data would skew the results of existing calibration approaches which are based on the less robust least-square estimator. To overcome this problem, we have recently developed a robust version [23] of our neural calibration approach, which is less sensitive to outliers. That version uses a Maximum-likelihood estimator (M-est) to reduce the influence of outliers on calibration accuracy.

3.3   Reconstruction Approach

The main difficulty in stereo vision is to establish correspondences between image pairs. Sensor planning guarantees a large overlapping area between the images acquired for the target and consequently reduced number of occluded points that often cause problems for any stereo matching algorithm. The information extracted by camera calibration imposes a set of geometrical constraints (epipolar constraints) between the frame of images. The additional constraints provided by the third camera help reduce the number of false matches found between the other two images. Once correspondences have been established, 3D reconstruction is easily done by intersecting the optical rays of the matched pixels.

Due to the different characteristics of object surfaces in the environment, a single stereo matching technique does not work well in all situations, and thus we employ multiple techniques to find pixel matches [7]. Our approach benefits from the accuracy of feature-based stereo and the richness of area-based stereo.

The system employs structured light to induce features on textureless objects that cannot be properly handled with feature- or area-based stereo.

Based on the acquired images, if the object surface appears to have enough texture as evident from some texture measures [24], the system uses correlation-based stereo to provide dense reconstruction of the surface. Several correlation scores have been tested, and the normalized cross-correlation has been found to give the best result. The candidate matches are those which maximize the correlation score. A match is considered reliable if correspondence could be established in the three images, with the correlation score between any pair of images exceeding a pre-selected threshold (say, 0.85). Points matched between only two images are considered if their score exceeds a higher threshold (about 0.95). Validation of matches is also performed by performing the correlation another time by reversing the order of checking on the images (e.g, starting with the third instead of the first). A match is kept if the triplet (or pair) matches obtained in the two times are the same. The whole algorithm was efficiently parallelized on our 24-processor supercomputer. More speed is also gained by computed the epipolar lines in the beginning of the algorithm and then storing them in a table. As such, we have been able to get very good results in less than 16 sec for three 320 × 242 images. One example is depicted in Fig. 9, which displays the obtained Euclidean reconstruction from the images previously shown in Fig. 7 after applying sensor planning. For textureless objects or those lack-

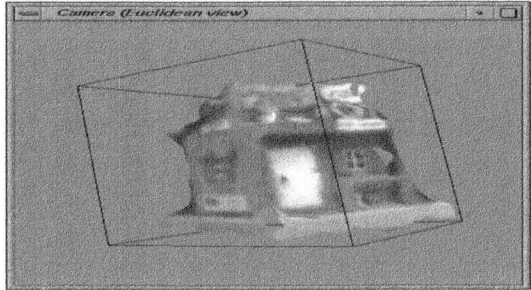

Fig. 9. Reconstruction result of correlation based stereo after surface fitting and adding texture.

ing enough texture through the whole surface, fewer point matches are usually obtained and the reconstructed model is thus not dense enough. Our system efficiently handles these objects using a multi-stage approach. A feature-based stereo algorithm reconstructs the visible edges in the scene. In the same time, artificial features are induced on the object using structured light generated by the system active light device. To make the reconstructed model denser, correlation stereo is performed to fill the gaps between the reconstructed features using the matches already obtained from feature-bases stereo as a guide.

A schematic diagram of our approach is illustrated in Fig.10. First, three images of the scene are snapped and used as reference images. All straight line segments are then extracted from the three images, matched and validated for matching using some feature descriptors (e.g., line orientation and existence of common segments) and epipolar constraints [8]. The theme of our work is similar to Ayache's work [25]. Both fall under the category of prediction and verification techniques, as classified by Faugeras [26]. However, our approach differs from Ayache's approach in three points. First, we work directly on the obtained, unrectified images to avoid the distortion results from rectifying the images. Second, we do not consider the relative length of the line segments as a matching criterion. Thus, our approach can handle the foreshortening problem. Third, we eliminate the dependency on predefined thresholds by verifying the matching using a global optimization process.

Then a set of artificial lines are added by having the active lighting device project one laser line at a time. The line in each images is extracted using the reference images, thinned, and reconstructed in 3D. The location of the projected line is incrementally updated by the system at each time. The number of used lines is selected by the user. However, if a line is projected onto a textured enough region (according to the measure for textureness [24]), this line location is skipped since the points in that region can be reconstructed by the subsequent correlation algorithm.

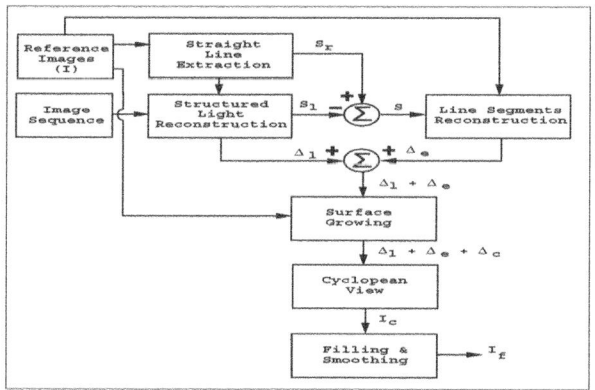

Fig. 10. Schematic diagram of the multi-stage reconstruction technique.

All found line matches are used to guide a correlation matching technique. The correlation technique is used to match the gap points (i.e., unmatched points located between matched points along the epipolar lines) and grow a surface around the matched points. The final output is a dense set of match points that can be represented as a disparity map or projected onto the cyclopean view.

Fig. 11 illustrates the different stages of the reconstruction algorithm. More results are shown in Figs. 12,13.

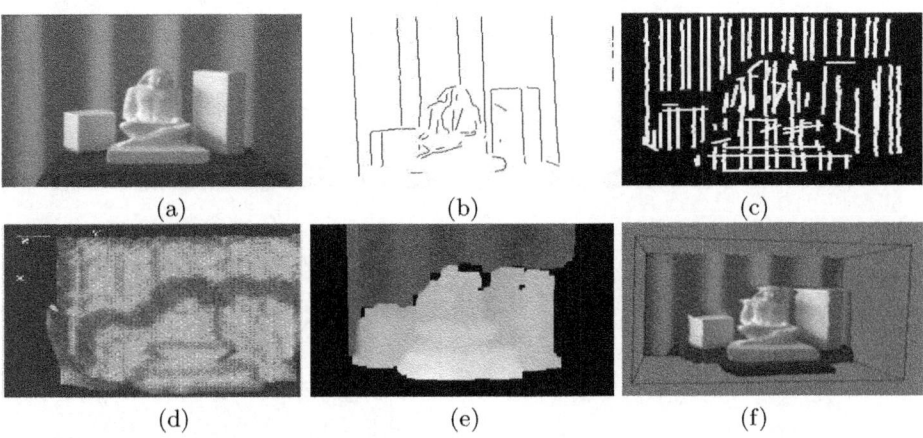

Fig. 11. Some reconstruction steps of a test scene: (a) an image of the original scene (after sensor planning), (b) actual and (c) artificially induced edges, (d) a free form surface fitted to the final reconstruction, (f) the cyclopean view of the reconstruction after adding texture.

The approach successfully produced good quality 3D models for objects with various characteristics in about 3 minutes (most time is lost during acquisition of more images with laser line markings). Moreover, a quantitative assessment of the reconstructed models has been obtained by reconstructing some objects with simple geometry (e.g., boxes), then comparing the metric dimensions of model to those of the original object as measured by a 3D digitizer arm. Fig. 14 shows the dimensions of one such object, the measured data in part (a) and the reconstructed data in part (b). The *rms* error between the reconstructed object dimensions and the ground truth values is within 5 millimeters. More details about the approach and performance analysis of the system can be found in [15].

4   Conclusion

In this paper, we presented the design and construction of the CardEye trinocular active vision system. The system has several degrees of freedom. Its flexibility and the availability of different sensors can assist in solving many problems in active vision research. In addition to its novel architecture, the contribution of this paper includes new sensor planning technique to the system variables that maximize the effectiveness of the reconstruction algorithm under a set of

Fig. 12. The reconstruction results of the 'Speakers' scene. (a) The original image,
(b) The cyclopean view as a range image, (c) The cyclopean view as a mesh (d) The
cyclopean view as a textured mesh.

desirable system constraints; accurate, general approach to calibrate the zoom-
lens cameras; and an efficient reconstruction approach that integrates area-based
and feature-based stereo techniques with structured light. The final contribution
is the integration of the hardware and the software algorithms in a working active
vision system that builds dense 3D models of objects in the system working space.

Our current research is directed to the second phase of the system in which
the CardEye head will be mounted on a robotic arm to expand the system
capabilities. Another direction to this research is to use and integrate more
image frames from different views to build a complete model of the whole scene.
Building a parallel network of DSP boards for real time applications is also a
possibility for future investigation.

Acknowledgment. This work was supported in part by grants from the US
Department of Defence (USNV N00014-97-11076) and NSF (ECS-9505674).

Fig. 13. The reconstruction results of the 'CarDog' scene. (a) The original image, (b) The cyclopean view as a range image, (c) The cyclopean view as a mesh (d) The cyclopean view as a textured mesh.

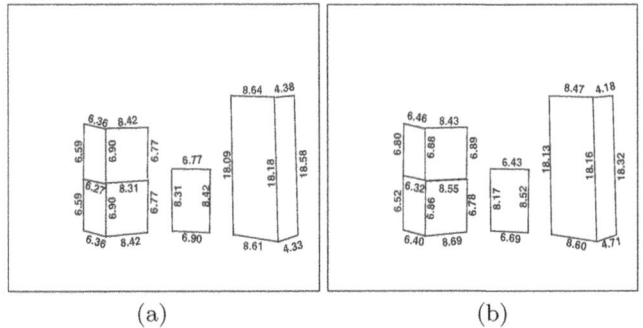

Fig. 14. Schematic diagram of the Boxes scene. The apparent sides are shown only. (a) The ground truth measured by a 3D digitizer. (b) The reconstructed data.

172   E.E. Hemayed, M.T. Ahmed, and A.A. Farag

References

1. R. Bajcsy, "Active perception vs. passive perception," *Proceedings: Workshop on Computer Vision*, 1985.
2. M.J. Swain and M. Stricker, *Promising directions in active vision*, Technical Report CS 91-27, University of Chicago, 1991.
3. A. L. Abbott and N. Ahuja, "Active surface reconstruction by integrating focus, vergence stereo and camera calibration," *ICCV*, 1990.
4. T. Vieville, *A few steps towards 3D active vision*, Springer-Verlag, Information Sciences Series, 1997.
5. P. Lehel, E. E. Hemayed, and A. A. Farag, "Sensor planning for a trinocular active vision system," *CVPR*, 1999.
6. M. Ahmed and A. Farag, "A neural optimization framework for zoom-lens camera calibration," *CVPR*, 2000.
7. E. Hemayed and A. Farag, "Integrating edge-based stereo and structured light for robust surface reconstruction," *Int. Conf. Intelligent Vehicles*, 1998.
8. E. Hemayed and A. Farag, "A geometrical-based trinocular vision system for edges reconstruction," *ICIP*, 1998.
9. C. M. Brown, "The rochester robot," 1988.
10. W. N. Klarquist and A. C. Bovik, "Fovea: A foveated vergent active stereo vision system for dynamic three-dimensional scene recovery," *IEEE Trans. Robotics and Automation*, vol. 14(5), October 1998.
11. B. C. Madden and U. C. Seelen, *PennEyes: A binocular active vision system*, Technical Report, University Of Pennsylvania, 1995.
12. C. Weiman and M. Vincze, "A generic motion platform for active vision," *SPIE Conf 2904*, Nov 1996.
13. T. Vieville, E. Clergue, R. Enciso, and H. Mathieu, "Experimenting with 3-d vision on a robotic head," *Robotics and Autonomous Systems*, vol. 14(1), Jan/Feb 1995.
14. Y. Ohta, M. Watanabe, and K. Ikeda, "Improving depth map by right-hand trinocular stereo," *ICPR*, pp. 519–521, 1986.
15. E. E. Hemayed, *A 3D Trinocular Active Vision System for Surface Reconstruction*, Ph.D. Thesis, CVIP Lab, University of Louisville, August 1999.
16. E. Hemayed, Moumen Ahmed, and A. Farag, "Cardeye: A 3d trinocular active vision system," *Proc. 3rd IEEE Conference on Intelligent Transportation Systems (ITSC'2000)*, pp. 398–403, Oct. 2000.
17. R. G. Wilson, *Modeling and calibration of automated zoom lenses*, PhD dissertation, CMU, 1994.
18. M. Li and J. Lavest, "Some aspects of zoom lens camera calibration," *IEEE Transactions on Pattern Analysis and Machine Intelligence*, vol. 18(11), pp. 1105–1110, November 1996.
19. K. Tarabanis, R. Tsai, and D. Goodman, "Calibration of a computer controlled robotic vision sensor with a zoom lens," *CVGIP: Image Understanding*, vol. 59(2), pp. 226–241, Jan 1994.
20. A. G. Wiley and K. W.Wong, "Geometric calibration of zoom lenses for computer vision metrology," *Photogrammetric Engineering and Remote Sensing*, vol. 61(1), pp. 69–74, January 1995.
21. S. W. Shih, Y.P. Hung, and W. S. Lin, *Calibration of an active binocular head*, vol. 28(4), IEEE Trans. Man, Sys. and Cybernetics, July 1998.
22. M. Ahmed, E. Hemayed, and A. Farag, "Neurocalibration: a neural network that can tell camera calibration parameters," *ICCV*, 1999.

23. M. T. Ahmed and A.Farag, "Zoom-lens camera calibration from noisy data with outliers," *To appear in Proc. the 11th Britich Machine Vision Conference, Bristol, UK*, Sept. 2000.

24. G. Cochran, S.D.; Medioni, "3-d surface description from binocular stereo," *PAMI*, vol. 14(10), pp. 981–994, October 1992.

25. N. Ayache and F. Lustman, "Trinocular stereo vision for robotics," *IEEE Trans. on Pattern Analysis and Machine Intelligence*, vol. 13(1), pp. 73–85, Jan. 1991.

26. O. Faugeras, *Three-Dimensional Computer Vision - A Geometric Viewpoint*, the MIT Press, 1993.

RPV-II: A Stream-Based Real-Time Parallel Vision System and Its Application to Real-Time Volume Reconstruction

Daisaku Arita and Rin-ichiro Taniguchi

Department of Intelligent Systems, Kyushu University
6-1 Kasuga-koen, Kasuga, Fukuoka 816-8580 Japan
{arita,rin}@limu.is.kyushu-u.ac.jp
http://limu.is.kyushu-u.ac.jp/

Abstract. In this paper, we present RPV-II, a stream-based real-time parallel image processing environment on distributed parallel computers, or PC-cluster, and its performance evaluation using a realistic application. The system is based on our previous PC-cluster system for real-time image processing and computer vision, and is designed to overcome the problems of our previous system, one of which is long latency when we use pipelined structures. This becomes a serious problem when we apply the system to interactive applications. To make the latency shorter, we have introduced stream data transfer, or fine grained data transfer, to RPV-II. One frame data is divided into small elements such as pixels, lines and voxels, and we have developed efficient real-time data transfer mechanism of those. Using RPV-II we have developed a real-time volume reconstruction system by visual volume intersection method, and we have measured the system performance. Experimental results show better performance than that of our previous system, RPV.

1 Introduction

Recently, especially in computer vision community, image analysis using multiple cameras has been extensively researched[1,2]. When we use multiple cameras, distributed systems are indispensable because a single or centralized system can not handle a large amount of image data[3,4,5,6,7]. When we require real-time analysis of those images, the problem becomes much more serious because of their large bandwidth and their huge computation demand. To solve the problems, we have developed a parallel/distributed real-time image processing system, RPV (Real-time Parallel Vision), on a PC-cluster, which consists of multiple off-the-shelf PCs connected via very high speed network[3,4]. The PC-cluster strategy has an important merit of scalability, which means that putting additional PCs into the network we can easily acquire larger number of sensors, or cameras, and larger computation power with low cost. The key issues of such distributed real-time image processing systems are synchronization among distributed PCs, the performance of network, the end-to-end latency at user level, the programming framework and the cost of the system.

B. Schiele and G. Sagerer (Eds.): ICVS 2001, LNCS 2095, pp. 174–189, 2001.
© Springer-Verlag Berlin Heidelberg 2001

The biggest problem of RPV is its long latency when we employ pipelined structures to acquire higher throughput. This is because, for real-time data transfer in RPV, we have developed synchronization mechanism based on the timing of image frame in an video sequence, and, as a result, the latency becomes $2N \times one\ frame\ period$, when we use N PCs arranged in a pipeline structure. This becomes a serious problem when we apply the system to interactive applications.

To make the latency smaller, we have introduced stream data transfer, or fine grained data transfer, to RPV-II, the next version of RPV. One frame data is divided into small elements such as pixels, lines and voxels. When each PC finishes processing an element, it starts sending it to the succeeding PC and then starts processing the next element. This mechanism can make the latency $1/M$, where M is the number of elements in one frame period.

Using RPV-II, as a realistic application, we have developed real-time volume reconstruction system by visual volume intersection method[8], and we have measured the system performance. The main part of this system consists of three steps: silhouette extraction, visual cone generation and volume construction by intersecting the visual cones. Each of three steps are executed by multiple PCs and voxel data representing the visual cones and the object shape are transfered in stream among the PCs. In this paper, at first, we overview RPV and outline RPV-II emphasizing on its stream data transfer. Then we describe real-time volume reconstruction using RPV-II, and, finally, the performance evaluation based on the developed application.

2   Real-Time Parallel Vision

2.1   Overview

Our PC-cluster system consists of 14 PCs, each of which has Pentium-III×2(see Fig 1 and Fig. 2). All the PCs are connected via Myrinet, a crossbar-switch based gigabit network, and six of them have IEEE1394-based digital cameras[9], each of which can capture an uncompressed image sequence in real-time. On our PC-cluster, we support the following parallel processing schemes and their combinations. From the viewpoint of program structure, each PC corresponds to a component of a structured program of image processing.

Pipeline parallel processing. As shown in Fig. 3(a), the whole procedure is divided into sub-functions, and each sub-function is executed on a different PC sequentially.

Data parallel processing. As shown in Fig. 3(b), a set of data is divided into sub-data, and each sub-data is processed on a different PC in parallel. There are two approaches in data parallel processing:

- Image is divided into sub-images, and each sub-image is processed on a different PC in parallel.

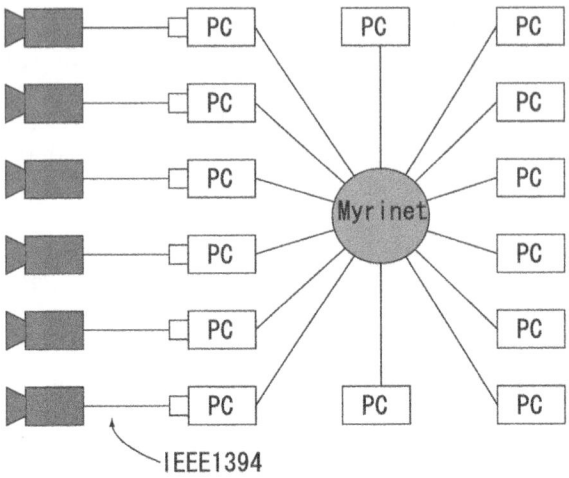

Fig. 1. Configuration of PC-cluster

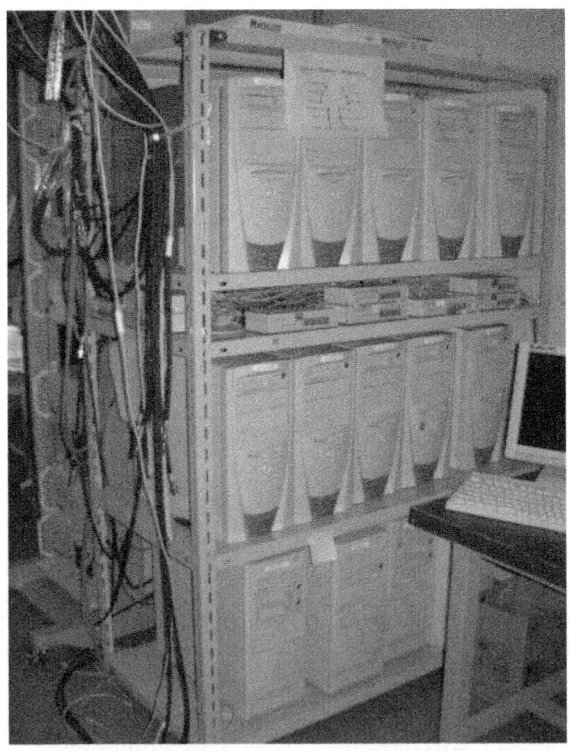

Fig. 2. PC-cluster

(a) Pipeline parallel processing

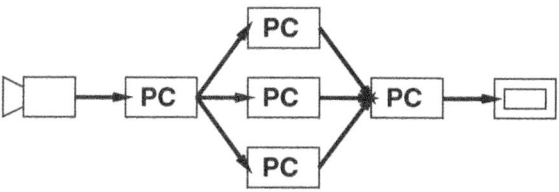

(b) Data parallel processing

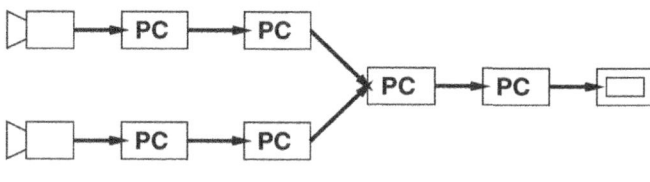

(c) Data gathering

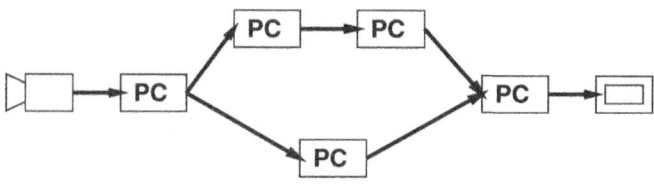

(d) Function parallel processing

Fig. 3. Parallel processing schemes

- Different frames are processed on different PCs. The longer[1] processing time can be secured, but the latency also becomes longer.

Data gathering. As shown in Fig. 3(c), images captured by multiple cameras are processed by PCs and integrated on the succeeding processing stage.

---

[1] It is proportion to the number of pipelined PCs. When N PCs are used the secured processing time is up to $N \times one\ frame\ period$.

Function parallel processing. As shown in Fig. 3(d), images are multicast
to multiple PCs, on which different procedures are executed in parallel, and
their results are unified in the succeeding processing stage.

2.2   Mechanisms for Real-Time Parallel Processing

For supporting the real-time parallel processing schemes described before, the
system must have such mechanism as follows[3].

Real-time data transfer. We have used PM library[10] as communication
primitives on Myrinet, and its actual network bandwidth is enough high
to transfer image data in real-time. Since PM library supports DMA transfer between a main memory and a buffer on Myrinet board, it is able to
reduce waste of CPU power for data transfer.
Synchronization. To inform all PCs when they start processing a frame data,
we introduce Frame Synchronization Signal (FSS), which notifies the time
to start processing, and which is received by all the PCs.
Error recovery. If data processing has not been finished or data receiving has
not been finished when FSS is received by a PC, it is necessary to invoke an
error recovery function. According to the image processing algorithm in each
PC, programmers can select an error recovery mode from data missing mode,
incomplete data mode or complete queuing mode. In data missing mode,
only complete data are sent to the following PCs but some data are lost.
In incomplete data mode, no data are lost, but incomplete data, which are
intermediate result data, previous frame data or default data, are sometimes
sent. In complete queuing mode, no data are lost and all data are completely
processed, but the latency of data increases and a certain size of queue is
required.

2.3   Implementation

In each PC, the following four modules are running concurrently to realize the
mechanisms described before(see Fig. 4). Each of the modules is implemented
as a UNIX process.

Data Processing Module(DPM). This module is the main part of the image
processing algorithms, and is to process data input to the PC. It receives
data from a DRM and sends data to a DSM via UNIX shared memory.
In DPM, any programs should consist of the following three elements:
  1. A main loop is to process image sequence, in which one iteration is
     executed per one frame time. The main loop is executed according to
     the following procedure to process image sequence continuously.
     a) Wait for a signal from FSM to start processing. If a signal arrives
        before processing of previous frame is not finished, an error recovery
        function is invoked.

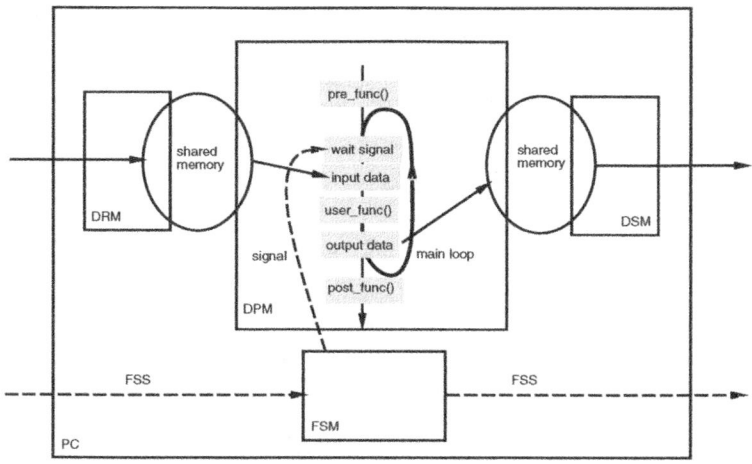

Fig. 4. Modules and functions in RPV

b) Get input data. Actually pointers to input data are transferred in
order to avoid copying data. If input data has not been received, an
error recovery function is invoked.

c) Execute a user-defined function representing one iteration of the
main loop, which is named user_func here. Function user_func receives synchronous input data I and asynchronous input data A and
sends output data O. Synchronous input data I are main streams of
data, which originates from image capture cards and are transferred
between PCs synchronously. They are synchronized at the beginning
of function user_func (described at previous step). Asynchronous
input data A can be used for feedback data and irregular data in
cooperative processing. They are not synchronized at the beginning
of function user_func and are reloaded with the newest ones at any
timing a programmer indicates.

d) Put output data. Because output data are directly written to shared
memory in order to avoid copying data, only a notification of write-
done is sent to DSM.

2. Before entering the main loop, a pre-processing function is executed. It
is named pre_func here. Function pre_func is a user-defined function,
which is used, for example, to load data necessary for the main loop such
as a background image and calibration parameters.

3. After exiting the main loop, a post-processing function is executed. It is
named post_func here. Function post_func is a user-defined function,
which is used, for example, to save results.

Data Receiving Module(DRM). This module is to receive data from other
PCs via messages, and has buffers for queuing data. When a data request
demand arrives from its succeeding DPM, it returns pointers to data.

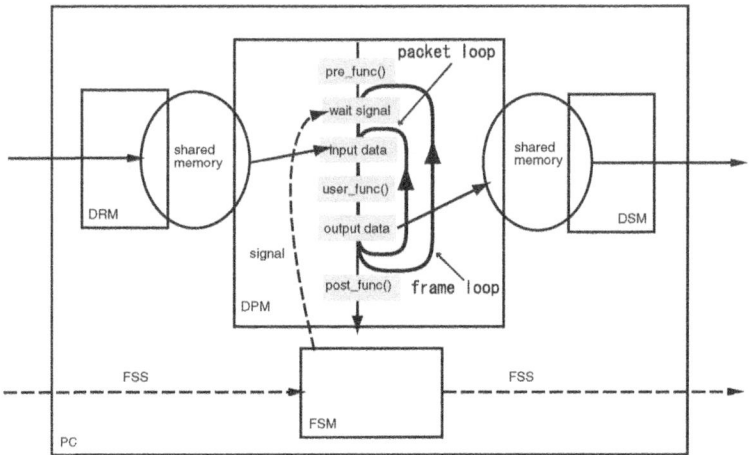

Fig. 5. Modules and functions in RPV-II

Data Sending Module(DSM). This module is to send data to other PCs via messages, and has buffers for queuing data. When processed data arrives from its preceding DPM, it sends the data to the succeeding PCs.

Frame Synchronization Module(FSM). To realize synchronization among PCs, FSS is introduced, which is a time quantum signal of 1/30 second cycle. FSS, which originates in an image capturing component, is transfered via Myrinet network from upper PCs to lower PCs of the data flow. FSM sends FSSs to the succeeding FSM, and/or receives FSSs from the preceding FSM. FSM also sends start signals to activate the DPM in the PC. This framework makes executions of different DPMs synchronize with one another.

3   Stream Data Transfer on RPV-II

RPV has been designed to achieve quite high throughput of real-time image processing. However, its biggest problem is the long latency when we employ pipelined structures to acquire higher throughput. This is because, for real-time data transfer in RPV, we have developed synchronization mechanism based on the timing of image frame in an video sequence. For each pipeline step, one frame period τ, which is 33msec in case of NTSC-based camera signal, is allocated to process one image frame and one frame period is allocated to transfer one image frame to the succeeding PC (see Fig. 6 (a)). Therefore, when we use N PCs arranged in a pipeline structure, the latency becomes $2N\tau$ (τ is a frame period and is 33msec for NTSC-based camera signal). For example, 3 stage pipeline causes about 0.2 sec. Thus, the latency problem becomes a serious problem when we apply the system to interactive applications. However, in general it is not easy to solve the tradeoff between high throughput and low latency.

To solve this problem, i.e., to make the latency smaller keeping high through-put, we have introduced stream data transfer, or fine grained data transfer, to the next version of RPV, RPV-II. One frame data is divided into small packets consisting of pixels, lines, voxels, or other image features, and data processing and transfer are applied to each packet. When each PC finishes processing a packet, it immediately starts sending it to the succeeding PC and then starts processing the next packet. Therefore, when the packet arrives at the succeed-ing PC, the processing of the packet can be started immediately. Fig. 5 shows the processing procedure implemented in RPV-II. The key difference is that, in RPV-II, function `user_func` is executed for every packet. This mechanism can greatly reduce the latency (see Fig. 6 (b)). Of course, the tradeoff between throughput and latency sill remains. When the size of the packet becomes too small, the communication overhead exhibits apparently. Therefore, we have to decide the adequate size of the packet, with which reduction of the throughput is small.

Compared with the previous framework, stream data transfer mechanism has the following features.

- Keeping high throughput, in general, the latency can be drastically reduced, i.e., $1/M$. It is $2N\tau/M$, instead of $2N\tau$, where M is the number of packets in one frame period.[2]
- In the succeeding PC, the packets should be processed in the order that the packets are received. When the data should be reordered or reorganized for processing, the latency for the reorganization is added.

4   Real-Time Volume Reconstruction

For evaluation of effectiveness of stream data transfer on RPV-II, we have devel-oped a real-time volume reconstruction system on our PC-cluster. The volume of an object is reconstructed via visual cone intersection using multi-perspective view of the object. A visual cone is defined as a cone whose vertex is the view point and whose cross section coincide with the silhouette of the object (see Fig. 7). Since the object is included in the visual cone, intersecting visual cones constructed from multiple view points makes the volumetric data of the object.

4.1   System Configuration

This method consists of four stages as follows (see Fig. 8).

1. **Extraction of object silhouette (EOS)**
   Background subtraction is employed to extract the silhouette of the object in each view. We use a simple method, i.e., thresholding of difference between pixel values of a captured image and those of a pre-acquired background image.

---
[2] Here, we assume that data transfer time is equal to data processing time.

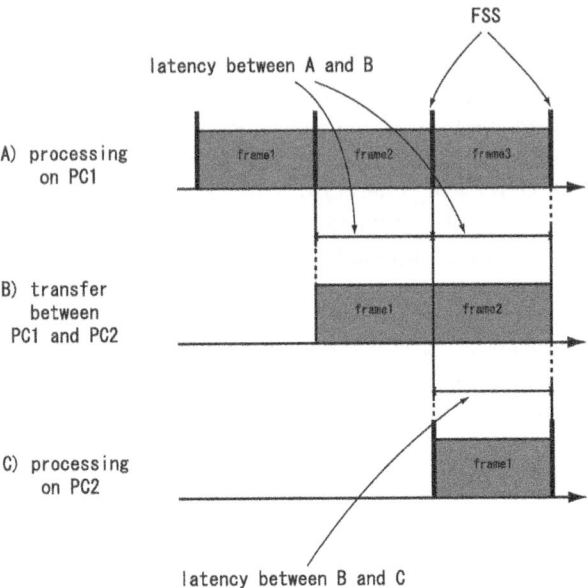

(a) Synchronous (Frame-based) Data Transfer

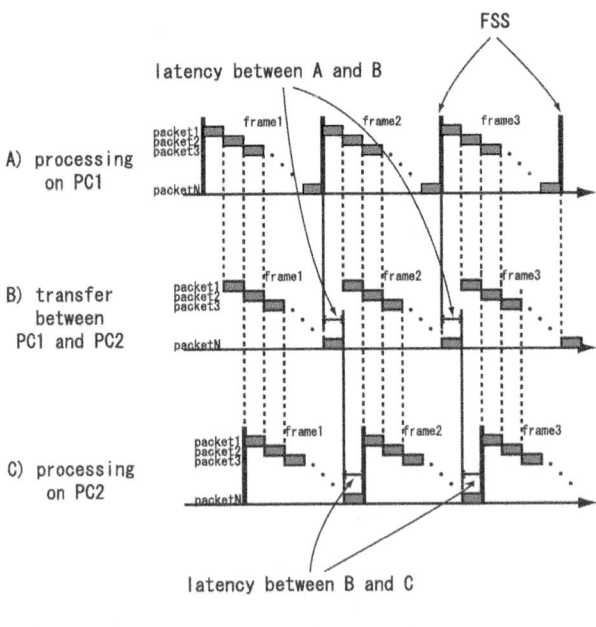

(b) Stream Data Transfer

Fig. 6. Comparison of data transfer mechanism

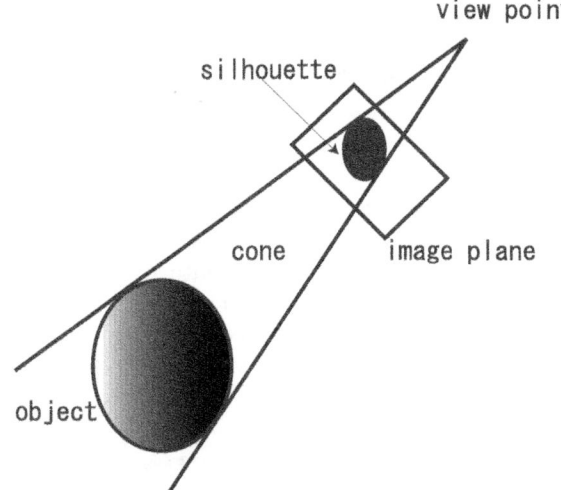

Fig. 7. Visual Cone

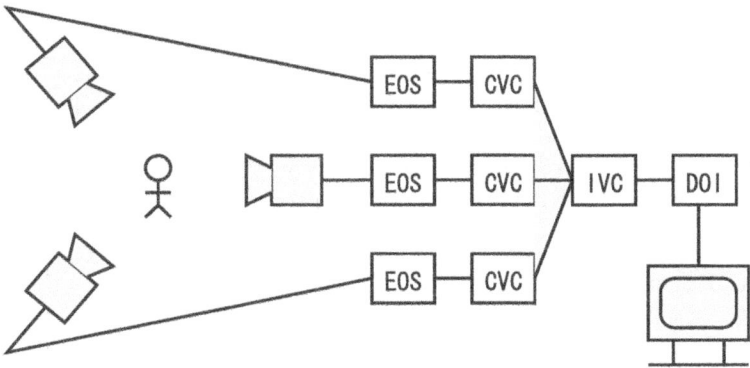

Fig. 8. System Configuration

Essentially a silhouette image can be calculated and sent to the succeeding PC in pixel-wise order, and therefore its latency should be τ/M_p, where M_p is the number of packets of pixels in one frame image. However, in this system, an image captured by a camera is received frame by frame, not pixel by pixel, and the silhouette calculation can not be started after one complete image frame has been received. This inconsistency makes an additional latency τ.[3] As a result, the latency caused in this stage becomes $\tau + \tau/M_p$.

2. **Calculation of visual cone (CVC)**

A visual cone represented in terms of voxels is constructed from the object silhouette of each view point. For each voxel, the system examines whether

---

[3] This can be easily reduced by modifying the camera interface with which image data can be acquired line by line.

a pixel corresponding to a voxel is included in the object silhouette or not[4]. This process consists of two subprocesses, voxel projection to a silhouette image and inclusion test on it. The voxel projection can be optimized by using a pre-computed lookup table representing correspondence between voxels and pixels. Using this lookup table improves the speed of the visual cone calculation drastically.

A silhouette image is received in a pixel-wise order, but visual cone construction is executed in a voxel-wise order. Because of this inconsistency the latency between data receiving and data processing becomes τ. On the other hand, since voxel space representing visual cone is generated and sent in a voxel-wise order and there is no inconsistency, the latency between data processing and data sending is τ/M_v, where M_v is the number of packets of voxels in one voxel space. Total latency at this stage becomes $\tau + \tau/M_v$

3. **Intersection of visual cones (IVC)**
   Visual cones from multiple view points are gathered and intersected to generate a volumetric data of the object represented in terms of voxels. Since receiving a voxel space, intersecting all voxel spaces and sending a generated voxel space are executed in a voxel-wise order, both the latency between data receiving and data processing and the one between data processing and data sending are τ/M_v.

4. **Display of object image (DOI)**
   Reconstructed volumetric data is projected to an image plane to generate an object image and the image is displayed on a screen.
   Since receiving a voxel space and projecting it to an image plane is executed in a voxel-wise order, the latency between receiving and processing is τ/M_v.

The total latency becomes $\tau/M_p + 4\tau/M_v + 2\tau \simeq 2\tau$ (suppose M_p and M_v is large enough). It is much reduced compared with the case of frame-based data transfer where the total latency becomes 7τ. Again, the decline of the throughput is very little.

4.2   Performance Evaluation

First, Table 1 shows throughput, the number of frames which the volume reconstruction system process in one second. The amount of its computation is proportional to the number of voxels. In case that the number of packets is small, or the size of the packet is large, the throughput is in inverse proportion to the number of voxels, which is an ideal characteristic. However, in case that the number of packets is large, or the size of the packet is small, the throughput is not in inverse proportion to the number of voxels. This is because the overhead of data transfer is getting large. Since the maximum frame rate of our cameras 30 fps, the maximum throughput of the system becomes 30 fps.

Second, Table 2 shows latency. Throughput in this experiment is lower than that in previous one because of probing overhead. The results are nearly equal

---

[4] Though multiple pixels are usually corresponding to one voxel, only one pixel is selected for simplification and speed up.

Table 1. Throughput(fps)

# voxels	M_v (M_p is fixed on 10)			
	125	1000	2500	5000
$40 \times 40 \times 40 = 64000$	30.00	30.00	30.00	30.00
$80 \times 80 \times 80 = 512000$	28.57	25.00	11.11	6.67
$100 \times 100 \times 100 = 1000000$	14.27	12.46	10.99	5.71

Table 2. Latency(msec)

stage	M_v (M_p is fixed on 10)			
	125	1000	2500	5000
EOS	10.154	11.163	11.140	11.070
EOS–CVC	0.309	0.337	0.350	0.329
CVC	156.260	182.816	201.501	384.612
CVC–IVC	9.904	0.143	1.644	38.518
IVC	0.187	0.073	1.107	23.135
IVC–DOI	0.315	0.155	0.501	42.939
DOI	6.407	6.326	6.390	7.195
Total(L)	183.536	201.013	222.696	507.793
Frame rate($1/\tau$)	12.5	11.1	10.0	4
Frame period(τ)	80.000	90.000	100.000	250.000
L/τ(experimental)	2.294	2.233	2.227	2.031
L/τ(designed)	2.132	2.104	2.102	2.101

to the designed values, which shows that the system works correctly. Assuming that the experimental values (L/τ) are effective in case of no probes, the latency L may be equal to $1000/14.27 \times 2.294 = 160.8$ msec.

These experiments are preliminary ones and, because of the limitation of physical space and camera calibration, we have used three cameras. According to the experiments, for real-time volume reconstruction, the number of voxels should be around $100 \times 100 \times 100$. In this case, the throughput is about 14.27 fps and the latency is 184 msec with an optimal packet size. In other words, the number of packets in one frame is 125, or the size of the packet is 8000 bytes. The low latency exhibits the effectiveness of our method.

Fig. 9 shows input image sequences of three views and Fig. 10 shows reconstructed volumetric representation. Since we have only three cameras in this experiment, the reconstructed 3D shape is not very accurate. We are making large scaled experiments with more cameras, which can produce more precise 3D shape.

(a) Viewpoint 1

(b) Viewpoint 2

(c) Viewpoint 3

Fig. 9. Input Images

vp   frame a   frame b

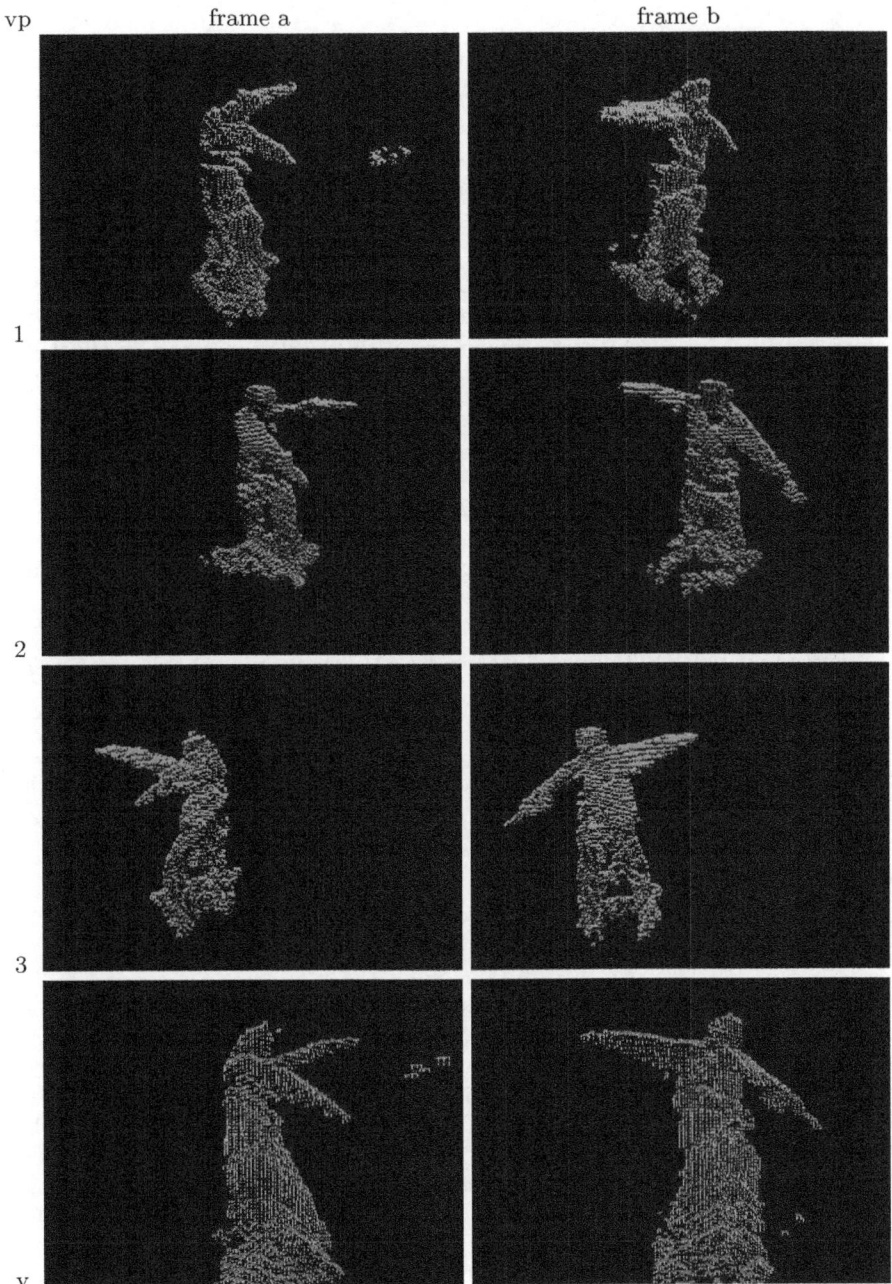

Fig. 10. Output Images: The first column is viewpoint. Viewpoint v means a virtual viewpoint. The second and the third columns are output images on different frames

5 Conclusion

In this paper, we have presented a stream-based real-time parallel vision system on PC-cluster and its application to a real-time volume reconstruction system. The motivation of this research is to develop a large-scaled real-time computer vision system with high performance, i.e., high throughput and low latency. The low latency is quite important especially for interactive application such as human interface systems. The key idea is that real-time data processing and transfer is established not on image frames but on finer grained data packets consisting of pixels, lines, voxels, or other image features. This enables the systems to have much less latency with little decrease of throughput, compared with ordinary frame-based real-time image processing and transfer. The effectiveness of our idea has been also shown by a realistic application of real-time volume reconstruction from multiple views. The throughput of the experimental system is about 14 fps for a $100 \times 100 \times 100$ voxel space, and the latency is only about 160 msec, which can be improved by further refinement.

The future works remaining are as follows.

– Evaluation with larger scaled applications: we are constructing a 20 camera systems to acquire more precise volumetric representation.
– System construction with cheaper cost: we are developing a PC-cluster whose network is IEEE1394 bus, not Myrinet[11]. Evaluation of this system should be done, too.

Acknowledgment. This work has been supported by R&D activities in the info-communication area, Telecommunication Advancement Organization (TAO) of Japan(No.10080).

References

1. T. Kanade, R. T. Collins, A. J. Lipton, P. Burt, and L. Wixson, "Cooperative multi-sensor video surveillance," in Proc. of Image Understanding Workshop, pp.3–10, 1997.
2. T. Matsuyama, "Cooperative Distributed Vision – Integration of Visual Perception, Action, and Communication –," in Proc. of Image Understanding Workshop, pp.1–39, 1998.
3. D. Arita, Y. Hamada, and R. Taniguchi, "A Real-time Distributed Video Image Processing System on PC-cluster," in Proc. of Int. Conf. of the Austrian Center for Parallel Computation(ACPC), pp.296–305, 1999.
4. D. Arita, S. Yonemoto, and R. Taniguchi, "Real-time Computer Vision on PC-cluster and Its Application to Real-time Motion Capture," in Proc. of IEEE Workshop on Computer Architectures for Machine Perception, pp.205–214, 2000.
5. T. Kanade, H. Saito, and S. Vedula, "The 3D room: Digitizing time-varying 3D events by synchronized multiple video streams," in Technical Report, CMU-RI-TR-98-34, Carnegie Mellon University, Dec. 1998.

6. T. Wada, X. Wu, S. Tokai, and T. Matsuyama, "Homography Based Parallel Volume Intersection: Toward Real-time Volume Reconstruction Using Active Cameras," in Proc. of IEEE Workshop on Computer Architectures for Machine Perception, pp.331–339, 2000.

7. E. Borovikov, and L. Davis, "A Distributed System for Real-time Volume Reconstruction," in Proc. of IEEE Workshop on Computer Architectures for Machine Perception, pp.183–189, 2000.

8. W. N. Martin and J. K. Aggarwal, "Volumetric Description of Objects from Multiple Views," in IEEE Trans. PAMI, Vol.5, No.2, pp.150–158, 1987.

9. 1394 Trade Association, in 1394-based Digital Camera Specification Version 1.20.

10. H. Tezuka, A. Hori, Y. Ishikawa, and M. Sato, "PM: an operating system coordinated high performance communication library," High-Performance Computing and Networking, P. Sloot and B. Hertzberger, in Springer-Verlag, pp.708–717, 1997.

11. H. Yoshimoto, D. Arita and R. Taniguchi, "Real-Time Image Processing on IEEE1394-based PC Cluster," in CD-ROM Proc. of International Parallel & Distributed Processing Symposium, 2001.

A Real-Time Vision Module for Interactive Perceptual Agents

Bruce A. Maxwell, Nathaniel Fairfield, Nikolas Johnson, Pukar Malla,
Paul Dickson, and Suor Kim

Swarthmore College
500 College Ave.
Swarthmore, PA 19081
maxwell@swarthmore.edu

Abstract. Interactive robotics demands real-time visual information about the environment. Real time vision processing, however, places a heavy load on the robot's limited resources, and must accommodate other processes such as speech recognition, animated face displays, communication with other robots, navigation and control. For our entries in the 2000 American Association for Artificial Intelligence robot contest, we developed a vision module capable of providing real-time information about ten or more operators while maintaining at least a 20Hz frame rate and leaving sufficient processor time for the robot's other capabilities. The vision module uses a probabilistic scheduling algorithm to ensure both timely information flow and a fast frame capture. The vision module makes its information available to other modules in the robot architecture through a shared memory structure. The information provided by the vision module includes the operator information along with a confidence measure and a time stamp. Because of this design, our robots are able to react in a timely manner to a wide variety of visual events.

1 Introduction

This year Swarthmore College entered robots in two events--Hors d'Oeuvres Anyone? [HA] and Urban Search and Rescue [USR]--at the American Association for Artificial Intelligence [AAAI] robot competition. The Hors d'Oeuvres Anyone? event requires the robot(s) to serve food to the conference attendees at the main conference reception with over 500 people in attendance. The robots are evaluated based upon their ability to cover the room, manipulate food, and interact with the people they are serving. The robot-human interaction is weighted most heavily of the three.

The USR event requires the robot(s) to explore a test arena designed by the National Institute of Standards and Technology [NIST]. The test arena simulates the inside of a building after some type of disaster situation and contains three sections of increasing difficulty. The simplest level is navigable by a wheeled mobile robot, the other two sections require a tracked or 4-wheel drive robot. Robots are evaluated on their ability to explore the arena, detect humans--simulated by motion, heat, and skin-colored mannequins--and exit the area within the allotted time (25 minutes).

B. Schiele and G. Sagerer (Eds.): ICVS 2001, LNCS 2095, pp. 190–200, 2001.

Both events benefit greatly from the use of visual input. The HA event, in particular, requires the robot to sense and react to people and various related features, such as colored conference badges in a timely and appropriate manner. The more information the visual sensing can provide, the more interactive and responsive the robot can be to the people it is serving. In the USR event, visual sensing gives the robots one method of detecting and labeling important features in the environment. In some cases it is the only sensing modality able to reliably detect the simulated people.

Rather than have custom vision processing and robot architectures for each event/platform, we used a single software architecture for all of our intelligent agents, with different controlling modules for the different events. Both the general architecture and the vision module were shared between three different platforms--a Nomad Super Scout II mobile robot, a Magellan Pro mobile robot, and a workstation that acted as the Maitre'd for the HA event. All three participated in the HA event; the Magellan Pro worked by itself in the USR event.

The robots work under significant processing constraints. The Nomad uses a 266MHz Pentium MMX processor, and the Magellan uses a 350MHz Pentium II. For the HA task, the Nomad's capabilities include speech recognition, speech synthesis, visual processing, a sliding arm controller, navigation, control, facial animation, and inter-robot communication. The Magellan possesses similar capabilities but does not attempt speech recognition or possess a moving arm. The workstation is better equipped with dual 400MHz Pentium II's, but gets a correspondingly heavier load with real-time facial animation and synchronization of the lips with speech.

Because of the wide array of capabilities demanding processor time, the vision module has to avoid monopolizing the processor while still capturing video in real-time and providing timely information. The combination of our overall architecture and the vision module achieves this goal. In part because of this design, our robots won both events as well as the Ben Wegbrait award for the integration of AI technologies at the 2000 AAAI robot contest. The remainder of this paper gives a brief overview of the overall architecture and a detailed description of the vision module.

2   REAPER: An Intelligent Agent Architecture

The overall system architecture--hereafter referred to as REAPER [REflexive Architecture for PErceptual Robotics]--is based on a set of modules. The purpose of each module is to handle one specific task, which include: sensing, reflexes, control, communication, and debugging. The fundamental concept behind REAPER is that the central control module--whether it is a state machine or other mechanism--does not want a flood of sensory data. Nor does it want to have to make low-level decisions like how fast to turn each wheel. At the same time it needs real-time updates of symbolic information indicating what the world around it is doing. The sensor and reflex modules gather and filter information, handling all of the preprocessing and generating intermediate actions required to achieve high-level commands or goals. This is similar to the way our brain seems to deal with a request to pick up an object. While we consciously think about picking up the object, our reflexes deal with actually moving our hand to the proper location and grasping it. Only then does our conscious mind take control to decide what to do next. This approach has some biological justification [1].

Two sensing modules, vision and speech, handle all vision and speech-based inter-action. Their main task is to act as filters between the sensory data and the symbolic information required by the rest of the system. Two reflex modules, navigation and face, handle the motion and appearance of the robot. Central control of the robot is handled through a state module, and communication between robots is handled through its own module. Finally, the architecture has two modules for debugging pur-poses. One, the monitor, shows text fields that represent all of the information available to the system. The other, the visual monitor, is designed to show graphically the information being provided by the vision module.

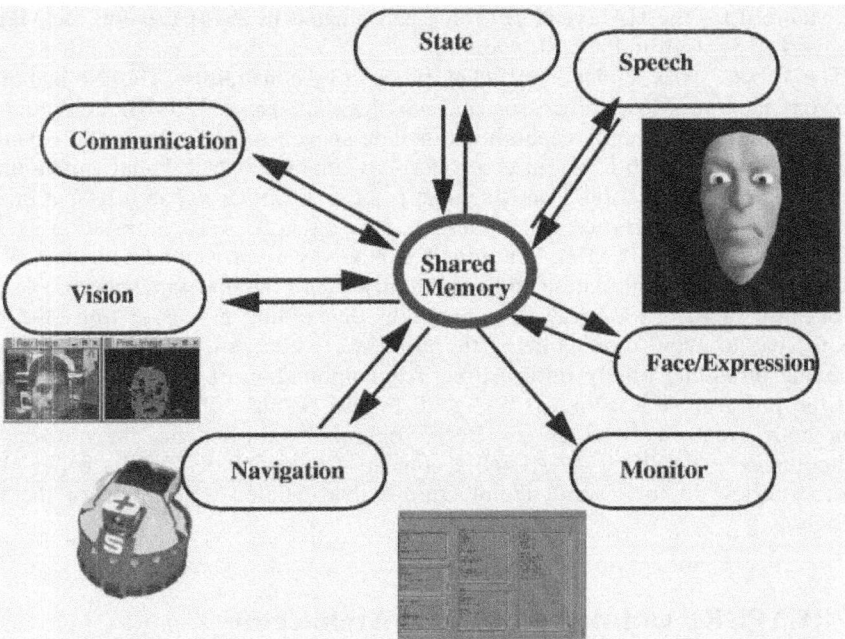

Fig. 1 Logical diagram of the REAPER Architecture. Each module takes inputs from and writes its outputs to the shared memory. The State module is the central controlling unit.

The modules in the architecture communicate through a shared memory structure, which provides a computationally efficient means of sharing information. They use a common framework for communicating and programming, including a handshaking protocol to ensure that information and commands are passed and read correctly. Communication between robots occurs through sockets between the agents' communication modules over a wireless ethernet system.

The REAPER design methodology follows a number of the lessons learned about robot architectures over the past two decades. In particular, it follows the recommendations of Bryson that an autonomous agent architecture needs:

- a modular structure,
- a means to control action and perception sequences for complex tasks, and
- a mechanism for reacting quickly to changes in the environment [4].

REAPER is related to behavior-based systems, such as those proposed by Brooks, in that it distributes low-level interpretation and control of sensors and actuators to modules [3]. REAPER is not a pure behavior-based system, however, because it is designed to facilitate the mixing of symbolic and subsymbolic, reactive strategies. Thus, REAPER is also related to hierarchical architectures, which facilitate the development of action and perception sequences for complex tasks.

The real strength of the system, however, is REAPER's modular design which facilitates cross-platform and multi-platform development and simplifies debugging and testing of the individual modules. This is particularly true in the case of the vision module, which we extensively tested on its own before putting it on the robot platform.

At the most fundamental level, the REAPER approach evolved because it enables the agent to gather information at a tremendous rate from a large number of sensors and present that information in a useful, symbolic form to the controlling module. This overall architecture for a perceptive agent is the framework within which we developed the real-time vision module. Our goals in designing the vision module were to avoid dominating the robot's processor, provide easy access to a wide variety of information about the world, and maintain as fast a frame rate as possible to avoid time lags between sensing and action. The remainder of the paper describes how we balanced these goals within an integrated robot system.

3   Vision Module

From the command module's point of view, the vision module is an information provider. The command modules specifies a general action mode and then specifies the operators from which it wants information. The vision module then begins processing images and continually updates information associated with each active operator.

The vision module itself begins with an initialization routine that sets up its shared memory and alerts the other modules it is active. It then enters an event loop--initially in an idle state. Each time through the event loop, the module tests if the controller has issued it a new command, either a new mode or a new set of operators to apply. If so, the transition to executing that command takes place. Otherwise, the module continues executing the current mode and operator set. The module continues to process and update sensory information until told to do something else. The goal of the vision module is to maintain 30Hz, or real-time visual processing, for any given operator set.

3.1   Modes and Operator Scheduling

The vision module includes a rich set of operators for converting images into symbolic information. The three general classes of operators are: object detection, motion detection, and object characteristic analysis. Each command to the vision module indicates a general mode and the set of operators that should be turned on. Other modules within the REAPER architecture can then scan the relevant output fields of the vision module for positive detections, motion, or object characteristics. Each output field includes information about where an object was detected in the image and when it was detected as determined by a time stamp. Based on the time stamp and the operator information, other modules can decide what information requires a response.

The set of operators provided by the vision module include:

- Person detection based on skin color and gradients
- Moving area detection across multiple frames
- Color blob detection, focused on colored conference badge detection
- P-similar pattern detection
- Red, white, and green flag detection
- Palm detection
- Orange arrow detection
- Green ring detection
- Shirt color analysis (dependent upon detecting a person)
- Person identification (dependent upon detecting a person)
- Calculation of how much food was on the robot's tray (using the tray camera)
- Take a panoramic image (on the Magellan robot only)

Which operators are available depends on the mode the controller selects. The major modes are: IDLE, LOOK, TRAY, and PANO. The LOOK mode is the primary mode of operation and permits all but the last two operators to be active. The TRAY mode activates the second camera input and analyzes how much of the robot's serving tray is filled. The PANO mode works with a pan-tilt-zoom camera to generate a 180° panoramic image that concatenates eight frames together while simultaneously applying the motion and person detection operators.

While in the LOOK mode, there is clearly no way to maintain a high frame rate and execute all of the operators on each image. To solve this problem the vision module uses a probabilistic scheduling algorithm that applies at most two operators to each frame. This solution works because the robot usually doesn't usually need to know that there is a pink blob in view--or whatever other object--30 times per second. Frame rate is usually a lot faster than the robot can react to things since reactions often involve physical actions or speaking. Likewise, most of the other operators do not benefit from continuous application in most human-robot interactions.

The scheduling algorithm is based on the premise that running two operators per frame will not reduce the frame rate. This puts an upper bound on operator complexity, although we can get around the limitation somewhat by pipelining the process. In the standard LOOK mode, the module randomly selects two of the active operators based on a programmer-defined probability distribution. To create the probability distribution, each process gets a weight associated with it, with processes requiring higher frame rates receiving higher weights. Most of the vision operators have small, relatively equal weights. Once selected, the module executes the two operators and updates their information. On average, each operator is executed according to the probability distribution defined by the manually supplied weights.

Since not all operators are applied on each frame, there can be a time lag between operator applications. To communicate the freshness of data to other modules, the vision module supplies a time stamp with each piece of information. The information persists until the next application of the operator, and the controller can decide based on the time stamp whether it is recent enough to warrant a response.

A secondary mode within the LOOK mode permits tracking--or consistent application of an operator--using one operator in addition to looking for other objects. To
engage tracking, the controller specifies one tracking operator and the regular list of
active operators. The vision module scheduler puts the tracking operator in one of the
execution slots and randomly selects the other operator from the active list. This guarantees the vision module will look for the object being tracked every frame, providing
the fastest update rate possible. In the tracking mode the navigation module can look
directly at the vision module output and adjust its control of the robot accordingly.
Mario, the Magellan Pro robot, could use this ability to follow pink badges.

The scheduling algorithm and overall structure were a successful way to manage
our robot vision system. Even with all of the robot modules running, the vision
module was able to maintain a frame rate of at least 20Hz during the competition.
Information updates occurred often enough that the robots could attend to multiple
aspects of their environment with real-time reactions.

To help us debug and monitor the vision module we developed a vision monitor
module that watches the vision module output and graphically displays current information using color and bounding boxes. This enables us to determine how well the
different operators are working.

A brief description of each operator follows. The new capabilities we developed
for the 2000 competition included a new face detector, a short-term person identifier,
a shirt-color identifier, a vertical Italian flag detector, and the ability to estimate how
much food was left on the robot's tray. For more complete descriptions of the other
capabilities, see [11] and [12].

3.2 Motion-Based Person Detection

The motion detection operator is the most difficult operator to integrate within this
framework because it requires multiple frames--at least three for robust processing--
and requires a significant amount of processing for each frame. Our algorithm uses
Sobel gradient operators to calculate edge images, and then subtracts adjacent (in
time) edge images to locate edges that moved. It then locates the bounding box of
areas of motion that exceed a certain threshold. We have found this algorithm to be
quite successful at locating people in the hors d'oeuvres event [11][11][12].

To avoid breaking the overall structure of the vision module, we pipeline the algorithm across multiple event loops. The motion algorithm takes five event loops to
complete--with the first three capturing images and calculating the Sobel results. To
ensure the motion algorithm is called frequently enough, it has a high weight in the
probability distribution. On average, the motion algorithm completes 5-6 times per
second and the overall vision module maintains a frame rate of at least 20Hz. When
the motion operator is active, it is usually selected as one of the operators.

3.3 Skin-Based Person Detection and Identification

We used two independent techniques, motion and face detection, to detect people.
Our motion detector is described above, but we took a somewhat novel approach to
face detection that resulted in a robust technique in the HA domain.

The basis of our face detection system is skin-color blob detection. The key to skin
detection is effective training (or good color constancy, which is hard), since lighting

conditions strongly affect colors. We developed a fast, interactive training program, shown in Figure 2(c), that gives the user direct feedback about how well the system is going to perform under existing conditions. The output of the training algorithm is an rg fuzzy histogram, where r and g are defined as in (1).

$$r = \frac{R}{R + G + B} \qquad g = \frac{G}{R + G + B}. \tag{1}$$

A fuzzy histogram is a histogram with entries in the range [0, 1] that indicate membership in the colors of interest. To create a fuzzy histogram we generate a standard histogram and divide each individual bucket by the maximum bucket value [18].

We use fuzzy histograms to convert standard images into binary images that contain only pixels whose colors have high fuzzy membership values. For skin-color blob detection we train the fuzzy histogram on skin-color regions of several training images and then keep only pixels with membership values above a specified threshold. To get blobs we run a 2-pass segmentation algorithm on the binary image and keep only regions larger than a certain size [16].

The result of the blob detection is a set of regions that contain skin-color. In previous competitions we ran into trouble using just blob detection because the walls of the HA competition areas in 1998 and 1999 were flesh-tones. While this was not the case in 2000, there were other sources of skin-color besides people in the environment.

Our solution for distinguishing between background flesh-tones and true faces is to multiply the gradient magnitude of the image with the skin-color probability image prior to segmentation. The gradient magnitude image, however, is pre-filtered to remove high gradient values (i.e. strong edges). The result is a gradient image where mild gradients are non-zero and all other pixels are zero or close to it. Faces are not flat and contain mild gradients across most of their surface. However, they do not tend to contain strong edges. Thus, including the mid-range gradient values effectively eliminates walls--which are flat and tend to be featureless--but leaves faces. We found the combination to be robust and it reduced our false positive rate to near zero for the event while still reliably locating people.

3.4 Short-Term Person Identification

In the 1999 competition our robot, Alfred, tried to remember people based on texture and color histograms from a fixed portion of the image. Unfortunately, this relied on the person standing directly in front of the camera, which was rarely the case. This year we integrated the person identification with face detection and shirt color identification, described below. We did not store a permanent database of persons, but instead used a 100 entry buffer to recall people for a short time period. The purpose, therefore, of the person identification was to discover if a particular person was standing in front of the robot/agent for an extended period of time.

After a successful face detection the memory algorithm extracts a bounding box around the person's body based on the location of their face, as shown in Figure 2(a). It then extracts a short feature vector from that box to represent that person's identity. The feature vector is the top five buckets in an rg histogram--as defined in (1)--the top five buckets in an IB (Intensity, Blue) histogram, the average edge strength as determined by X and Y Sobel operators, the number of strong edge pixels, and the number of significant colors in the rg histogram. These 12 numbers provide a nice key with which we can compare people's appearance.

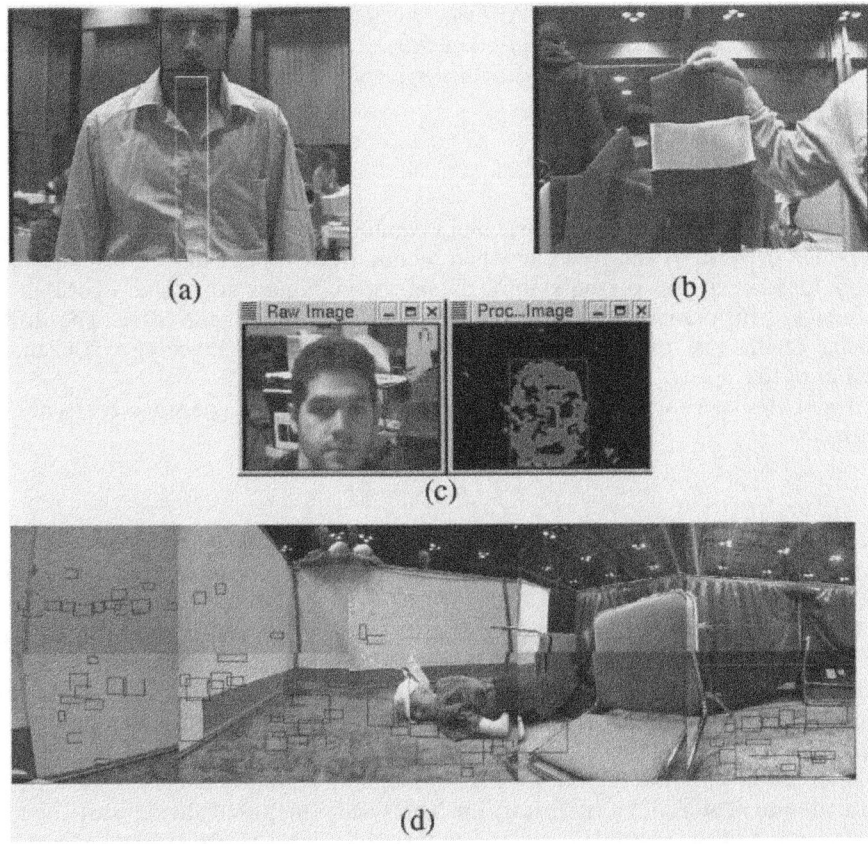

Fig. 2 Examples of the vision module in action. A) Successful face detection and the corresponding box used for shirt color and person identification. B) Successful flag detection. C) Training system for face detection system. D) Panoramic image from the USR contest: the green and blue boxes indicate possible motion and skin color respectively. Note that the skin-color on the mannequin's arm--on which we trained--was grey, which is why the walls and floor get highlighted.

To compare two keys, we use standard histogram intersection with the top five buckets in the rg and IB histograms, and then percentage difference in the average edge strength, number of strong edge pixels, and number of significant colors. Appropriate normalization provides a single number which indicates the degree of match.

Once the system extracts a key, it compares the key to all other keys recently seen. The system stores the 100 most recent unique keys. If it finds a probable match, then it will send the matching ID to an output filter. If it finds no match, it will add the key to the data base and then call the output filter with the new ID value. The output filter simply returns the most common key identified in the past 10 calls. However, if no single key has at least three matches in the past 10, it returns a null result (no match).

The output filter guarantees that, even in the presence of a moving person and schizo-phrenic face detection results (jumping between people), if a person is standing in front of the camera for an extended period of time their key will register consistently.

We used this capability with Alfredo, the maitre'd. If a person was standing in front of Alfredo for a minimum period of time, it would comment that they should go do something else. Clearly there are other applications, but we did not pursue them in the competition setting.

3.5 Shirt Color Identification

Like the memory operator, the shirt color operator waits for a successful person detec-tion (face or motion) and then extracts a section of the image that corresponds to the likely location of the person's shirt, as shown in Figure 2(a). The algorithm then generates a histogram of this region and selects the dominant color. The difficult aspects of this task are selecting the histogram space, and attaching color labels to regions of that space.

Based on experimentation, we selected the rgI histogram space to represent color, where

$$I = \frac{1}{3}(R + G + B) \qquad (2)$$

I is intensity, and r and g are normalized color as defined by (1). (R, G, B) are the raw pixels values returned by the camera. We used 20 buckets in each of r and g, and 4 buckets in I.

Because different camera settings and different lighting affect where a color sits in the rgI space, we calibrate the system using a MacBeth™ color chart prior to each sit-uation in which the robot interacts--i.e. once prior to the competition. Using a picture of the color chart under the appropriate illumination we identify the centroid in the rgI space for each of the 24 colors on the chart.

After identifying the region of interest--the shirt region--the system identifies the most common color in the rgI histogram. The system then finds the closest color cen-troid in a Euclidean sense and returns its text color label as the output. Alfredo cor-rectly identified numerous shirts during the competition, including Dr. Maxwell's mother, who was wearing a purple shirt. It made the computer appear cognizant of its surroundings in an engaging manner and provided it with something intelligent to talk about.

3.6 Food Tray Analysis

The food tray analysis is a simple, but effective algorithm. We have two cameras on the robot connected to an Osprey 100 framegrabber card which has multiple composite video inputs that are software selectable. Upon entering the TRAY mode, the vision module switches to analyzing the input from a small greyscale camera mounted on top of the food tray looking across it. During the competition we used a white napkin to cover the tray and served dark brown or black cookies.

The tray analysis algorithm works on the middle 1/2 of the image, in which the tray dominates the scene. The operator counts the number of dark pixels and calculates the percentage of the visible tray that is full. Using pre-calculated minimum and maxi-mum values, the operator sets a flag that specifies FULL, EMPTY, or a percentage in between. This is a good proxy for how many cookies remain on the tray. Since the small camera includes an auto-gain feature, this method works even when someone blocks the direct lighting by leaning over the tray or standing so it is in shadow. This feature worked well and enabled the robot to respond to how much food was left on its tray by heading towards its food refill station in an appropriate manner.

3.7 Vertical Italian Flag (Red-White-Green) Detection

Finally, we gave the robots for the hors d'oeuvres event the ability to strike up conversations with one another. To make this capability realistic it should only happen when the robots can "see" one another, which means they must be able to visually recognize each other. Since our theme was an Italian restaurant, we used the italian flag colors--red, white, and green--as our identifying feature. Santino had a flag draped vertically from his serving tray, and Mario had one placed on an antenna about 4 feet above the ground. To differentiate the two mobile robots we reversed the order of the colors for Mario and Santino from top to bottom.

The technique we use for flag recognition is based on traversing columns in the image with a state machine that tracks the order and color of the pixels. The state machine only outputs a positive identification if it finds a vertical series of red, white, and green pixels (or in reversed order). Each color has to be mostly continuous and contain at least a specified number of pixels. The state machine allows a certain number of invalid (not red, white, or green) pixels as it traverses the colors. However, too many invalid pixels invalidates that particular recognition and resets the state machine. This method, since it is based on single columns, is robust and easy to execute in real time. The recognition system worked well both in test runs and in the competition.

4 Summary

The products of our experience that we will continue, and are continuing to use are the overall REAPER architecture, the navigation modules, the face module, and the vision module. All of these provide us with generic scaffolding on top of which we are building other capabilities and systems. All of them are extendable and easily integrated with one another. We also now have excellent debugging tools that permit us to track all of the information and messages that pass between modules during execution. For us, this infrastructure is the real outcome of this project.

In particular, we have continued to use and develop the vision module for research purposes. It is straightforward to add capabilities to the module and use it for a variety of tasks. The probabilistic scheduling algorithm and wide variety of capabilities make it ideal for a mobile robot that is processor limited but must continuously monitor and react to multiple aspects of its environment.

As shown by the motion operator, the vision module is not limited to simple operations. We can use more complex operators by pipelining the processing across multiple event loops. Ultimately we are limited by the processing power of the robot, but clearly operators of moderate complexity are feasible within the real-time vision module approach.

Finally, the tracking capability gives the module the ability to focus on one operator and provide fast updates while still actively monitoring the environment. The combination of fast image capture, the application of operators in a probabilistic manner, pipelining of complex operations, and the ability to track, avoids bogging down our robot's processor and permits it to respond appropriately to the visual world.

References

[1]   E. Bizzi, S. Giszter, E. Loeb, F.A. Mussa-Ivaldi, and P. Saltiel, "Modular organization of motor behavior in the frog's spinal cord", *Trends in Neuroscience*, 18:442-446.

[2]   R. P. Bonasso, R. J. Firby, E. Gat, D. Kortenkamp, D. P. Miller, and M. G. Slack, "Experiments with an architecture for intelligent, reactive agents", *J. of Experimental & Theoretical Artificial Intelligence*, 9(2/3):237-256, 1997.

[3]   R. A. Brooks, "A robust layered control system for a mobile robot", *IEEE J. of Robotics and Automation*, vol. 2, no. 1, 1986.

[4]   J. Bryson, "Cross-Paradigm Analysis of Autonomous Agent Architecture", *J. of Experimental and Theoretical Artificial Intelligence*, vol. 12, no. 2, pp 165-190, 2000.

[5]   D. R. Forsey and R. H. Bartels, "Hierarchical B-spline refinement", in *Computer Graphics (SIGGRAPH '88)*, 22(4):205-212, August, 1988.

[6]   E. Gat, *Reliable Goal-Directed Reactive Control of Autonomous Mobile Robots*, Ph.D. thesis, Virginia Polytechnic Institute and State University, 1991.

[7]   *IBM ViaVoice™ Outloud API Reference Version 5.0*, November 1999.

[8]   E. C. Ifeachor and B. W. Jervis, *Digital Signal Processing. A Practical Approach*, Addison Wesley Publishing Company, 1995.

[9]   D. Kortenkamp, R. P. Bonasso, and R. Murphy (ed.), *Artificial Intelligence and Mobile Robots*, AAAI Press/MIT Press, Cambridge, 1998.

[10]   B. A. Maxwell, L. A. Meeden, N. Addo, P. Dickson, N. Fairfield, N. Johnson, E. Jones, S. Kim, P. Malla, M. Murphy, B. Rutter, E. Silk, "REAPER: A Reflexive Architecture for Perceptive Agents", *AI Magazine*, spring 2001.

[11]   B. A. Maxwell, L. A. Meeden, N. Addo, L. Brown, P. Dickson, J. Ng, S. Olshfski, E. Silk, and J. Wales, "Alfred: The Robot Waiter Who Remembers You," in Proceedings of *AAAI Workshop on Robotics*, July, 1999. To appear in *J. Autonomous Robots*, 2001.

[12]   B. Maxwell, S. Anderson, D. Gomez-Ibancz, E. Gordon, B. Reese, M. Lafary, T. Thompson, M. Trosen, and A. Tomson, "Using Vision to Guide an Hors d'Oeuvres Serving Robot", *IEEE Workshop on Perception for Mobile Agents*, June 1999.

[13]   H. P. Moravec, A. E. Elfes, "High Resolution Maps from Wide Angle Sonar", *Proceedings of IEEE Int'l Conf. on Robotics and Automation*, March 1985, pp 116-21.

[14]   J. Neider, T. Davis, and M. Woo, *OpenGL Programming Guide: The Official Guide to Learning OpenGL*, Addison-Wesley, Reading, MA, 1993.

[15]   F. I. Parke and K. Waters, *Computer Facial Animation*, A. K. Peters, Wellesley, MA, 1996.

[16]   A. Rosenfeld and J. L. Pfaltz, "Sequential operations in digital picture processing", *ACM*, 13:471-494, October 1966.

[17]   D. Scharstein and A. Briggs, "Fast Recognition of Self-Similar Landmarks", *IEEE Workshop on Perception for Mobile Agents*, June 1999.

[18]   H. Wu, Q. Chen, and M. Yachida, "Face Detection From Color Images Using a Fuzzy Pattern Matching Method", *IEEE Transactions on Pattern Analysis and Machine Intelligence*, vol. 21, no. 6, June 1999.

A Fault-Tolerant Distributed Vision System Architecture for Object Tracking in a Smart Room*

Deepak R. Karuppiah, Zhigang Zhu, Prashant Shenoy, and
Edward M. Riseman

Department of Computer Science,
University of Massachusetts,
Amherst, MA - 01003, USA
{deepak|zhu|shenoy|riseman}@cs.umass.edu

Abstract. In recent years, distributed computer vision has gained a lot of attention within the computer vision community for applications such as video surveillance and object tracking. The collective information gathered by multiple cameras that are strategically placed has many advantages. For example, aggregation of information from multiple viewpoints reduces the uncertainty about the scene. Further, there is no single point of failure, thus the system as a whole could continue to perform the task at hand. However, the advantages arising out of such cooperation can be realized only by timely sharing of the information between them. This paper discusses the design of a distributed vision system that enables several heterogeneous sensors with different processing rates to exchange information in a timely manner in order to achieve a common goal, say tracking of multiple human subjects and mobile robots in an indoor smart environment.

In our fault-tolerant distributed vision system, a resource manager manages individual cameras and buffers the time-stamped object candidates received from them. A User Agent with a given task specification approaches the resource manager, first for knowing the available resources (cameras) and later for receiving the object candidates from the resources of its interest. Thus the resource manager acts as a proxy between the user agents and cameras, thereby freeing the cameras to do dedicated feature detection and extraction only. In such a scenario, many failures are possible. For example, one of the cameras may have a hardware failure or it may lose the target, which moved away from its field of view. In this context, important issues such as failure detection and handling, synchronization of data from multiple sensors and sensor reconfiguration by view planning are discussed in the paper. Experimental results with real scene images will be given.

---

* This work is supported by DARPA/ITO Mobile Autonomous Robots S/W (MARS) (Contract Number DOD DABT63-99-1-004) and Software for Distributed Robotics (SDR) (Contract Number DOD DABT63-99-1-0022)

B. Schiele and G. Sagerer (Eds.): ICVS 2001, LNCS 2095, pp. 201–219, 2001.

1   Introduction

In the recent years, rapid advances in low cost, high performance computers and sensors have spurred a significant interest in ubiquitous computing. Researchers are now talking about throwing in a lot of different types of sensors in our homes, work places and even on people. They hope that the wealth of information from these sensors when processed and inferred carefully would significantly enhance our capacity to interact with the world around us. For instance, today, humans rely largely on their innate sensory and motor mechanisms to understand the environment and react to the various situations arising thereof. Though our intelligence is far superior to today's AI, the memory and number crunching capacity of an average person leaves much to be desired. But with a distributed backbone of processors and sensors augmenting our brain and senses, elaborate information gathering and complex and systematic decision-making could become possible for everyone. A smart environment could assist humans in their daily activities such as teleconferencing, surveillance etc. The smart environment idea is therefore not to replace a human but to augment one's capacity to do things in the environment. An interesting perspective into this area from the machine vision point of view has been provided in [14].

Distributed computer vision forms a vital component in a smart environment due to the rich information gathering capability of vision sensors. The collective information gathered by multiple cameras that are strategically placed has many advantages. For example, aggregation of information from multiple viewpoints reduces the uncertainty about the scene. Further, there is no single point of failure, thus the system as a whole could continue to perform the task at hand. However, the advantages arising out of such cooperation can be realized only by timely sharing of the information between them. The distributed system can then share the information to carry out tasks like inferring context, updating knowledge base, archiving etc. A distributed vision system, in general, should have the following capabilities

- Extraction of useful feature sets from raw sensor data
- Selection and fusion of feature sets from different sensors
- Timely sharing of information among the sensors
- Fault-tolerance and reconfiguration

This paper discusses the design of such a distributed vision system that enables several heterogeneous sensors with different processing rates to exchange information in a timely manner in order to achieve a common goal, say tracking of multiple human subjects as well as mobile robots in an indoor environment, while reacting at run-time to various kinds of failures, including: hardware failure, inadequate sensor geometries, occlusion, and bandwidth limitations. Responding at run-time requires a combination of knowledge regarding the physical sensorimotor device, its use in coordinated sensing operations, and high-level process descriptions.

1.1   Related Work

The proposed work is related to two areas in literature - multi-sensor network and distributed self-adaptive software. Research on multi-sensor network devoted to human tracking and identification can be found in [4], [13], [12], [14] and [15]. An integrated system of active camera network has been proposed in [16] for human tracking and face recognition. In [2], a practical distributed vision system based on dynamic memory has been presented. In our previous work [17], we have presented a panoramic virtual stereo for human tracking and localization in mobile robots. However, most of the current systems emphasize on vision algorithms, which are designed to function in a specific network. Important issues concerning fault-tolerance and sensor reconfiguration in a distributed system of sensors are seldom discussed.

These issues are addressed to some extent in the second area namely distributed self-adaptive software. Much of current software development is based on the notion that one can correctly specify a system a priori. Such a specification must include all input data sets, which is impossible, in general, for embedded sensorimotor applications. Self-adaptive software, however, modifies its behavior based on observed progress toward goals as the system state evolves at run-time [8]. Current research in self-adaptive software draws from two traditions, namely control theoretic and planning. The control theoretic approach to self-adaptive software treats software as a plant with associated controllability and observability issues [7]. Time-critical applications require the ability to act quickly without spending large amounts of time on deliberation. Such reflexive behavior is the domain of the control theoretic tradition. Drawing from the planning community, a generic software infrastructure for adaptive fault-tolerance that allows different levels of availability requirements to be simultaneously supported in a networked environment has been presented in [6]. In [1], a distributed control architecture in which run-time behavior is both pre-analyzed and recovered empirically to inform local scheduling agents that commit resources autonomously subject to process control specifications has been presented.

1.2   Architecture Overview

The proposed distributed vision system has three levels of hierarchy - sensor nodes $(S_1...S_N)$, resource managers $(RM_1...RM_K)$, and user agents $(UA_1...UA_M)$, as shown in Fig. 1. The lowest level consists of individual sensors like omni-directional cameras and pan-tilt-zoom cameras, which perform human and face detection using motion, color and texture cues, on their data streams independently in (near) real-time. Each sensor reports its time-stamped object candidates (bearing, sizes, motion cues) to one or more resource managers at the next level. The communication protocol between the sensor and the resource manager could be either unicast or multicast. A resource manager acts as a proxy by making these object candidates available to the user agents at the topmost level. Thus the resource manager could serve many user agents simultaneously, freeing the sensors to do dedicated feature detection and extraction only. The user agent, in our application, matches the time-stamped object candidates from the most favorable sensors, estimates 3D locations and extracts tracks of moving objects in the environment. There could be other user agents that use the same or different sensor information but with a different task specification as well.

All the components of the system communicate using the Ethernet LAN. Thus Network Time Protocol (NTP) is used to synchronize the local clocks of the nodes after justifying that the synchronization resolution provided by NTP is sufficient for our task. For further details in implementation and applications of NTP, the reader is referred to [10] and [11].

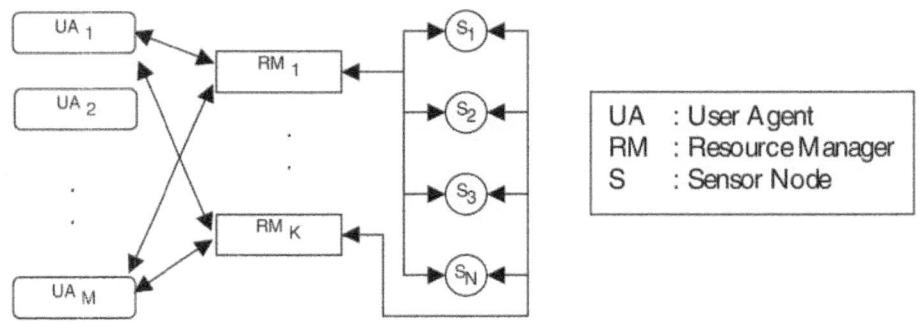

Fig. 1. System Architecture

2   Sensor Nodes

The typical flow of information at a sensor node is shown in Fig. 2. The lowest level is the sensor layer. A sensor node consists of a physical sensor and a processor. In general, the sensor node could also have motor capabilities, for example, a camera that could pan or a camera that is mounted on a robot. The processor could be a desktop computer or a simple embedded processor depending on the computational needs of the sensors. For example, a 68HC11 processor is sufficient for a simple pyro-electric sensor, which detects temperature changes. But a powerful desktop computer is needed for running algorithms for motion detection using vision sensors in real-time. In any case, the nodes should be able to connect to a Local Area Network (LAN). This enables them to communicate with the layer immediately above in hierarchy. Two such vision sensor nodes used in our human tracking system will be discussed in Sec. 6.

At the sensor level, the physical sensor perceives the environment, typically within a certain frequency spectrum of electromagnetic waves. The raw data is then, digitized by the device drivers of the sensor. The digitized data is pre-processed to get rid of random and systemic noise (if the noise models are available). The noise-free data is then used to extract useful features of interest. The features thus extracted are streamed out to the resource manager via the Resource Manager Interface (RM-Interface), shown in Fig. 2. The extracted feature

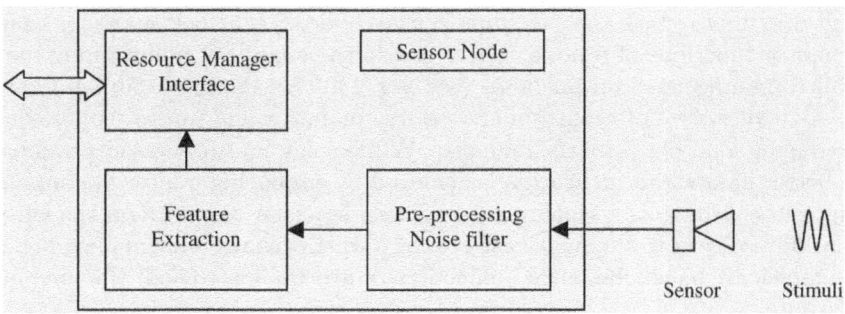

Fig. 2. Sensor Node

set falls into two classes namely basic features and special features. Typically, basic features are common to all the sensor nodes, require low bandwidth and are streamed by default to the resource manager while the special features are node specific, require high bandwidth and are provided on-demand by user agents. For the task of tracking and localization of human subjects in a smart room, the basic features include the bearing and size of moving subjects while special features include their texture, color and motion cues. The special features can be used to match the objects across two cameras and thereby determine their 3-D location. Object matching using special features is further elaborated in Sec. 6.

When a sensor comes online, its RM-Interface reports to a resource manager, the sensor's unique ID followed by its location and geometry in a global reference frame. On receiving a confirmation from the RM, it activates the sensor's processing loop, which does the motion detection and periodically reports the feature. The RM-Interface is capable of receiving commands from the resource manager. Some commands are general like pausing operation or changing the reporting rate. Others are specific to the resource like motion commands to a PTZ platform or a mobile robot.

3   Resource Manager

A resource manager structure is shown in Fig. 3. The resource manager (RM) is the via-medium between the producers of information (the sensor nodes) and their consumers (the user agents). The resource manager keeps track of the currently available sensors and reports their status to the user agent periodically. The user agent chooses the best sensor subset from the available pool to accomplish its goals. The resource manager, therefore, acts as a proxy between the sensors and user agents. Thus the resource manager could serve many user agents simultaneously, freeing the sensors to do dedicated feature detection and extraction only. This way the sensors are not committed to a single agent, but could be shared among many agents. However, the motor functions of a node cannot be shared because they cause conflicts when more than one agent attempts to perform a motor task on the same sensor node. So, a lock manager manages the motor functions of a node. There is also the facility of maintaining multiple resource managers simultaneously (see Fig. 1). This improves fault-tolerance in the event of failure of a particular resource manager and improves performance in reducing load per resource manager. While using multiple resource managers, the better bandwidth utilization is achieved by employing multicast communication protocol. In such a scenario, a sensor node pushes the data on the wire only once addressing it to the multicast group to which the resource managers belong. The multicast backbone, then, efficiently routes the data to all the members of the group.

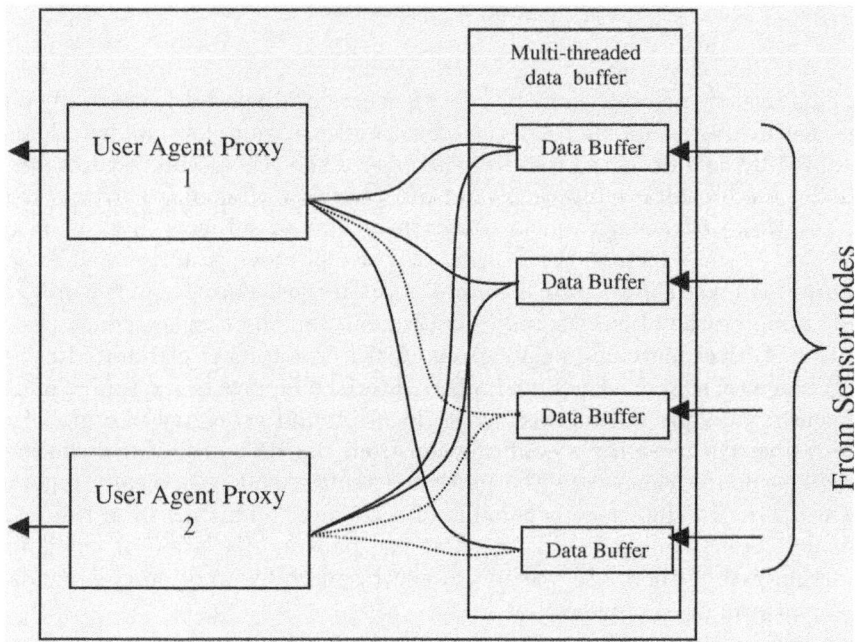

Fig. 3. Resource Manager

3.1 Multi-threaded Data Buffer

In the RM, the Multi-threaded Data Buffer (MDB) collects these time-stamped feature sets from different sensors and buffers them. When the RM-Interface of a sensor begins the registration process by sending its unique sensor ID, the MDB checks for the validity of the ID (i.e. if it is a trusted and known sensor). This simple security check prevents the MDB from being flooded by unscrupulous requests for service. After validation, a thread is spawned to serve that particular type of sensor. The buffering process that is crucial for synchronization of data from different sensors is discussed in Sec. 5.

3.2   User Agent Proxy

User Agent Proxy (UA-proxy) is the end point in the RM, which serves the user agents. Similar to MDB, UA-proxy registers and validates a user agent and a thread is spawned to begin the information exchange with the user agent. UA-proxy provides the user agents with the list of currently available sensors. Depending on a user agent's choice from this list, the UA-proxy delivers the corresponding sensor parameters and their time synchronized feature sets to the user agent. In Fig. 3, the solid lines between the UA-proxies and the data buffers in MDB indicate the respective user agent's choice of sensors.

The states of sensors are pushed to the user agents when one of the following occurs

- A new sensor has registered or,
- A sensor has failed.

Depending on this information, the User Agent modifies its choice set and informs the UA-Proxy which then responds accordingly. The User Agent can also request special features in addition to the default feature set from sensors via the Resource Manager.

4   User Agents

User Agents are processes that achieve a specific goal by using multiple sensori-motor resources. When they go about doing this, the availability of the required resources is not always guaranteed. Even if all the resources are available, the environmental context may prevent them from reaching the goal. This may require some action in the form of redeployment of sensors to handle the new context. User agents are thus adaptive to hardware, software and environmental contexts. A straightforward way to realize a user agent is to identify useful system configurations and assign a behavior to each configuration. Since the combinatorics of this procedure is prohibitive when there are a large number of sensors, an inductive method could be used. In this method, the system could learn from past behavior and identify useful system configurations by itself. An example of user agent used in our system will be given in Sec 7.

5   Time Synchronization Mechanism

The Resource Manager plays a vital role in making the sensors available to the user agents in a timely and fault-tolerant fashion. In this section we discuss how the features from multiple sensors are synchronized in time. A simple way to solve this would be to synchronize all the cameras using an electronic trigger signal.

However, this hardware solution is not general enough to handle heterogeneous sensors and mobile sensors, which are an inevitable part of a smart environment. Even in the case of an all camera network, such synchronization could prove to be difficult and expensive, especially when there are many cameras scattered over a wide area. With the objective of providing a simple, inexpensive yet general solution, we propose a software solution exploiting the existing time synchronization protocol (NTP) running in today's computer networks.

Once the computer nodes are synchronized by NTP, the sensors attached to them could work independently and time-stamp their dataset based on their local clocks. These datasets are buffered at the multi-threaded data buffer (MDB) in the resource manager. When a report has to be sent to a UA, its UA-proxy in the resource manager queries the MDB for the current data from the user agent's sensor set. The query is parameterized by the current time. Each sensor's feature set that is closest in time may be returned. This method works when different sensors process at approximately the same rate. However, if their processing rates differ by a wide margin, this procedure could lead to errors.

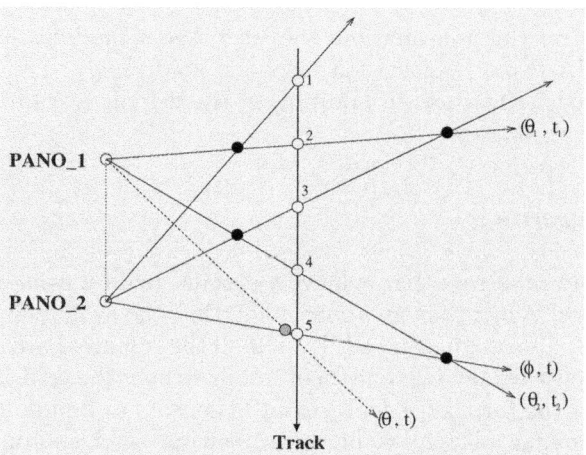

Fig. 4. Illustration of errors due to lack of synchronized matching across two sensors. PANO_2 detects the object at white circles 1, 3, & 5 while PANO_1 does at 2 & 4. The dark circles show the location estimates using the most recent bearings from the sensors while the gray circle shows the estimate at time t when interpolation is used

Let's demonstrate this by a simple example in which only the bearing angles to the moving subjects from the sensors are used. Suppose, two panoramic sensors PANO_1 and PANO_2 are registered in the RM and they report their bearings (to a single moving object in the scene) at different rates as shown in Fig. 4. If UA-proxy were to push the latest reported feature sets from the sensors to the UA, the result of fusion would be inaccurate, as shown in Fig. 4, because of timing discrepancy between the two sets. The white circles show the real positions of the moving object along the track. The dark circles show the error in triangulation caused due to matching datasets not synchronized in time.

So in such situations, using suitable interpolation techniques (polynomials or splines), the feature sets must be interpolated in time. Interpolation algorithm must also be aware of certain properties of the feature sets like the angular periodicity in the case of bearings. MDB is capable of interpolating the data buffer to return the feature set values for the time requested by the UA-proxy (see Fig. 5). This ensures the feature sets being used to fuse are close in time. However, it should be noted that for doing the interpolation, we need to assume that a linear or spline interpolation will approximate the motion of a human subject between two time instants, t_1 and t_2. In a typical walk of a human subject, the motion track can be approximated to be piecewise linear, so the bearing requested for time t in PANO_1 can be calculated as

$$\theta = \frac{(\theta_1 - \theta_2)}{(t_1 - t_2)} (t - t_1) + \theta_1. \tag{1}$$

where θ_1 and θ_2 are bearings measured in PANO_1 at time t_1 and t_2 respectively. The time t used in the above equation is the time for which a measurement of bearing, ϕ, is available from PANO_2. The angular periodicity of bearing angles has not been shown in Eqn. 1 for the sake of simplicity. However it has been incorporated in the interpolation calculations on the real system. We can see that the result of triangulation using bearings θ (in PANO_1) and ϕ (in PANO_2), represented by a gray circle in Fig. 4, has reduced the error considerably. Real scene examples will be given in Sec. 7.

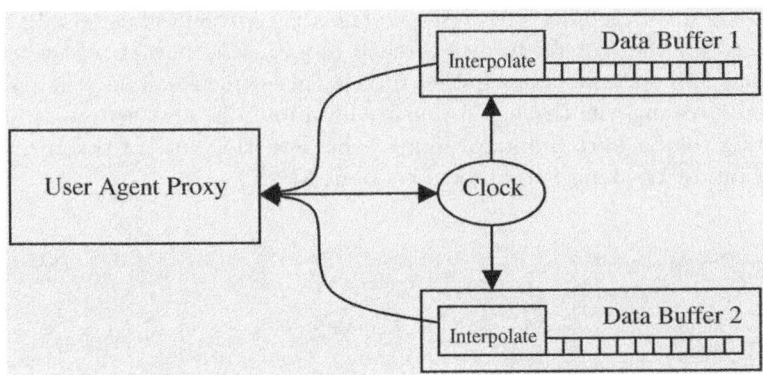

Fig. 5. Interactions between User Agent Proxy and Data Buffer

This algorithm will work provided all the different layers in the hierarchy have a global notion of time. Using Network Time Protocol (NTP), one could achieve time synchronization resolution of the order of 5ms among the nodes of a Local Area Network (LAN). If the fastest sensor in the system would take at least twice this time (every 10ms) to produce a report, then this resolution is acceptable. Typically this is valid because cameras have a frame rate of 25Hz with added overload in processing (i.e. a report at every 40ms at most from a camera).

6   Vision Sensor Nodes

6.1   Panoramic Camera Nodes

Effective combinations of transduction and image processing is essential for operating in an unpredictable environment and to rapidly focus attention on important activities in the environment. A limited field-of-view (as with standard optics) often causes the camera resource to be blocked when multiple targets are not close together and panning the camera to multiple targets takes time. We employ a camera with a panoramic lens [3] to simultaneously detect and track multiple moving objects in a full 360-degree view.

Figure 6 depicts the processing steps involved in detecting and tracking multiple moving humans. Four moving objects (people) were detected in real-time while moving in the scene in an unconstrained manner. A background image is generated automatically by tracking dynamic objects though the background model depends on the number of moving objects in the scene and their motion. Each of the four people were extracted from the complex cluttered background and annotated with a bounding rectangle, a direction, and an estimated distance based on scale from the sensor. The system tracks each object through the image sequence as shown in Fig. 6, even in the presence of overlap and occlusion between two people. The dynamic track is represented as an elliptical head and body for the last 30 frames of each object. The human subjects reversed directions and occluded one another during this sequence. The vision algorithms can detect change in the environment, illumination, and sensor failure, while refreshing the background accordingly. The detection rate of the current implementation for tracking two objects is about 5Hz.

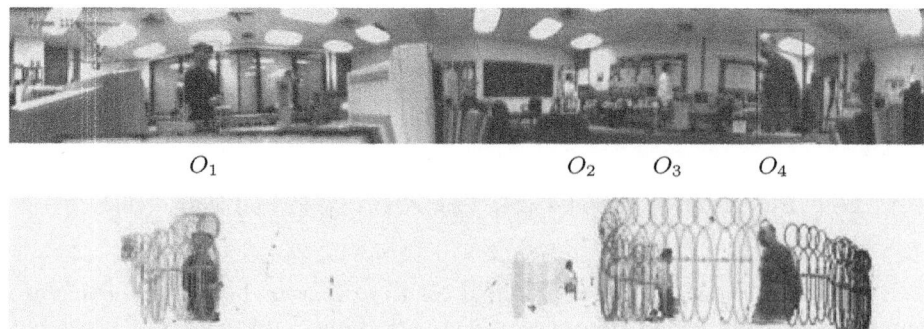

O_1 O_2 O_3 O_4

Fig. 6. Motion detection & tracking in a panoramic camera

With a pair of panoramic sensor nodes, 3D location of multiple moving objects can be determined by triangulation. This pair could then act as a virtual sensor node which reports the 3D location of moving objects to the resource manager. But there are two issues that must be considered namely, matching objects from widely seperated viewpoints and triangulation accuracy when the object is collinear with the cameras. Robust matching can be done by using special features from the sensor nodes like size, intensity and color histogram of the motion blobs in addition to the basic features [17]. When the object is in collinear configuration with the cameras (and if they are the only ones available at that instant), we employ the size-ratio method described in [17]. By using the ratio of the size of objects as seen from the two cameras, their distances from each camera could be calculated (see Fig. 7a). Figure 7b shows two subjects (walking in opposite directions on a rectangular track) being successfully tracked by the algorithm. There are outliers in the track caused due to false detections and mismatches which can be rejected using the fault-tolerance mechanism described later in Sec. 7.1

6.2   Pan-Tilt-Zoom Camera Nodes

The PTZ cameras are another type of sensors used in our system. A PTZ camera can function in two modes - 1) motion detection, and 2) target tracking. In mode 1, the camera remains still and functions in exactly the same way as a panoramic camera, except that now it has a narrow field of view with high resolution. Though the area covered is very limited due to narrow field of view, it is better than panoramic camera for face detection. In mode 2, the camera gets information about a moving target from the higher level and tries to pursue the target. In this mode, it could continuously receive information from the higher level for target location, or it could take over tracking itself (see Fig. 8). Whenever a face is detected in its field of view, it could zoom in and snap a face shot of the moving person immediately. Face shots fall under the catergory of special features for this sensor node and are sent to user agents on demand.

7   Experimental Results

In this section, the implementation of the system as well as preliminary experimental results has been described. The smart room consists of four vision sensors to monitor the activities of human subjects entering the room. Our experiments were conducted using different arrangements of sensors which are shown in Figs. 11 & 13. Two of the sensors are panoramic cameras represented as Pano-I and Pano-II respectively, while the other two are Sony Pan-Tilt-Zoom (PTZ) cameras represented as PTZ-I and PTZ-II respectively. A single resource manager coordinates the cameras and reports their availability to the Track User Agent (Track-UA). The goal of this user agent is to track multiple humans in the smart environment and get face shots of the human subjects (see Fig. 9

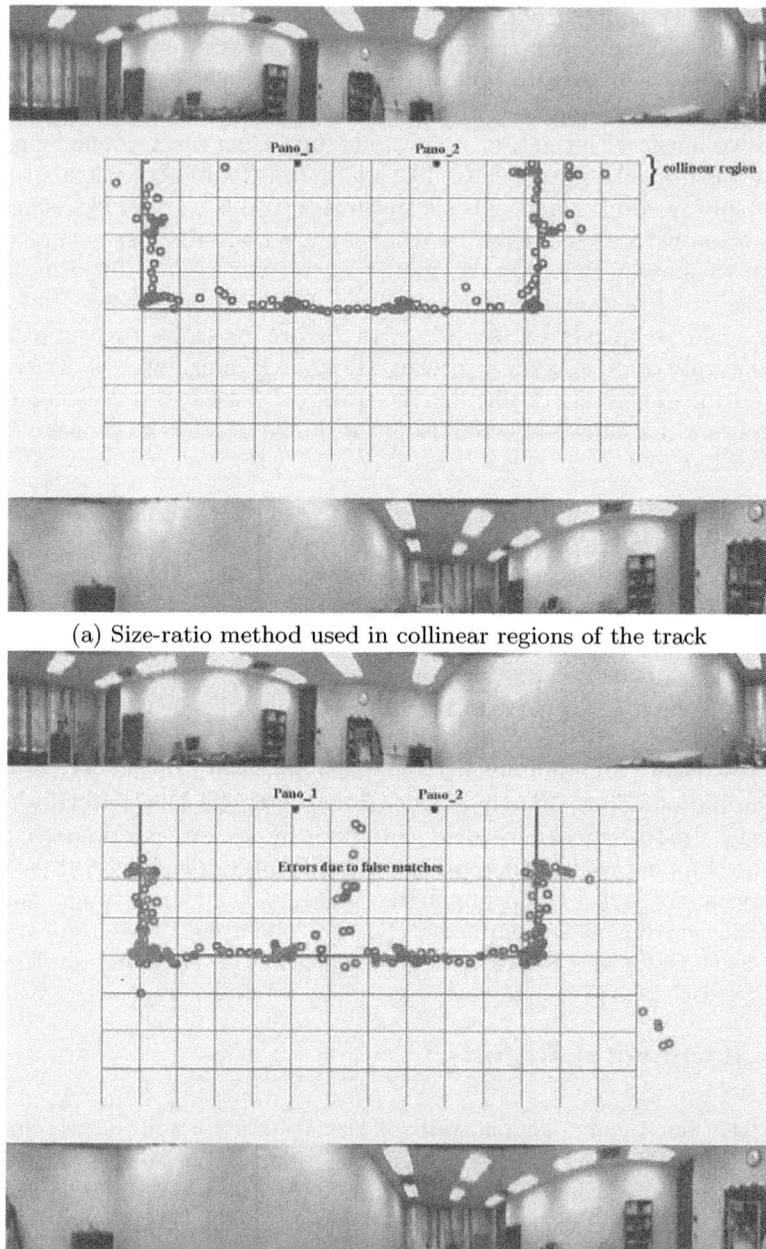

(a) Size-ratio method used in collinear regions of the track

(b) False matches in the center of the track could be rectified by a third camera

Fig. 7. A virtual sensor node comprising of two panoramic cameras providing 3D locations of objects in the scene

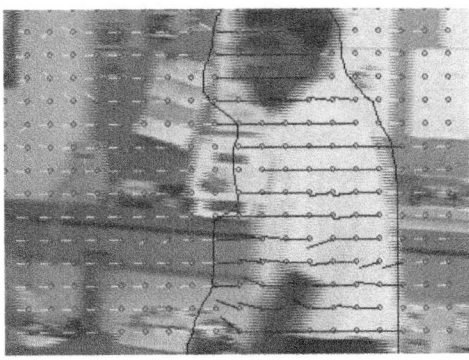

Fig. 8. Illustration of using flow to track moving object in a PTZ camera node

and Fig. 10). The efficacy of the system can be evaluated based on two crite-ria, namely fault-tolerance and accuracy of the tracking. The former criterion evaluates the usefulness of hierarchical design while the latter evaluates vision algorithms and synchronization between multiple sensors.

7.1 Fault-Tolerance Evaluation

The first criterion was evaluated by generating faults at the sensor nodes and ob-serving how the system reacts. As explained in Sec. 3, the resource manager is at the core of the fault-tolerant operation of the system. In our system, the resource manager maintains an availability list. This list is pushed to the Track-UA upon occurrence of certain events like a sensor coming online or a sensor failure. The Track-UA uses the rule-based decision making engine shown in Table 1 to take appropriate actions.

Table 1. The rule-based decision making engine in Track-UA

Availability	Action
At least one camera	Keep track of the heading of the human subjects
Panoramic PTZ pair that are close to each other	Use the bearing information from panoramic camera to pan the PTZ towards the most dominant human subject
Two Panoramic and one PTZ	Match objects across the panoramic cameras. Triangulate to find the 3-D location of each matched object. Use the PTZ to look at one of the objects
Two Panoramic and two PTZ	Same as previous state, except assign the two of the ob-jects to the two PTZ

The system reacting to the event of Pano-II failing is shown in Fig. 11. When both the panoramic cameras are available, the 3-D location of the moving subject

214   D.R. Karuppiah et al.

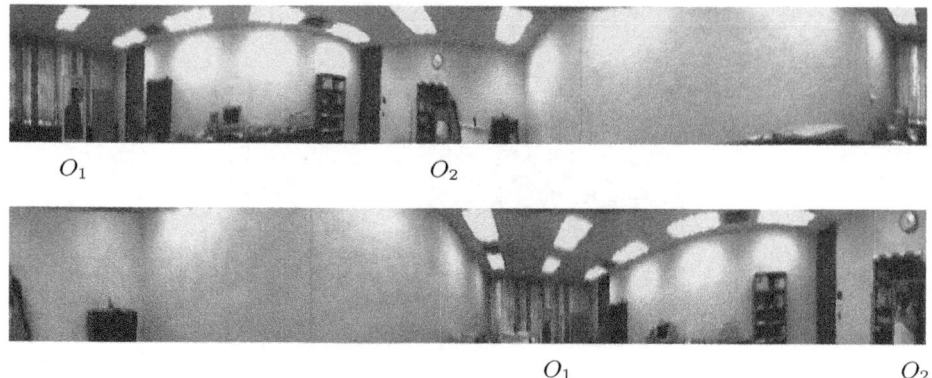

O_1 O_2

O_1 O_2

Fig. 9. Frames from PANO-I & PANO-II showing objects O_1 & O_2 being tracked

Fig. 10. Face shots of O_1 from PTZ-I and O_2 from PTZ-II respectively

can be estimated by triangulation (Fig. 11(a)). In this case any PTZ camera
(PTZ-I or PTZ-II) can be assigned to focus on the human subject. However if
Pano-II fails, we can only use Pano-I to estimate the bearing of the subject. If
no other cameras are available for 3-D localization via triangulation, we can only
use PTZ-I that is closely placed with Pano-I to obtain the face of the human
subject.

In Sec. 6.1, we showed two kinds of failures when only a pair of panoramic
cameras is used for 3D-localization namely, poor triangulation at collinear conditions and stereo mismatches. Both these errors can be detected and can be
easily handled by a third camera as shown in Fig. 12. Collinear conditions can
be detected easily from the bearing angles. The triangulation accuracy under
such conditions can be improved by either using a third camera or by using the
size-ratio method when one is not available. A more difficult problem is the detection of false objects due to stereo mismatches. Again by verifying each object
candidates with a third camera, false ones can be rejected.

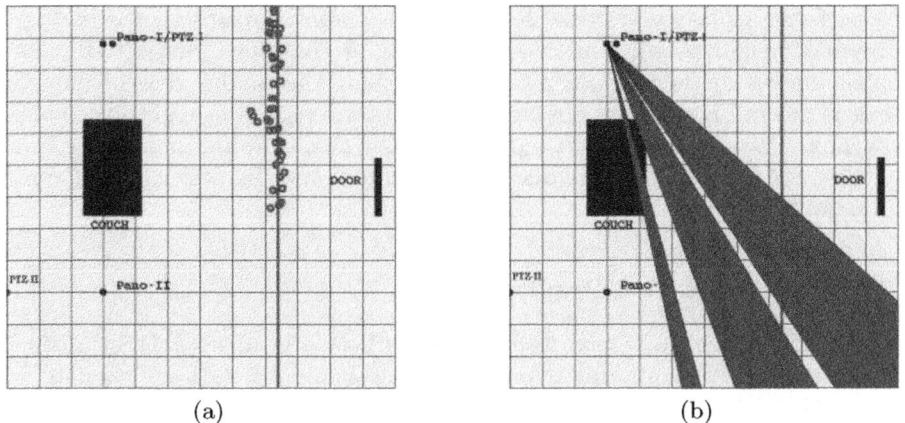

Fig. 11. Pano-I and Pano-II are available in (a). Pano-II failed in (b)

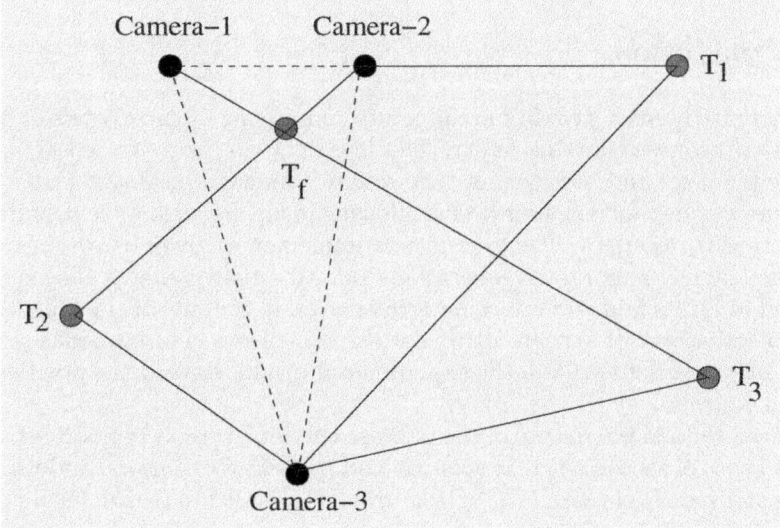

Fig. 12. Object T_1 is collinear with Camera-1 and Camera-2 but can be localized by (Camera-1,Camera-2) pair using size-ratio method or better by either (Camera-1,Camera-3) pair or (Camera-2,Camera-3) pair using triangulation method. A mismatch could result in the false object T_f which can easily be discarded when verified by Camera-3

In a multi-sensor network, information from many cameras can thus provide a better degree of fault-tolerance and allow for dynamic resource reconfiguration to perform a particular task. Results from a real run are shown in Fig. 13. Figure 13a shows two sensors triangulating at the moving object. But as the object moves further to the right, it is occluded from the view of one of the sensors. So in Fig. 13b, we observe that another sensor is brought in to continue tracking. The same process is repeated for the case of collinear sensor geometry in Figs. 13c & 13d. We have discussed fault-tolerance by sensor reconfiguration in more detail in [5].

7.2   Synchronization Results

In this experiment, a person walked along a pre-determined path at a constant velocity and two panoramic cameras - Pano-I and Pano-II are used to track the motion (Fig. 14). Before the start of the experiment, the local clocks on all the sensor nodes are synchronized using NTP. In this experiment, Pano-II is set to process twice as fast as Pano-I. The result of target tracking under this situation is shown in Fig. 14a. We can notice that the error in the track result is quite large with a mean of around 60cm due of lack of synchronization. After we employed the interpolation method discussed in Sec. 5, the mean localization error is reduced within 15cm (Fig. 14b).

8   Conclusion

A distributed sensor network architecture comprising of three levels of hierarchy has been proposed in this paper. The hierarchy consists are sensor nodes, resource manager and user agents. The resource manager acts as a proxy between the sensor nodes and the user agents allowing many user agents to simultaneously share sensor resources. The system was implemented using two types of vision sensors, namely panoramic cameras and pan-tilt-zoom cameras. The system was evaluated for its fault-tolerance performance and accuracy of tracking. A simple, cost-effective way of synchronizing data streams from heterogeneous sensors using NTP was discussed and the experimental results showed the practical utility of this approach.

Given the general nature of the proposed architecture, it is possible to add different types of sensors such as acoustic and pyroelectric sensors, and use them to perform a variety of tasks. The system will be extended to realize its full potential of having multiple user agents, each pursuing a specific goal in the smart environment, simultaneously using multiple resource managers in the multi-sensor framework. The system could be further extended to provide a human interface by building semi-autonomous user agents. A semi-autonomous user agent could interact with a human who can make decisions. While acting under guidance, the agent can learn and increase its confidence in handling certain situations. When it encounters similar situations in the future it can autonomously act without guidance.

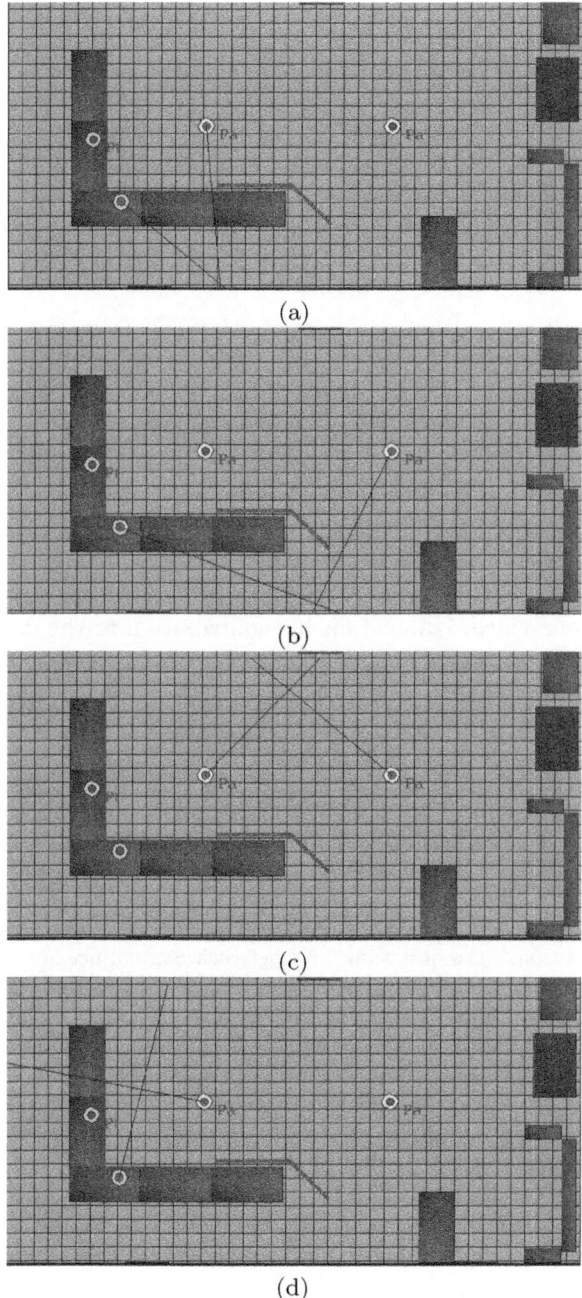

Fig. 13. Frames from a tracking task demonstrating pair-wise sensor mode changes induced on occurrence of faults like object track lost by one of the sensors (a-b), or collinear sensor geometry (c-d)

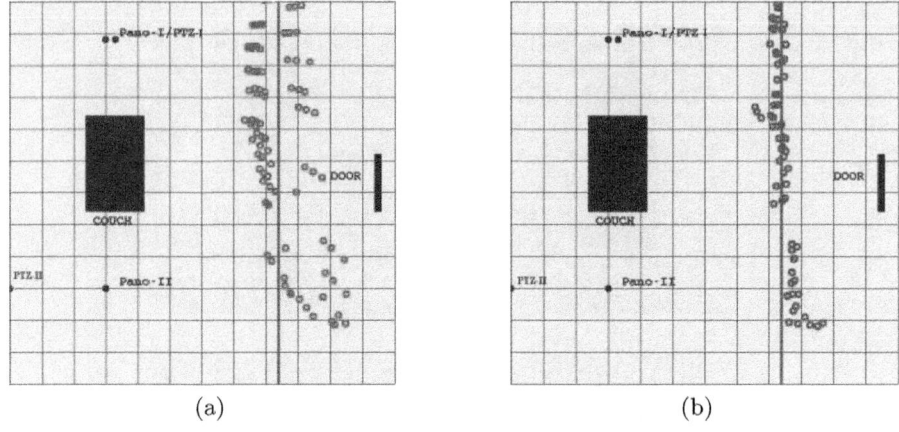

(a)   (b)

Fig. 14. (a) Unsynchronized tracking and, (b) Synchronized tracking

Acknowledgements. We would like to thank other members of our research team - Gary Holness, Subramanya Uppala, S. Chandu Ravela, and Prof. Roderic Grupen - for their involvement in the development of this research. We would also like to thank Yuichi Kikuchi for his contribution to the development of the Pan-Tilt-Zoom sensor node.

References

1. D. R. Karuppiah et al. Software mode changes for continuous motion tracking. In P. Robertson, H. Shorbe, and R. Laddaga, editors, *Self-Adaptive Software*, volume 1936 of *Lecture Notes in Computer Science*, Oxford, UK, April 17-19 2000. Springer Verlag.
2. T. Matsuyama et al. Dynamic memory: Architecture for real time integration of visual perception, camera action, and network communication. In *Proceedings of IEEE Computer Society Conference on Computer Vision and Pattern Recognition*, volume 2, Hilton Head Island, SC, June 2000.
3. P. Greguss. Panoramic imaging block for three-dimensional space. U.S. Patent 4,566,763, January 1986.
4. I. Haritaoglu, D. Harwood, and L. S. Davis. W4: Real-time system for detection and tracking people in 2.5d. In *Proc. of the 5th European Conf. on Computer Vision*, Freiburg, Germany, June 1998.
5. G. Holness, D. Karuppiah, S. Uppala, R. Grupen, and S. C. Ravela. A service paradigm for reconfigurable agents. In *Proc. of the 2nd Workshop on Infrastructure for Agents, MAS, and Scalable MAS*, Montreal, Canada, May 2001. ACM. To appear.
6. Z. T. Kalbarczyk, S. Bagchi, K. Whisnant, and R. K. Iyer. Chameleon: A software infrastructure for adaptive fault tolerance. *IEEE Transactions on Parallel and Distributed Systems*, 10(6):1–20, June 1999.
7. M. Kokar, K. Baclawski, and Y. A. Eracar. Control theory based foundations of self controlling software. *IEEE Intelligent Systems*, 14(3):37–45, May 1999.

8. R. Ladagga. Creating robust-software through self-adaptation. *IEEE Intelligent Systems*, 14(3):26–29, May 1999.
9. K. Marzullo and S. Owicki. Maintaining the time in a distributed system. *ACM Operating Systems Review*, 19(3):44–54, July 1985.
10. D. L. Mills. Internet time synchronization: The network time protocol. *IEEE Transactions on Communications*, 39(10):1482–1493, October 1991.
11. D. L. Mills. Improved algorithms for synchronizing computer network clocks. *IEEE/ACM Transactions on Networks*, 3(3):245–254, June 1995.
12. A. Nakazawa, H. Kato, and S. Inokuchi. Human tracking using distributed vision systems. In *In 14th International Conference on Pattern Recognition*, pages 593–596, Brisbane, Australia, 1998.
13. Kim C. Ng, H. Ishiguro, Mohan M. Trivedi, and T. Sogo. Monitoring dynamically changing environments by ubiquitous vision system. In *IEEE Workshop on Visual Surveillance*, Fort Collins, Colorado, June 1999.
14. A. Pentland. Looking at people: Sensing for ubiquitous and wearable computing. *IEEE Transactions on Pattern Analysis and Machine Intelligence*, 22(1):107–119, January 2000.
15. T. Sogo, H. Ishiguro, and Mohan. M. Trivedi. *Panoramic Vision: Sensors, Theory and Applications*, chapter N-Ocular Stereo for Real-time Human Tracking. Springer Verlag, 2000.
16. Mohan M. Trivedi, K. Huang, and I. Mikic. Intelligent environments and active camera networks. *IEEE Transactions on Systems, Man and Cybernetics*, October 2000.
17. Z. Zhu, K. Deepak Rajasekar, E. Riseman, and A. Hanson. Panoramic virtual stereo vision of cooperative mobile robots for localizing 3d moving objects. In *Proceedings of IEEE Workshop on Omnidirectional Vision - OMNIVIS'00*, pages 29–36, Hilton Head Island, SC, June 2000.

Compiling SA-C Programs to FPGAs: Performance Results

Bruce A. Draper[1], A.P. Willem Böhm[1], Jeff Hammes[1], Walid Najjar[2],
J. Ross Beveridge[1], Charlie Ross[1], Monica Chawathe[1], Mitesh Desai[1], and
José Bins[3]

[1] Department of Computer Science
Colorado State University
Fort Collins, CO 80523, USA
draper,bohm,…@cs.colostate.edu
[2] Department of Computer Science,
University of California at Riverside
Riverside, CA 92521-0304, USA
najjar@cs.ucr.edu
[3] Faculdade de Informática
Pontifícia Universidade Católica (RS)
Porto Alegre, RS 90619-900, Brazil
bins@inf.pucrs.br

Abstract. At the first ICVS, we presented SA-C ("sassy"), a single-assignment variant of the C programming language designed to exploit both coarse-grain and fine-grain parallelism in computer vision and image processing applications. This paper presents a new optimizing compiler that maps SA-C source code onto field programmable gate array (FPGA) configurations. The compiler allows programmers to exploit FPGAs as inexpensive and massively parallel processors by writing high-level source code rather than hardware-level circuit designs. We present several examples of simple image-based programs and the optimizations that are automatically applied to them during compilation, and compare their performance on FPGAs and Pentiums of similar ages. From this, we determine what types of applications benefit from current FPGA technology, and conclude with some speculations on the future development of FPGAs and their expanding role in computer vision systems.

1   Introduction

Over the past several years, field-programmable gate arrays (FPGAs) have evolved from simple "glue logic" circuits into the central processors of reconfigurable computing systems [1]. For readers who are not familiar with FPGAs, they are grids of reprogrammable logic blocks, connected by reconfigurable networks of wires. For example, the Xilinx XV-1000 Virtex FPGA contains 12,288 logic blocks, each con-

B. Schiele and G. Sagerer (Eds.): ICVS 2001, LNCS 2095, pp. 220–235, 2001.
© Springer-Verlag Berlin Heidelberg 2001

taining a four-bit lookup table (LUT) and two bits of memory. Additional circuitry allows pairs of logic blocks to be configured as 5-bit LUTs. The reconfigurable network on the Virtex is essentially a mesh, with one router for every four logic blocks. Reconfigurable computing systems combine one or more FPGAs with local memories and bus connections to create reconfigurable co-processors. An example of such a coprocessor is the Annapolis Microsystems (AMS) Starfire, which has a Xilinx XV-1000 Virtex chip, six 1 MBytes local memories and a PCI interface.

The economics of FPGAs are fundamentally different from that of other parallel architectures proposed for computer vision. Because of the comparatively small size of the computer vision market, most special-purpose vision processors are unable to keep up with advances in general purpose processors. As a result, researchers who adopt them are often left with obsolete technology. FPGAs, on the other hand, enjoy a multi-billion dollar market as low-cost ASIC replacements. Consequently, increases in FPGA speeds and capacities have followed or exceeded Moore's law for the last several years, and researchers can continue to expect them to keep pace with general purpose processors.

Recently, the computer vision and image processing communities have become aware of the potential for massive parallelism and high computational density in FPGAs. FPGAs have been used for real-time point tracking [2], stereo [3], color-based object detection [4], video and image compression [5] and neural networks [6]. Unfortunately, to exploit FPGAs programs have to be implemented as circuits in a hardware description language such as VHDL or Verilog. This has discouraged many researchers from exploiting FPGAs. The intrepid few who do are repeatedly frustrated by the process of modifying or combining complex logic circuits.

The goal of the Cameron project at Colorado State University is to change how reconfigurable systems are programmed from a hardware-oriented circuit design paradigm to a software-oriented algorithmic one. To this end, we have developed a high-level language (called SA-C) for expressing computer vision and image processing algorithms, and an optimizing SA-C compiler that targets FPGAs. Together, these tools allow programmers to quickly write algorithms in a high-level language, compile them, and run them on FPGAs. While the resulting run-times are still greater than the run-times for hand-coded logic circuits, there is a tremendous gain in programmer productivity. Moreover, because SA-C is a variant of C, it makes FPGAs accessible to the majority of programmers who are not skilled in circuit design.

This paper briefly reviews SA-C and then describes the compiler that maps SA-C programs onto FPGA configurations. We compare the run-times of SA-C programs on an AMS Starfire to equivalent programs from Intel's Image Processing Library (IPL) running on a 450 MHz Pentium II. (These machines are approximately the same age.) Based on these comparisons, we draw conclusions about what types of applications can benefit from this technology, and what future advancements in FPGA technology might make them more broadly interesting to computer vision researchers.

2   SA-C

SA-C is a single-assignment variant of the C programming language designed to exploit both coarse-grained (loop-level) and fine-grained (instruction-level) parallelism. Roughly speaking, there are three major differences between SA-C and standard C: 1) SA-C adds variable bit-precision data types (e.g. int12) and fixed point data types (e.g. fix12.4). This exploits the ability of FPGAs to form arbitrary bit precision logic circuits, and compensates for the high cost of floating point operations on FPGAs. 2) SA-C includes extensions to C that providing parallel looping mechanisms and true multi-dimensional arrays. These extensions make it easier for programmers to operate on sliding windows or slices of data, and also make it easier for the compiler to identify and optimize common data access patterns. 3) SA-C restricts C by outlawing pointers and recursion, and restricting variables to be single assignment. This prevents programmers from applying memory models that do not map well onto FPGAs. A full description of the SA-C language can be found in [7], while a reference manual can be found at http://www.cs.colostate.edu/cameron.

```
uint11[:,:] prewitt(uint8 Image[:,:])
// Declare constant Prewitt masks
int2 H[3,3] = { {-1, 0, 1},
                {-1, 0, 1},
                {-1, 0, 1}} ;
int2 V[3,3] = { {1, 1, 1},
                {0, 0, 0},
                {-1, -1, -1}} ;
// Compute mask responses and edge magnitude
uint11 R[:,:] =
    for window W[3,3] in Image {
        int11 dx, int11 dy = for w in W dot h in H dot v in V
            return( sum(h*(int11)w), sum(v*(int11)w );
        uint11 edge = sqrt(dx * (int22)dx + dy * (int22)dy);
    } return( array(edge) );
} return R;
```

Fig. 1. SA-C source code for computing edge magnitudes using horizontal and vertical Prewitt masks.

As an example, Figure 1 shows the SA-C code for computing edge magnitudes using horizontal and vertical Prewitt edge masks. At first glance, the code may seem unlike C, but the differences are motivated by the three criteria above, and programmers adapt quickly. The heart of the program is a pair of nested loops. The outer loop executes once for each 3x3 window in the source image. It contains the inner loop, which convolves the Prewitt masks with the image window; and also computes the edge magnitude as the square root of the sum of the squares of the mask responses. This demonstrates SA-C's looping mechanisms in terms of "for window" and "for element" loops, as well as the ability to combine loops through dot products that run generators in lock step[1].

Many of the other syntactic differences between SA-C and C in this example concern data types. In this case, the source image has unsigned 8-bit pixels, but of course the Prewitt mask values only require two bits each (one for sign, one for value). This is significant because FPGA configurations are special-purpose circuits, and it takes less time and space to multiply an 8-bit value by a 2-bit value (producing a signed, 9-bit value) then it does to multiply two signed 16 bit values (the closest alternative in C). In this example, we have carefully specified the smallest data types possible, for demonstration purposes. This creates efficient circuits, but requires a lot of casting to set the data types of intermediate values, and is often a source of programming errors. In practice, we tend to set the input and output types of a function precisely, while using larger values for intermediate values. In most cases, the compiler can infer maximum sizes and remove unnecessary bits automatically, without the risk of introducing software bugs.

Figure 2 shows another example, this time of a dilation operator. In particular, we show a program designed to compute a gray-scale dilation using a 3x3 mask of 1s. This example is written so as to demonstrate SA-C's ability to take a "slice" of an array (i.e. part of a row or column), in this case by using `array_max(W[:,0])` to compute the maximum of the first row of a window. It also demonstrates the array operators (in this case, `array_max`) that are predefined for simple loops.

```
uint8[:,:] dilate (uint8 A[:,:]) {
    uint8 R[:,:] =
    for window W[3,3] in A {
        uint8 m0 = array_max(W[:,2]);
        uint8 m1 = array_max(W[:,1]);
        uint8 m2 = array_max(W[:,0]);
        uint8 V[3] = {m0,m1,m2};
        uint8 mx = array_max(V);
        uint8 val = array_min((uint9)(mx)+1,255);
    } return (array(val));
} return (R);
```

Fig. 2. SA-C source code for computing a gray-scale dilation with a 3x3 mask of 1's.

---

[1] Loops can also be combined through cross products that generate all combinations of data elements.

3   The SA-C Compiler

3.1   Overview

The SA-C compiler translates high-level SA-C code into data flow graphs, which can be viewed as abstract hardware circuit diagrams without timing information [8]. Nodes in a data flow graph are either simple arithmetic, simple control (e.g. selective merge), or array access/storage nodes; while edges are data paths that correspond to variables. Figure 3 shows an unoptimized data flow representation of the Prewitt code from Figure 1. Note that the variables in Figure 1 turn into edges in the data flow graph; instead of memory locations as with a von Neumann processor. The operators are simple arithmetic operators that can be implemented in circuitry.

The two exceptions to the "simple operator" rule in Figure 3 are the window generator and window collector nodes. Large arrays and unbounded arrays (i.e. arrays whose sizes are not known at compile time) are stored in local memory on the reconfigurable processor, and window generators[2] are used to incrementally feed them into the FPGA. Window collectors gather output values and store them in memory as arrays (if needed). Both of these node types are themselves broken down into graphs of simple primitives, such as read word, write word, and increment address. However, because these subgraphs include registers (to hold addresses and values), they are not stateless, and therefore are not traditional data flow nodes. They must be handled specially within the compiler.

The SA-C compiler optimizes data flow graphs before generating a VHDL hardware description. Some optimizations are traditional while others were specifically designed to suit the language and reconfigurable hardware. Traditional optimizations include: Common Subexpression Elimination (CSE), Constant Folding, Invariant Code Motion, Dead Code Elimination, Function Inlining, and Loop Unrolling. The specialized optimizations include Loop Stripmining, Array Value Propagation, Loop Fusion, Lookup Tables, Temporal CSE, Window Narrowing, Size Propagation Analysis, and Pipelining. We show examples of some of these optimizations below.

Once the SA-C compiler has translated the data flow graph into VHDL, commercial compilers map the VHDL onto an FPGA configuration. The SA-C compiler also automatically generates all the necessary run-time code to execute the program on a reconfigurable processor. This includes downloading the FPGA configuration, data and parameters, and uploading results.

---

[2] Or slice generators, or element generators.

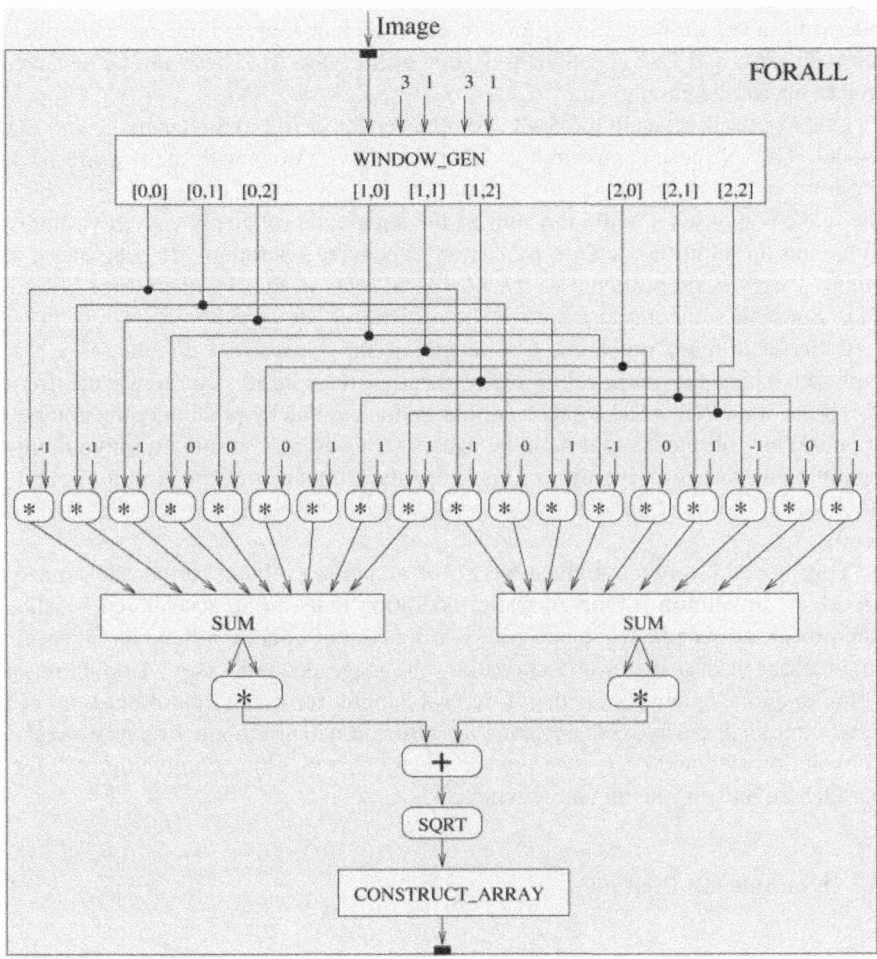

Fig. 3. Naïve mapping of the SA-C source code in Figure 1 to a data flow graph.

3.2   Example #1: Edge Magnitude

Part of the power of SA-C's compiler comes from traditional optimizations. Consider, for example, the inner loop of the Prewitt operator in Figure 1. This loop convolves a 3x3 data window with two 3x3 masks. Implemented naively (as in Figure 3), it would require 18 multiplications and 16 additions to compute the two responses. However, the SA-C compiler is aggressive about constant propagation and constant folding; in particular, it propagates constants through arrays. Six of the 18 multiplications are with the constant zero, and can be eliminated (along with the subsequent additions, since there is no reason to add zero.) Six more are multiplications with the constant 1; and can also be removed. Finally, the last six are with the constant −1; these are replaced by a negation operator. As a result, the inner loop requires no multiplications, ten additions, and five negations[3], as shown in Figure 4. These can be arranged in a tree to maximize parallelism.

Other optimizations in the SA-C compiler are specific to the language and machine model. One of these is pipelining. After the convolutions with the Prewitt masks, the program in Figure 1 still has to compute the square root of the sum of the squares of the mask responses. While the sum of the squares is relatively easy (two multiplications and an addition), square root is an expensive operation. It generates a circuit whose length is proportional to the number of bits in the argument (see [9], Chapter 21). Since there is only one square root operation per window, the size of the square root circuit is not a problem. The length of the square root circuitry is a problem, however, since the propagation delay through the circuit determines the frequency (MHz) of the FPGA. The SA-C compiler addresses this by pipelining the computation. It puts layers of registers through the square root circuitry, turning it into a multi-cycle operation as shown in Figure 5. This keeps the frequency of the circuit up, and introduces a new form of parallelism, since all stages of the pipeline are executed concurrently.

Together, these two optimizations solve a classic problem for parallel image processors. Convolution is a data-parallel operation that can be accelerated by allocating one processor per pixel. Square root is a sequential operation that can be accelerated by breaking it into stages and allocating one stage per processor. Combining a convolution and a square root is therefore problematic for many multiprocessors. FPGAs have enough logic blocks, however, to allocate a (sub)circuit to every pixel in the convolution step and every stage of the square root pipeline, combining both forms of parallelism and eliminating any bottleneck.

3.3 Example #2: Dilation

The dilation example in Figure 2 is also optimized using language-specific techniques. Dilating a gray-scale image by a 3x3 mask of 1s requires taking the maximum of nine values in every 3x3 data window. Once again, the naïve implementation is to arrange the nine max operators in a binary tree to maximize parallelism. The code in Figure 2 was organized so as to emphasize a point, however: the computation can be structured hierarchically into columns, by first taking the max of each column, and then taking the maximum of the three column maximums. Structuring the code in this way makes it clear how the compiler can take advantage of image windowing. As the data window slides from left to right, the same column-wise operations are being repeated. The maximum of the right-most column at time step #1 ($m0$ in Figure 2) is the maximum of the middle column ($m1$) at time step #2 and the maximum of the left-most column ($m2$) at time step #3. Instead of recomputing these values, the compiler can insert

---

[3] There are five negations, not six, because of common subexpression elimination.

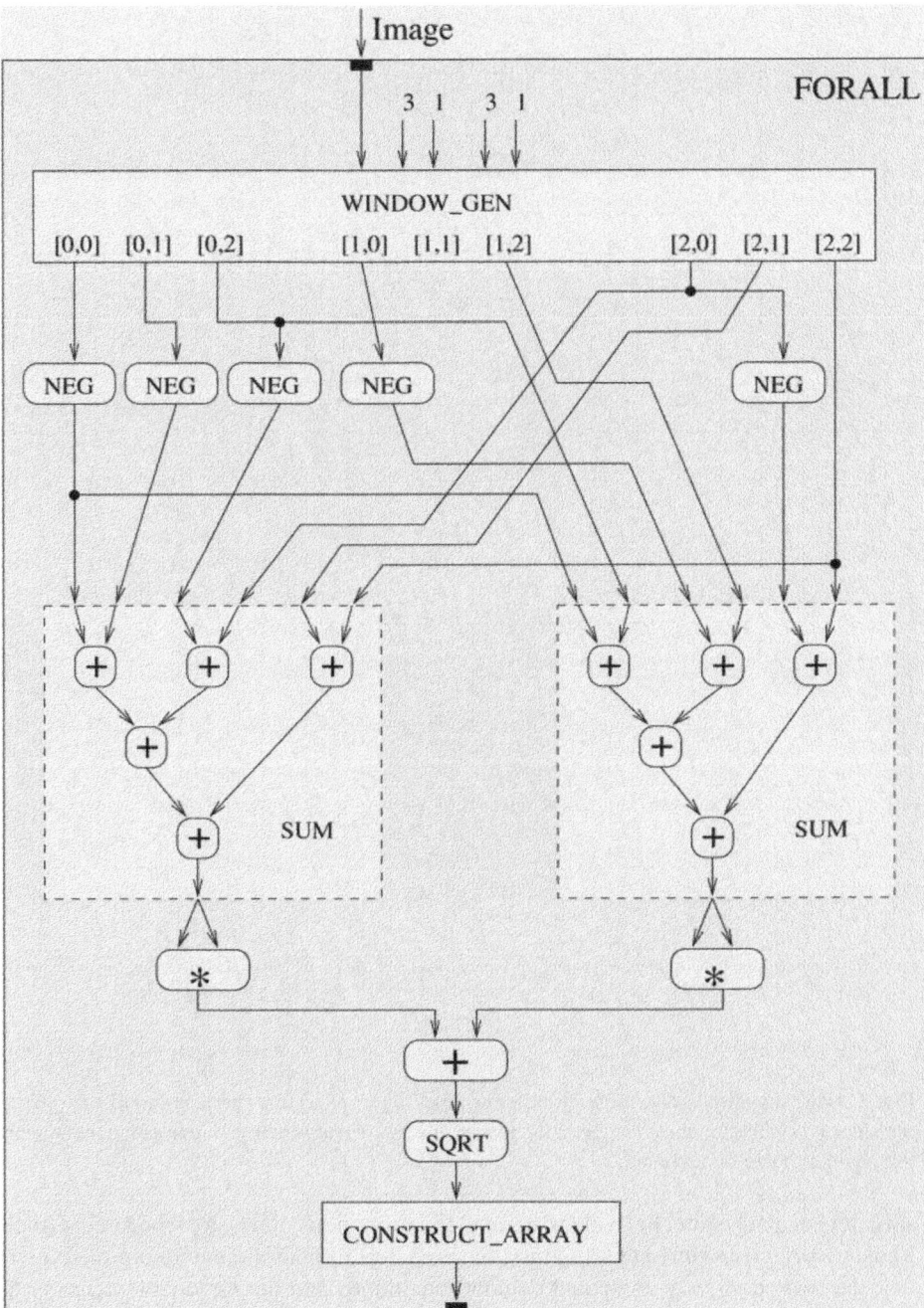

Fig. 4. Data-flow graph for source code in Figure 1, after constant propagation, constant folding, and common subexpression elimination.

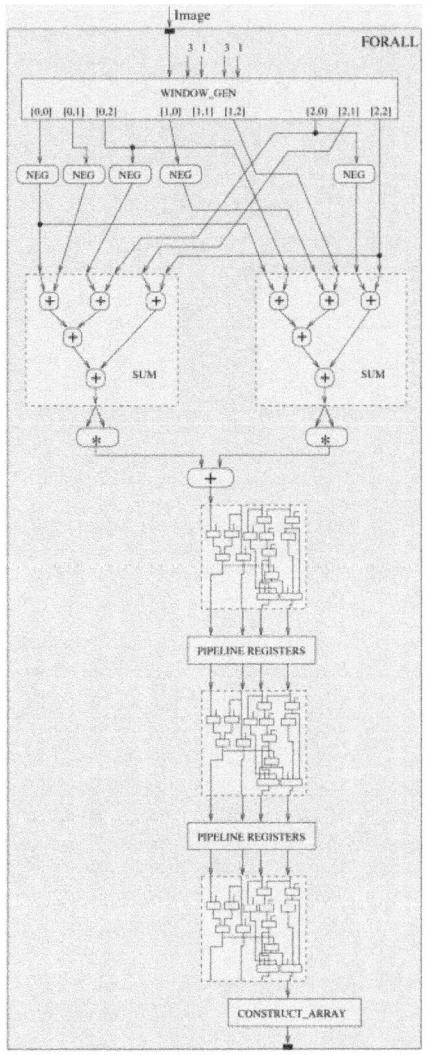

Fig. 5. Edge magnitude data flow graph after pipelining. Note that the position of the pipeline registers is symbolic; they are actually placed so as to equalize the propagation delays and thereby maximize frequencies.

shift registers to store the values computed at previous time steps and reuse them. Thus, at any given time step, the program only has to take the maximum of five values: the two previously computed column maximums and the three new values in the right-most column. This results in a smaller and faster binary tree of max operators. This general optimization of reusing values computed on previous iterations is known as *Temporal Common Subexpression Elimination*, or Temporal CSE.

Temporal CSE has a second, less obvious benefit. The only pixels being accessed are now those in the right-most column; the pixels in the middle and left columns are not accessed, since their maximum was computed and stored on a previous iteration. As a result, the window size can be reduced from 3x3 to 3x1, saving registers in the window generator. In and of itself, there is only a modest savings in this step, which we call *window narrowing*. Simple procedures like dilation, however, are almost never executed alone; they are components of larger programs. Another optimization, called *loop fusion,* minimizes the number of passes over the data by fusing loops that have producer/consumer relationships. For example, if a program dilates an image twice with a 3x3 mask, it can be implemented as a single pass with a 5x5 window.

The disadvantage of loop fusion is that the size of the image window grows as more loops are fused. In the example from Figure 2, the window is 3x3, so fusing two iterations produces a 5x5 window, and fusing four iterations produces a 9x9 window. Implementing a 9x9 sliding window requires buffering 81 8-bit values, at a cost of at least 648 logic blocks. If the window size or pixel size is larger, the buffering requirements get worse. Fortunately, Temporal CSE and window narrowing reduce the window size of the dilation operator in Figure 2 to 3x1; fusing four iterations of the dilation operator therefore produces a window of only 9x1. In other words, the size of the buffers grows linearly with the number of loops fused, not quadratically.

In other programs the computation may be less regular, in the sense that the computation over the pixels in one column may be distinct from the computation in any other. In this case, it may still be possible to "push the computation to the right" by computing values as soon as the source pixels appear in the image window and then shifting the result to the left via registers. In this case, window narrowing can still be applied prior to loop fusion.

3.4 Example #3: I/O

One disadvantage of FPGAs is their limited I/O facilities. Although we can compute many things in parallel, we can only read or write 32 bits per cycle per memory (64 on some machines). As a result, very simple operations that do not do much computation per pixel will be I/O bound and perform poorly on FPGAs (see Section 4.1). This problem is exacerbated by the redundancy inherent in sliding a window across an image. Although we use shift registers to avoid reading any pixel more than once as we slide the image window from left to right, at the end of the row we have to drop the window one row and start sliding again (like the carriage return on a typewriter). As a result, if the processing window is m by n, each pixel is read m times.

An optimization that reduces this problem in both the edge magnitude and dilation examples is called vertical *stripmining.* The general idea is that instead of sliding a 3x3 window across the image, we slide a 4x3 window instead. By adding an extra row to the data window, we can compute two instances of the 3x3 operator (either edge magnitude or dilation) at once, one above the other. This adds another level of parallelism to the system. More importantly, because we are computing two windows worth of data at each step, when we reach the end of a row we can drop the data window two rows instead of one. This halves the amount of I/O by halving the number of times each pixel is read. In general, for a window of height n, if we stripmine it q times, we reduce the memory I/O by a factor of $(n+q)/(q+1)$.

4   Image Processing

The SA-C language and compiler allow FPGAs to be programmed in the same way as any other processor. Programs are written in a high-level language, compiled and debugged on a local workstation, and then downloaded to a reconfigurable processor. The compiler produces both the FPGA configuration and all necessary host code to download the configuration onto the FPGA, download the data onto the recongifurable processor's local memory, trigger the FPGA, and upload the results. SA-C therefore makes reconfigurable processors accessible to applications programmers with no particular expertise in FPGAs or circuit design.

The question for applications programmers is which tasks will benefit from reconfigurable technology. To answer this question, we have compiled image processing programs of varying complexity to an Annapolis Microsystems StarFire, with a Xilinx XV-1000 Virtex FPGA and six local memories of 1 MByte each. We compare its performance to a general-purpose processor of similar age, a 450 MHz Pentium II with 128 MBytes of RAM.

4.1   Simple Image Processing Operators

Our first instinct was to write the same program in SA-C and C, and compare their performance on the Starfire and Pentium II. Unfortunately, this would not have been a fair comparison, since neither the Microsoft nor Gnu C++ compilers exploit the Pentium's MMX technology. Instead, we wrote SA-C programs corresponding to a set of simple image operators from the Intel Image Processing Library (IPL), since the IPL was written by Intel in assembly code and optimized for MMX. We then compare the performance of the Starfire to the Pentium II with MMX acceleration, as shown in Table 1. As can be seen, the Pentium outperforms the FPGA on these tasks by factors ranging from 1.2 to 5.8.

This result is not surprising. Although the FPGA has the ability to exploit fine grained parallelism, it operates at a much slower clock speed than the Pentium. (The clock speed of an FPGA depends on the configuration; these programs were clocked at between 30 and 40 MHz.) These simple programs are all I/O bound, and the slower clock speed of the FPGA is a major limitation when it comes to fetching data from memory.

Table 1. Execution times in seconds of simple IPL routines on a 512x512 8-bit image. The comparison is between a 450Mhz Pentium II and an AMS Starfire with one Xilinx XV-1000 (Virtex) FPGA. The ratio is between the execution times (Pentium/Starfire).

	Routine	Pentium II	Starfire	Ratio
1	AddS	0.00120	0.00687	0.17
2	OrS	0.00127	0.00628	0.20
3	SubtractS	0.00133	0.00617	0.22
4	Not	0.00140	0.00650	0.22
5	AndS	0.00146	0.00628	0.23
6	Or	0.00241	0.00822	0.29
7	And	0.00243	0.00822	0.30
8	Subtract	0.00253	0.00841	0.30
9	Open	0.01147	0.03493	0.33
10	Close	0.01158	0.03280	0.35
11	Add	0.00246	0.00688	0.36
12	Multiply	0.00300	0.00816	0.37
13	Dilate	0.00857	0.01441	0.59
14	Erode	0.00902	0.01463	0.62
15	Square	0.00529	0.00659	0.80
16	Gaussian	0.00538	0.00625	0.86

The first eight routines in Table 1 are pixel-wise operators with very simple logic, and the Pentium is three to six times faster than the FPGA. Six of the last eight are neighborhood operators, and here the Pentium is 1.2 to 3 times faster. One reason for this relative improvement is that the SA-C compiler is able to vertically stripmine neighborhood operations, minimizing the number of read operations, as discussed in Section 3.4. Another is that the SA-C compiler knows the neighborhood masks at compile time, and is able to reduce the total number of operations by constant propagation and constant folding, as discussed in Section 3.2.

4.2 Application Tasks

Next we look at the edge magnitude function in Figure 1, which is more complex then the IPL routines above. Edge magnitudes can be computed using the Prewitt masks with a single function call (iplConvolve[4]) in the IPL. The execution times for the edge magnitude operator are on the top line of Table 2. This time it is the FPGA that is faster by a factor of four. This is because the slower clock rate of the FPGA is offset by its ability to do more work per cycle by exploiting parallelism.

The FPGA compares even better as we look at more complex operations. The ARAGTAP pre-screener was developed by the U.S. Air Force as the initial focus-of-attention mechanism for a SAR automatic target recognition application [10]. It in-

---

[4] iplConvolve can apply multiple masks and return the square root of the sum of the squares of the mask responses at each pixel, as required for computing edge magnitudes.

cludes operators for down sampling, dilation, erosion, positive differencing, majority thresholding, bitwise "and", percentile thresholding, labeling, label pruning and image creation. Most of the computation time is spent in a sequence of eight gray-scale morphological dilations, and a later sequence of eight gray-scale erosions. Both the dilations and erosions alternate between using a 3x3 mask of 1's (as in Figure 2) and a 3x3 mask with 1's in the shape of a cross and zeros at the corners.

In principle, the SA-C compiler should be able to fuse a sequence of eight dilations into a single operator that passes only once over the image. Unfortunately, a problem with our place and route mechanism prevents us from fusing all eight dilations (or all eight erosions) into a single operation. We are able to fuse four dilations into a single loop, however, and therefore divide the eight dilations into two sets of four. Table 2 shows the run-times for four dilations and four erosions on the FPGA and Pentium II. In both cases, the FPGA is fifteen times faster than the Pentium. If we go further and run the dilations, erosions, positive differencing, majority threshold and bitwise "and" on the FPGA, the run-time drops from 1.07 seconds on a Pentium to 0.041 seconds, an twentysix-fold speed-up.

In this experiment, we did not use the Intel IPL library to evaluate the Pentium. The IPL's dilate and erode routines cannot alternate masks, nor do they match the definitions of gray-scale dilate and erode used by ARAGTAP. Therefore we used an implementation of ARAGTAP by Khoral Research, Inc., compiled with optimizations using g++ and timed on an Intel Pentium II running Linux. As a result, the Pentium II was not exploiting its MMX technology for this evaluation.

Table 2. Run-times for complex operators. The comparison is between a 450Mhz Pentium II and an AMS Starfire with one Xilinx XV-1000 (Virtex) FPGA. The ratio is between the execution times (Pentium/Starfire).

Routine	Pentium II	Starfire	Ratio
Prewitt	0.057	0.013	4.38
Open (4)	0.20	0.00612	32.68
Close (4)	0.20	0.00610	32.79
ARAGTAP	1.07	0.04078	26.24

4.3 FLIR Probing

The most computationally intensive algorithm we have studied to date is a probing algorithm developed by the U.S. Army Night Vision Laboratory. The underlying idea is simple: a "probe" is a pair of pixels that should straddle the boundary of a target when viewed from a known position. If the difference between the two probe values in an image exceeds a threshold, the probe fires. A "probe set" is a set of probes arranged around the silhouette of a target, as shown in Figure 6. The positions of probes in a probe set are specified relative to a window, and the window slides across the image. At any image position, if the number of firing probes in a probe set exceeds a (second) threshold, the target is detected at that location.

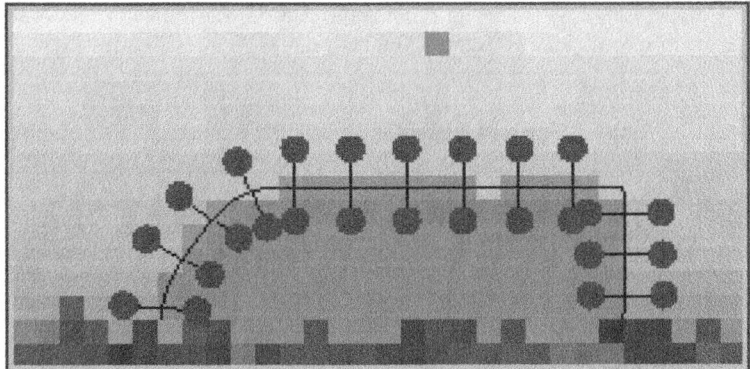

Fig. 6. A set of probes outlining the silhouette of a target. The positions of probes in a probe set is relative to a sliding image window. If at any point the number of firing probes exceeds a threshold, the target is detected at that location.

What makes this algorithm difficult is the quantity of probes and the time constraint. A typical probe set consists of twenty to twenty-five probes. Each target requires one probe set for each possible view, and the viewing hemisphere is divided into eighty-one canonical views. Multiple distinct targets may have to be recognized in real-time ($1/30^{th}$ of a second). Currently, the goal is to detect four targets via 324 probe sets of 20-25 probes each at every image location, 30 times a second. Doing this on traditional hardware requires a bank of processors, with the associated space, weight and power requirements thereof.

This algorithm is well suited to SA-C and FPGAs. The basic computational model is a sliding window. Moreover, it is easy to program SA-C to evaluate N probe sets at each image position before sliding the window, which takes advantage of the parallelism inherent in FPGAs. We are currently investigating how many FPGAs will be required to compute 324 probe sets in real-time.

The probing algorithm exploits the strengths of the SA-C compiler. If two probe sets have a probe in common, common subexpression elimination (CSE) will prevent it from being computed twice. If two probe sets share the same pair of probes, CSE will also reuse the sum of the probe responses. More importantly, if one probe is a horizontally translated version of another probe, temporal common subexpression elimination (TCSE) will compute the probe response only once, and insert shift registers to reuse the result, as discussed in Section 3.3. Finally, window narrowing will compute all probe responses as soon as the data appears in the image window, reducing the number of registers needed to implement the sliding window.

Execution times for one, two, four and eight probe sets on the AMS Starfire with a single Xilinx XV-1000 FPGA are shown in Table 3. The run-times were computed on a 100x256 12-bit image. The execution times for the AMS Starfire are a bit erratic as a function of the number of probe sets, for reasons we do not understand yet. Unfortunately, we do not have a C implementation of this algorithm by a neutral party to use as a fair comparator.

Table 3: Comparison of run-times for probing on an AMS Starfire and Pentium II. The execution times are in seconds on a 100x256 12-bit image.

Number of Probe Sets	Total Number of Probes	Execution (Starfire)	Percent of FPGA used
1	22	0.0015	14%
2	43	0.0039	15%
4	87	0.0016	17%
8	186	0.0043	20%

5   Conclusion

Should applications programmers rush out and adopt FPGA technology? Sadly, no (or at least not yet). To run an operator on an FPGA, the image has to be downloaded to the reconfigurable systems' memory, and the results must be returned to the host processor. A typical upload or download time for a 512x512 image is about 0.019 seconds on our system. As a result, the data transfer time almost cancels the gain in execution time for the edge magnitude example. Even with data transfer times included, the FPGA is still faster than the Pentium II on the dilate and erode examples, but the gain is reduced to a factor of 4.5. Generally it is not worth adopting new hardware technology unless the speed-up is a full order of magnitude.

Worse still, current FPGAs cannot be reconfigured quickly. It takes about 0.1 seconds to reconfigure a Virtex over a PCI bus. It is therefore not feasible to dynamically reconfigure it during an application. This is a problem, for example, when running the ARAGTAP pre-screener, where more than half of the one second improvement in execution time is negated by the need to reconfigure the FPGA six times. Applications programmers need to select one operator sequence to accelerate per reconfigurable processor and pre-load it with the appropriate FPGA configuration. In the case of the ARAGTAP pre-screener, it would be best to have two reconfigurable processors, and use one to accelerate the dilations and the other to accelerate the erosions.

As a result, FPGAs are currently well suited to only a small fraction of computer vision applications. In particular, they are suited to applications where a small speed-up (e.g. by a factor of five) matters, and where most of the processing time is spent in a single sequence of image processing operators. In addition, this sequence of operators must be able to fit on an FPGA (although FPGAs get larger all the time). Applications that meet these criteria can be accelerated by FPGAs, and should continue to be accelerated as both FPGAs and general purpose processors get faster.

The future trend in FPGA design is to build processors that 1) can be quickly reconfigured and 2) have a general-purpose RISC processor on-board. Chameleon, for example, is a new company building FPGAs that can be reconfigured in a single clock cycle (see http://www.chameleonsystems.com). This will greatly expand the application domain of FPGAs, since they will no longer be constrained to applications with a single computational bottleneck. In addition, Xilinx has announced (but not yet released) the Virtex II, which puts a RISC processor on every FPGA chip. This will eliminate the data transfer time, making FPGAs much faster than standard processors for many operations, and making it easier to interleave processing between an FPGA and a general-purpose processor. The Virtex II will also include floating point arithmetic units distributed throughout the FPGA grid, making floating point operations much more efficient. When this next generation of chips are available, FPGAs should become a standard part of every computer vision system.

The contribution of the Cameron project to this future is a language and compiler for mapping high-level algorithms to FPGA configurations. Currently, FPGAs are rarely applied even for applications that fit the criteria above; it is just too difficult to implement complex algorithms in circuit design languages. SA-C and the SA-C optimizing compiler eliminate this barrier, allowing FPGAs to be easily and quickly exploited.

Acknowledgements. This work was sponsored by DARPA and the U.S. Air Force Research Laboratory under contract F33615-98-C-1319.

References

1.	DeHon, A., *The Density Advantage of Reconfigurable Computing.* IEEE Computer, 2000. **33**(4): p. 41-49.
2.	Benedetti, A. and P. Perona. *Real-time 2-D Feature Detection on a Reconfigurable Computer.* in *IEEE Conference on Computer Vision and Pattern Recognition.* 1998. Santa Barbara, CA: IEEE Press.
3.	Woodfill, J. and B.v. Herzen. *Real-Time Stereo Vision on the PARTS Reconfigurable Computer.* in *IEEE Symposium on Field-Programmable Custom Computing Machines.* 1997. Napa, CA: IEEE Press.
4.	Benitez, D. and J. Cabrera. *Reactive Computer Vision System with Reconfigurable Architecture.* in *International Conference on Vision Systems.* 1999. Las Palmas de Gran Canaria: Springer.
5.	Hartenstein, R.W., *et al. A Reconfigurable Machine for Applications in Image and Video Compression.* in *Conference on Compression Technologies and Standards for Image and Video Compression.* 1995. Amsterdam.
6.	Eldredge, J.G. and B.L. Hutchings. *RRANN: A Hardware Implementation of the Backpropagation Algorithm Using Reconfigurable FPGAs.* in *IEEE International Conference on Neural Networks.* 1994. Orlando, FL.
7.	Hammes, J.P., B.A. Draper, and A.P.W. Böhm. *Sassy: A Language and Optimizing Compiler for Image Processing on Reconfigurable Computing Systems.* in *International Conference on Vision Systems.* 1999. Las Palmas de Gran Canaria, Spain: Springer.
8.	Dennis, J.B., *The evolution of 'static' dataflow architecture,* in *Advanced Topics in Data-Flow Computing,* J.L. Gaudiot and L. Bic, Editors. 1991, Prentice-Hall.
9.	Parhami, B., *Computer Arithmetic: Algorithms and Hardware Designs.* 2000, New York: Oxford University Press.
10.	Raney, S.D., *et al. ARAGTAP ATR system overview.* in *Theater Missile Defense 1993 National Fire Control Symposium.* 1993. Boulder, CO.

Identification of Shapes Using A Nonlinear Dynamic System

S. Hoque, S. Kazadi, A. Li, W. Chen, and E. Sadun

Jisan Research Institute; 28 N. Oak Ave.; Pasadena, CA 91107; USA

Abstract. We describe a nonlinear system capable of use as a recognition system. This system is composed of a set of coupled oscillators, connected by linear springs. Images are overlaid on the system by altering the masses and spring constants of the oscillators, thereby modifying the detailed behavior of the system. Signatures extracted from the system using FFT of the individual oscillator positions show coherance, relative continuity, and translational and rotational invariance. These properties are discussed in the context of the eventual use of this system as a general identification system.

Keywords: nonlinear dynamic system, pattern recognition

1 Introduction

Historically, visual object detection has tended to fall into one of two basic methodologies, template matching and approaches based on image pattern relationships, such as light intensity (Papageorgiou, 1997). One of these methodologies is the set of methods which depend on gross properties of images such as the intensity distribution as a function of wavelength or the overall average luminosity. Another is *generalized template matching* in which small features are extracted from the image in question, and their positional relationships are used to identify the image. These features can correspond both to features representing physical structure and to features representing regional variations.

Characteristically, systems dependant on relationships view images as a whole rather than a combination of the individual parts which comprise it. Such a process generates a single value for a given characteristic. In the classification of lumber, for example, it may be advantageous to detect wood-type by the brightness of a sample. By using a "training set" of lumber to generate a frequency distribution for brightness of a given variety of lumber, unknown samples can be classified based on correlations with these distributions (Duda and Hart, 1973).

Contrary to relationship systems, template matching employs algorithms to partition images into desireable regions. The positions of these individual portions relative to one another are the basis for recognition. In cases when it is only necessary to locate objects rather than classify them, such as the problem of finding humans in a given scene, template matching is often used. Once many

B. Schiele and G. Sagerer (Eds.): ICVS 2001, LNCS 2095, pp. 236–255, 2001.

parts of an object have been detected from the same region in a picture, it is assumed that the object in question is present in that area (Mohan, 1999).

A third process created as an extension of standard template mathing was found by attempting recognition through the use of "template ratios," whereby a human face is represented by the relationships between the average intensities of specified regions, such that changes in illumination were not of significance (Sinha, 1994). Although this proved relatively successfull, it suffers from the same problem as all other template systems. The characteristics by which regions are located are not based on any rigorous scientific or mathematical foundation. Rather, these regions are found through pre-determined assumptions of the user. Therefore, the reliability of such a system is limited to the accuracy of the human-defined regions.

We investigate in this paper the use of a highly nonlinear system as an object recognition system. This system uses the system's inherant structure to generate a single signature, which itself will be a unique representation of the system's structure. It is very much like both methods, and may be viewed as a combination of both, as it is capable of incorporating features of the system into an overall measurement.

The choice of a nonlinear system is not arbitrary. It stems from some of the limitations inherent in the use of linear systems. The chief attractive feature of a linear system is the linear independence. Linear independence is concisely expressed by the superposition principle which basically states that

$$O\left(\sum_i \vec{x_i}\right) = \sum_i O\left(\vec{x_i}\right) \tag{1}$$

for some operator O and some set of vectors $\{\vec{x_i}\}$. The use of the superposition principle enables a much easier analysis of a linear system than that of a non-linear system. If a system has N inputs, the system's response can be determined by adding the individual responses of the system due to each input. Also, multiplication of an input by a scalar number will result in a scalar multiplication of the response by the same number. Linear systems work well when inputs are independent of one another, and there are no interactions between them. However, if the inputs are not independent, and there are interactions between inputs, the system response is non-linear, and linear systems are not well suited in this case. In image recognition problems, the pixels which make up the image can be thought of as a set of inputs. Since the patterns in the image represents relationships among pixels, the inputs are not expected to be independent of one another.

Non-linear systems are capable of producing complex behavior. This complex behavior may seem random at first, but when they are viewed in phase space, they can display very high level complex patterns. The patterns produced by a non-linear system are contained in an attractor. An attractor may be defined as the set of trajectories traced by the system's states as the system evolve under the influence of the system's dynamics. The most interesting features of an attractor are:

1. attractors are bounded,
2. there can be infinite number of trajectories in an attractor,
3. and small differences in the initial conditions produce very different trajectories.

Although the trajectories in the attractor are sensitive to the initial conditions, the attractor themselves are remarkably consistent. For a given system, the attractor is the the same regardless of the initial condition.

For image recognition problems, the relationships among the pixels can be modeled as the interactions among inputs. The interactions among inputs will create non-linear dynamics which, under certain circumstances, will generate an attractor. Since the attractor is unique for a given dynamics, the dynamics is the result of the interactions among the inputs which represents the relationships among the pixels, the relationships are defined by the pattern in the image, the attractor can be used to identify the pattern in the image.

Inasmuch as an attractor represents its generating system, one may think of using attractors to identify the system it generates. In this paper, we present the use of chaotic attractors in the identification of images. We generate dynamic systems using a system of coupled linear oscillators whose properties are generated in part by the image. This system produces a chaotic attractor, and the properties of this attractor may be used to identify the image.

2   Theory

2.1   Measurements

The use of nonlinear dynamic systems requires an understanding of the underlying dynamics of the system at such a level as to produce a useful property or set of properties. Our goal is to understand chaotic attractors at such a level as to be able to utilize their properties in the identification of images. We therefore begin with definitions clarifying these properties. We assume that the reader is familiar with the concept of phase space, and take this to be the launching point of our work.

Suppose that we have a system S defined by a set of n degrees of freedom $\{x_1, ..., x_n\}$. We can represent this system as a point in the n-dimensional real space. Thus, we may represent the system as $\vec{x} \in \Re^n$. The use of the time-derivative gives the complete state of the system, and we may think of a system as its combined position and time derivative of the position. This gives us a system description such as $\left(x, \frac{dx}{dt}\right)$. From this, we may define an attractor.

Given our system S and its equations of motion and constraints, the set of points in phase space corresponding to allowed configurations of the system are set. We may denote this set as Γ and define it as

$$\Gamma = \{x \mid S(x) \text{ is allowed}\}$$

The set of all allowed initial points to a trajectory are the set of all allowed points which are not exclusively the final points in trajectories. That is, any trajectory may be thought of as a set of initial points, which each start the trajectory consisting of those points which follow the point. These will not include the points that make up point attractors. Thus,

$$I = \{\boldsymbol{x} \in \Gamma \mid \boldsymbol{x} \text{ is not an attractor of the system}\} .$$

Then we may define a propagator of the system. Given the dynamic equations of motion, there exists a propagator P_S which maps the set of all initial points in phase space to their corresponding points in phase space at later times. This propagator acts on the initial point $\boldsymbol{x}_0$ and maps it into another point $P_S(\boldsymbol{x}_0, t) = \boldsymbol{x}_t$ where t represents some time in the future after the time at which the system was at $\boldsymbol{x}_0$.

A **trajectory** $\tau_{S,\boldsymbol{x}_0}$ is defined as the set of all points arising from the action of the system on points in phase space. More formally,

$$\tau_{S,\boldsymbol{x}_0} = \{\boldsymbol{x} \mid \exists\, t \in \Re \,.\, \ni \,.\, \boldsymbol{x} = P(\boldsymbol{x}_0, t)\} .$$

We say that a trajectory is **bounded** if there exists an ϵ-ball $B(\boldsymbol{x}; \epsilon)$ which contains the trajectory.

From these trajectories arise attractors. As a stable system evolves trajectories in phase space, these trajectories will tend to clump, forming a region in space, known as an attractor. This region typically has a well defined multidimensional shape and extent. We may define it as follows:

$$A = \{\tau_{S,\boldsymbol{x}_0} \mid \boldsymbol{x}_0 \in I\} .$$

we define the attractor as stable and bounded if there exists an $\epsilon > 0$ and an $\boldsymbol{x}'$ such that $A \subseteq B(\boldsymbol{x}'; \epsilon)$.

Each attractor is defined by the trajectories that define it. However, it may be the case that each trajectory is unique. Thus, a single trajectory cannot define the attractor. On the other hand, each trajectory may be viewed as a sampling of the attractor that creates it, and it can be easily shown that any attractor will come arbitrarily close to each point off the attractor.

Given a particular trajectory in phase space, one may have a number of different measurements which depend only on that trajectory. The most notable one, of course is the length of the trajectory. This is given by

$$M_l = \oint_\tau d\vec{s} \tag{2}$$

where $\vec{s}$ is a unit vector along the length of the trajectory τ. However, one may imagine other measurements which are defined by the trajectory as well. These measurements are defined by

$$M_f = \oint_\tau f(\vec{s}) \, d\vec{s} \tag{3}$$

where f may or may not be a vector function of the position in the trajectory.

Empirically, it has been found that many measurements done on different trajectories in chaotic systems are identical. Such a property is extremely useful if the system is dependant on the image. This means that different instances of the same system should be expected to generate the same measurement despite differences in initial conditions. This we take to be a necessary property of any chaotic system to eventually be used in an object recognition system. This, of course, comes out of the fact that many chaotic systems are indeed ergodic, and thus different trajectories will have similar statistical properties.

At present, it is does not seem to be known under which conditions chaotic systems become ergodic. We defer this discussion to another paper. However, we present a dynamical chaotic system which we believe to be ergodic. This system may be used, as we shall show, to identify different images used to modify the basic system.

2.2   Clustering of Measurements

We have already commented on the ergodicity of the system we intend to describe. Such ergodicity gives us a way of identifying the system despite the detailed initial conditions, and despite the later deviations of trajectories in phase space. However, an ergodic system with such an invariance property cannot be used to differentiate between different objects. This is because every image will tend to have only minor differences in the system behavior, making identification impossible. Thus, the use of a single invariant system in order to generate the measures that yield identification would not seem to be fruitful.

It is well known that different systems of the same type have the capability of exhibiting very significant changes due to a change in the detailed parameters of the system. This change can happen due to a very small change in the detailed parameters describing the system. Our system, although chaotic, is quite different from this. In our system, changes in the system cause commensurate changes in the measure, though these changes occur continuously. Thus, the system empirically seems to represent a continuous mapping between image space and signature space, with various invariences becoming consequences of this mapping. This is known as *clustering*, and it allows a simple threshold to be used in determining the identity of the system.

This is a very desirable state of affairs in image recognition, when objects of the same class are clustered in the same group in signature space. That is, two oak trees will tend to be more alike than, say, two ginko trees. By the same token, it is desirable if two people are clustered together far from two lions, which are wholly different. This same state of affairs may allow one to group large numbers of pictures of the same person in the same area of signature space, allowing the identification of the same person through many different stages of life and allowing uninterrupted identification.

More rigorously, we report work on a system that represents a two step procedure. The first step consists of a mapping of images onto a system in such a way that they create chaotic dynamics. Thus

$$c : I \to A \tag{4}$$

where I is the set of images, and A is the set of attractors to which it is mapped. Moreover, we develop a measurement M which maps the set of attractors to a signature space

$$M : A \to S \tag{5}$$

in which the desired properties occur. Thus, our desired mapping is

$$M \circ c : I \to S \ . \tag{6}$$

In the next section, we describe a system in which the mapping appears to behave in this way.

3 Incorporating an Image in a Dynamic Nonlinear System

We are interested in studying the construction of a nonlinear system with the properties outlined above. Most importantly, we wish to develop a system which exhibits basic characteristics of a continuous mapping between picture and signature space. This means that, given a $\delta > 0$, $\exists$ a resolution and a positive number ϵ at which a sufficiently small alteration to the picture may be made which will cause the signatures of any given pictures differing by less than ϵ to have a distance smaller than δ. Moreover, basic desired properties of the system include scale invarience, as well as translational and rotational invariance of a given image in a given visual field.

We use a toroidal lattice of linear oscillators as the basic element in our system, depicted in Figure 2.1.

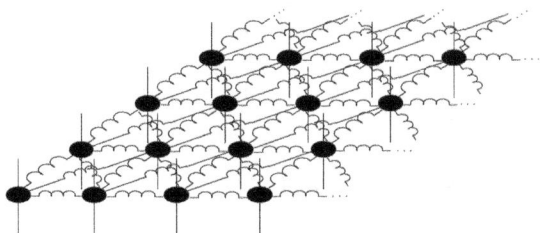

Fig. 2.1: A lattice of coupled oscillators. Each oscillator oscillates in the z-coordinate, and is connected to eight neighboring oscillators via springs.

Each node contains a single oscillator, whose oscillation is constrained to the axis perpendicular to that of the toroid. Each node corresponds to a single image pixel. This means that an image of size $n \times m$ requires an identically-sized lattice of nodes. The nodes are located in Euclidean plane. Each node is connected by springs to adjacent nodes, yielding eight neighbors per node. Nodes are equidistant from their neighbors. Nodes on edges are connected to nodes on the opposite edges, completing the toroid.

Pictures may be overlaid on the system of oscillators by choosing a characteristic in the picture and using this characteristic to modify the properties of the oscillators. The property under modification may range from the mass of the oscillator to its spring characteristics. We consider black and white pictures, whose pixels are either on or off. Pixels that are on correspond to oscillators with higher masses and different spring constants than those that are off. This allows the system's dynamics to reflect the image.

The system is initialized in a state in which all oscillators are motionless and located at their equilibrium point, with the exception of the oscillators corresponding to image elements. These latter pixels are pulled to a height above their equilibrium point commensurate with some characteristic in the picture – in our case whether or not the pixel is turned on, as we use only black and white images. In order to allow the system to produce consistent signatures, the oscillators are run for some measure of time. This removes any measurements that might depend on a transient response of the system produced as a result of starting from rest. Once the system has reached a steady state, the positions of each of the oscillators is recorded for a predetermined number of iterations. Each sequence of positions if subjected to a fast fourier transform (FFT). The logarithm of all resulting FFTs are summed, producing the signature of the image. This signature may then be compared with those from other images.

It is worth noting, in view of the previous theory, that each step in this process occurs via a continuous transformation. Only one process, that of summing the individual FFTs may be seen to be a possible discontinuous action, whose discontinuity might arise from the discreteness of an individual space. It may be possible to demonstrate that in the limit of infinite resolution, the fourier transforms themselves are continually varying across the image, and so summing them represents a multidimensional integral of continuous functions. In this limit, the mapping between image space and signature space may be seen to be continuous. Although we consider this to be plausible, we do not assert that it is true. Rather, we view it as an important component of future research.

4   Pictures and Signatures

The above procedure was applied to several different data sets, of which representative data sets will be presented. The data falls into five distinct categories: that which demonstrates the uniqueness of pictures of different classes, invariance in the identification of different size pictures in the same class, invariance in the identification of pictures with different orientations, invariance in the identification of pictures of the same class at different positions , and continuity between two different objects. We present the data, and discuss its implications as to the nature of the system. We defer to the next section a discussion of the importance of these properties in terms of identification systems.

4.1   Translational Invariance

The design of our system implies that translations of identical images should produce identical signatures. At any position on the lattice, the system will be identical, differing by a simple rotation compared to the original system. This will tend to produce images that differ at most by rounding errors. This is desirable in a recognition system.

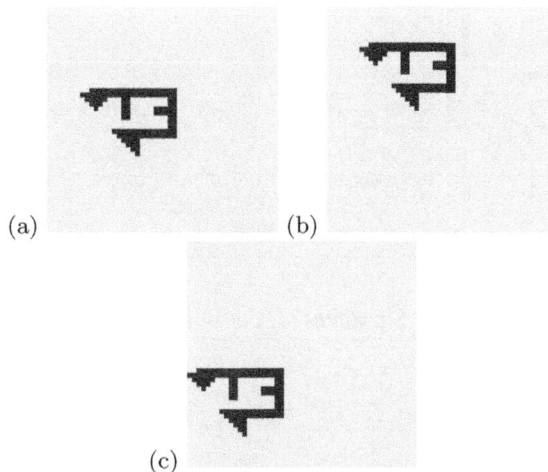

(a)   (b)

(c)

Fig. 3.1: These pictures are typical of images used to test the translational invariance. The pictures are moved across the lattice, yet the final signatures are nearly identical.

We utilize several sets of data, of which one representative set is presented. Each of the objects in these images is displaced relative to other images. As expected, in Figure 3.2, we find almost perfect overlap of the signatures. Only a very small variation in the zoomed graph is apparent.

4.2   Rotational Invariance

The system has obvious rotational symmetry. That is, an image imposed on the system will interact with an identical grid despite any rotation that occurs. This again is an extremely advantageous property. This may be illustrated by using images rotated by $\frac{\pi}{2}$, as in Figure 3.3.

Figure 3.4 illustrates the overlap of the signatures created from these images. Note that the signatures are so alike, that only differences due to rounding errors are detected.

One difficulty with the system arises from the particular geometry of the system. As illustrated in Figure 3.5, the neighborhood structure of a simple pair of pixels changes dramatically if the pixels are rotated by $\frac{\pi}{4}$. This causes significant differences in the signatures, as in Figure 3.6.

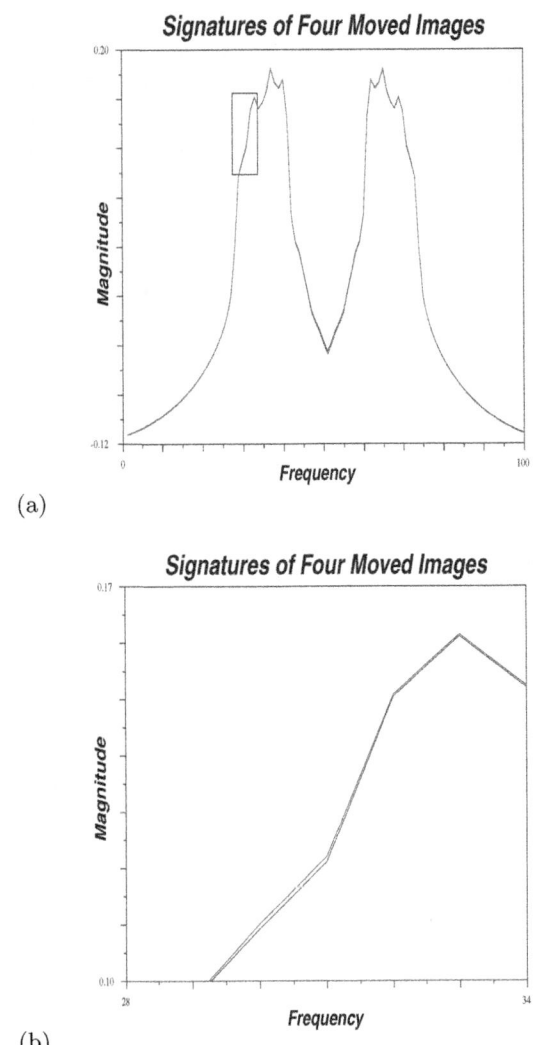

(a)

(b)

Fig. 3.2: These graphs depict the signatures of the system created by translating a simple image across the grid. As expected, the images nearly overlap.

Low resolution is the key, however. At higher resolutions, the differences tend to disappear. This indicates that in the high resolution limit, we have true rotational invariance.

Practical use of such a lattice would seem to require one to determine the difference resulting from such a rotation, and to verify that different images have sufficiently different signatures to distinguish them from simple rotations.

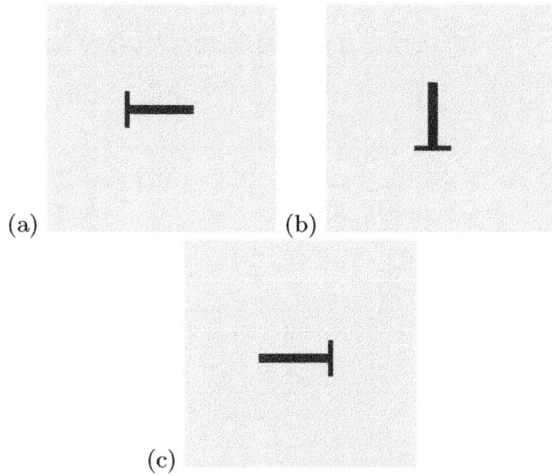

(a)   (b)

(c)

Fig. 3.3: These pictures illustrate the rotation of an object found on our grid.

Although Figure 3.8 illustrates that increases in image resolution do not lead monotonically to improved rotational invariance in the signature, as the resolution is increased, the system tends to allow for greater freedom of rotation without variation in signatures. Thus we expect rotational invariance to be found, as asserted, at high resolution.

4.3   Uniqueness

The foundation of any visual recognition system is some form of uniqueness. This establishes the ability to distinguish between different objects. For uniquness to exist in our system, the attractors generated by two pictures must be distinctively different. This means that the time-variant behaviors of differing images should be significantly different, allowing the signature of the pictures to have evident differences. In order to demonstrate show this property, we plot the signatures of four different pictures in Figure 3.9. As is evident, the signatures are significantly deviant, and may easily be identified as different.

4.4   Continuity

In examining continuity we cannot make claims of an $\epsilon - \delta$ nature. Images are made up of a specific resolution, making the determination of a given δ for any specific ϵ impossible. In order to make claims about continuity, we must therefore view δ as a minimum resolution, and rewrite the definition of continuity using this.

Definition: We define an *infinite resolution continuous mapping* ψ between image space and signature space, assumed to be a normed vector space with norm $\|\|_s$, to be one such that given any $\epsilon > 0$, $\exists \ \delta > 0$ such that if the images have a *resolution* of δ and if $|I - I'|_i < \delta$, then $|\psi(I) - \psi(I')|_s < \epsilon$.

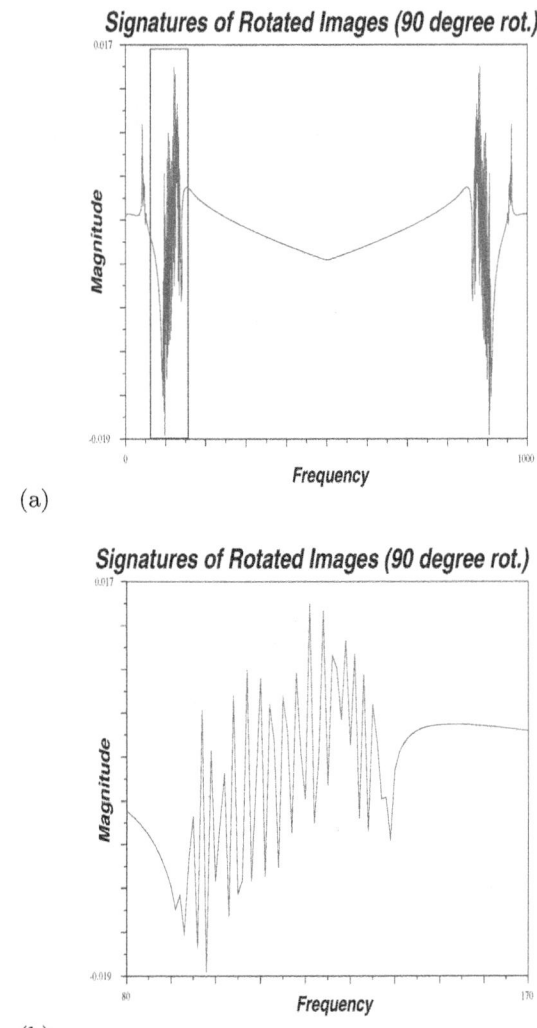

(a)

(b)

Fig. 3.4: These signatures result from the rotated images depicted in Figure 3.5. The overlapping signatures confirms the rotational invariance of the system.

Note that any two images, the distance between which is δ or must have a resolution of δ or less. In the absence of this condition, it is not possible to have two different images whose difference is less than δ. Using this definition of an infinite resolution continuous mapping between the image space and the signature space, we can talk about whether or not the mapping between image space is indeed continuous. As the mathematical proof of this property is beyond

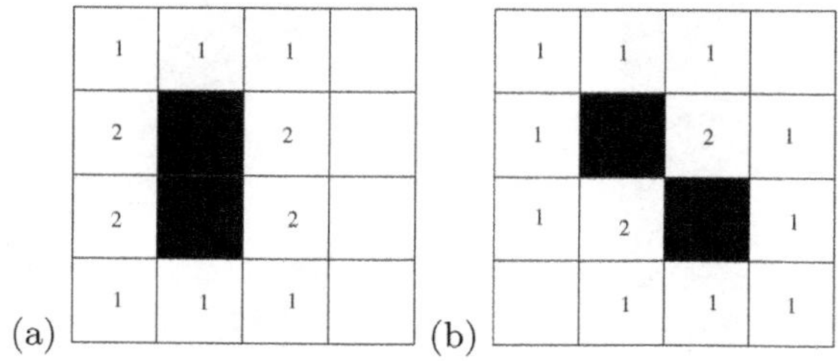

(a)

1	1	1
2	■	2
2	■	2
1	1	1

(b)

1	1	1	
1	■	2	1
1	2	■	1
1	1	1	

Fig. 3.5: The neighborhood structure changes when the image is rotated. In these images, a dark square indicates a pixel which is turned on, while the numbers indicate how many activated pixels the square is adjacent to.

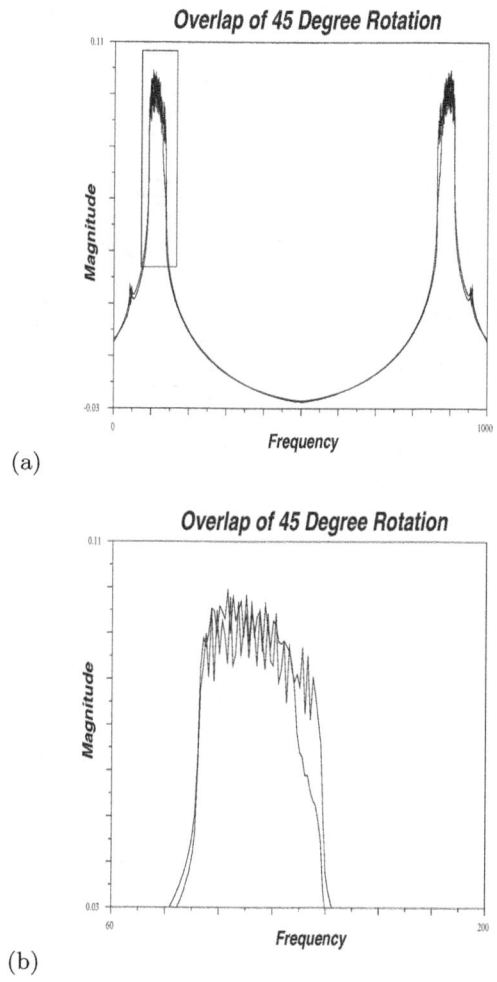

(a)

(b)

Fig. 3.6: The signatures of rotated images are significantly different at rather low resolution.

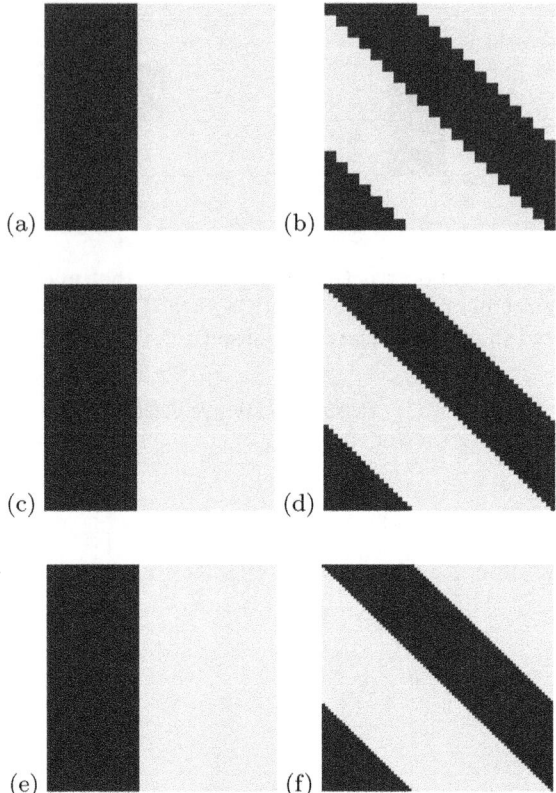

(a)   (b)

(c)   (d)

(e)   (f)

Fig. 3.7: These images depict the same object in two rotational states in different resolutions. The higher resolution images would seem to differ less significantly from their counterparts than the lower resolution images.

the scope of this study, we demonstrate empirically that the system appears to behave in a way consistent with the existence of a continuous mapping.

We accomplish this by investigating the effects of random changes to a given image at different resolutions. Random variations are introduced by altering individual bits and calculating new signatures. We present representative data at resolutions of 30×30, 60×60, and 90×90 in Figure 3.10. In this figure, it is evident that single changes, expected also to be representative of multiple changes, generally decrease in relative magnitude as the resolution increases.

Interestingly, this mapping does not seem to be uniformly continuous. This means that different alterations would seem to cause different changes in the signature. This may be related to why the increase of resolution does not produce a monotonic decrease in rotational variance. Despite this phenomonon, we have yet to observe any case that contradicts that the mapping is indeed an infinite dimensional continuous mapping. In the absence of such data, we may state that

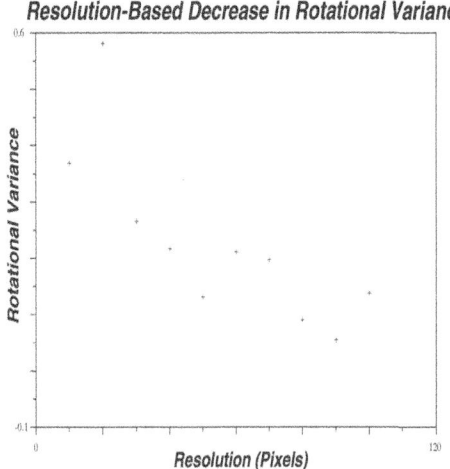

Fig. 3.8: This figure illustrates the reduction in differences between rotated images at different resolutions. Clearly, high resolution creates significantly smaller variations.

this mapping, and therefore this system, satisfies the final condition, and await theoretical verification.

Indeed, in Figure 3.11, we plot several different signatures generated from similar images.

These data support our assertion of continuity in our system, though as discussed above, this is not true $\epsilon - \delta$ continuity.

5   Discussion and Conclusions

Many recent visual recognition systems have typically been designed around a specific class of objects of interest. This requires one to build feature detectors which find specific predetermined features in a particular object. For instance, one may find eyes, noses, mouths, ears, eyebrows, etc. when finding a face. However, a face is not made up entirely by the simple features found within it. The tilt of the eyes, the cheekbones, indentations on the cheeks, length of the forehead, etc. all contribute to the overall understanding one obtains when viewing a face.

We have developed a system that takes a first step in this direction. Continued work in this direction may lead to the development of a somewhat different method of performing identification. Rather than requiring the scientist to determine what makes up the important set of features found within the picture, the entire picture may be used in its identification. This means that although the eyes and nose and mouth would be important constituents of the image, they are by no means the only constituents. Indeed, though we are a far distance from

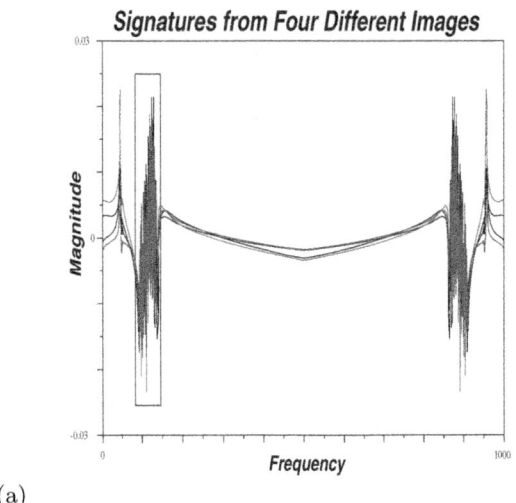

(a)

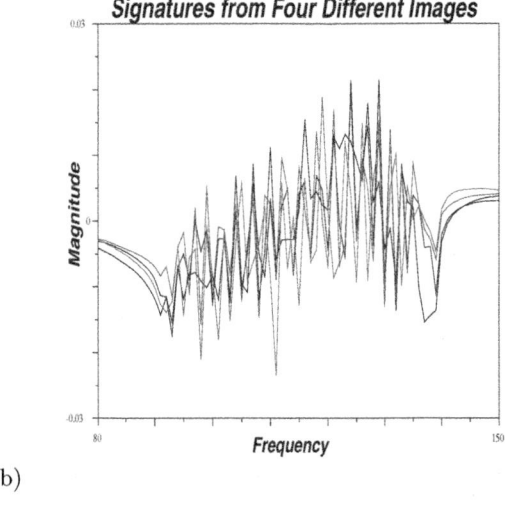

(b)

Fig. 3.9: Signatures from four different images. Each pair of similar images produces a pair of similar signatures, which are distinct from one another. The level of distinction is sufficient to allow rudimentary identification.

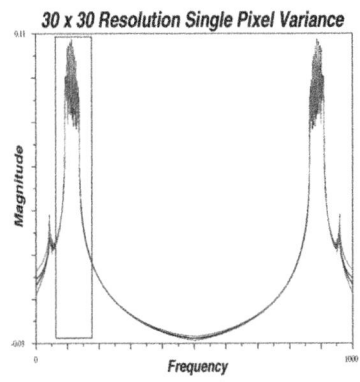

(a)

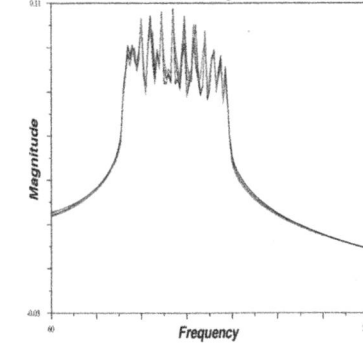

(b)

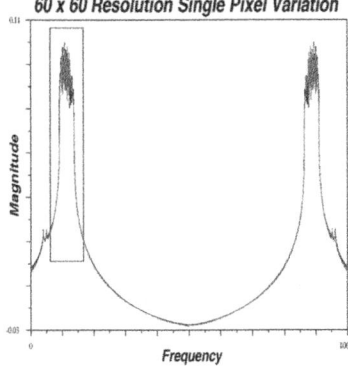

(c)

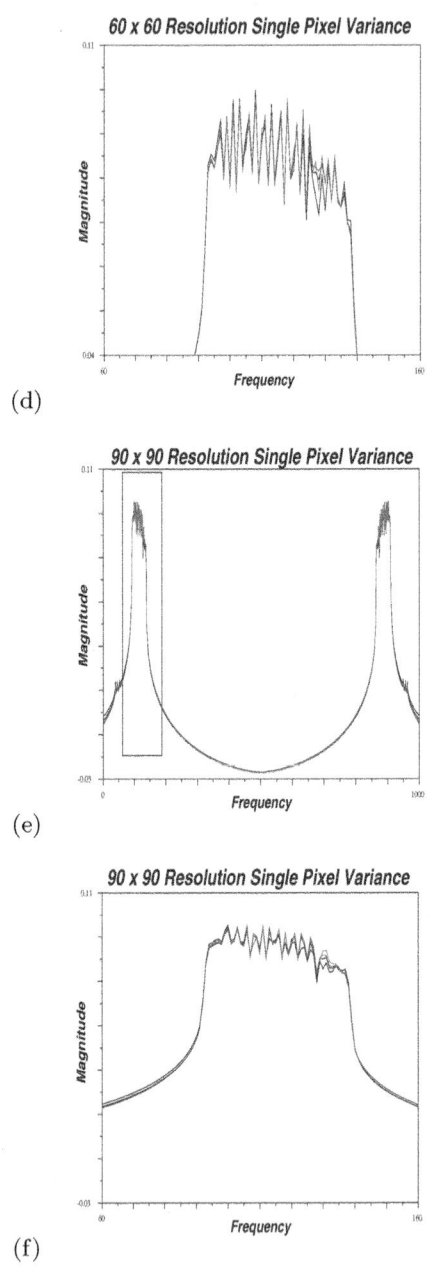

(d)

(e)

(f)

Fig. 3.10: As the resolution increases, there is a concommittant decrease in the variance among signatures created by similar images differing by single pixels.

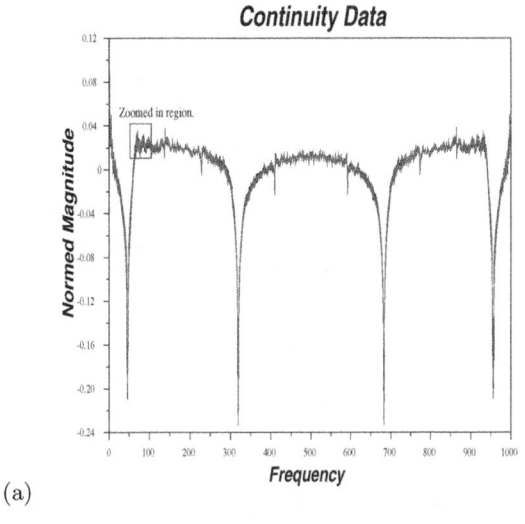

(a)

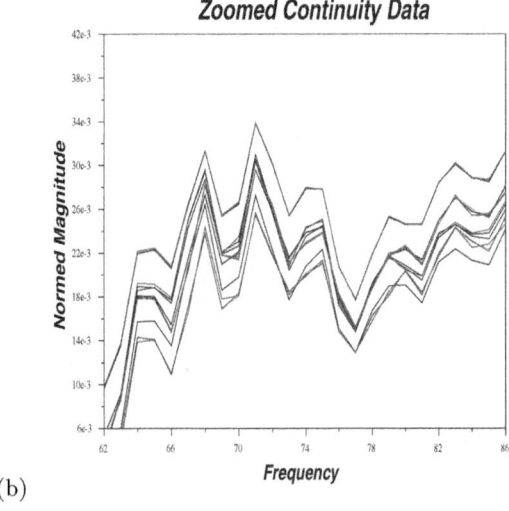

(b)

Fig. 3.11: These images show the signatures of several different images of the same general design. As one can see, thought these do not overlap, the images are quite similar.

this desirable goal, we have been able to demonstrate some of the features one might want to have in such a system.

Firstly, our system demonstrates some measure of rotational invarience and true translational invarience, with rotational invariance subject to the constraints of the system's resolution. At high resolution, the variation due to rotations is expected to become negligible. This expectation is well supported by our data, though a theoretical verification of this fact is outside the scope of this paper. This particular characteristic is useful if the object or objects of interest may not be placed in the same orientation with respect to our sensors. This might be true if the objects are not fixed, say as a person approaching an ATM, or if the sensor is not fixed, say as a camera mounted on an aircraft. Second, the use of translational variation allows us to recognize the object without requiring it to be in the center of a visual field. Such a characteristic is also advantageous in a number of applications in which the field of view is expected to be larger than the object.

Continuity is a tricky subject in discrete object recognition. It cannot be demonstrated empirically that the system obeys continuity. At best, we can demonstrate that the sequence of differences in characteristic signature is Cauchy as the resolution increases. This would also seem to indicate that variations in a picture of a given resolution would produce signatures of a given maximum difference, with this maximum depending heavily on the magnitude of the change in the picture. Thus, as long as the changes in the picture were small, we would be able to create an acceptable difference in the magnitude of the change signature, and be able to identify the object.

Despite the fact that this system is promising, there are still several problems to be overcome before it might be used to implement real object recognition. The first problem arises from the true rotational invariance we would like to have in the system. As discussed above, this would seem to be only approximately possible, due to the difference in neighborhood structure upon changing the orientation of an image. However, possible improvements in the design of the lattice itself and its connectivity may reduce the impact of rotations. For instance one might utilize a hexagonal lattice rather than a rectangular lattice, and the maximum rotational variation would seem to come about at a rotation of 30 degrees rather than 45 degrees.

Other problems include ways in which to achieve true scale invariance. The design of a scale invariant system might require some form of fractal design for the lattice, which would allow the image to have the same design despite its scale. This would seem to work if the image was truly fractal, but of course could only approximately be accomplished using real discrete lattice components. Careful design of such a system would seem to be an interesting future research direction.

While there are many challenges to the creation of practical systems based on this design, the possible uses of this work are relatively wide open. Of particular interest would be the use of this system in any kind of security system including ATM systems, door lock systems, etc. Uses of large numbers of these systems functioning in parallel would seem to provide sufficient individuality to the different images to be able to be used in real security systems.

Other uses of this technology are also more practical. As this might be able to be used to identify different regions of space and landmarks, this might provide an extremely low computation method of determining precise locations as part of a topographic map in autonomous robots. Moreover, very detailed identification of the visual scene might be possible, allowing very precise behavioral switching necessary for applications such as swarm engineering (Kazadi, 2000) which would require simple agents to be able to understand their environment, despite rather stringent computational cost requirements. This technology might provide a cost effective, lightweight alternative to time consuming computations based on high resolution cameras and rather quick processors.

Acknowledgements. This work was carried out at the Jisan Research Institute, and funded by the Institute. The idea, originally proposed by S. Hoque, was entirely investigated by the students and faculty at the Jisan Research Institute. This project represents an exciting new venue for scientific investigation, whereby training and research are coupled.

References

[1] Duda R. and Hart P. **Pattern Classification and Scene Analysis**. New York: John Wiley & Sons, 1973.

[2] Eckmann, J. P. and Ruelle D. *Ergodic theory of chaos and strange attractors.* **Reviews of Modern Physics**. 57 (3): 617-656, 1985.

[3] Kazadi, S. **Swarm Engineering**. PhD Thesis, California Institute of Technology, 2000.

[4] Papageorgiou, C. **Object and Pattern Dectection in Video Sequences.** Master's Thesis, Massachusettes Institute of Technology, May 1997.

[5] Mohan, A. *Object Detection in Images by Components.* **MIT AI Lab-Memo**, No. 1664, June 1999.

[6] Sinha, P. **Object Recogntion via Image Invariants: A Case Study.** *Investigative Ophthamology and Visual Science*, 35, 1735-1740, 1994.

[7] Sinha, P. *Object Image-based Representations for Object Recognition.* **MIT AI Lab-Memo**, No. 1505, 1994.

[8] Goldstein, H. **Classical Mechanics**. Amsterdam: Addison-Wesley, 1980.

[9] Baker G. and Gollub J. **Chaotic Dynamics, an Introduction**. New York: Cambridge University Press, 1996.

[10] Ott E. **Chaos in Dynamical Systems**. New York: Cambridge University Press, 1993.

[11] Strogatz S. **Nonlinear Dynamics and Chaos with Applications to Physics, Biology, Chemistry, and Engineering**. Reading: Pereus Books, 1994.

[12] Williams G. **Chaos Theory Tamed**. Washington D.C.: Joseph Henry Press, 1997.

Adapting Object Recognition across Domains: A Demonstration

Bruce A. Draper[1], Ulrike Ahlrichs[2], and Dietrich Paulus[2]

[1] Department of Computer Science
Colorado State University
Fort Collins, CO 80523, USA
draper@cs.colostate.edu
[2] Lehrstuhl für Mustererkennung
Universität Erlangen-Nürnberg
91058 Erlangen, Germany
ahlrichs,paulus@informatik.uni-erlangen.de

Abstract. High-level vision systems use object, scene or domain specific knowledge to interpret images. Unfortunately, this knowledge has to be acquired for every domain. This makes it difficult to port systems from one domain to another, and therefore to compare them. Recently, the authors of the ADORE system have claimed that object recognition can be modeled as a Markov decision process, and that domain-specific control strategies can be inferred automatically from training data. In this paper we demonstrate the generality of this approach by porting ADORE to a new domain, where it controls an object recognition system that previously relied on a semantic network.

1 Introduction

High-level vision systems can be defined as those that use object, scene or domain knowledge to control the recognition process. By this definition, the first working high-level vision system may have been Nagao and Matsuyama's aerial image analysis system [1]. Since then, high level vision systems have been built using production systems [2-4], blackboard systems [5, 6], semantic networks [7-9] and Bayesian networks [10, 11], not to mention hybrid combinations of these techniques above, e.g. [12, 13]. Although much of the work on high-level vision originated in the 1980's, research continues today (e.g. [9, 14]); see [15] for a recent review.

There are good intellectual reasons to pursue high-level vision. There are currently no general-purpose object recognition techniques, only techniques that can recognize limited classes of objects in restricted domains. It is therefore natural to speculate that a general-purpose vision system might be built by selecting among or combining multiple techniques. Moreover, there is no reason to believe that any single technique should work for all objects – some objects are defined by their shapes, while others are defined by their colors, subparts, textures or contexts. This suggests that object knowl-

B. Schiele and G. Sagerer (Eds.): ICVS 2001, LNCS 2095, pp. 256–267, 2001.

edge should help in selecting the most efficient and robust method for interpreting a scene. Finally, there is psychological evidence for the use of object-specific *signal features* to categorize objects (see, for example, [16] pg. 114).

Unfortunately, high-level vision systems have proved to be problematic. They are difficult and time-consuming to build, and are often brittle once built. (See [17, 18] for discussions of knowledge engineering and vision.) Worse still, it is difficult to conclude anything from the behavior of these prototype systems, since changing the knowledge base can alter almost any success or failure. Of particular importance to this paper, the dependence of high-level systems on domain-specific databases makes it difficult to port them from one domain to another, since the databases have to be re-engineered for every task. This limits their utility, since no high-level system is really general. Moreover, since they cannot be ported without fundamentally changing their behavior, direct comparisons are impossible, undermining the improvements that are supposed to come from competition and refinement.

In the last several years, a new class of high-level vision systems have emerged that avoid many of the problems above, while still using object, scene and domain information to direct processing. These systems use machine learning techniques to acquire information from training images. This simplifies system construction, and makes it possible to port them from domain to domain. Examples of these systems include [19-22].

For the last several years, the first author has advocated the use of Markov models for high-level computer vision, with reinforcement learning as the training method [18, 23]. As a prototype, ADORE (for *Ad*aptive *O*bject *Re*cognition) was built and trained to find buildings in aerial imagery [19]. In this paper we demonstrate that ADORE really can be ported from one domain to another, by training it to recognize objects in a new domain (office supplies), using images and routines developed at another university (Erlangen-Nürnberg). The system was ported by two people in the span of one week, and required no significant changes in the underlying learning algorithms or control systems. The routines of the Erlangen System are also used in an object recognition system on the same task domain [24].

2 ADORE

The adaptive object recognition (ADORE) project at Colorado State University approaches object recognition as a supervised learning task. Developers train ADORE to recognize specific objects by providing training images and training signals, where a training signal provides rewards based on how closely the output matches the desired output for a training image. ADORE learns control strategies that maximize the expected value of the reward signal, given a library of visual procedures. These control strategies can then be used to hypothesize new object instances in novel images. Thus ADORE is a method for learning and applying high-level visual control strategies, as depicted in Figure 1.

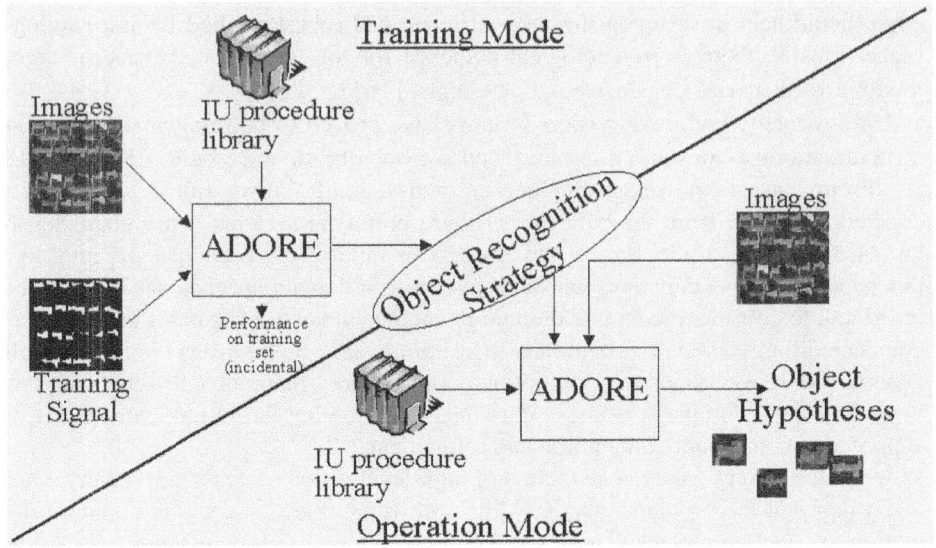

Fig. 1. Overview of ADORE. The system learns an object-specific recognition strategy that controls vision procedures by comparing training images to an ideal training signal. Once learned, these recognition strategies are then used to find object instances in novel test images.

ADORE learns control strategies by modeling object recognition as a Markov decision process. In general, a Markov decision problem is defined in terms of a set of states and a set of actions; the goal is to find a control policy that maps states onto actions so as to maximize the expected total reward. In the case of ADORE, the state of the system is determined by data tokens produced by vision procedures. For example, the state of the system might be a region of interest (ROI), a set of 2D line segments, or a 2D contour. The actions are vision procedures, such as correlation or line extraction. Actions change the state of the system by producing new data tokens from old data tokens. A control strategy (or control policy) is a function that maps states onto actions. In the context of ADORE, control policies map data tokens onto vision procedures, thereby selecting the next action in the recognition process. (See [19] for a software-level description of ADORE.) It should be noted that ADORE controls vision procedures, not physical sensors, so the strategies learned by ADORE are not active vision strategies. Instead, they are knowledge-directed strategies that use learned information to direct the recognition process.

The control strategies learned by ADORE are dynamic. In other words, ADORE does not choose a fixed sequence of actions (vision procedures) to apply to all images in a domain. Instead, it learns to select the next vision procedure based on attributes is measures of the previous result. In the past, this capability was used mostly to recover from unreliable actions. For example, if a segmentation routine returned too many regions, the control strategy could respond by invoking a region merging procedure. In this paper, however, it is used to select among different object labels.

One of the strengths of ADORE is that it is a very general mechanism for learning visual control strategies, and is not limited to one style of visual processing or another. In [19], the objects to be recognized were rigid geometric shapes, and the routines in the procedure library grouped regions, points and lines into geometric structures. In [25], the procedure library contained focus of attention routines and preprocessing routines for a principal components analysis (PCA) recognition system. In this paper, the procedure library contains more traditional pattern recognition routines that segment images and classify regions based on size, color and texture (see Section 4).

3   ANIMALS

The ANIMALS[1] system (shown in Figure 2) was developed at the University of Erlangen-Nürnberg as a prototype for systems combining active vision with knowledge-based object recognition [9]. In particular, the goal in ANIMALS was to combine data-driven and knowledge-based techniques so as to enable goal-directed exploration under the guidance of an explicit knowledge base. As a result, ANIMALS is a complex, multi-part system. It includes a bottom-up subsystem that uses sensor movements along a rail to compute 3D depth maps of scenes that are registered to color images. It has an active vision component that responds to cues (typically colors) in the image data by panning and zooming the camera to produce high-resolution images at known scales (based on the depth data) centered on potential objects in the scene. Finally, it has a knowledge-based object recognition component that uses a semantic network to interpret and label high-resolution images. These three components are combined in a loop, so that the system can get a low-resolution but 3D view of a large scene, select promising locations, and then iteratively zoom in and interpret each region of interest until a target object is found.

Of interest to this paper is the knowledge-based object recognition component of ANIMALS. The goal of this system is to determine whether an image contains an instance of one of a set of target objects; in this paper, a hole punch, tape dispenser or glue stick. Because of its role within the larger ANIMALS system, the object recognition subsystem is always given a high-resolution image that is centered on a potential target. However, since color is not a perfect cue, some of these images are centered on other similarly colored objects found in office scenes, such as books or staplers. The accuracy of the depth computation is sufficient to determine the required focal length of the active camera such that close-up views of objects can be captured in which the objects have approximately the same size. Using scale invariant features for object recognition, these images can be classified reliably. However, the images differ in scaling up to 20%.

As described in [9], one of the available object recognition components of ANIMALS is a knowledge based system for recognizing 3D objects in 2D images. It begins by segmenting the image into regions, and then measures properties of those

---

[1] ANIMALS is an acronym for "An Image Analysis System".

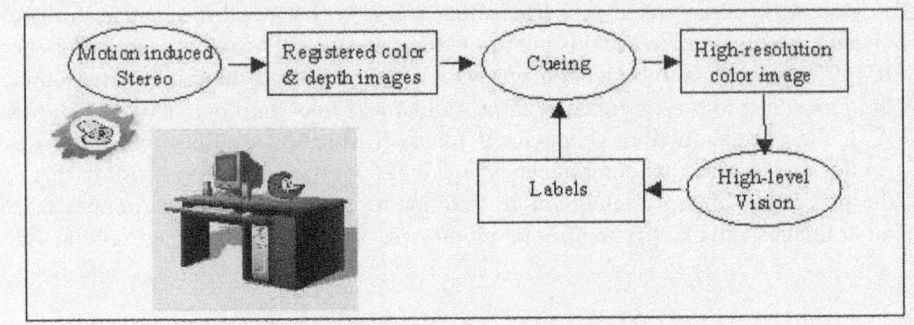

Fig. 2. The ANIMALS active object recognition system [9]

regions such as size and color to find the most likely object label. A semantic network relates objects to each other, and provides the basis for an A* search that matches features to object types [24].

4   Porting ADORE to ANIMALS

The goal of this exercise is to test the claim that ADORE is a general-purpose, high-level vision system that can be ported from domain to domain. In principle, all ADORE needs is a library of vision routines, a data set and a training signal; it will learn the best strategy possible for that library and task. This has never been demonstrated, however, by actually porting it to another domain. (Nor, to our knowledge, has it been demonstrated for any other high-level vision system.) In this paper, we port ADORE to the University of Erlangen-Nürnberg and apply it to high-resolution images captured by the active imaging component of ANIMALS. The task assigned to ADORE is to apply ANIMAL's segmentation and recognition components to compute an optimal object recognition strategy.

4.1   The Vision Procedure Library

The vision procedures for this exercise were extracted from the ANIMALS object recognition system. Each procedure consumed and/or produces one of four data representations: *image, segmentation, feature vector* or *label*. The system is given attributes it can measure about segmentations, feature vectors and labels. These attributes form the basis for its decisions about what procedure to execute at each choice point.

There are a total of twelve vision procedures. One of the procedures is *grabimage,* which is used to read in an image and start the process. Three of the procedures are *reject* procedures used to stop processing and signal to the user that that image con-

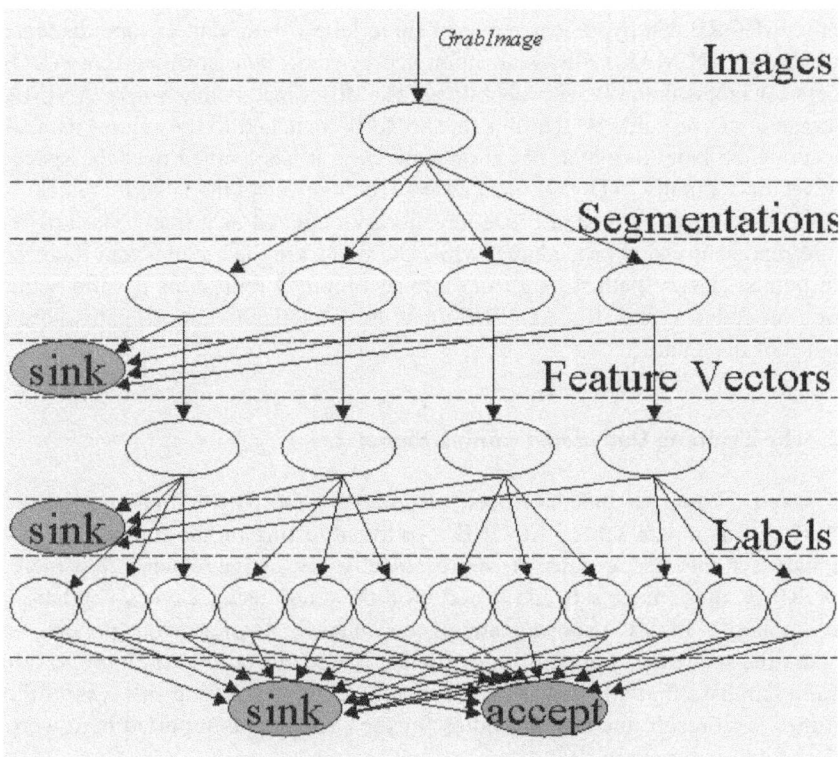

Fig. 3. The Visual Procedure Library depicted as a tree. Arrows represent procedures, while ovals represent data tokens. The individual procedures and representations are described in the text.

tains no known object[2]. Four of the procedures are segmentation procedures resulting in four segmentation results (see Fig. 3), although there are only two underlying color-region segmentation algorithms. The two color segmentation algorithms are applied that were programmed to have uniform interfaces. One is a split and merge algorithm extended to work on color similarity measures. The other is the so-called CSC segmentation algorithm [26]. There are a total of four segmentation options in the procedure library because both segmentation algorithms are parameterized, and it is the goal of this experiment to determine the best sets of parameters. We therefore included two parameterizations of each algorithm in the database, giving ADORE four methods of segmenting images.

Once an image is segmented, there is only one procedure for reducing a segmentation to a feature vector, although ADORE also has the option of rejecting the segmentation if it does not contain a region that might be the target object. Given a feature

---

[2] Since every procedure in ADORE can only be applied to one datatype, it takes three different procedures to reject segmentations, feature vectors and labels.

vector, ADORE can hypothesize one of three labels (hole punch, tape dispenser, glue stick) using ANIMAL's Bayesian inference system. The attribute that ADORE can access for labels is the label probability. The difference is that where ANIMAL used a semantic net to guide which objects should be matched to the region data, ADORE selects which label to match based on a function it has learned over the space of feature vectors. Finally, ADORE must either accept or reject the label it creates.

Figure 3 shows the vision procedure library depicted as a tree. The arrows in the figure represent vision procedures, while the ovals are data tokens and therefore decision points. Every path through the tree in Figure 3 represents a valid sequence of vision procedures, and it is ADORE's task to dynamically choose paths based on attributes of the data.

4.2   The Training Data and Training Signal

We saved 57 images that had been acquired by the active imaging component of ANIMALS as a data set for ADORE. To avoid testing on the training data, we split the data set into ten groups of approximately six images each. We then trained ADORE on nine image sets and tested it on the tenth, using a cross-validation testing methodology[3]. Figure 4 shows some of the images. As in previous papers, we tested all possible sequence of actions on every test image (according to Figure 3) in order to build a database that allowed us to efficiently simulate running the system thousands of times; as a result, the training times for the experiments reported here were on the order of one-half hour each.

For a training signal, we manually labeled each image by object type. During training, when ADORE accepted an object label it received a reward of 0.9 if the label was correct, and 0.1 if the label was erroneous. If ADORE correctly concluded that the image did not contain a target object, it received a reward of 0.2, in order to bias it toward selecting object labels.

5   Experimental Results

The most important result of this demonstration is not the output of ADORE on any given image, but rather the fact that ADORE could be ported to a new domain with a new vision procedure library in two people-weeks (one calendar week). Moreover, porting it did not require any significant changes to the learning algorithms or control mechanisms of ADORE. It did require writing a new library file to describe the new vision procedures to ADORE, and it took some effort to extract the relevant vision algorithms from ANIMALS and convert them into stand-alone programs. This process was greatly helped by the fact that ANIMALS was developed using the ζππος

---

[3] Due to time limitations, only 36 of the 57 images (six of ten groups) were used as test images.

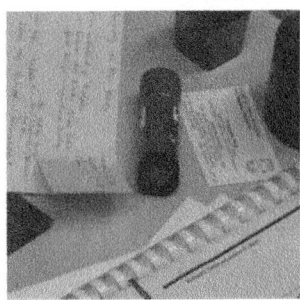

Fig. 4. Three images captured by the active imaging component of ANIMALS. These three images show the tape dispenser, hole punch and glue stick, respectively.

(HIPPOS [27]) system. Most of the porting effort was spent writing shell scripts to support the cross-validation training and testing protocols, which have never been automated in ADORE.

The purpose of the cross-validation study, however, was to see if ADORE performed well in this new domain. Table 1 gives a summary of the results in the form of a confusion table. Overall, ADORE correctly identified 28 out of 36 images. It had the most trouble with the glue stick, which it identified correctly only once in four images. Most likely this is because long and narrow regions can also be produced by oversegmenting the hole punch or other objects such as the spines of books. The errors in Table 1 might be reduced by adding better attributes to describe segmentations, or by introducing new procedures to verify hypothesized labels.

A better way to judge ADORE's performance is in terms of rewards. The goal of ADORE's learning algorithm is to maximize the total expected reward. In this domain, the maximum possible reward is 0.9 for any image that contains a hole punch, tape dispenser or glue stick, and 0.2 for any other image. For the 36 images tested, the maximum possible total reward was 25.4.[4] The reward received by ADORE was 21.1, or 83% of maximum.

The results above (including Table 1) were generated by running ADORE in a traditional Markov process mode. In particular, it is not possible to "undo" an action in a traditional Markov process. The control policy selects the action with the best expected total future reward, but the actions are probabilistic, and in some instances the results of an action are worse than expected. In this case, a Markov process must carry on from the new, undesired state because it cannot backtrack. This traditional model was developed for the control of physical devices, where it is not possible to go back in time and undo the effects of previous actions. Object recognition, however, is a computational process. As long as the system has memory, it can always return to a

---

[4] Note that the maximum possible reward for a Markov system with this action & state space – i.e. the optimal control policy -- is unknown, but must be less than or equal to this number.

Table 1. Confusion table for ADORE applied to the office supply domain describes in [9]

	Hole Punch	Tape Dispenser	Glue Stick	Other
Hole Punch	13	0	0	0
Tape Dispenser	0	7	1	3
Glue Stick	0	0	1	0
Other	2	0	2	7

previous state. For example, if a vision procedure oversegments an image, it is not necessary to proceed with the overly fractured segmentation; the system can go back to the original image and select another segmentation routine instead. In other words, backtracking is possible.

If we let ADORE backtrack while interpreting test images, it does more work in the sense that it executes more procedures. However, its performance improves. Table 2 shows the confusion table with backtracking. Overall, it interprets 26 of 36 images correctly – two less than without backtracking. It does a better job of maximizing its reward function, however. The total reward with backtracking improves to 23.0, compared to 21.1 without backtracking. This brings ADORE to within 91% of the maximum possible reward. The reward increases because the reward function is biased to prefer mislabeling an image that contains no object over failing to label an image that contains an object. With backtracking enabled, ADORE segments images multiple times if the first segmentation does not include a viable target region. In this way, it tries repeatedly to generate plausible labels. This maximizes the reward function by correctly labeling 26 of the 28 images that contain objects[5], as opposed to 21 of 28 without backtracking. The penalty is that it only correctly labels 2 of 10 images without target objects, but this is a good trade-off in terms of the reward function. Of course, ADORE could be retrained with other reward functions.

---

[5] One of the two mislabeled hole punch images is an imaging failure, in the sense that only part of the punch is in the field of view.

Table 2. Confusion table for ADORE with backtracking applied to the office supply domain.

	Hole Punch	Tape Dispenser	Glue Stick	Other
Hole Punch	13	0	0	0
Tape Dispenser	0	7	0	7
Glue Stick	0	0	4	1
Other	2	0	0	2

6 Conclusions

A major problem with traditional high-level vision systems is that they cannot be ported from domain to domain without manually re-engineering their knowledge bases. In theory, newer systems that use machine learning techniques to infer their knowledge bases overcome this problem. However, their ability to be ported has never (to our knowledge) been tested in practice. This paper reports on an experiment in which ADORE was ported from one domain to another (and one university to another) by two people in a single week, and successfully learned to recognize objects in a new domain. We find it significant that ADORE was able to adapt to a new domain and procedure library so quickly, and also that the routines of ANIMALS allowed for such an export to another system.

Acknowledgements. This work was partially supported by DFG Ni 191/12 and SFB 603.

References

1.   Nagao, M. and T. Matsuyama, *A Structural Analysis of Complex Aerial Photographs.* 1980, New York: Plenum Press.
2.   Ohta, Y., *A Region-oriented Image-analysis System by Computer*, Ph.D. thesis, 1980, Kyoto University: Kyoto, Japan.

3.   McKeown, D.M., W.A. Harvey, and J. McDermott, *Rule-Based Interpretation of Aerial imagery.* IEEE Transactions on Pattern Analysis and Machine Intelligence, 1985. **7**(5): p. 570-585.

4.   Clement, V. and M.Thonnat, *A Knowledge-Based Approach to Integration of Image Processing.* Computer Vision, Graphics and Image Processing, 1993. **57**(2): p. 166-184.

5.   Draper, B.A., *et al., The Schema System.* International Journal of Computer Vision, 1989. **2**(2): p. 209-250.

6.   Andress, K.M. and A.C. Kak, *Evidence Accumulation & Flow of Control in a Hierarchical Spatial Reasoning System.* AI Magazine, 1988. **9**(2): p. 75-94.

7.   Freuder, E.C. *A Computer System for Visual Recognition using Active Knowledge Sources.* in *International Joint Conference on Artificial Intelligence.* 1977. Cambridge, MA.

8.   Niemann, H., *et al., Ernest: A Semantic Network System for Pattern Understanding.* IEEE Transactions on Pattern Analysis and Machine Intelligence, 1990. **12**(9): p. 883-905.

9.   Paulus, D., *et al. Active Knowledge-Based Scene Analysis.* in *International Conference on Vision Systems.* 1999. Las Palmas de Gran Canaria, Spain: Springer-Verlag. p. 180-199.

10.   Rimey, R.D. and C.M. Brown, *Control of Selective Perception using Bayes Nets and Decision Theory.* International Journal of Computer Vision, 1994. **12**: p. 173-207.

11.   Mann, W.B. and T.O. Binford. *SUCCESSOR: Interpretation Overview and Constraint System.* in *Image Understanding Workshop.* 1996. Palm Springs, CA: Morgan Kaufman.

12.   Hwang, V.S.-S., L.S. Davis, and T. Matsuyama, *Hypothesis Integration in Image Understanding Systems.* Computer Vision, Graphics and Image Processing, 1986. **36**(2): p. 321-371.

13.   Stilla, U., E. Michaelson, and K. Lütjen, *Structural 3D-Analysis of Aerial Images with a Blackboard-based Production System,* in *Automatic Extraction of Man-made Objects from Aerial and Space Images,* A. Gruen, O. Kuebler, and P. Agouris, Editors. 1995, Birkhäuser: Basel. p. 53-62.

14.   Thonnat, M., S. Moisan, and M. Crubézy. *Experience in Integrating Image Processing Programs.* in *International Conference on Vision Systems.* 1999. Las Palmas de Gran Canaria, Spain: Springer. p. 200-215.

15.   Crevier, D. and R. LePage, *Knowledge-based Image Understanding Systems.* Computer Vision and Image Understanding, 1997. **67**(2): p. 161-185.

16.   Kosslyn, S.M., *Image and Brain: The Resolution of the Imagery Debate.* 1994, Cambridge, MA: MIT Press. 516.

17.   Draper, B.A. and A.R. Hanson, *An Example of Learning in Knowledge Directed Vision,* in *Theory and Applications of Image Analysis,* P. Johansen and S. Olsen, Editors. 1992, World Scientific: Singapore. p. 237-252.

18.   Draper, B.A., A.R. Hanson, and E.M. Riseman, *Knowledge-Directed Vision: Control, Learning and Integration.* Proceedings of the IEEE, 1996. **84**(11): p. 1625-1637.

19.   Draper, B.A., J. Bins, and K. Baek, *ADORE: Adaptive Object Recognition.* Videre, 2000. **1**(4): p. 86-99.

20.   Peng, J. and B. Bhanu, *Closed-Loop Object Recognition Using Reinforcement Learning.* IEEE Transactions on Pattern Analysis and Machine Intelligence, 1998. **20**(2): p. 139-154.

21.   Au, W. and B. Roberts. *Adaptive Configuration and Control in an ATR System.* in *Image Understanding Workshop.* 1996. Palm Springs, CA: Morgan Kaufman. p. 667-676

22.   Maloof, M.A., *et al. Learning to Detect Rooftops in Aerial Images.* in *Image Understanding Workshop.* 1997. New Orleans: Morgan Kaufman. p. 835-846

23.   Draper, B.A., *Learning Control Strategies for Object Recognition,* in *Symbolic Visual Learning,* K. Ikeuchi and M. Veloso, Editors. 1997, Oxford University Press: New York. p. 49-76.

24.   Ahlrichs, U., D. Paulus, and H. Neiman. *Integrating Aspects of Active Vision into a Knowledge-Based System.* in *International Conference on Pattern Recognition.* 2000. Barcelona.

25.   Draper, B.A. and K. Baek. *Unsupervised Learning of Biologically Plausible Object Recognition Strategies,.* in *IEEE International Workshop on Biologically Motivated Computer Vision.* 2000. Seoul: IEEE CS Press.

26.   Priese, L. and V. Rehrmann. *On Hierarchical Color Segmentation and Applications.* in *IEEE Conference on Computer Vision and Pattern Recognition.* 1993.

27.   Paulus, D. and J. Hornegger, *Pattern Recognition of Images and Speech in C++,* in *Advanced Studies in Computer Science.* 1997, Vieweg: Braunschweig.

A System to Navigate a Robot into a Ship Structure

Markus Vincze[1], Minu Ayromlou[1], Carlos Beltran[3], Antonios Gasteratos[3],
Simon Hoffgaard[2], Ole Madsen[2], Wolfgang Ponweiser[1], and Michael Zillich[1]

[1]Institute of Flexible Automation, Vienna University of Technology
Gusshausstr. 27-29/361, 1040 Vienna, Austria, e-mail: vm@infa.tuwien.ac.at
[2]Aalborg University, Department of Production, 9220 Aalborg DK
[3]Lab for Integrated Advanced Robotics of the University of Genova, 16145 Genova, IT

Abstract. A prototype system has been built to navigate a walking robot into a
ship structure. The robot is equipped with a stereo head for monocular and
stereo vision. From the CAD-model of the ship good viewpoints are selected
such that the head can look at locations with sufficient features. The edge
features for the views are extracted automatically. The pose of the robot is
estimated from the features detected by two vision approaches. One approach
searches in the full image for junctions and uses the stereo information to
extract 3D information. The other method is monocular and tracks 2D edge
features. To achieve robust tracking of the features a model-based tracking
approach is enhanced with a method of Edge Projected Integration of Cues
(EPIC). EPIC uses object knowledge to select the correct features in real-time.
The two vision systems are synchronised by sending the images over a fibre
channel network. The pose estimation uses both the 2D and 3D features and
locates the robot within a few centimetres over the range of ship cells of several
metres. Gyros are used to stabilise the head while the robot moves. The system
has been developed within the RobVision project and the results of the final
demonstration are given.

1 Project Overview

Robot navigation is a common problem in mobile robotics. In most cases, the problem
is considered a 2D problem. The sensor data is projected to the ground plane and then
used for path planning and robot control. The task of navigating a climbing robot into
a ship structure requires 3D navigation, since the robot shall be also able to climb
walls.

The objective of the RobVision project is to develop a vision system that finds and
measures the location of 3D structures with respect to a CAD-model for the purpose
of robot navigation. The project focused on using the vision system for guiding a
robotic vehicle to enable it to navigate and position itself in order to deliver work
packages for inspection, welding and other tasks for the structure/body of a large
vessel during production. The main motivation for this project is the demand of the
end user Odense Shipyard, DK, who are ultimately looking for a robotic operator that
can replace human workers to perform the task outlined within a shipyard

B. Schiele and G. Sagerer (Eds.): ICVS 2001, LNCS 2095, pp. 268–283, 2001.
© Springer-Verlag Berlin Heidelberg 2001

environment. Of particular interest is to execute the final welding task at the dock, where conditions for the human worker are exhausting and dangerous.

The integration of a CAD-model to visual measurement and direct feedback of measurement results is the key aspect. In terms of system requirements the major concern is reliability. Other needs are fast operation, sufficient accuracy, autonomous behaviour, automated operation and a simple to use interface to the customer.

Reliability is tackled by developing a method of robust visual finding and tracking by integrating redundant low level image cues and high level object knowledge. Image cues and object knowledge are exploited and integrated both at a local and global level. For the extraction of basic visual cues independent and complimentary modules have been designed.

The paper presents the system layout (Section 2), the main components for feature extraction (Section 3), control of the head and 3D feature measurement (Section 4) and tracking 2D features and pose estimation (Section 5). Section 6 presents part of the demonstrations, which saw the walking robot enter and walk through the vessel structure and gives example results of tracking and pose estimation.

1.1   Related Work

The work of this project is related to navigating mobile robots in indoor environments or grasping parts with a robot. Autonomous robots hold a CAD-map of the building and use landmarks, such as walls or pillars, for navigation (e.g. [15,14,7]). The robot assumes a rough position and matches the landmarks of its map to those detected by the vision system. The main problems are a changing background and high computational demands. For example, a space application where background is dark and the object consists of parts of different surface characteristics, requires dedicated hardware to run at frame rate [23]. Probably the most successful system that uses vision to control a mechanism is the automatic car and air-vehicle approach using dynamic vision [9]. It integrates the dynamic aspects of a continuously operating system and image data to update the model description of the world.

Another series of technique that can be used for 3D navigation relate to object recognition. Object recognition matches image features to features in a data base of multiple objects [11,24]. The match reports object hypotheses, which are subsequently verified to report the most likely object. As a by-product of this process, most approaches report an estimate of the object pose. Impressive results have been shown using edge features (e.g., [11,24,3,6]). However, object recognition suffers from two common problems. (1) Matching requires extensive search and cannot be scaled to operate in real-time for 3D objects of reasonable complexity [4]. Newest results on using indexing [3,6] still require several seconds in simple cases and minutes in more complex images. Therefore most approaches are not used for navigation. An exception is a noticeable work that realises fast indexing by exploiting image and stereo lines, though the authors concede the "reliability-bottleneck" introduced by using one type of feature [7]. And (2), the recognition rates are high under the assumption of good feature extraction. Invariant (to perspective distortion [24] or to illumination [1]) features enable robust recognition, however this requires a solution to the equally difficult problem of robust feature segmentation.

Regarding reliable feature extraction, cue integration has been found in a few approaches as feasible approach (see upcoming book from Dagstuhl Seminar 421 Oct.

2000 in Springer Lecture Notes in Computer Science). An approach studied most closely is voting in cue integration. Voting is a model-free approach and requires a common classification space. Plurality voting gives best results when using four simple blob trackers [PiCh98]. In [16] the authors show that weighted consensus voting of five cues for view-based tracking performs better than a fuzzy fusion method and the single cues. The approach in [2] uses voting to integrate four cues to find planar surfaces but requires a good initial start segmentation to give good results.

2   System Layout

The goal of the project is to define a path and to navigate the robot through this path. Figure 1 shows the system components that have been built to fulfil this task. To summarise, the system works as follows.

From the shipyard's CAD database a 3D model is generated. The model seen in the top left corner of the Figure is a representative example of the typical geometries that can be expected. The model is also similar to the final mock-up that has been built. An operator will then interact with this model to specify intermediary points (IPs), which roughly describe the path along which the robot should move. Whilst each IP describes a pose, additional attributes attached to these IPs describe specific properties applicable to either the robot or the environment. For example, one of these attributes provides the robot with information about what type of walking gait it should adopt (for example, high gait to step over a truss, or narrow gait to step out the hole of the mock-up). For each IP the CAD system searches for good views to look for the vision system. These views present expected views that are seen by the vision system at each respective IP. From these views the CAD to Vision (C2V, developed by AAU) system extracts all significant features and sends them to the two vision components PRONTO and V4R (Vision for Robotics). The goal is to automatically select features that are expected to be robust and can be used by the vision system to reliably calculate pose.

Using the view direction, PRONTO (developed by DIST) controls the head to look at the specified directions. Figure 2 (right) shows the head mounted on the robot. PRONTO also searches for junctions features and measures the 3D pose of these features.

The feature list is also used by Vision for Robotics (V4R, developed by INFA) to find 2D line, junction and arc features. To assure that the two vision systems are synchronised, the images from the head are submitted via messages using the fibre channel network from PRONTO to V4R. Due the optical network this is done in a few milliseconds. Furthermore, the two vision systems mutually report about features found to increase the reliability of finding and tracking features.

Finally V4R estimates at each tracking cycle the pose of the head and the pose of the robot with respect to the coordinate system of the ship. Knowing its present pose from the message of V4R and the path described by the IP, the robot can calculate its trajectory and can travers to the next IP and finally the final target pose.

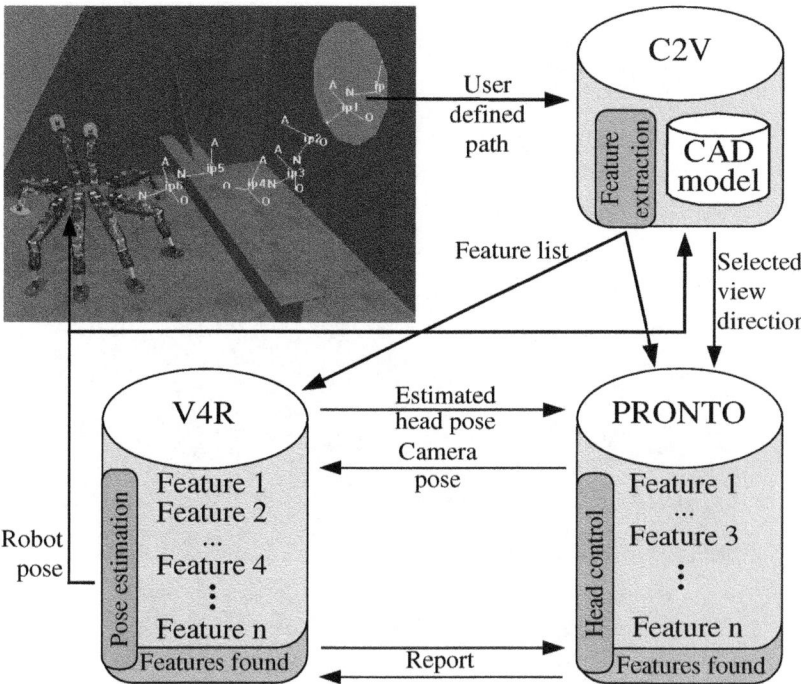

Fig. 1. Principal approach of the RobVision project indicating the main functions of the system components C2V (CAD to Vision, view generation and feature extraction), PRONTO (head control and 3D feature finding) and V4R (Vision for Robotics, 2D feature tracking, pose estimation). In the top left picture, the white co-ordinate systems are the intermediate target poses defined by the user. The trajectory between these intermediate target poses is calculated automatically by V4R. The robot uses this information and the robot pose message of the V4R system to stay on the trajectory.

The robot Robug IV has been developed by Portech, Portsmouth, UK. The robot can carry a weight of 50 kg and is actuated pneumatically. The body of the robot is designed to carry a robot arm for the welding or inspection task. Figure 2 (left) shows the robot at the entrance hole of the mock-up. The right part of the Figure shows the stereo head, called Eurohead, developed by DIST and here mounted on the robot.

2.1   Simulating and Integrating Communication

The stable communication between several components is of utmost importance for systems integration. A communication tool has been developed that provides the *capability to simulate the components*, test each component individually *and to conduct hardware tests in the loop*.

The core of the communication tool is a supervisor process running on a computer with a Windows operating system. The components need to be specified only once. For each component it is then possible to run a simulation or the actual system, which can both run on the same or another computer. The communication protocol utilises

Fig. 2. The Robug IV robot entering the mock-up (left) and a close-up of the Eurohead mounted on the robot front (right).

the TCP/IP standard. Therefore, the components can run on any operating system. The *system components are detected automatically*, therefore no reconfiguration is needed when switching from the simulated component to the actual component.

This communication tool has been successfully applied within RobVision to test the communication of individual components and to enable rapid integration of the components.

2.2   Summary of System Specifications

The project presented a demonstrator to enable autonomous robots in ship building. The approach is flexible, because it can operate in any environment that has distinct features and that is modelled or that can be modelled.

The path of the robot can be planned off-line using the ship model and the *PathPlanner* tool to easily specify the path (for more details on the tools contact the authors). The tool shows the robot and the ship section graphically in one display as the user enters or modifies the position descriptors in a dialog. Each robot position is defined by a pose, a tolerance, and a gait. The tolerance specifies the required accuracy that the robot controller needs to achieve before changing focus to the next position in the path.

The accuracy of the pose estimation of the demonstrator has been 5 to 35 mm for three test series at distances to the features of two to three meters. The pose is continuously estimated along the path in the ship section. The accuracy does not depend on the path length, but on the distance to features at the final location. Therefore this pose accuracy can be reached also after long paths.

Robustness of feature tracking is attempted with appropriate visual processes (Hough transform and a method for Edge Projected Integration of Cues) and the integration of several 2D and 3D line and junction features. The egomotion of the robot is compensated using gyros.

The update cycle time of the pose estimation is presently 120 milliseconds, however, the visual tracking system is capable of lowering this cycle time to 40 milliseconds (if not executing several other tools for system evelopment). The rate of this feedback allows a robot speed of 25 cm/s.

The following sections will now give more detail on the subsystems.

3   Feature Extraction: CAD to Vision (C2V)

The basic idea of C2V is to select good view points, to send new view points along the path, and to provide model and feature information to the vision systems, which then find features in the images and determine pose from the features found. Sending and supervising the present view point operates at a rate of about 1s.

The C2V component *automatically extracts distinct features from the object model* to enable visual navigation. It also automatically evaluates the quality of view points to look at for the vision system. The CAD subsystem concentrates on determining the reference features, which are defined as a coherent set of an intermediate point (IP), the corresponding robust features that should be seen in a view and a robot gait. The features are geometric references determined from the CAD model of the work piece, i.e. surface boundaries and intersections, represented as lines, circles, half circles, junctions (intersections of edges), regions, etc. By robust we mean features, which will not be confused by the vision subsystem when viewed from the specific intermediate point or which are too small to be significant. C2V consists of 3 major systems:

- C2VoffLine (RobCad): C2VoffLine is the part of the AAU system that simulates the motion of the robot and cameras from the path created by the Odense shipyard. During this simulation of the movements the features are collected, which the camera will to see during the execution of the task (Figure 3 gives an example desk top view). To simplify the system and make it available to a large number of customers, a simplified version has been developed: C2VoffLine (Windows NT), described next.

- C2VoffLine (Windows NT): The kernel (C2Vkernel) used in the RobCad version is implemented in an NT-based version of C2VoffLine. The NT version does not have all the functionality and the same degree of automation, which is found in the RobCad solution, but this version is fully capable of creating features for demos and can be used by any user.
- C2VonLine: C2VonLine is the specially designed communication software of C2V that communicates with the entire RobVision network at the demanded rate. The software is used to send Models and Features generated by C2VoffLine depending on the present pose of the robot.

The loop between the vision subsystem and the CAD subsystem will then be as follows:
1. After a small robot motion, the knowledge of the former pose and the direction of the movement the vision subsystem predicts the robot pose, which is also passed on to the CAD subsystem.
2. The CAD subsystem provides 3D geometric features detected in the CAD model from these poses and the present view of the camera(s) if the view changed considerably due to the robot movement.
3. If the features or images are recognised by the vision subsystem, a the view direction is kept and the robot moves towards its target. Go to 2 and continue the loop from here.
4. If the features or images are not recognised by the vision subsystem, the cameras move to another direction of view. This view point is suggested by the CAD subsystem evaluating areas that are rich with features to render the task of the vision system more easy.
5. Go to 3 and continue the loop from here.

The model just described is very generic, which enable the use to track any object that is represented with a CAD model. Details on the method to extract features can be found in [Del00].

4   Head Control and 3D Feature Measurement: PRONTO

The PRONTO system fulfils several tasks, which in brief are:
- Head control and calibration.
- Inertial sensor data acquisition, distribution to other systems and use for head stabilization.
- Image acquisition and delivery to other systems and image processing.
- Communications and synchronization with V4R vision system.

PRONTO, therefore, performs a large number of complex and interrelated task that need to be synchronized. For these reasons the software is implemented in C++ as a *multithread object oriented distributed application* with the aid of the distributed programming technology DCOM (Distributed Component Object Model) to create a

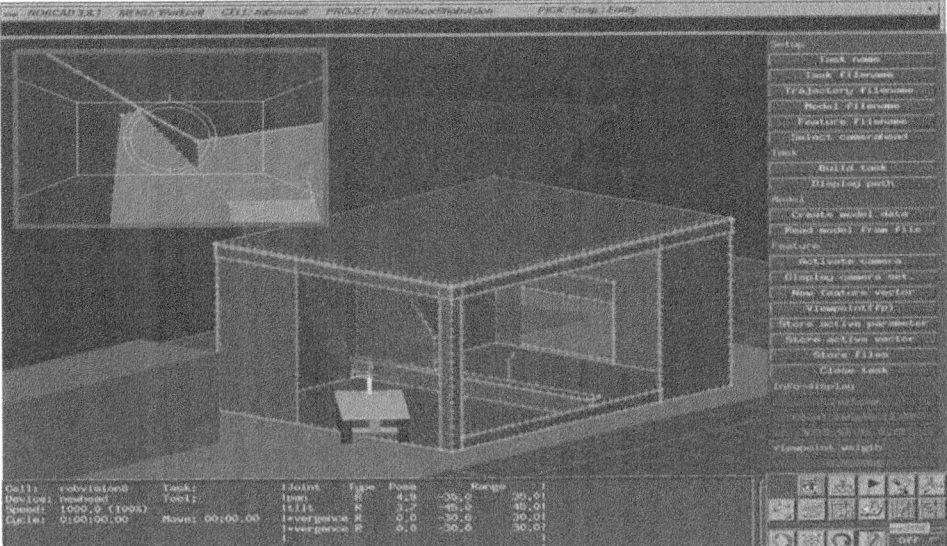

Fig. 3. Example of mock-up in the C2Voffline system. For part of the demonstration a cart was used since the robot was not always available. The top left is the view as seen from the left camera of the stereo head. From this view features are extracted automatically.

software architecture that tries to simplify the complexity of this subsystem. From the hardware point of view PRONTO consists of a two processors computer running Windows NT and, of course the Eurohead (the head is shown in Figure 2 above)

The accuracy of the Eurohead has been evaluated in detail in [10]. To find and measure the 3D junctions a Hough technique is used to extract the lines on the image planes of a stereo pair using the features from C2V. The extracted lines and the junctions are related to the CAD model using a weighted least mean squares method. Then a closed loop method follows, such that by simultaneously moving the three degrees of freedom of the head the junction is fixated at the principal point of the image in both images. When this is the case the two cameras are verging on the certain junction and the direct kinematics of the head are applied in order to determine the 3D position of the junction relative to the head.

5   2D Feature Tracking and Pose Estimation: Vision for Robotics (V4R)

The task of the vision system is to extract features from the cues of images and relate them to the features provided by C2V. C2V provides geometric features such as line, arc, junctions, region, and attributes connected to these features. The attributes of a line can be, for example, welded or not welded, chamfered, or rounded. Regions can have attributes such as intensity, texture, or colour.

The V4R software package is a well tested prototype, which is available to interested researchers from the authors. V4R provides a tool for tracking using images from video (mpeg), life camera, or image sequences. V4R contains two major components, which can be exploited separately: (1) *framework for tracking of features and* (2) *pose estimation* using a model and the feature found in the image. The tracking tool within V4R is capable of following line, junction and ellipse features at field rate. The tracking method is edge based and uses a scheme of Edge Projected Integration of Cues (EPIC) to obtain robustness against varying background and continuous illumination changes [20]. The goal of tracking is to be able to follow fast motions. Therefore fast cycle rate and a windowing approach have been adopted as formally derived in by considering the dynamics of the robot - vision system [17]. The entire vision system of INFA is designed in C++ and presents a generic structure for any model-based vision method [20]. Its development pays tribute to the developments of the XVision system by Greg Hager [12].

The pose estimation tool of V4R uses the object model and the features found in the image to determine an optimal pose. The following features are utilised for pose estimation: line, 2D point (junction), 3D point, and surface normal. Outliers are detected and a least squares procedure over all remaining features gives a best pose fit.

Figure 4a shows the windows projected into the image. Yellow lines present found features, red line features not found. Figure 4b gives the pose found in green as a re-projection into the image.

5.1   Performance Evaluation of 2D Feature Finding Methods

To track the edges (lines, ellipses) a method for cue integration (Edge Projected Integration of Cues, EPIC) is used, which has been proposed in [20]. EPIC uses cues (intensity, colour, texture, …) to distinguish object from background edgels. However, the initialisation of the feature cannot use this information and is therefore the most critical event.

For first finding the edge feature several methods can be used. This section introduces a comparison of methods to find the edges. The next section then outlines how topological knowledge from the model can be used to discriminate candidate edges.

During the project the following methods have been evaluated when the model is first projected into the image. The two references are tracking, where previous information can be taken into account. This is simpler than finding the feature for the first time. The second reference is only using the edge information from a classical edge extractor. For all methods the warped image approach of [12] has been used.

1. Only-edge: Edge finding only using an edge filter as in [12] and least squares fit to find line.
2. Tracking: Using information from a simulated previous finding.
3. LMedS: uses zero crossings to find edgels and a Least Median Square regression to fit the line.
4. EPIC-centre: Integrating the Using the centre location as most likely source to indicate edgels.

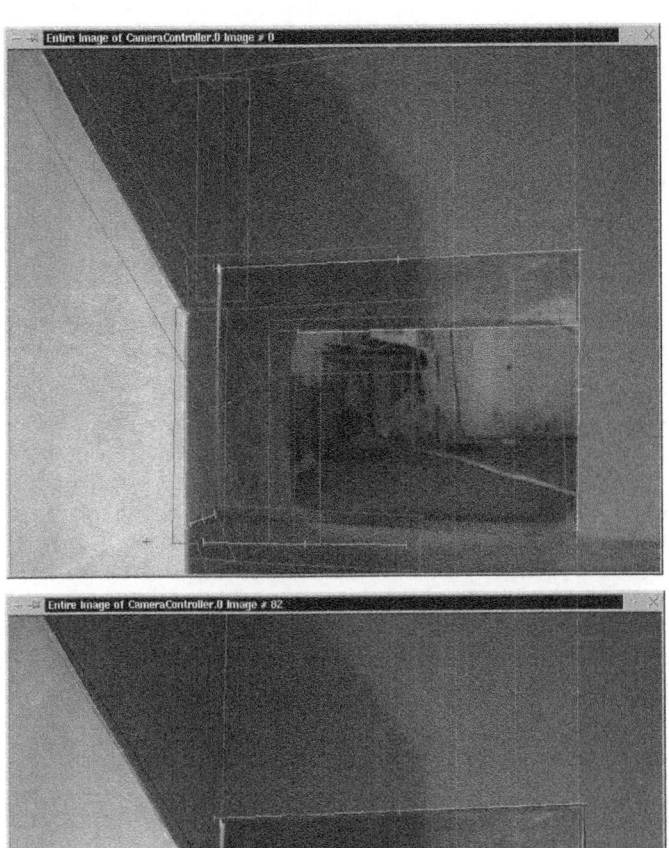

Fig. 4. Top: Tracking windows to search for features. Bottom: Blue is the projection into the image, yellow features found, red are features not found (due to poor contrast in this case), and green is the re-projection of the estimated pose into the image.

The methods have been evaluated on real images of typical ship sections. Figure 5 shows a typical example. The detection of features has been tested by moving the images in the horizontal and vertical axis. This renders the initialisation inaccurate by a know range covering plus and minus 30 pixels to the correct centre position.

The four algorithms have been tested. The results are summarised in Figure 6. The detection rate gives the percentage of lines found of all lines initialised. Each data point corresponds to about 120 lines in two dozen images. The next figure then shows

Fig. 5. Initialisation (left) and detection results (right) when horizontally displacing the image of the ship section in ten pixel steps. The EPIC-centre algorithm is used in this example.

the percentage of the detected lines that has been detected correctly. It shows that the Only-edge method detects many lines but also many incorrect lines. The LMedS improves the performance, but adding the centre information is better even if the displacement becomes larger.

A significant problem is the false detection of feature due to ambiguities in the image. The introduction of probabilistic likelihood values to evaluate the quality of a line did not proof successful. Lines have been found with many edgels along the line. Therefore other measures has to be taken. The basic approach is to integrate the topological knowledge from the CAD model.

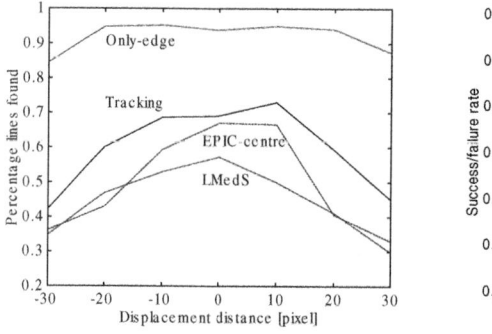
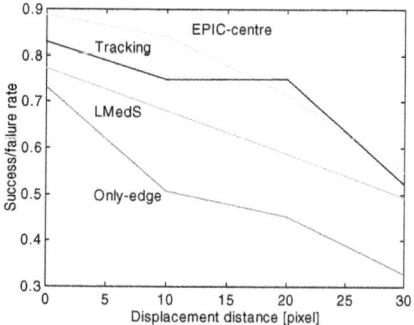

Fig. 6. The detection rate (left) and the success/failure rate of the "Only-edge", the "LMedS", the "EPIC-centre" and the "Tracking" algorithms over the distance relative to correct localisation. The S/F rate is given by the relation of correctly versus falsely found features over the features found.

5.2   Integrating Object Topology

Double lines cause severe problems due to ambiguity. Displacements of junctions on both image planes due to either wrong estimation of the robot position or bad construction also causes problems.

On the other hand, exactly this information can be exploited to discriminate features: parallel lines and lines intersecting at a junctions must show some specific properties. The use of this topological information is referred to as validation. It helps to disambiguate local ambiguities.

Figure 7 shows a tracking example and also an example of using parallelity information. The bottom front of the images shows the T-truss with three parallel line. By defining a "parallel line" relation between two lines, the lines can be ordered locally. By applying the method two times (to the top pair of lines and the bottom pair of lines, the centre line of the three lines is an element of both pairs) the lines are discriminated most of time. Therefore the ends of lines in a tracking window need to be found. This seems to be the most feasible extension and should be considered for implementation.

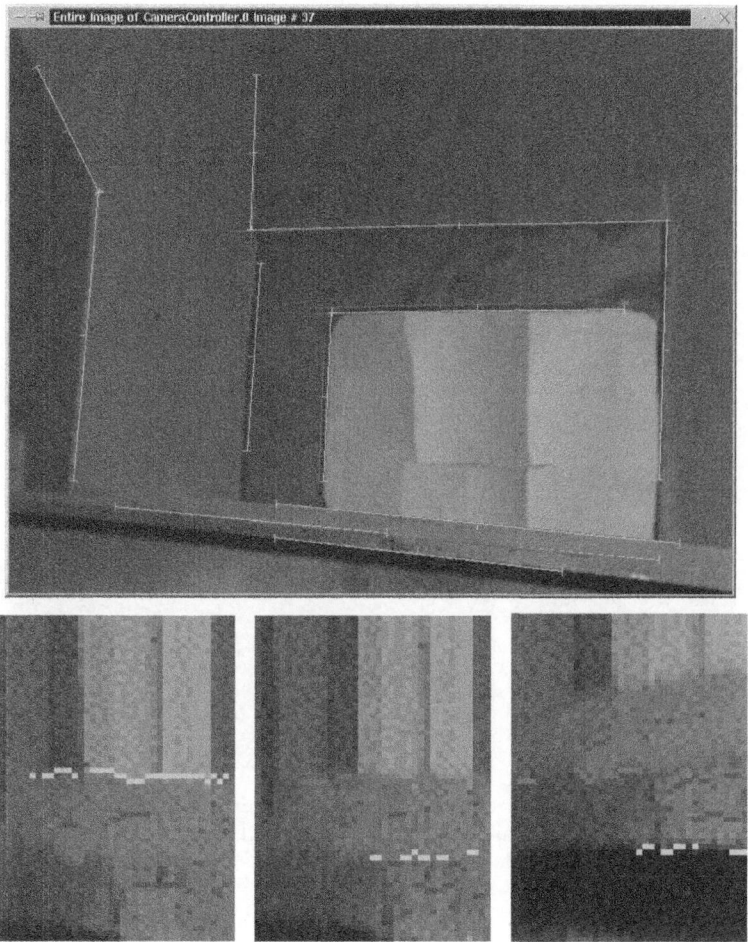

Fig. 7. Discriminating between close parallel lines. The small windows in the bottom line show the warped tracking images of the three lines from top to bottom in the above image. Yellow indicates the selected edge, cyan a candidate, red are all edgels found.

280   M. Vincze et al.

A second method is to use the information of a junction. When intersecting potential candidate lines at one junction, only the two lines that form the junction will lead up to the junction point. This can be validated locally in the image without requiring expensive computations.

Using these simple validation methods it is possible to track complex scenes as given here with a standard Pentium PC 500 MHz at frame rate. In the project only 120 ms have been used to run several other tools to improve the system performance.

6   Demonstration Results

The final demonstration of the RobVision project brought together all of the tools to demonstrate the integrated system at the demonstration site at Odense Shipyard in Odense, DK. Figure 8 gives an example of the tracking performance from the robot. The robot moves towards its goal and the vision system tracks the features to estimate the robot pose continuously.

The motion of the robot is depicted in Figure 9. The jerky motion of the robot can be clearly seen. While tracking is fast and shows good robustness, the maximum allowed object motion is still restricted. The use of inertial sensors proved effective to compensate fast angular motions. This aspect will be investigated more closely by integrating a full 6D inertial sensor suit with the optical tracking methods.

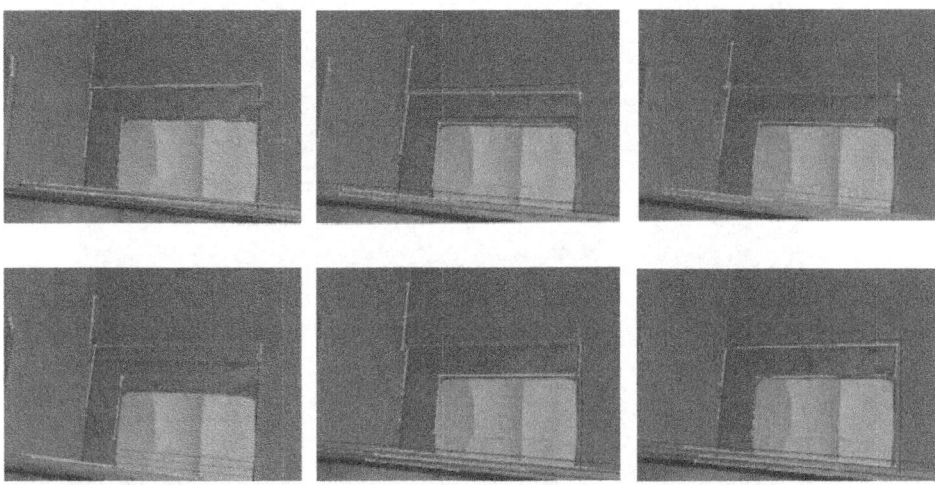

Fig. 8. 6 images from a sequence of more than 300 images of tracking from the moving robot. The colours are used as in Figure 4. Note that a short jerk of the robot body due to its pneumatic actuators is compensated after two cycles and tacking regained.

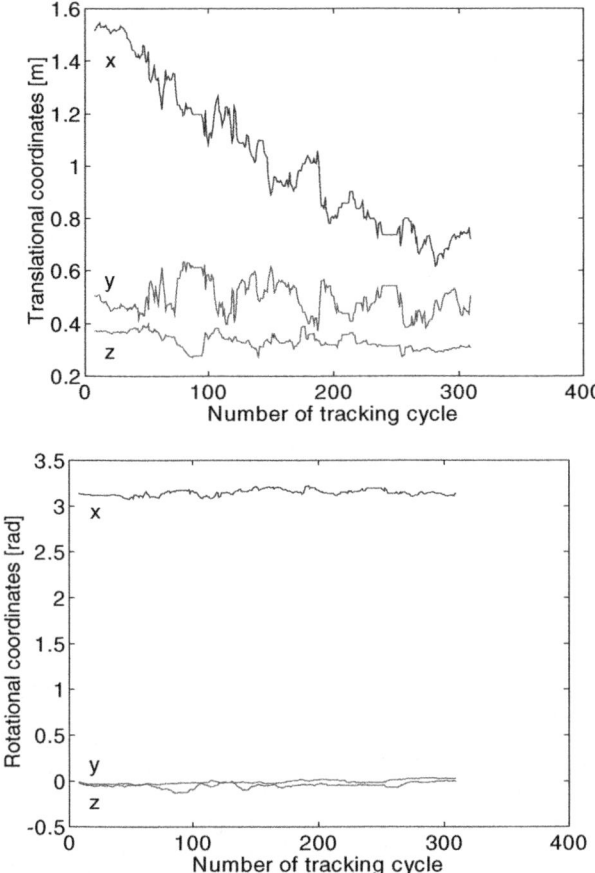

Fig. 9. The result of pose estimation during a tracking sequence from the walking robot.

7   Summary of Results

The objective of the RobVision project is to navigate a walking robot into ship sections using visual feedback. The system consists of the components walking robot, CAD-system, and two redundant vision systems that provide the feedback to steer the robot. The system demonstrated the following.

- A modular walker is able to operate with 6 or 8 legs without any hardware or software changes and can carry a work package of 50 kg into the cell.
- The CAD-model can select, evaluate and deliver significant features that the cameras on the robot should see along the path of the robot.
- The redundancy of two vision systems can be used to improve the reliability to find and track features.

- Features such as lines, 2D and 3D points and junctions, ellipses, or surface normals can be integrated with one algorithm to determine the pose of the object.
- Image processing is executed in 120 ms (and can be improved to obtain frame rate, 40 ms), which allows fast real-time operation.
- The approach is ready to be applied to locate and measure any object that has been described with a standard CAD-system.

This technique opens up other potential applications. The model-based approach enables to measure any modelled object and to feed back the measurement data directly into the CAD-system. The impact of this capability is manifest. The industrial partners in the ship building and the construction industry can supervise the production quality and consequently reduce production time.

Acknowledgements. This work has been mainly supported by the RobVision project Esprit 28867 and is partly supported by the Austrian Science Foundation (FWF) under grant P13167-MAT and Project GRD1-1999-10693 FlexPaint.

References

[1]   Alferez, R., Wang, Y.F.: Geometric and Illumination Invariants for Object Recognition, IEEE Transactions on PAMI 21(6), 1999, pp. 505-536.
[2]   C. G. Bräutigam: A Model-Free Voting Approach to Cue Integration, Dissertation, KTH Stockholm, 1998.
[3]   J.S. Beis, D.G.Lowe, Indexing without Invariants in 3D Object Recognition, Pattern Analysis and Machine Intelligence, Vol.21, No.10, 1999, pp. 1000 - 1015.
[4]   J.R. Beveridge, E.M. Riseman, How Easy is Matching 2D Line Models Using Local Search?, Pattern Analysis and Machine Intelligence, Vol.19, No.19, 1997, pp.564 - 579.
[5]   H.I. Christensen, D. Kragic: Robust Vision for Manipulation and Navigation, in: Markus Vincze (ed.): Proc. Robust Vision for Industrial Applications 1999, 23rd Workshop ÖAGM/AAPR.
[Del00]   Deliverable of the RobVision project, also available from robvision.infa.tuwien.ac.at, 2000.
[6]   Dickinson, S.J., Wilkes, D., Tsotsos, J.K.: A Computational Model of View Degeneracy, IEEE Transactions on PAMI, vol.21, no.8, 1999, 673-689.
[7]   C. Eberst, M. Barth, et.al., Robust Vision-based Object Recognition Integrating Highly Redundant Cues for Indexing and Verification, IEEE ICRA 2000, pp. 3757-3764.
[8]   Förstner, W. and Gülch, E., (1987): A Fast Operator for Detection and Precise Location of Distinct Points, Corners and Centers of Circular Features; ISPRS Intercommission Workshop, Interlaken.
[9]   Fuerst, S., Dickmanns, E.D.: A Vision Based Navigation System for Autonomous Aircraft; Robotics and Autonomous Systems 28, pp.173-184, 1999.
[10]   A. Gasteratos and G. Sandini, On the Accuracy of the Eurohead, LIRA – TR 2/00, July 2000.
[11]   Grimson, W.E.L.: Object Recognition by Computer, MIT Press, 1990.
[12]   Hager, G. and Toyama, K. (1998): The XVision-System: A Portable Substrate for Real-Time Vision Applications, Computer Vision and Image Understanding, 69 (1), 23-37.
[13]   Garding, J. and Lindeberg, T. (1994): Direct Estimation of Local Surface Shape in a Fixating Binocular Vision System, in: J. O. Eklundh, Lecture Notes in Comp. Science, 800, 365-376.

[14] D.S. Kim, R. Nevatia, Recognition and localization of generic objects for indoor navigation using functionality, Image and Vision Computing 16(11), Special Issue SI, 1998 Aug 1, 729-743.

[15] Kosaka, A., Nakazawa, G.: Vision-Based Motion Tracking of Rigid Objects Using Prediction of Uncertainties; ICRA, pp.2637-2644, 1995.

[16] D. Kragic, H.I. Christensen, Cue Integration for Manipulation, in [21], pp. 1 - 16.

[17] P. Krautgartner, M. Vincze: Optimal Image Processing Architecture for Active Vision Systems; Int. Conf. on Vision Systems, Gran Canaria, S. 331-347, January 13-15, 1999.

[18] P. Pirjanian, H.I. Christensen, J.A. Fayman, Application of Voting to fusion of Purposive Modules: An Experimental Investigation, Robotics & Autonomous Sys., Vol.23, 1998, pp. 253-266.

[19] Smith, S. M. and Brady, J. M. (1997): SUSAN - a new approach to low level image processing, Int. Journal of Computer Vision, 23, (1), 45-78.

[20] M. Vincze, M. Ayromlou, W. Kubinger: An Integrating Framework for Robust Real-Time 3D Object Tracking; Int. Conf. on Vision Systems, Gran Canaria, S. 135-150, January 13-15, 1999.

[21] M. Vincze, G.D. Hager, Eds., Robust Vision for Vision-Based Control of Motion, IEEE Press, 2000.

[22] M. Vincze: Robust Tracking of Ellipses at Frame Rate; Pattern Recognition 34(2), 487-498, 2001.

[23] Wunsch, P., Hirzinger, G.: Real-Time Visual Tracking of 3-D Objects with Dynamic Handling of Occlusion; ICRA, pp.2868-2873, 1997.

[24] A. Zisserman, D. Forsyth, et.al., 3D object recognition using invariance, Artificial Intelligence, Vol.78, 1995, pp. 239 - 288.

Reconstructing Textured CAD Model of Urban Environment Using Vehicle-Borne Laser Range Scanners and Line Cameras

Huijing Zhao[1] and Ryosuke Shibasaki[1]

Center for Spatial Information Science, Univ. of Tokyo
{chou,shiba}@skl.iis.u-tokyo.ac.jp

Abstract. In this paper, a novel method is presented to generate textured CAD model of out-door urban environment using a vehicle-borne sensor system. In data measurement, three single-row laser range scanners and six line cameras are mounted on a measurement vehicle, which has been equipped with a GPS/INS/Odometer based navigation system. Laser range and line images are measured as the vehicle moves ahead. They are synchronized with the navigation system, so that can be geo-referenced to a world coordinate system. Generation of CAD model is conducted in two steps. A geometric model is first generated using the geo-referenced laser range data, where urban features like buildings, ground surface and trees are extracted in a hierarchical way. Different urban features are represented using different geometric primitives like planar face, TIN and triangle. Texture of the urban features is generated by projecting and re-sampling line images on the geometric model. An out-door experiment is conducted, and a textured CAD model of a real urban environment is reconstructed in a full automatic mode.

1   Introduction

Up to now, many research groups in photogrammetry community have been devoted to the analysis of aerial based imageries for the reconstruction of 3D urban object (e.g. [4,8]). Normally, aerial survey can cover relatively wide area, but fail in capturing details of urban objects such as sidewall (facade) of buildings. On the other hand, most of the existing systems in computer vision field have been demonstrated at small scales, using simple objects, under controlled light condition. (e.g. [1,5,12]). With the development of automobile navigation system, 3D GIS (*Geographic Information System*), and applications using virtual and augmented reality, details of urban out-door objects are found to be of importance, as user viewpoints are involved on the ground, not in the air. An efficient reconstruction method exploiting ground-based survey technique at large scale, for complicated and unexpected object geometries, under uncontrolled light condition is required.

B. Schiele and G. Sagerer (Eds.): ICVS 2001, LNCS 2095, pp. 284–297, 2001.
© Springer-Verlag Berlin Heidelberg 2001

1.1   Related Works

Several systems aiming at generating 3D model of real world have been developed during the last few years. According to the major data source being used for reconstructing object geometry, the systems can be broadly divided into two groups. One is called image-based approach. Another is called range-based approach. In the first group, 3D model of urban scene is reconstructed using still or moving images. Image-based approach is also called indirect approach since object geometry has to be automatically or human-assistedly extracted using stereo or motion techniques. Debevec, et al. [3] presented an interactive method of modeling and rendering architectural scenes from sparse sets of still photographs, where large architectural environment can be modeled with far fewer photographs than using other full-automated image-based approaches. MIT City Scanning Project [7] developed a prototype system of automatically reconstructing textured geometric CAD model of urban environment using spherical mosaic images, where camera's position and orientation of each spherical image is first initialized using positioning sensors, then refined through image matching. Geometric representation is extracted either using feature correspondence or by identifying vertical facades. Uehara and Zen [13] proposed a method of creating textured 3D map from existing 2D map using motion technique, where a video camera is mounted on a calibrated vehicle and the image streams that captured are geo-referenced to the existing 2D map using GPS data. Through the above research efforts, it is demonstrated that image-based approach can be used in reconstructing 3D model of urban out-door environment. Whereas, the difficulties in reliable stereo matching, distortion from limited resolution and unstable geometry of CCD cameras are the major obstacles to reconstruct a 3D model of complicated environment with necessary accuracy and robustness. In the second group, 3D model of urban scene is reconstructed using range image. Range-based approach is also called direct approach since object geometry can be directed measured using range scanner. In recent years, as the development of laser technique, range scanners using eye-safe laser with high accuracy, large range distance and high measurement frequency are being used for the modeling of urban environment. Sequeira et al.[11] and El-Hakim et al.[2] developed systems on reconstructing indoor environment of rather large scale. Stamos and Allen [10], Zhao and Shibasaki [15] aimed at generating 3D model of urban out-door objects. In these systems, range scanners are mounted on stationary platforms (called stationary system). Range images produced by the systems are typically rectangular grids of range distances (or 3D coordinates after conversion) from the sensor to the objects being scanned. Objects are measured from a number of viewpoints to reduce occlusions, where location and direction of viewpoints are unknown or roughly obtained using GPS, Gyro sensors and/or other navigation systems. Range data obtained in different viewpoints are registered and integrated, and a completed model of urban environment is reconstructed. There are several drawbacks of stationary systems. First, in data acquisition, successive range views have to keep a degree of overlay, so that location and direction of viewpoints can be traced (or refined) by registering range data. Planning for viewpoints and directions in data acquisition becomes difficult when measuring large and complicated scene, since a balance between the degree of overlay and the number of viewpoints has to be decided according to both target objects and registration method. Secondly, there is still no registration method that could succeed in automatically registering range data of all kinds. When the number of range views increases, registration while keeping necessary accuracy becomes difficult. Updating stationary systems to moving platform ones (called vehicle-borne system) for reconstructing 3D model of large real scene is very important.

1.2   Outline of the Research

In the sensor system developed by Konno et al. [14], three single-row laser range scanners and six line cameras are mounted on a measure vehicle (GeoMaster), which has been equipped with a GPS/INS/Odometer based navigation system. The sensor system outputs three kinds of data sources. They are laser range data, line images, and navigation data. Either laser range data or line images are in the sensor's local coordinate system at the moment of measurement. They are synchronized with the navigation data using the sensors' local clock. This research contribute to a method of reconstructing textured 3D model of urban out-door environment by fusing the data outputs of the sensor system. It has two procedures. A geometrical surface model is first generated using the integrated model of laser range data, where laser range data in the sensor's local coordinate system at the moment of measurement are geo-referenced to a world coordinate system using both the navigation data and the calibration parameters of the sensor system. Texture data are then generated by projecting line images onto the surface model, where line images are geo-referenced to a world coordinate system in the same way with that of laser range data. In the following, we will first briefly describe the hardware system and the way for geo-referencing each kind of data sources. We then present the method for surface model reconstruction and texture mapping. An outdoor experiment is conducted in a real urban environment, Kirigaoka Apartment Complex, where the measurement vehicle ran a course about 1.5km at a speed of 20~40km/h. A textured CAD model including the urban features like buildings, trees, roads etc. along the measurement route is generated in a full-automated mode. The experiment results and discussions are presented subsequently.

2   Sensor System and Geo-Referencing of Data Outputs

The sensor system consists of three different kinds of sensors and each for a specific purpose. They are laser range scanners - the sensor for measuring object geometry, line cameras - the sensor for capturing object texture, and GeoMaster - the moving platform.

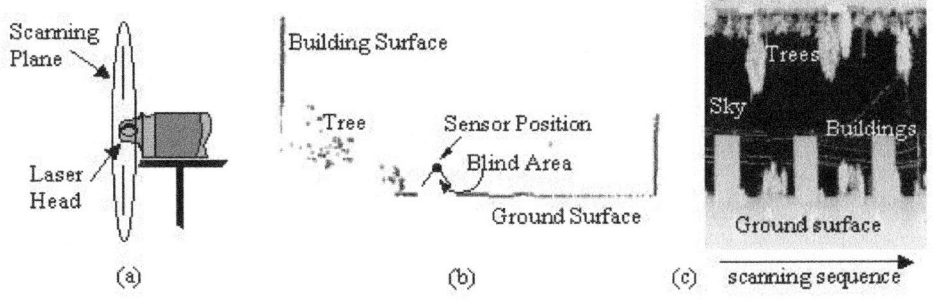

Fig. 1. Laser range finder (LD-A) and examples of range data (a) configuration of LD-A, (b) range points in a scan line, (c) a piece of range image.

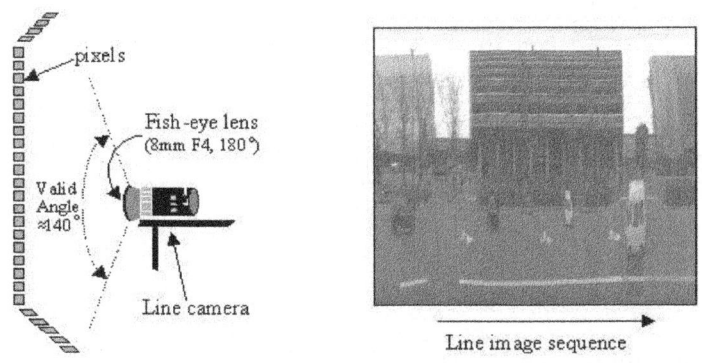

Fig. 2. Line Camera and an example of line image strip

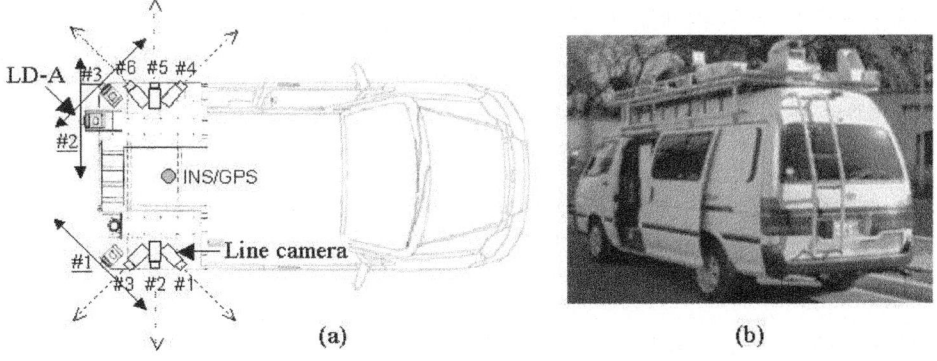

Fig. 3. Sensor system (a) sensor alignment, (b) measurement vehicle (GeoMaster).

Laser range scanner - Sensor for measuring object geometry. Single-row laser range scanners, LD-A, produced by IBEO Lasertechnik, are exploited in the sensor system (see Fig.1(a)). In one scanning (a range scan line), LD-A profiles 480 range points of the surroundings on the scanning plane within 300 degrees. A blind area of 60 degree exists due to the hardware configuration (see Fig.1(b)). LD-A has a maximum range distance of 70 meter and an average error of 3cm. Frequency of LD-A is 20Hz, implying that it profiles 20 range scan lines per second. Fig.1(c) shows a piece of range image, where each column corresponds to a range scan line, and range scan lines are aligned in the order of measurement sequence.

Line camera - sensor for capturing object texture. Line cameras are implemented in the sensor system. Each has a 8mm F4 fish-eye lense with a vision field of 180 degree on it (see Fig.2(a)). In each snapshot, a single-row image (line image) of 1×2048 pixels are captured on the scanning plane. Among the 2048 pixels, about 1600 pixels (≈ 140 degree) are valid due to the hardware configuration. Fig.2 shows a strip of the line images, where each column corresponds to the valid pixels of a line image.

GeoMaster - moving platform. The measurement vehicle (Fig.3(b)) - GeoMaster is equipped with a high accurate GPS/INS/Odometer based navigation system - HISS [14]. A method of improving the accuracy of the navigation system in highly dense urban area is addressed in [16]. In this paper, we assume the navigation error of the moving platform is small enough to be neglected.

Sensor alignment. Three LD-As and six line cameras are mounted on the roof of GeoMaster as shown in Fig.3(a). Both LD-As and line cameras are installed with their scanning planes at different angles to reduce occlusion. In this research, all exterior calibration parameters (relative angles and distances) between the sensors' local coordinate system are obtained through physical measurement; all interior calibration parameters (e.g. focus length) are obtained from maker or sensors' specification. For data measurement, all the sensors keep recording data sources as the vehicle moves ahead. When GeoMaster moves at a speed of 20km/h, line images are captured at an interval of about 2cm by each line camera, range scan lines are profiled at an interval of about 15cm by each LD-A, and navigation data (location and direction of the vehicle at the local coordinate system of HISS) are measured at an interval of 20cm. Navigation data is associated to each line image and range scan line through linear interpolation using the sensors' local clock.

Geo-referencing data sources. Fig.4 shows the conceptual figures of geo-referencing range scan lines and line images in each sensor's local coordinate systems at the moment of measurement to a world coordinate system. According to the navigation data associated to each range scan line and line image, a

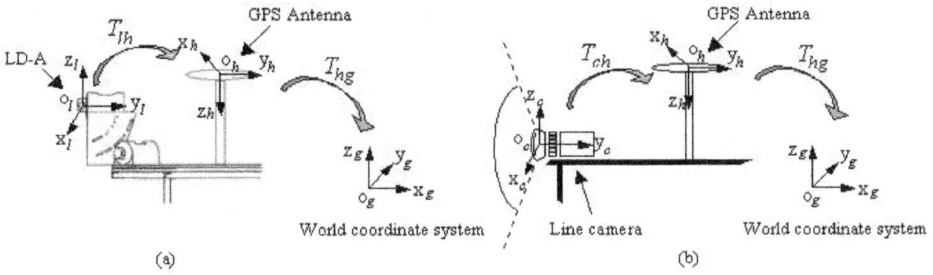

Fig. 4. Conceptual figures of Geo-referencing data sources (a) geo-referencing of range scan line, (b) geo-referencing of line image.

transformation matrix T_{hg} from the coordinate system of HISS to a world co-ordinate system is calculated, where the origin of HISS is at the center of GPS antenna. On the other hand, a transformation matrix T_{lh} from the coordinate system of LD-A and a transformation matrix T_{ch} from the coordinate system of line camera to the coordinate system of HISS are calculated based on the exterior calibration parameters. In the case of LD-A, a right-hand coordinate system is defined with its origin at the center of the laser head. The laser head of LD-A does a clockwise rotation with its starting angle downward. Z-axis and X-axis are defined composing the scanning plane, at the angles of $180°$ and $270°$ from the starting angle. A range point with a range distance of r at the angle of α is geo-referenced to the world coor-dinate system as follow,

$$(x, y, z)^t = T_{hg}T_{lh}(-r\sin\alpha, 0, -r\cos\alpha)^t. \tag{1}$$

In the case of line camera, a right-hand coordinate system is defined with its origin at its projection center. Z-axis is defined to the upward of the line camera, and Y-axis is reverse to the projection axis. Focus length (f) of the line camera as well as a formula defining the relationship between the index of image pixel (h) and its projection angle (ω) towards the projection axis is obtained from the sensor's specification.

$$\omega = 2 \times \arcsin((h - o)/2/f). \tag{2}$$

where o is the image center, which is obtained by doing physical measurement using sample images. Using formula 2, the projection vector of image pixel (h) is geo-referenced to the world coordinate system as follows,

$$(x, y, z)^t = T_{hg}T_{ch}(0, -\cos\omega, \sin\omega)^t. \tag{3}$$

3   Creating Geometric Mode

The goal of geometric modeling is to generate a surface representation of ur-ban features with small data size for the use of commercial applications. In the present research, urban features are reconstructed in three levels. They are buildings, trees, and ground surfaces, where buildings are further divided into vertical and non-vertical building surfaces. Geometric modeling is conducted in two interrelated procedures. They are classification of range points and geometric feature extraction. Fig.5 is an overview of the data and processing flows. Range points are classified by first segmenting each range scan lines into line segments, then grouping the range points in a hierarchical procedure based on the following simple and intuitive rules.

1. The range points belonging to vertical linear features of range scan line might be the measurement of vertical building surface.
2. Since the ground surface is always smooth and flat, and the elevation values near by vehicle's positions can be deduced using the height of GPS antenna and navigation data, the range points with small gradient values, and their elevation values within a pre-defined range might be the measurement of ground surface.
3. The range measurement of trees always has a high distribution variance among the neighboring range points of successive range scan lines.
4. The range points of small clusters always have low reliability.

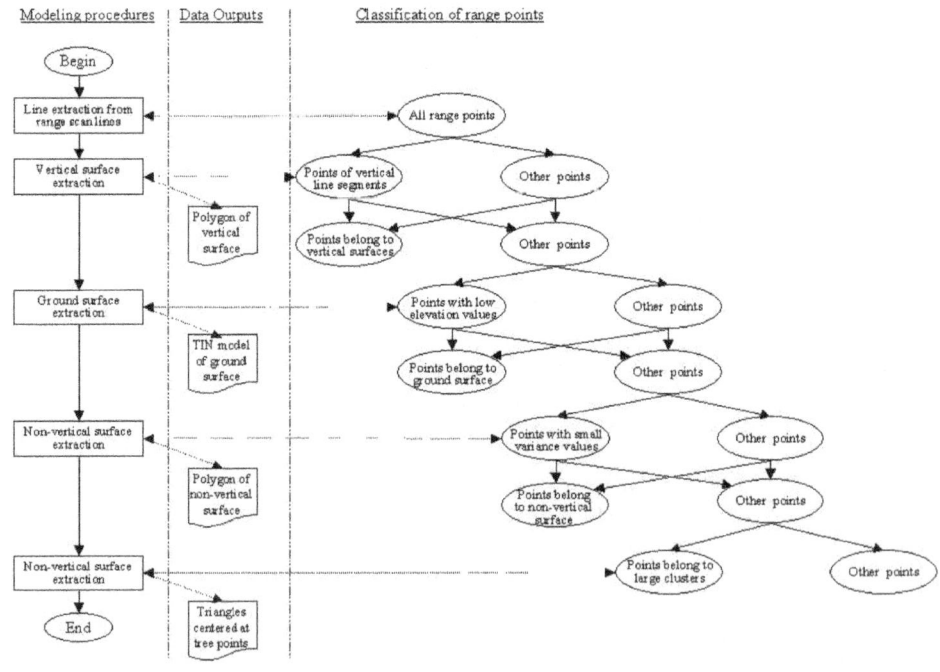

Fig. 5. Data and processing flows of geometric modeling

Segmentation of range scan lines is conducted in a two-dimensional way. Coordinate system is defined consistent with the one in Fig.4(a), where Y-axis is omitted. The method presented in [9] is applied in this research to extract line segments from range scan lines. Fig.6 shows two examples of line segment extraction. With the result of line segment extraction, range points are broadly divided into four groups, the measurement of vertical building surface, ground surface, non-vertical building surface, and others (trees). However mis-classification exists in practice. For example, many line segments are extracted in the measurement of trees (see Fig.6(b)), whereas they are not linear feature characterized objects. The above classification result is used as a start point of the subsequent procedures in geometric modeling, through which geometric characteristics of range measurements are tested and verified.

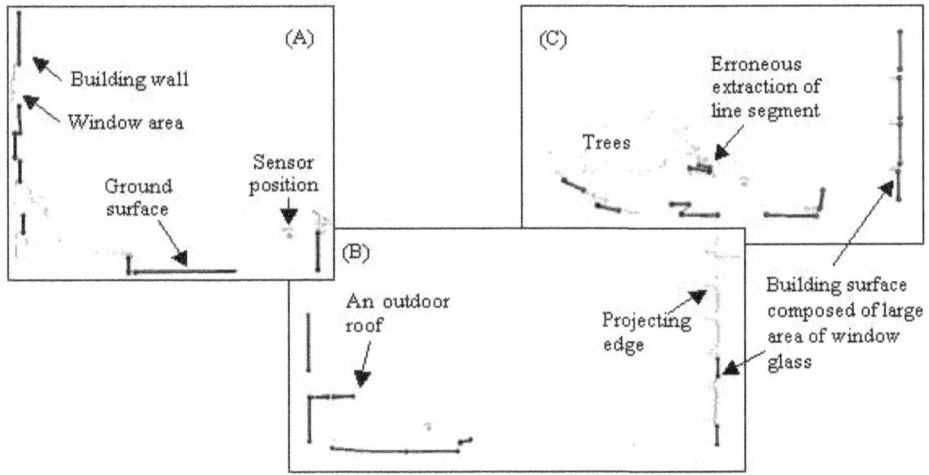

Fig. 6. Segmentation of range scan lines

Geometric extraction of vertical building surfaces, ground surfaces, non-vertical building surfaces and trees is conducted in a subsequent way as shown in Fig.5 using the corresponding group of range points. On the other hand, classification of range points is validated and refined using the extracted geometric features. For example, the range points near to a vertical planar face are classified to the measurement of vertical building surface. On the other hand, the range points belong to vertical line segments might be discarded, if no vertical planar face is extracted from the range points. In the extractions of vertical building surfaces, Z-image is exploited, which has been defined and demonstrated with efficiency in urban out-door area in [15], so that a three-dimensional extraction is converted to a two-dimensional problem. Line segments are first extracted from the Z-image of the range points belonging to the group of vertical building

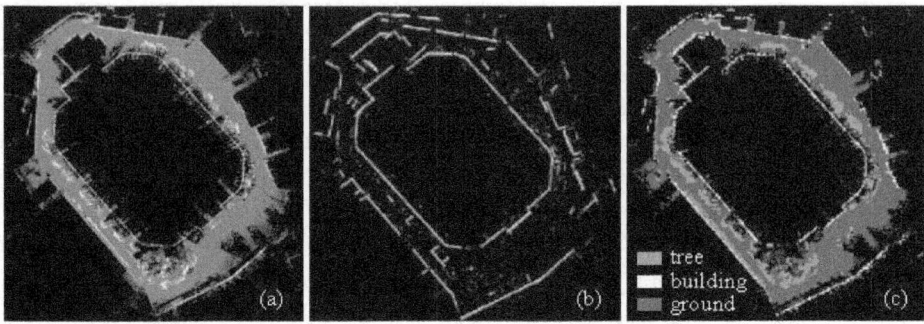

Fig. 7. Extracting geometric features (a) a Z-image of all range points, (b) extracting vertical planar faces using Z-image, (c) classification result.

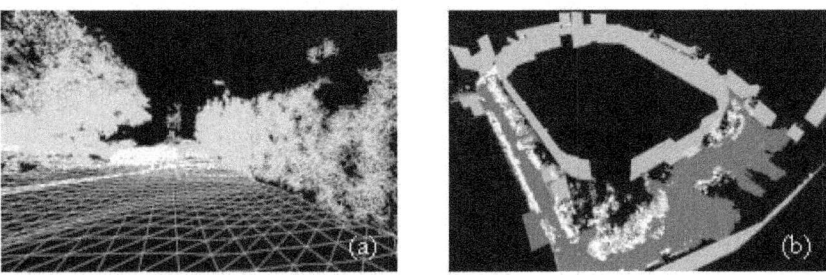

Fig. 8. Modeling geometric features (a) ground surface in TIN model, (b) a perspective view of the geometric model.

Fig. 9. Texture mapping onto the geometric model (a) positions and principle axes of line camera, (b) the strip of line images, (c) texture mapping using geo-referenced line images.

surface (see Fig.7(a,b)). Line segments are then recovered to vertical polygons using the corresponding range points to define boundaries (see Fig.8(b)). As for the extraction of ground surface, range points are projected onto a regularly tessellated horizontal plane, and an elevation map of the ground surface is generated using the minimal Z-value of the range points in each grid cell. A TIN (*Triangulated Irregular Network*) model is constructed on the elevation map to represent the surface geometry (see Fig.8(a)). Non-vertical building surfaces are extracted using an existing three-dimensional approach, USF segmentation algorithm. A detailed technical explanation can be found in [6]. After extracting building and ground surface, the left set of range points are a mixed data of trees, parking cars, utility poles, irregular points and so forth. One of the major differences between trees and others is the measurement of trees always yields a large cluster of range points. Z-image of the left set of range points is generated. The range points that corresponding to isolated or small cluster of image features in Z-image are removed. Triangular cells are used to model trees, where each range point of the measurement of trees is amplify into a small triangle. Shape of the triangle is decided in a random way, whereas, surface normal is pointing to the center of the range scan line, and distances from each vertex to the range point are limited in a given range (see Fig.8(a)).

4 Texture Mapping

Fig.9 explains the principle of line image measurement, where trajectory of the line camera #5, i.e. positions and principle axes, is shown in Fig.9(a), the corresponding strip of line images is shown in Fig.9(b). Distortion in the strip of line images is obvious. It is caused by the change of relative distance and direction from line camera to the objects. In order to correct the distortions and generate a texture of direct proportion to each object, line images are re-sampled as follows.

1. Texture of each building surface is generated by projecting and re-sampling line images on each planar face. The projection vector of each line image pixel is calculated using the formula 3.
2. Texture of TIN-based ground surface is generated in two steps. First projecting and re-sampling line images on a horizontal plane at almost the same elevation level with the ground surface, to generate a texture of the ground surface. Secondly projecting each vertex of TIN model along the direction of range beams to the horizontal plane to create a connection between TIN-model and the texture image.
3. Texture of trees is generated using synthetic colors, since the projection of line images onto the range points of trees is not reliable due to occlusions.

An example of texture mapping onto geometric model of Fig.8(b) is shown in Fig.9(c).

5   Experimental Results and Discussion

An experiment is conducted in a real urban out-door environment, KIRIGAOKA apartment complex in Tokyo. The measurement vehicle run a course about 1600m at a speed of 20km/h~40km/h. A map of the testing site and the vehicle trajectory is shown in Fig.10. Over 7000 range scan lines and 30000 line images are measured by each LD-A and line camera respectively as the vehicle moves ahead. As an example, the range image measured by LD-A#2 and the strips of line images captured by line camera #2 and #5 are shown in Fig.11. It can be seen that except distortions, buildings, trees, as well as other urban facilities are captured clearly by each kind of data sources with rather high resolution. Arrows in Fig.11 denotes the same objects that being measured in different data sources. All range scan lines and line images are geo-referenced using the calibration parameters and navigation data. As has been addressed before, the major purpose of exploiting multiple LD-As and line camreas is to reduce occlusion. It is testified in Fig.12. Fig.12(a), (b) and (c) demonstrate the range points measured by LD-A#1, #2 and #3, respectively. It can be found that by a single LD-A, only the building surfaces of angles within a specific range can be measured. Fig.12(d) show an integrated model of range points, from which all the building surfaces facing to the road can be extracted with more reliability. Perspective views of extracted surfaces are shown in Fig.12(e) and (f). Textured CAD model of KIRIGAOKA apartment complex is reconstructed by first extracting geometric urban features using the integrated model of range points. In this experiment, there are totally 7,613,502 range points from LD-A measurement (see Fig.13(a)). 155 pieces of vertical building surfaces are extracted as shown in Fig.13(b). Texture mapping is conducted subsequently using the geo-referenced line images. Two perspective views of the textured CAD model are shown in Fig.13(c,d), with their viewpoint from the ground and on the air respectively. All the processing are conducted in a Windows PC with a Pentium III Processor, CPU 500MHz, RAM 256MB. Time cost of the total processing is about 3~4 hours.

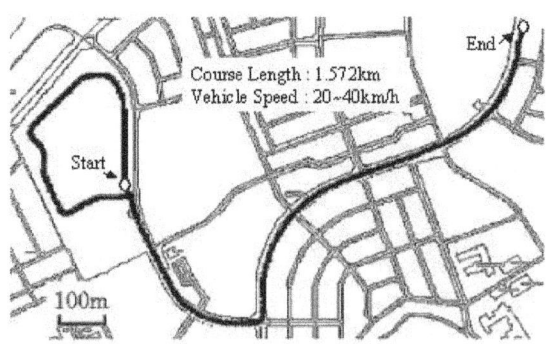

Fig. 10. A map of the testing site

6   Conclusion

In this paper, a novel method is presented to efficiently generate textured CAD model of urban out-door environment using vehicle-borne laser range scanner and line cameras. Both laser range scanners and line cameras are synchronized with a GPS/INS/Odometer based navigation system, so that the range and line images that measured by different devices can be geo-referenced to a world coordinate system. Generating a textured CAD model of urban out-door environment is conducted in two procedures, where range data are first exploited to generate a geometric model of urban features, line images are then projected and re-sampled on the geometric model. Through an experiment, it is demonstrated that urban out-door environment can be reconstructed with high automation and efficiency. Future studies will be focused on two topies. They are 1) extracting and modeling other urban features such as parking cars, telegram poles, traffic signals, and so on; 2) fusing the textured CAD model by vehicle-borne system with that by aerial survey for the purpose of updating urban spatial database.

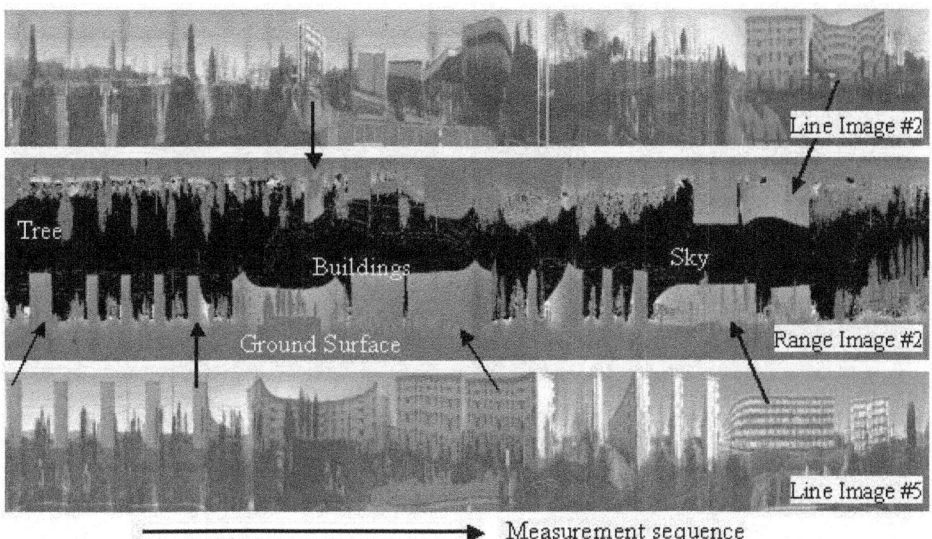

Fig. 11. An example of range and line images measured in urban environment

Acknowledgement. The authors would like to express their appreciation to Asia Air Survey Co. Ltd. for their cooperation.

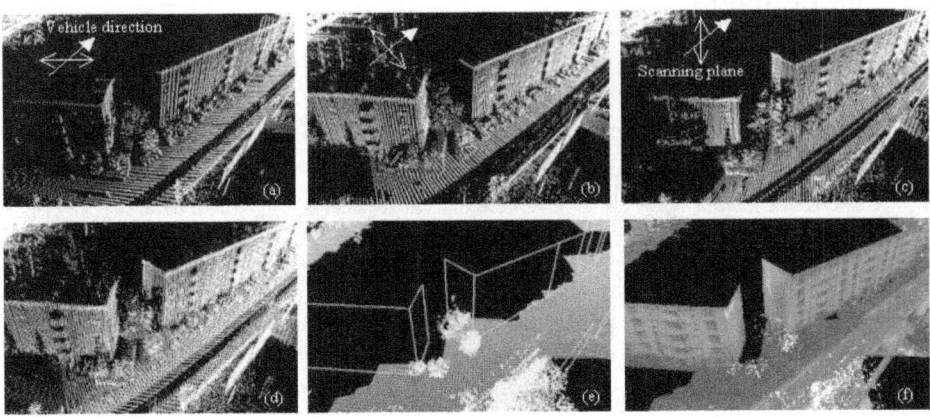

Fig. 12. Reducing occlusion using multiple laser range and line images (a) range points by LD-A#1, (b) range points by LD-A#2, (c) range points by LD-A#3, (d) integrated model of range points, (e) geometric surface model, (f) texture surface model.

Fig. 13. Perspective views of the textured CAD model of KIRIGAOKA apartment complex (a) integrated range points, (b) geometric surface model, (c) textured surface model (viewpoint on the air), (d) textured surface model (viewpoint on the ground).

References

1. Chen,Y., Medioni,G.: Object Modelling by Registration of Multiple Range Images, Image and Vision Computing,Vol. 10, No. 3, Apr. pp.145-155, 1992.
2. El-Hakim, S.F., Brenner,C., Roth,G.: A Multi-sensor Approach to Creating Accurate Virtual Environments, JSPRS Journal of Photogrammetry & Remote Sensing, vol.53, pp.379-391, 1998.
3. Debevec, P.E., Taylor,C.J., Malik,J.: Modeling and Rendering Architecture from Photographs: A hybrid geometry- and image-based approach, SIGGRAPH1996.
4. Gruen, A.: TOBAGO - a semi-automated approach for the generation of 3-D building models, ISPRS Journal of Photogrammetry and Remote Sensing, vol.53, issue 2, pp.108-118, 1998.
5. Higuchi, K., Hebert,M., Ikeuchi,K.: Building 3-D Models from Unregistered Range Images, Graphical Models and Image Processing, vol.57, No.4, pp.315-333, 1995.
6. Hoover, A., et.al.: An Experimental Comparison of Range Image Segmentation Algorithms, IEEE Trans. on Pattern Analysis & Machine Intelligence, vol. 18(7), pp. 1-17, July 1996.
7. http://city.lcs.mit.edu//city.html, MIT City Scanning Project: Fully Automated Model Acquisition in Urban Areas.
8. http://vis-www.cs.umass.edu/projects/radius/radius.html, The U. Mass RADIUS Project.
9. Rosin, P.L., West,G.A.W.: Nonparametric Segmentation of Curves into Various Representations, IEEE PAMI, vol.17, no.12, 1995.
10. Stamos, I., Allen,P.K.: 3-D Model Construction Using Range and Image Data, CVPR 2000.
11. Sequeira, V., et al.: Automated Reconstruction of 3D Models from Real Environments, ISPRS Journal of Photogrammetry & Remote Sensing, vol.54, pp.1-22, 1999
12. Shum, H., Ikeuchi,K. Reddy,R.: Virtual Reality Modeling from a Sequence of Range Images, Proc. IEEE/RSJ Int. Conf on Intelligent Robots and Systems, pp.703-710, 1994.
13. Uehara, M., Zen,H.: From Digital Map to 3D Map: Creating 3D Map by Motion Stereo Utilizing 2D Map, IAPR Workshop on Machine Vision Applications, pp.592-595, 2000.
14. Konno, T, et al.: A New Approach to Mobile Mapping for Automated Reconstruction of Urban 3D Model, proc. of Int. Workshop on Urban Multi-Media/3D Mapping, 2000.
15. Zhao, H., Shibasaki,R.: Reconstruction of Textured Urban 3D Model by Ground-Based Laser Range and CCD Images, IEICE Trans. Inf.& Syst., vol.E83-D, No.7, July, pp.1429-1440, 20001.
16. Zhao, H., Shibasaki,R.: High Accurate Positioning and Mapping in Urban Area using Laser Range Scanner, proc. of Int. Workshop on Urban Multi-Media/3D Mapping, 20002.

A Stereo Vision System for Support of Planetary Surface Exploration

Maarten Vergauwen, Marc Pollefeys*, and Luc Van Gool

K.U.Leuven ESAT-PSI, Kasteelpark Arenberg 10
B-3001 Leuven, Belgium
firstname.lastname@esat.kuleuven.ac.be

Abstract. In this paper a system will be presented that was developed for ESA for the support of planetary exploration. The system that is sent to the planetary surface consists of a rover and a lander. The lander contains a stereo head equipped with a pan-tilt mechanism. This vision system is used both for modeling of the terrain and for localization of the rover. Both tasks are necessary for the navigation of the rover. Due to the stress that occurs during the flight a recalibration of the stereo vision system is required once it is deployed on the planet. Due to practical limitations it is infeasible to use a known calibration pattern for this purpose and therefore a new calibration procedure had to be developed that can work on images of the planetary environment. This automatic procedure recovers the relative orientation of the cameras and the pan- and tilt-axis, besides the exterior orientation for all the images. The same images are subsequently used to recover the 3D structure of the terrain. For this purpose a dense stereo matching algorithm is used that – after rectification – computes a disparity map. Finally, all the disparity maps are merged into a single digital terrain model. In this paper a simple and elegant procedure is proposed that achieves that goal. The fact that the same images can be used for both calibration and 3D reconstruction is important since in general the communication bandwidth is very limited. In addition to the use for navigation and path planning, the 3D model of the terrain is also used for Virtual Reality simulation of the mission, in which case the model is texture mapped with the original images. The system has been implemented and the first tests on the ESA planetary terrain testbed were successful.

Keywords: Active Vision systems, Prototype systems, 3D reconstruction, Stereo calibration.

1 Introduction

The work described in this paper was performed in the scope of the ROBUST[1] project of the European Space Agency (ESA). In this project an end-to-end system is developed for a planetary exploration mission.

---

* Postdoctoral Fellow of the Fund for Scientific Research - Flanders (Belgium) (F.W.O. - Vlaanderen).

[1] The ROBUST consortium consists of the Belgian companies SAS and OptiDrive, the K.U.Leuven departments PMA and ESAT-PSI and the German companies DLR and vH&S.

B. Schiele and G. Sagerer (Eds.): ICVS 2001, LNCS 2095, pp. 298–312, 2001.

The ROBUST system consists of three important parts.

- the planetary rover: the Nanokhod, a small and simple rover, designed to carry instruments in the immediate surroundings of a lander. It is equipped with a tether cable, providing the rover with power and data connection to the lander which allows a very high ratio instrument-mass/rover-mass [10]. Figure 1 on the left shows an image of the Nanokhod.
- The Planetary Lander which contains the Imaging Head, an On-Board computer and the Control System for both Nanokhod and Imaging Head. The right image of figure 1 shows one of the cameras.
- The On Ground Control System

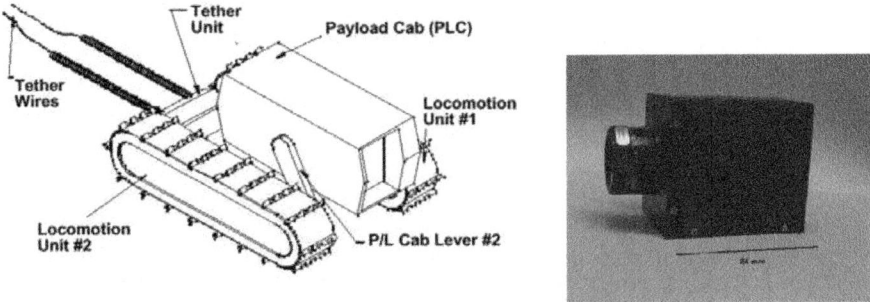

Fig. 1. Left: the Nanokhod; right: one of the cameras of the stereo rig

The Imaging Head is both used for recording images from which a reconstruction of the planetary terrain is computed and for controlling the motion of the rover, using Light Emitting Diodes on the payload cab of the rover for the latter. It consists of a stereo head, mounted on a unit which allows for pan and tilt motions and which is approximately 1.5 meter high. The two cameras of the stereo head are space approved 1024x1024 CCD cameras. The stereo head has a baseline of 0.5 meter.

A typical utilization scenario will deploy the Imaging Head as soon as possible after the landing of the planetary system. Because of the strain on the parts during launch and landing, the Imaging Head needs to be recalibrated. To accomplish this, it takes images of the terrain which are sent to earth where the calibration is performed using these images. From the same images a 3D reconstruction of the terrain is then computed. Since the cameras have a limited field of view (23x23 degrees) the entire environment is not recorded at once but it is segmented into rings according to the tilt angle and each ring is divided into segments according to the pan angle of the Imaging Head (see figure 2). The outermost boundary of the recorded terrain lies at twenty meters from the camera. For each of the segments a stereo image pair is recorded and sent down. The values of the actual pan and tilt angles can be read out from the encoders of the pan-tilt motors and are sent down together with the corresponding images.

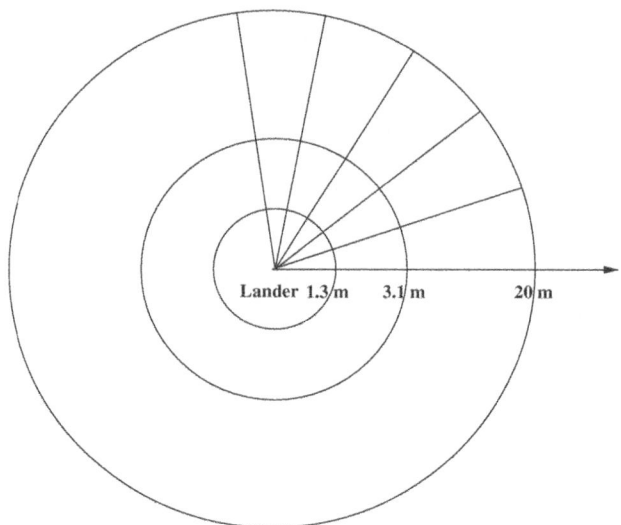

Fig. 2. Segmentation of the terrain into segments

2   Calibration

Every planetary mission is a high-risk operation. During launch and landing, the lander and its contents are subject to extreme forces. The mechanical properties of the Imaging Head are likely to have been affected by mechanical and thermal effects. For high accuracy equipment, such as the Imaging Head, a small change in these mechanical properties results in large degradation of the results, unless the new properties can be estimated. The cameras themselves are built so that the intrinsic parameters during the mission can be assumed identical to the parameters obtained through calibration on ground. If the camera housing were not so rigidly built and the camera intrinsics were likely to change during launch or landing. Algorithms exist that can retrieve these intrinsic parameters from images too [12,7].

Traditional calibration algorithms rely on known calibration objects with well-defined optical characteristics in the scene. If cameras take images of these artificial objects, the pose of the cameras can be computed, yielding the extrinsic (mechanical) calibration of the stereo rig. There are two reasons why this scheme is not suited in our case where the Imaging Head is deployed on a distant planet. First there is the problem of where to place the calibration objects. One needs to be absolutely sure of the pose of these objects for the calibration to have any meaningful result. It is of course impossible to add objects to the terrain, so one has to think of placing calibration "markers" on the lander itself. A typical lander consist of a "cocoon" which opens after landing, comparable to an opening flower. The markers could be applied to the opening "petals". However, one is never sure of the exact position of these petals which makes the markers much harder to use. Even if one did dispose of accurate markers on the lander, a second problem arises. During the design of the Imaging Head, robustness was a very important issue and therefore the number of moving items was minimized. Therefore, a fixed focus lens was chosen. Since the accuracy of the stereo matching decreases with the square of the distance, the cameras are focussed on the far range to gain as much accuracy in the far regions as possible. As a consequence, the images of near regions are blurred. Since the markers would be on the lander, images of the markers would always be blurred, reducing the accuracy of the calibration up to the point where the markers are useless. It is clear that standard calibration algorithms can not be used in our system. A new strategy had to be developed that only uses images of the terrain to calibrate the Imaging Head.

The calibration procedure that was implemented for the ROBUST project is able to calibrate the Imaging Head using images of the terrain only. This means that the images which are sent down from the planet to earth to reconstruct the terrain, can also be used for calibrating the Imaging Head. Therefore, the terrain based calibration causes no important overhead on transmission. The calibration of the extrinsic (mechanical) properties of the Imaging Head is split into two parts which are executed consecutively. First the relative transformation between the two cameras is computed. Once this relative calibration is performed, a procedure can be performed which computes the relative transformations between the cameras and the lander. This boils down to computing the pan and tilt axes of the pan-tilt unit.

2.1 Relative Calibration

The relative transformation between the two cameras of the Imaging Head can be computed from images of the terrain only. The algorithm to do this uses the concept of the essential matrix. This matrix represents the epipolar geometry between two views, including the internal parameters of the cameras as extra information. We make use of the fact that the relative transformation between the cameras does not change when the the different segments of the terrain are recorded, which allows for different measurements of the epipolar geometry to be combined to yield one accurate solution.

If the essential matrix between the two views is computed, the relative transformation (position and orientation) between the two cameras can be calculated up to the baseline (i.e. the distance between the two cameras).

Computing epipolar geometry. The first step in obtaining the relative calibration is the computation of the epipolar geometry of the stereo head. The epipolar geometry constraint limits the search for the correspondence of a point in one image to points on a line in the second image. Figure 3 illustrates this.

To find back the epipolar geometry between two images automatically, a feature detector, called the Harris Corner Detector [3] is applied to the images. Next, the corners are matched automatically between pairs of images using cross correlation. This process yields a set of possible matches which is typically contaminated with an important number of wrong matches or outliers. Therefore a robust matching scheme, called RANSAC[2], is used to compute and update epipolar geometry and matches iteratively.

In the case of the ROBUST Imaging Head the data of the different segments of the terrain can be combined to compute the epipolar geometry much more robustly because the relative transformation between the cameras does not change. Figure 4 illustrates this.

Fig. 3. Epipolar geometry of an image pair

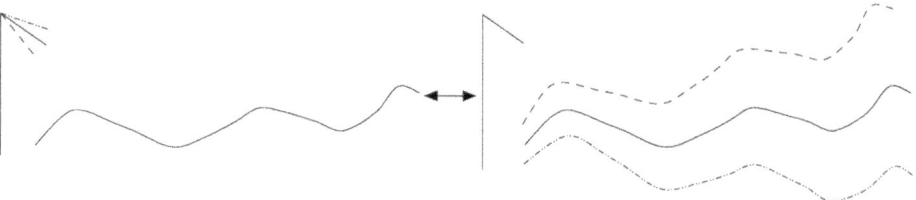

Fig. 4. Combining different segments

Stereo images of different rings are obtained by tilting the Imaging Head. However, one could imagine the camera to be kept steady and the terrain to be tilted. This would result in the same stereo images. That is why the possible correspondences of the different rings and segments can be combined to compute the epipolar geometry more accurately.

It is even the case that a specific degenerate case for the computation of the epipolar geometry is solved by the combination scheme we described. Computing the epipolar geometry of a pair of images of a planar scene is impossible from correspondences only. If the planetary terrain is planar or close to it, computing the epipolar geometry for one pair of images becomes an ill-posed problem. By combining correspondences from different segments, this problem is solved.

Computing relative transformation. Once the epipolar geometry is computed in the form of the fundamental matrix F, the relative transformation between the two cameras of the Imaging Head can be calculated. First the essential matrix is obtained as $\mathbf{E} = \mathbf{K}^\top \mathbf{F} \mathbf{K}$ with $\mathbf{K}$ the 3x3 matrix with the intrinsic calibration of the cameras. The relative transformation $(\mathbf{R}, \mathbf{t})$ (up to scale) can easily be obtained from it [6] since $\mathbf{E} = [\mathbf{t}]_\times \mathbf{R}$.

As mentioned, the absolute value of the distance between the two cameras, i.e. the baseline, can not be computed from the images. It is unlikely, however, that this value will deviate a lot from the original value. Since all measurements for 3D reconstructions and localization will consistently be carried out using the same stereo head, this has only very little influence. The only case where absolute measurements are really needed is for estimating tether consumption and the absolute size of obstacles to overcome. In these cases even a deviation of a few percent would be smaller than the uncertainty induced by other factors.

The computed values for $\mathbf{R}$ and $\mathbf{t}$ are used as an initialization for a non-linear Levenberg-Marquardt minimization which finds back the values of $\mathbf{R}$ and $\mathbf{t}$ that minimize sum of all distances between points and their corresponding epipolar lines. The result is a very accurate estimation of the relative transformation between the two images.

2.2   Pan-Tilt Calibration

To be able to bring all the measurements in a single frame, it is not sufficient to have the relative calibration between the cameras, but also the pan- and the tilt-axis are needed. Since for the same reasons as for the relative calibration these values can change due to the stress that occurs during launch and landing.

The evaluation of the pan- and the tilt-axis is more complicated, but can also be achieved from the image data, at least if some overlap exists between neighboring image pairs. This is guaranteed in the pan direction due to the fixed vergence set-up that does not allow 100% overlap between two views of the same stereo pair (and thus yields overlap with neighboring pairs). For the tilt axis care should be taken to foresee a sufficient overlap between the rings of Figure 2, at least for some image pairs.

To compute the different axes, the relative motion between stereo pairs is required. Matches can be obtained in a way similar to the one described in Section 2.1, however, in this case most features have already been reconstructed in 3D for one of the stereo pairs and a robust pose estimation algorithm (i.e. also based on RANSAC) can be used to determine the relative transformation between the stereo pairs. Once this has been done for all the overlapping pairs, the results can be combined to yield one consistent estimate of both pan and tilt axes. In this case available constraints such as the rotation angles (read from the encoders) are also enforced.

2.3   Synthetic Calibration Experiment

The calibration algorithm has been tested on artificial data. A planar scene with texture from a real image from Mars was constructed and pairs of images were generated with a visualization toolkit. First the relative calibration between the two cameras was computed. During calibration, data of 9 image pairs was combined and 2591 corners were matched to calculate the relative transformation. We could compare the result with the ground-truth value of the relative transformation. For comparison, the rotational part of the relative transformation is represented as a rotation around an axis (l, m, n) with a certain angle θ. The ground truth was

$$(l_0, m_0, n_0) = (0, 1, 0) \text{ and } \theta_0 = 10°$$

The computed values were

$$(l, m, n) = (0.000397, 0.99951, 0.00018) \text{ and } \theta = 10.093°$$

The angle between (l, m, n) and (l_0, m_0, n_0) was 0.0252 degrees. The difference between θ and θ_0 was 0.093 degrees. Both values are small, meaning that the rotation was estimated accurately because of the combination of data.

The pan and tilt axes were calibrated from the same data. The angle between the computed tilt axis and the ground truth was 0.138 degrees. The angle between the computed pan axis and the ground truth was 0.618 degrees. The larger error for the pan axis can be explained from the fact that only correspondences between three images are used to estimate it while correspondences from four images can be exploited to compute the tilt axis. During calibration of the real system, better results can be expected because much more image pairs of a non planar scene will be used.

3   3D Terrain Modeling

After the calibration of the IH is performed, the process of generating a 3D model or models of the planetary terrain can start. This modeling is vital to accomplish the goal of planetary exploration. Its input are all images of the terrain and the calibration of the Imaging Head. The output of the terrain modeling can have different forms but the most important is the Digital Elevation Map (DEM). In the following sections we will describe the different steps that are performed to obtain such a DEM.

3.1   Generation of Disparity Maps

On each pair of images recorded by the Imaging Head, a stereo algorithm is applied to compute the disparity maps from the left image to the right and from the right image to the left. Disparity maps are an elegant way to describe correspondences between two images if the images are **rectified** first. The process of rectification re-maps the image pair to standard geometry with the epipolar lines coinciding with the image scan lines [11,8]. The correspondence search is then reduced to a matching of the image points along each image scan-line. The result (the disparity maps) is an image where the value of each pixel corresponds with the number of pixels one has to move to left or right to find the corresponding pixel in the other image.

In addition to the epipolar geometry other constraints like preserving the order of neighboring pixels, bidirectional uniqueness of the match and detection of occlusions can be exploited. The dense correspondence scheme we employ to construct the disparity maps is the one described in [5]. This scheme is based on the dynamic programming scheme of Cox [1]. It operates on rectified image pairs and incorporates the above mentioned constraints. The matcher searches at each pixel in the left image for the maximum normalized cross correlation in the right image by shifting a small measurement window along the corresponding scan line. Matching ambiguities are resolved by exploiting the ordering constrain in the dynamic programming approach.

3.2   Digital Elevation Maps

A digital elevation map or DEM can be seen as a collection of points in a "top view" of the 3D terrain where each point has its own height or "elevation". The algorithm proposed for generating regular DEMs in the ROBUST project fills in a "top view" image of the terrain completely, i.e. a height value can be computed for every pixel in the top view image, except for pixels that are not visible in the IH because of occlusions. These occlusions are found in a very simple way.

The terrain is divided into cells: the pixels of the DEM. For each cell the stereo pair image is selected in which the cell would be visible if it had a height of zero. A vertical line is drawn and the projection of this line in the left and right image of the stereo pair is computed. Figure 5 illustrates the algorithm that is used to determine the height of the terrain on that line.

Fig. 5. Digital Elevation Map generation in detail. The figure contains the left rectified image (left), the corresponding disparity map (middle) and the right rectified image (right). The 3D line L corresponding to a point of the DEM projects to L_1 resp. L_2. Through the disparity map the *shadow* of L_1 on the right image can also be computed. The intersection point of L_2 and L_1 corresponds to the point where L intersects the surface.

- It is possible to detect occluded regions easily. This is the case for cells that are not visible in both stereo images. The height value of these cells can not be computed and these cells get a certain predefined value in the DEM which marks them as unseen.
- This particular scheme makes it possible to generate regular digital elevation maps at any desired resolution, interpolating automatically if needed.
- For the parts of the terrain close to the boundary of a ring, different parts of the vertical line will be projected in different stereo views. Therefore it is possible that data of two different stereo views has to be combined. This is not a problem because the transformation between the views can easily be computed since the calibration has been calculated.

4   Path Planning

Once the planetary terrain has been reconstructed, scientists can indicate sites of interest (Points Of Reference or PORs) which the rover should visit. Paths have to be computed between successive PORs. For this purpose, an path planning module has been developd. Given a terrain map, an initial rover position and heading and a desired rover position and heading, the path planner will find a path, using an A* framework, which takes the rover from the initial state to the goal state and which is optimal in terms of a series of parameters, like energy consumption, risk of tip-over, use of tether etc.

4.1   Travel Cost Map

The Travel Cost Map (TCM) provides a measure for the cost of traversal based on metrics inherent to the terrain. In the current implementation, a simple metric based on the gradient of the Digital Elevation Map (DEM) is used. Another metric characterizes the uncertainty of the terrain data, the farther from the lander camera the higher the uncertainty. Areas occluded by rocks also have high uncertainty.

4.2   The Hierarchical Approach

The rover can move according to a set of available operators (also called rover movements), which take the rover from one position and heading (this pair is also known as a state) to another position/heading. Each operator has an associated cost. The main term of this cost is computed from the above mentioned TCM. Given that A* is computationally very complex, finding a path in a reasonably large terrain, using complex operators for the rover movements, can take a long time. This has led to the choice of a hierarchical approach to the path planning problem.

Finding the Corridor. At the first stage, a traverse is planned between the start and goal states using A* covering the whole terrain but with reduced resolution, the cells being somewhat larger than the size of the rover so that it can move comfortable within the corridor. A low–resolution TCM is used for this. The transition operators are simple forward, backward, left and right, allowing to apply a highly optimized and fast version of A*. The result is a corridor (see figure 6) in which the rover may safely move.

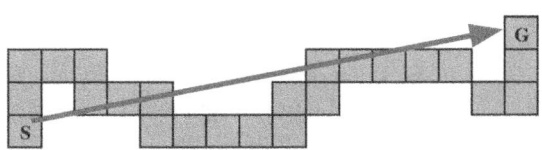

Fig. 6. Corridor

Refinement of the Path. At the second stage the path is refined using the high–resolution TCM. By restricting the search to cells marked in the Restrain Grid constructed in the previous stage more complex operators and full available resolution can be used within reasonable time constraints.

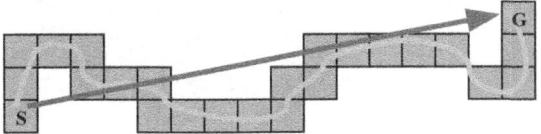

Fig. 7. Refined path

The representation of the operators to take the rover from one state to another is kept very general, i.e. a rotation followed by a translation. The cost of applying an operator is determined by using a number of cost evaluation points. The cost is calculated as a weighted sum of the costs at these points, evaluated at the resulting rover pose. The evaluation points represent parts of the 'virtual' rover during an after the completion of the corresponding move. The position of the evaluation points are calculated based on the rover dimensions, the parameters of the rover movement, the desired safety margin and the resolution of the TCM.

The result of the hierarchical A* algorithm is a high-resolution path (see figure 7), represented by an ordered list of rover poses, bringing the rover from its start pose to the desired destination.

5   System Test

A first test of the complete system was performed at the ESA-ESTEC test facilities in Noordwijk (The Netherlands) where access to a planetary testbed of about 7 by 7 meters was available. The Imaging Head was set up next to the testbed. Its first task was the recording of the terrain according to the setup shown in figure 2. A mosaic of the pictures taken by this process can be seen in figure 8.

Fig. 8. Mosaic of images of the testbed taken by the stereo head.

The autonomous calibration procedure was launched and it computed the extrinsic calibration of the cameras based on the images. Once the calibration had been computed the system rectified the images and computed dense disparity maps. Based on these, a Digital Elevation Map was constructed. The result can be seen in figure 9. Because of the relatively low height of the Imaging Head (approximately 1.5 meters above the testbed) and the big rocks in the testbed, a large portion of the Digital Elevation Map

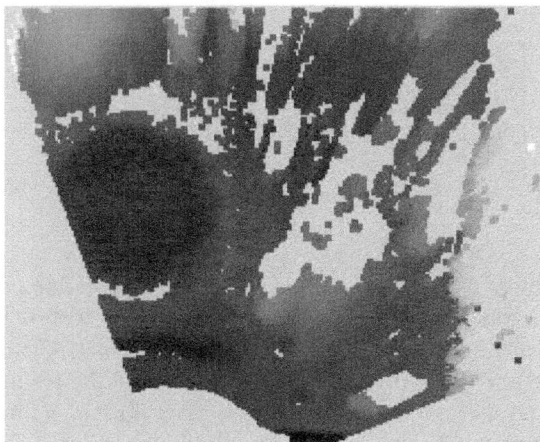

Fig. 9. Digital Elevation Map of the ESTEC planetary testbed. A significant amount of cells is not filled in because they are located in occluded areas.

could not be filled in because of occlusions. The Digital Elevation Map of figure 9 was then used to construct a textured triangulated mesh model. Some views of this model can be seen in figure 10. A striping effect is visible in the texture of the model. This is due to a hardware problem of the cameras which caused the images to suffer from an intensity gradient. Since the 3D model combines data from all images, the boundaries are visible.

Once the reconstruction was complete, the model was used to plan a trajectory for the Nanokhod rover. At that time, another component of the system came into play: the **Simulator**. This component allowed for the operator to simulate low-level commands on the Nanokhod and Imaging Head in a Virtual Reality environment. A simple gravitation model was used to predict the pose of the Nanokhod after a motion. An overview of the GUI of this component is shown in figure 11. The GUI is divided into 4 windows. The upper two show what the left and right camera of the stereo head are seeing. The bottom right window is a 3D interaction window and the bottom left window shows a picture of what a camera, mounted in the cab of the Nanokhod would see.

When the trajectory was simulated, the commands were uploaded to the lander system which executed them autonomously. The pose of the rover was observed using the Imaging Head. The lander needed the calibration parameters, computed on the ground station for this and made use of the LED's that are present on the Nanokhod. The telemetry, computed by the lander could then (after downlink to the ground station) be played back by the simulator and compared with the simulated pose of the Nanokhod.

6   Future Development

For the ROBUST project, calibration of the Imaging Head is a critical issue. Because of known specifics of the Imaging Head, the calibration algorithms can be targeted to this particular setup and take all known information on mechanics and intrinsics of the

Fig. 10. Three views of the reconstructed model of the ESTEC planetary testbed.

system into account. One can imagine situations where such information is not available. While the algorithms described in this paper can no longer be used, it is still possible to retrieve some calibration and 3D reconstruction.

6.1 Uncalibrated 3D Reconstruction

In [9] it is described how structure and motion can be retrieved from an uncalibrated image sequence. The 3D modelling task is decomposed into a number of steps. First successive images of the sequence are matched and epipolar geometry is computed using the same approach as described in section 2.1. The projection matrices of all views are computed by triangulation and pose estimation algorithms. The ambiguity on the reconstruction is then reduced from pure projective to metric (Euclidean up to scale) by self calibration algorithms (see also [7]). Finally textured triangular mesh models of the scene are constructed.

Fig. 11. Overview of the simulator. The upper two windows simulate the view of the two cameras. The bottom right window is a 3D interaction window and the bottom left window gives a view from the cab of the rover.

6.2   Experiment

The described technique could be of use during a planetary exploration mission. The most important instrument of the payload cab of the rover is probably a camera. This camera will make images of samples and rocks on the terrain but could also be used to perform close–range reconstruction of the terrain, helping the rover to "dock" precisely onto the desired position. The camera would take images of the area of interest during the approach. These images could then be used as input for the reconstruction algorithm described above to generate a 3D reconstruction. The resolution of this reconstruction would be far superior to the one of the DEM, obtained from the Imaging Head.

During testing of the *r*obust system on the planetary testbed at ESTEC, a preliminary test was performed. Images of some rocks on the testbed were taken by hand with a semi-professional digital camera. The images were processed by the 3D reconstruction system. The resulting 3D reconstruction of the rock can be seen in figure 12. The results are very good and show that this strategy could be an interesting extension of the *r*obust system.

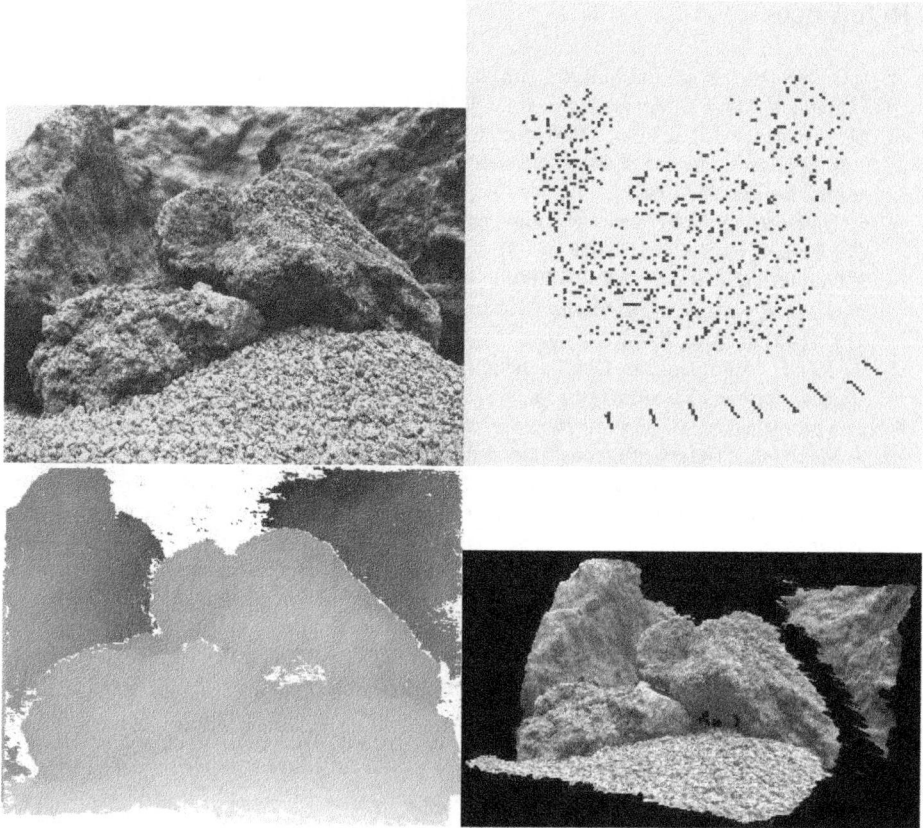

Fig. 12. Results of the reconstruction process of a rock on the planetary testbed. The upper left view shows one of the original images of the sequence. The upper right view displays reconstructed points and cameras. In the lower left view a dense depth map is shown. The lower right view shows an arbitrary view of the 3D reconstruction.

7   Conclusion

In this paper an approach for calibration and 3D measurement from planetary terrain images was proposed which allowed for an important simplification of the design of the imaging system of the lander. The components described in this paper are part of an end-to-end system which can reconstruct an unknown planetary terrain and guide a rover autonomously on the planetary surface. The system has succeeded a first test in a planetery testbed at ESTEC.

Acknowledgments. We acknowledge support from the Belgian IUAP4/24 'IMechS' project. We also wish to thank all partners of the ROBUST project for the collaboration. Special thanks go to Ronny Moreas of K.U.Leuven-PMA for his contribution on the path planning algorithm.

References

1. I. Cox, S. Hingorani and S. Rao, "A Maximum Likelihood Stereo Algorithm", In *Computer Vision and Image Understanding*, Vol. 63, No. 3, May 1996.
2. M. Fischler and R. Bolles: "RANdom SAmpling Consensus: a paradigm for model fitting with application to image analysis and automated cartography", In *Commun. Assoc. Comp. Mach.*, 24:381-95, 1981.
3. C. Harris and M. Stephens: "A combined corner and edge detector", In *Fourth Alvey Vision Conference*, pp. 147-151, 1988.
4. J. Knight and I. Reid, "Self-calibration of a stereo-rig in a planar scene by data combination", In *Proceedings International Conference on Pattern Recognition (ICPR 2000)*, pp. 411-414,Barcelona,2000.
5. R. Koch, "Automatische Oberflachenmodellierung starrer dreidimensionaler Objekte aus stereoskopischen Rundum-Ansichten", *PhD thesis*, University of Hannover, Germany, 1996 also published as *Fortschritte-Berichte VDI*, Reihe 10, Nr.499, VDI Verlag, 1997.
6. S. Maybank, "Theory of reconstruction from image motion", *Springer Verlag*, 1992.
7. M. Pollefeys, R. Koch and L. Van Gool. "Self-Calibration and Metric Reconstruction in spite of Varying and Unknown Internal Camera Parameters", *International Journal of Computer Vision*.
8. M. Pollefeys, R. Koch and L. Van Gool, "A simple and efficient rectification method for general motion", *Proc.ICCV'99 (international Conference on Computer Vision)*, pp.496-501, Corfu (Greece), 1999.
9. M. Pollefeys, R. Koch, M. Vergauwen and L. Van Gool, "Metric 3D Surface Reconstruction from Uncalibrated Image Sequences", *Proc. SMILE Workshop (post-ECCV'98)*, LNCS 1506, pp.138-153, Springer-Verlag, 1998.
10. R. Rieder, H. Wanke, H. v. Hoerner. e.a., "Nanokhod, a miniature deployment device with instrumentation for chemical, mineralogical and geological analysis of planetary surfaces, for use in connection with fixed planetary surface stations", In *Lunar and Planetary Science*, XXVI,pp. 1261-1262, 1995.
11. C. Loop and Z. Zhang. "Computing Rectifying Homographies for Stereo Vision". IEEE Conf. Computer Vision and Pattern Recognition (CVPR'99), Colorado, June 1999.
12. A. Zisserman, P. Beardsley and I. Reid, "Metric calibration of a stereo rig", *Proceedings IEEE Workshop on Representation of Visual Scenes*, Cambridge, pp. 93-100, 1995.

Author Index

GPSR Compliance

The European Union's (EU) General Product Safety Regulation (GPSR) is a set of rules that requires consumer products to be safe and our obligations to ensure this.

If you have any concerns about our products, you can contact us on ProductSafety@springernature.com

In case Publisher is established outside the EU, the EU authorized representative is:

Springer Nature Customer Service Center GmbH
Europaplatz 3
69115 Heidelberg, Germany

Batch number: 09624486

Printed by Printforce, the Netherlands